THE SUPPLY-BASED
Advantage

How to Link Suppliers to
Your Organization's
Corporate Strategy

Stephen C. Rogers

HarperCollins
Leadership

An Imprint of HarperCollins

Published by HarperCollins Leadership, an imprint of HarperCollins Focus LLC.

Any internet addresses, phone numbers, or company or product information printed in this book are offered as a resource and are not intended in any way to be or to imply an endorsement by HarperCollins Leadership, nor does HarperCollins Leadership vouch for the existence, content, or services of these sites, phone numbers, companies, or products beyond the life of this book.

Bulk discounts available. For details visit:www.harpercollinsleadership.com/bulkquotes

Email: customercare@harpercollins.com

ISBN 978-1-4002-4242-9 (TP)

To my parents and my wife.

To MY DAD, AL ROGERS, who taught me the value of debate over the dinner table on weekends when he came home after traveling in his sales job all week. Our spirited discussions about history, politics, the Vietnam War and even sports helped me learn how to think. I miss him.

To MY MOM, ELIA ROGERS (whose quote graces Chapter 5), for all the hours she spent teaching me how to read—those "see Spot jump" drills built the foundation. Her insistence that I read two or three books every week during summer vacation taught me to love what books can create in a person's mind. At ninety-four years old, she reads every day, and continues to lead her, as she puts it, "quiet life."

To MY WIFE, SUSAN, who bears the brunt of my writing. She has shown great patience dealing with my tying up the breakfast nook table, cluttering the basement and guest bedroom with research notes, and peering into a computer screen, pecking away at odd hours when inspiration struck. Not many would put up with so much.

Contents

Foreword

Why a Book on Supply and Competitive Advantage?

"Why write a book about business competitive advantage and inter-company relationships targeted for people in procurement and supply management?"

The speaker was business alliance expert, Robert Porter Lynch, and his reaction surprised me. His point was that senior management drives corporate direction and most senior executives (CEO, COO, CFO) would never pick up a book focused on what purchasing or supply management should do. They care about customer focus, not supplier focus, and rarely include procurement when formulating strategy.

Nevertheless, I continued to forge ahead and six months later submitted a book proposal to Christina McLaughlin (now Parisi), an editor with AMA-COM Publishing, on supply strategy/supplier management architecture. The proposal described the audience as general management and executives whose functions are major users of outsourcing providers, not just the "natural" supply manager audience.

Her response echoed Robert Lynch's: "If executive management or even mid- and lower-level managers don't already believe managing the supply base is an essential function, they won't pick up a book about it." Suppliers are often an afterthought, part of the business model's "givens" unless something major goes wrong. But if I was writing for supply professionals I would be just preaching to the choir. The sum of Robert and Christina's reactions caused me to pause and reflect—for three years!

I had to ask myself two questions:

1. Why did I still believe there was real insight in this topic regardless of its final audience?

2. What, specifically, does a "well-architected" supply base mean to a company's ability to compete?

The answer to the first question came from a career's worth of personal experiences that made me conclude: (1) in the hands of companies that know how to build a supply base, suppliers are critical to business success; (2) how to do that is not universally understood or practiced in business; and (3) even among those that have done it, their ability to forget how later on is amazing.

Seeing Is Believing

My education about this began the day I started working during the Arab oil embargo. I was given a phone list of every potential caustic soda and chlorine supplier or distributor in the United States and told to call them all and, if they had any material, buy it. We were running out. Later that same year, Procter and Gamble's (P&G) purchasing vice president addressed the annual corporate management meeting about working with suppliers during the rampant supply shortages to keep our products on the shelf more successfully than our competition.

Simultaneously, supplier research was engrained as an element of value as I watched peers work to commercialize and expand availability of new detergent builder molecules codeveloped by suppliers to replace phosphates. Shortly thereafter, cost control joined availability and innovation in the purchasing value equation when Nixon's wage and price controls ended and unbridled cost escalation erupted, especially for petrochemicals (remember, oil only cost $3/barrel in early 1973 but had quadrupled in price by 1974— previewing today's environment).

Over the next thirty years, I saw suppliers repeatedly make important contributions to business successes. Whether it was commercializing innovation, sustaining our presence on the store shelves, improving ingredient and packaging quality, or reducing costs to enable attractive price points for consumers, suppliers enabled P&G products to become preferred by end users.

Still, there were also times when we refused supplier ideas. Example: P&G entered the ready-to-serve cookie market with a patented manufacturing process for (only) "soft and chewy" Duncan Hines chocolate chip cookies. To win against entrenched competitors, however, a new entrant needed a broad line of cookies to offset their leverage with consumers across a broader variety of flavors and styles.

Realizing this, the cookie product development leader reached out to a small group of independent bakers, using their formulation skills and baking assets to broaden our line with sandwich and chocolate enrobed varieties. Unfortunately, when another food company lured him away, his more traditional replacement invoked NIH (not invented here) to reject supplier innovation. The broad line never saw the light of day.

Ultimately P&G's narrow cookie line became a brutally expensive failure, transforming a healthy food business into the least profitable unit in the company. Who knows if using supplier-designed products would have changed the outcome? But watching us refuse supplier help and then fail miserably made a huge impression on my thinking regarding suppliers.

In part, then, the answer to the first question was "seeing is believing." Over a thirty-plus-year career, both successes and failures repeatedly stemmed from acceptance or rejection of supplier ideas and our ability to productively use them even when accepted. I became a believer. Two other things stuck with me, adding to my conviction. One was a research study and the other, an eye-opening incident with a senior executive.

Surprising and Convincing Research

One of the almost ridiculous number of research papers that crossed my desk as a practitioner was a correlation study between corporate business success and the performance of various company functions. Single-variable correlations were no surprise—customer-facing functions (Product Design, Marketing, Customer Service, and Sales) consistently had the highest (but lower than I expected) statistical correlations to business success.

The surprise was that my expectation that combining customer-facing groups would drive the correlations even higher was simply wrong. Instead, combining any customer-facing function with either procurement or supply chain functions consistently delivered the higher correlations. The authors concluded that while product design, marketing, and sales are primary, when they are combined with strong supply chain flow and supplier management skills, the results are superior end-to-end performance delivery.

For me, this crystalized the importance of making the "line of sight" between suppliers and customers clear, so suppliers understand the value needed for their customer to win. No easy task given the obstruction internal hierarchies and miscommunication bring; done well it leads to competitive wins. When suppliers can help you make and sell a product your customers want more than those of your competition, and in the process grow their own business, it improves your odds of success by diversifying your portfolio of competencies, and like investment diversification, providing better long-term returns at lower risk.

Senior Management Doesn't Always Understand

The third experience occurred in the mid-1990s. I was a global director in charge of sourcing major spends, leading a dozen sourcing teams located in ten cities across the world. My boss, the head of Purchasing, reported to a manufacturing-based chief Supply Chain Officer. P&G was creating, documenting, and enforcing a series of relatively rigid supply chain work processes called CBAs (current best approaches). My boss was assigned a CBA on how to make sure we got the most out of suppliers.

Given that task, I wrote up a thought process with quite a bit of flexibility to change approaches as we better understood a supplier's needs. While it included standard steps, the thrust was situationally reading our leverage and dependence on a particular supplier and how their need for us might change over time. This CBA was quite different from those in other supply chain and manufacturing areas, substituting flexibility to change for closely defined work processes to drive success.

We sent my blend of science (process steps) and art (reading supplier reactions) up the line expecting a positive response. Instead, what came back was the word "Bullshit" scrawled across the top, some feedback about CBA process specificity, and a new deadline to "fix it." Convinced a rote process wouldn't work, this time I declined the task (probably a "CCI"—career crippling incident) and continued using approaches tailored to the particulars (supplier, market conditions, and both companies' needs).

Sometimes executives simply don't "get it" when dealing with suppliers. They envision suppliers sitting by the phone hoping for a call, regardless of the business opportunity's profit potential. This eye-opening experience helped me recognize that what had become second nature for me is not universally understood—that a situational, flexible approach will bring more supplier contribution to a company's value proposition than any unchanging, rote process ever will.

So, the rest of the first question's answer concludes that while suppliers can be integral to powerful value propositions, many executives simply do not intuitively understand how to engage them in a way that maximizes that contribution. Worse, sometimes their natural instinct to demand rather than discuss can lose those contributions. Senior managers who spend time listening to suppliers often come away with greater appreciation of what supplier capability can do for them—and greater advantage in the marketplace.

A number of consultants and academics recently began linking supply and competitive advantage. However, until practitioners actually pursue supply-based competitive advantage, nothing will change. This book tries to help practitioners do more than just "believe," and instead "do" supply-based competitive advantage.

Architecture and Advantage

Answering the second question—what the architecture of your supply base has to do with competitive difference—makes up the rest of this book. In addition to a framework for implementing a supply-based advantage, two additional perspectives emerge—recognition that supplier-based competitive advantage is not a single-function game, and that *people* still run businesses. Since most aspects of people interactions have not changed much over the years, communication, trust, revenge, and self-enrichment all still play out. A blend of both modern techniques and old-fashioned fundamentals are necessary to incorporate today's suppliers into your business strategy.

If you want to sustain supply-based competitive edge, supply management alone is not enough. Real competitive advantage takes a multifunctional mindset that "gets it" about the impact suppliers can have on business and uses it to apply the right skills in the right places at the right times by a broad set of the right people.

Acknowledgments

This book has been bouncing around in my head for a long time. It articulates my almost career-long belief in the importance of suppliers and those who work with them as sources of competitive advantage. As I sat down to write this (the very last) section of the book, my former administrative assistant, Mari Thompson, e-mailed me that Procter and Gamble won *Purchasing* magazine's 2008 Medal of Professional Excellence. As I read the articles, recognizing the names of people I worked with for years (and some new ones too), it helped me reflect on a thirty-year career's worth of colleagues. Much of my thinking was shaped by those P&G people—ranging from direct bosses (Dan Schuler, Peter Schmid, Bill Murphy, Bruce Stirling) who helped me "get" the importance of suppliers to another set of bosses (Ben Boor, Peter Adye, A. G. Lafley, Bob McDonald, Susan Arnold) in my manufacturing and advertising assignments who taught me about the business and about leading organizations.

Even more important were the people I worked with doing the real work of seeking and capturing supply-based advantage—the list is enormous (surely I will miss some). While many of them worked for me directly in my purchasing organizations, as peers in cross-business buying teams or as part of the global sourcing strategy teams that reported to me, their efforts were instrumental in the learning I did over the years. In particular, two groups accelerated my learning more than any others: my "green" coffee supply organization and my early group of global material strategy owners in the detergent business (who helped pioneer global sourcing at P&G). Never underestimate how much your own people can teach you. They helped write

xiii

this book more than they will ever know. Thanks to: Stew Atkinson, Stefan VanStraelen, Roberto Magana, Camille Chammas, Greg White, Mike Huber, Corrine Reich, Joelle Zilliox, Lisa Cooley, Rob Swift, Noel Faict, Mary Kostalansky, "Shin" Otsu, Bill Cortner, Javier Cajiga, Liliana Rodriguez, Bryan Edmonson, Dawn Bierschwal, Carol Rubeo, Pat Barger, Scott Workman, Art Tallas, Bill Kiel, Jerry Balkenhol—and so many more. Special thanks to my dear friend Tom Komura, who taught me a lot about Asian culture and to Roy Riedinger, who delayed retirement to teach me about global teams and international travel.

Then there were the many people in other functions who were kind enough to work with me when I showed up asking for their involvement in things their management often did not care much about. They taught me the power of internal alignment and collaboration. Thanks to: Lou Beland, Paul Smith, Mike Story, Dan Price, Joe Doner, Henry Mentle, Pat Schur, Jon Beers, JoAnn Hagopian, Glenn Bitzenhoffer, Dave Grayson, Ken Buell, Sharon Mitchell, Mike Noyes, Will Papa, Roger Stewart, Teri List, Melinda Whittington, Reba St. Clair—and many more. Special thanks to two R&D people who took the risk of joining purchasing at my request and helped suppliers better integrate into new product development at P&G: Jim Zeller and Ed Sawicki.

Finally, thanks to my suppliers and my peers at other companies who worked, benchmarked, and spoke at conferences, sharing their stories and knowledge with me (and many others). I especially remember suppliers like Pat Boyle (who passed away in 2007), the honorable president of Schulze and Burch, the baker that suffered when P&G's cookie business crashed; Cliff Simpson, a sales rep with Tredegar, who worked closely during some tough but energizing diaper and feminine product innovation projects years ago; Alejando de Maria, managing director of Quimir, a Mexican chemical company, with whom conversation always brought understanding; and Robert Lynch, a consultant I hired to help with retooling a supplier relationship management methodology and who became a friend. Many suppliers helped write this book too. Thanks to them all.

Now to the book-writing part. First, thanks go to Doug Smock, the guy who got me into this author stuff to begin with by dialing my number and asking if I would co-write a book with him and Bob Rudzki. He encouraged me to keep writing and read/critiqued the first several chapters. Special thanks to Karen White, who in a conversation gave me the "doors and windows" analogy to use with cross-functional work—greatly improving what I had come up with, and to Bill Cortner, who in another conversation about skills caused me to add some Practitioner's Takes on the impossibility of dealing with forty skills. To Martin Delahay, VP of procurement at the AMA, who kept telling me to get a proposal to their publishing arm, AMACOM. To Hank Kennedy, president of AMACOM, who gave me the chance to write a book. Finally, and very importantly, to my editors: Christina Parisi, who gave me some great feedback early on, allowed me to add a couple chapters at the last minute, and then helped me work through some big-time length issues at the end; Mike Sivilli, who ran the job so courteously and professionally; and special thanks to my copyeditor, Debbie Posner, who in addition to making my punctuation and grammar right, asked me lots of good questions that forced me to sharpen both my writing and my thinking. The AMACOM team has really been great to work with all along the way.

—Steve Rogers

CHAPTER 1

Competitive Advantage

Building a Supply-Based Framework

ADVANTAGE: any state, circumstance, opportunity, or means especially favorable to success, interest, or any desired end.

BUILD: to construct (something, especially, something complex) by assembling and joining parts or materials.

If you don't have a competitive advantage, don't compete.

—Jack Welch, former CEO of General Electric

"Our strategic goal is to deliver sustainable competitive advantage through supplier selection and management." The words rolled off Carlo Soave's tongue (as they had rolled off mine many times before) as he addressed a P&G Purchases' training class for new purchasing hires in Brussels, Belgium. At the time, Soave was the Purchases vice president for the Fabric and Home Care global business unit and overall leader of chemical sourcing for all of P&G. (Today he is a nonfamily CEO of a family-owned Italian nonwoven fabric producer, Albis.) Five concepts come together to define the business problem posed by "sustainable competitive advantage." Let's examine them one by one.

Concept 1: Sustainable Competitive Advantage

It wasn't until later that I questioned what the phrase "competitive advantage," especially *sustainable* competitive advantage, really means. Several ideas come to mind including value, capabilities, and innovation, and how they relate to marketplace competition. While researching this book, I quickly discovered there is no universal definition of competitive advantage and, more important, no agreement on the term "sustainable competitive advantage." Some say that all competitive advantage is temporary and as MIT Sloan School of Management professor Charles Fine once said, the faster the industry "clockspeed" (rate of change), the more temporary it is.

As with many strategic concepts, sustainable competitive advantage emerged in 1985 in Harvard professor Michael Porter's discussion of basic competitive strategies, although he neither discussed nor defined the concept in depth. Its meaning evolved to focus primarily on a company's distinctive, mostly internal, intangible capabilities like management skills, core competencies, ability to innovate, plus some tangible assets like financial strength, physical capital, and externally visible intellectual capital (patents, trademarks, etc.). These capabilities were viewed relative to which capabilities or resources one company has that its competitors do not.

Thus, a simple definition of sustainable competitive advantage becomes "an advantage that enables your business to survive against its competition over a long period of time."[1] Easily duplicated aspects drop out, leaving something that is:

- Unique.
- Superior to competition.
- Sustainable.
- Applicable to multiple businesses or situations.
- Hard to copy.

These attributes allow a disproportionate contribution to shareholder value, open doors to new opportunities, and include implicit, not just explicit, knowledge.

While many companies see the customer facing implications of competitive advantage like branding (P&G), customer service (Nordstrom), shopping experience (Target), or shopping convenience (Amazon), it is the unique, difficult-to-replicate, broad application aspect of sustainable competitive advantage that allows supply to be an important source of competitive edge.

Establishing unique relational assets—bonds between firms and their customers, suppliers, and comarketing partners—is one of the most difficult business tasks to replicate. Customer relations are frequently cited as an advantage, but the ability to develop intimate supplier business relationships is extremely difficult, in part because suppliers are typically viewed as part of the firm's cost structure, not its assets. Too quickly the goal becomes squeezing money from suppliers, leveraging volume to get lower prices. Such financial advantages are hardly unique and can be duplicated. The adversarial mindset that this creates is not conducive to suppliers becoming a sustainable competitive advantage for many companies. Instead, short-term savings equate to temporary advantage. The challenge is sustainable advantage over time, leading to a second major concept.

Concept 2: Value

At P&G, George Perbix, the father of modern purchasing, defined purchase of "total value," the combination of price, quality, total system cost, supply assurance, service, and supplier R&D, as supply's real goal. Like beauty, value often lies in the eyes of the beholder.

The traditional measures of supply value are cost, quality, and service. Academics, consultants, and practitioners alike go on about value chains and the "value-add" at each step along a supply chain. But the everyday low-cost value proposition of Wal-Mart is not the same as the value proposition of a Target or a Nordstrom's. So, just what is value anyway and how does it relate to competitive advantage and, in this book, supply-based competitive advantage? A simple definition results in a basic value equation:

$$V = P \div C$$

where V is value, P is performance of the product (good and/or service) as seen by the customer, and C is the total cost of ownership from the customer's viewpoint.

The Numerator: Performance

Performance is more than just how the product works, typically including components like quality, delivery, speed to market, and easy availability along with postpurchase service and customer satisfaction response. It also includes intangible factors like corporate reputation (supply chain ethics, legitimate "green-ness," and overall corporate "persona"); emerging customer expectations and needs—the unknown component that ongoing end user research and contact must determine (innovation); and other factors that can truly matter in the course of business.

In January 1995, Kobe, Japan, was hit by a massive earthquake that devastated the city. P&G's Asian headquarters were located on a small island (Rokko Island) just a short elevated train ride off the coast, near Kobe. The power of the quake cracked P&G's twenty-six-story building (constructed to earthquake standards) from the ground to its top floor, causing significant internal damage. A number of us, including then Director of Asia Purchases Jim Dempsey, had left Kobe the afternoon before the earthquake for China, and awakened to CNN videos of the destruction on Chinese television. The rest of the story is Jim's.[2]

Dempsey and his key lieutenants booked flights back to Osaka. What they found was devastating. P&G's offices were not usable. Worse, the quake eliminated all transportation on or off Rokko Island, destroying both the elevated train and the roadway bridge. An enormous number of P&G employees and expatriate families were trapped on the island with no way off. The company was able to rent a small tug boat on which a few leaders, including then Asian President, current CEO, A. G. Lafley, and Dempsey traveled to the island to attend to their employees.

That's when a Japanese supplier of contract packaging placed a cell phone call. Its parent company had a small ship and offered to take all the P&G people, their families, and salvageable possessions/luggage off the island. The local government (and P&G) had not been able to find any other way off and, given the quake-damaged infrastructure, the situation was becoming critical. The supplier ferried the people and possessions to Osaka in three trips. They made no request for payment. They didn't just drop the people at the Osaka pier, either, Dempsey recalls. They rented a building and served food and drink to the hungry and tired refugees.

The supplier's president got up and gave a brief welcoming speech (through an interpreter) that had enormous impact on the P&G people. He said that he wanted to welcome them, that his company was very happy to help, and that he understood how they felt because his own house was gone, lost in the quake as well. When your organization is knocked out of commission, the ability to get back up and running is critical to withstanding competitors' situational advantage. The key to staying focused is to have your people and their minds on the business. This supplier provided enormous value on both fronts—rescuing P&G's people took away many immediate worries, and focus on rebuilding the business could begin.

An interesting aside to this story is that months later, after completing the construction of a Chinese plant for P&G's business expansion, the business changed. P&G canceled the product launch (for good business reasons). The supply contract allowed P&G to cancel without penalty, leaving the supplier with an empty plant and significant economic disruption. A newly appointed procurement leader in China, without the background, began to do just that. But Dempsey and several other Asian managers stepped in, related the story, and supported the supplier. As a result, the two companies went outside the contract to reach a fair settlement. Value comes in many forms and can flow both ways.

The Denominator: Cost

Cost, the value equation's denominator, is too often simplified to price because, on the surface, price is a big part of cost and easy to see. However, the cost portion of value must go beyond invoice price to the buyer's total cost of ownership and the final customer's perspective. Total cost of ownership gives an extended view that exposes hidden value-stealing costs that reduce profit, while the customer's perspective flows from paying for the product, both economically and emotionally (dissatisfaction or delight).

Tangible cost elements include freight and transport; taxes (trade tariffs, local sales, inventory, excise taxes, etc.); cash-to-cash cycle costs arising from inventory levels and payment terms; waste, including inventory obsolescence, yield losses, and damage; supply overhead costs; quality inspection and warranty costs; and the popular catchall "other" ancillary costs (including related cost to use and maintain the item, e.g., gas, oil, spare parts, and mechanic labor for a car). More insidious are the intangible costs, perhaps the most dangerous of which is customer dissatisfaction that results in negative advertising, eroded brand image, and revenue loss.

Thus, in today's "flat, globally competitive world," value has great breadth. Elements like ancillary or dissatisfaction costs in the denominator and innovation or emerging needs in the numerator can shape long-term success or failure. All this is not a new concept, but it is operationally challenging because these elements hide in different parts of the value chain and are often hard to ferret out. Worse, some of them resemble a mathematical "unknown unknown"—a factor that exists but that no one can easily find.

Perhaps the best picture of value is an iceberg (see Figure 1.1.), easily visible at the top (price and specification), less clear but faintly visible at the water line (freight, duty, quality, on-time delivery, speed, responsiveness) and nearly invisible at the bottom deep below the water line (innovation, value

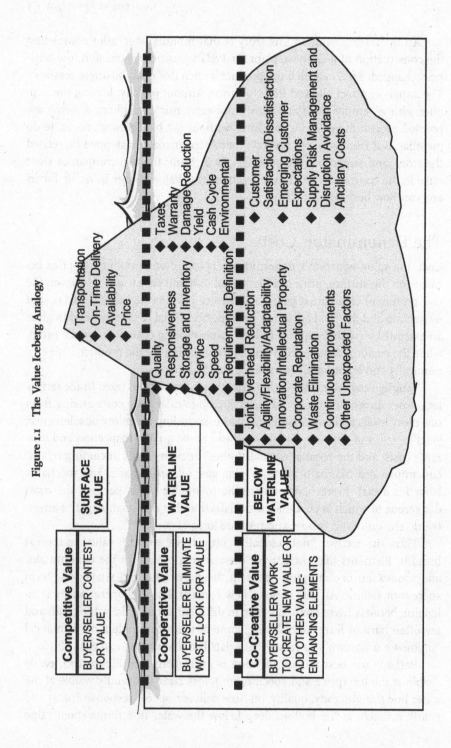

Figure 1.1 The Value Iceberg Analogy

chain waste, changing user expectations . . . and rescuing people from a devastated island). Less than 15 percent of an iceberg's mass lies above water and it is 20 to 30 percent wider underwater than above it—a perfect value analogy.

Unfortunately, while many buyers give lip service to value, typical supply metrics are savings dollars and not much else (more about metrics later). Many senior executives rate purchasing organizations only on cost reduction, which is fairly easy to measure relative to total value, because it becomes quickly evident, unlike innovation, flexibility, or latent quality aspects. This metric often defines the firm's reward structure for procurement operations. "You get what you measure" is clearly true as powerful retailers like Wal-Mart, with a marketing message of ever lower prices, emphasize the message that price equals value. This, in turn, reinforces short-term, price-motivated opportunistic procurement behavior, generating "falsely sustainable" competitive advantage because cost, for all but a few giants, is an easy value element to copy.

Three Levels of Supply Value

Returning to the iceberg analogy, supplier value revolves around the iceberg's three levels—surface, waterline, and underwater value. At the surface, cost savings are the measure and expectation. Think of this as a "value competition" between suppliers and buyers. While most trumpeted and easiest to see and measure, it has least to do with *sustainable* competitive advantage but is still critical for success! Cost control is the ticket to the sustainable competitive advantage game. Unless value's cost denominator is under control relative to its performance numerator, the overall equation simply does not work. The implications of a supply base that takes advantage of you relative to your competition are grave indeed. Your suppliers need to keep you competitive, but it is your job to enforce that expectation. That, in turn, often requires using market competition to understand what "competitive" really means and then capturing it.

At the waterline, value is less clear and harder to harvest, but often still visible. Projects like Supply Base Lean and Six Sigma exemplify this. Think of it as cooperative value found by jointly improving process efficiency and reducing waste at suppliers. In the auto industry, this kind of work was made famous by the Japanese—particularly Honda and Toyota—as an alternative cost reduction strategy to margin squeezing. Waterline value increases the size of the pie for the participants, sometimes at the expense of those in the chain that don't participate or aren't efficient. Think of it as either lowering the pie's cost-to-value ratio or, through waste elimination, taking pieces of pie away from firms that don't really deserve it. Its challenge is the need to work more openly with suppliers, especially for buyers who historically have overemphasized the competitive value "tip" of the iceberg. The payoff is that it is a bigger factor in competitive edge, harder to copy, and more sustainable than surface cost.

Finally, value beneath the water is much harder to find and harvest. Innovation and supplier-enabled customer service superiority fall here, typically impacting value's performance aspect and sometimes reducing cost as well. Tangible effort must be paired with a "win-win" mindset because harvesting supplier ideas and resources suffers unless the supplier sees something in return for its investment of intellectual, financial, or physical capital. This is where the "sustainable" in sustainable competitive advantage is most frequently found. Think of it as *co-creative value.* (By "co-creative," we mean that both the supplier and the buyer work together to create something different than either team could do alone.)

Harnessing sustainable competitive advantage from the supply base takes all three parts of this iceberg. The competitive element sustains base value, the cooperative element differentiates and tailors supplier value to each organization's unique situation, while the co-creative element takes supplier contribution to a new level. Importantly, both cooperative and co-creative value are less transparent, thus harder to copy, than competitive value—and that is part of the definition of competitive advantage.

Concept 3: Complexity

Thomas Friedman's bestseller, *The World is Flat,* while describing the impact of massive optical fiber capacity on the Internet to increase "line of sight" global "flatness," also describes some of the complexity this flatness creates. As they extend around the world, global supply chains follow truly complex routes. They incorporate emerging country interior logistical complexities, congested port operations, governmental trade regulations, tariff charges, and 9/11 terrorist attack–induced security requirements. Add to that conflicting safety and environmental laws between trading countries and almost universal customer expectations for "we want it when we want it" supply availability despite the distances and time zones these chains span. Friedman's example (written in 2004/05) of the makeup of his laptop (notebook) computer is a case in point, with Dell's supply matrix comprising a veritable global "symphony" of suppliers.[3]

A complex series of multisourced operations with capacity for about

150,000 computers per day and the reliability necessary for Dell's renowned fast delivery model, it included suppliers from seventeen countries (United States, Taiwan, Malaysia, Philippines, Brazil, Ireland, Costa Rica, Germany, China, South Korea, Japan, Mexico, Singapore, Thailand, Indonesia, India, and Israel). In turn, these facilities were owned by companies from ten countries (United States, Taiwan, Germany, China, Korea, Japan, Ireland, Thailand, U.K., and Israel).

Expand logistical complexity to encompass cultural and currency differences as well. Complexity isn't just geographical either. New technologies are no longer simple. Those that once delivered advantage are becoming commodities. In the pharmaceutical industry, straight chemistry is being supplanted by biotechnology because generic drug makers can duplicate off-patent chemical-based drugs. Business models are growing in complexity, too. Silicon-based microchips are behind the merging (or collision) of computer, TV, gaming, entertainment, telecommunication, and advertising industries. Planning strategy and competitive advantage in these industries is incredibly complex. Companies once considered untouchable leaders face seismic market shifts (Motorola as of this writing, in cell phones) or exit an industry all together (IBM in PCs).

New invention is being driven by technology convergence or hybridization across disciplines often in different companies, many of which are suppliers. The combinations of inorganic nanotechnology, biology, and medicine (biomedical nanotechnology), genetics and computers (genomics), or mathematics, biology, and chemistry (bioinformatics) require experts from multiple fields to understand and collaborate, making the complexity of commercialization more exacting. I recently toured a John Deere exhibit in Moline, Illinois, and from the cab of a huge piece of Deere farm equipment, used a simulator to "virtually farm" with a blend of huge machines, global positioning satellites, satellite surveillance, and agricultural chemical deposition. This level of supplier technology integration means crossing corporate, cultural, and core competency boundaries. All this illustrates the complexity factor in competitive edge.

Concept 4: Rapid Change

Complexity introduces the next factor in sustaining competitive advantage—speed of change. The use of global outsourcing, once the province of large multinationals, is now done by midsize companies (even small mom-and-pop shops) for everything from call centers and software support to manufacturing and marketing services. They have to, in order to compete. In less than five minutes on the Chinese website Alibaba.com, I can locate 1,334 zipper makers in China, an impossible task five or ten years ago (vetting those you find is sometimes quite another story, however). What was a sourcing coup then is a workable option today.

Historically stable elements like employee tenure now churn rapidly, making institutional memory suffer. Rote tasks steeped in unconscious competence erode into unconscious incompetence when the implications of a change are not recognized. This can happen at the buying company, its suppliers, and their suppliers. Simple example: In 2004 P&G introduced Hewlett Packard, its information technology outsourcing supplier, to a business OGSM for the information technology organization. An OGSM is a strategy matrix with objectives (in words), goals (in numbers), strategies (in words), and measures (in numbers). HP was unfamiliar with it. But P&G had originally gotten the methodology in a benchmarking session with HP, who had developed it fourteen years before.

Using a company's institutional memory can help a great deal, with finding it becoming the challenge. In November 2007, Pat Paolino won a Phoenix Award—P&G's career award in procurement—for his efforts managing P&G's surfactant chemical supply base for seven years.

In our conversation after the awards ceremony, Paolino reinforced this "past is future" perspective on competitive advantage from suppliers, commenting, "Over the last five or ten years, we applied some new approaches to help us work with suppliers, but as oil and petrochemical markets skyrocketed and supplies got tight, many of the techniques we use are eerily similar to those used twenty-five years ago—tailored for some current realities, but still eerily similar. The key is finding the people with experiences and knowledge and then tapping that expertise."

Rapid change represents yet another complication in gaining sustainable supply-based competitive advantage. As they compete, supply chains constantly change even as benchmarking exercises cause their current incarnations to be copied by competitors. Members of one supply chain show up in those of many companies, bringing techniques learned elsewhere. Rapid change reinforces the temporary nature of competitive advantage and the need to constantly change in order to stay ahead.

Concept 5: Risk

We will talk about risk in Chapter 12, but the concept of risk is integral to sustained competitive advantage in successful businesses. In Friedman's Dell example, the use of multiple sources (up to four production locations for single source items; three or four suppliers of most components) was a risk management approach to maintain supply reliability and supplier competitiveness in cost and technology. Basic supply risk, like *E. coli* contamination of spinach, can quickly undermine a business proposition. Example: Chiquita Brands' U.S. bagged salad business dropped almost 30 percent after bagged spinach from two competitors was found to have *E. coli* contamination in 2006. Chiquita has never had the problem. But their business certainly did!

Enterprise-wide supply risk management looks across a number of risk elements in a world where competition, value, technology, and complexity constantly change. Simplistically, four major categories of supply risk interact: *financial risks,* including national or international economic downturns, value shifts, currencies, costs, and price changes; *business risks,* including sales volume, regulatory change, competitor actions, profit pressures, project uncertainty, supplier strategy changes, and corporate reputation; *operational risks,* caused by human mistakes, fraud, miscommunication, and poor internal controls or processes; and *physical risks,* such as plant disruptions, disasters, terrorism, product contamination, supply chain dislocations, and labor strikes.

Innovation is the lifeblood of sustainable competitive advantage. It is also extremely risky. Not every new idea is a winner—in fact many fail. Supplier ideas are no different; they do not always pan out the way they were envisioned. A classic example occurred at Interstate Bakeries, the producer of such traditional American brands as Wonder Bread and Hostess Twinkies.[4]

One of the largest cost centers in the bread business is product shelf life. For a baker, finding a way to modify the formula to extend freshness, synchronize plant capacity with real demand, and reduce losses and truck delivery frequency is the "holy grail." A successful formula change on snack cakes caused Interstate to reapply it to their bread business. However, bread packaging, different than snack cakes, only supported a three-day shelf life, so the snack formula change had to be further modified.

An Interstate supplier, Innovative Cereal Systems, developed an enzyme that would bind water molecules to the bread, making it softer and last longer before going stale. Interstate used it to double shelf life to seven days—only to later discover that in some markets the extra water seemed to make the bread gummy, while in others there were no bread quality issues at all, but that the less frequent deliveries resulted in sloppy shelves in all markets. (Delivery drivers reset store shelves to keep them looking attractive for shoppers.) The project never fully delivered the savings, and sales dropped while competitors' sales increased—part of what led to Interstate's Chapter 11 bankruptcy filing in 2004.

Interestingly, the same supplier provided the same material to another baker, whose project only targeted an extension of shelf life from one day to four days. It was successful. Supplier ideas and capabilities do not flow unchanged through the buying company. Combining supplier innovation with internal plans, goals, ideas, and capabilities can create unexpected risk. In this case one company's choices led to problems while a competitor's use of the same supplier technology was a winner. Supply-based advantage requires strong integration and risk mitigation to ensure competitive edge.

The challenge becomes managing supply risks, not avoiding them. Introduction of a second company (the supplier) into the risk planning mix can raise complications. This fact can lead to risk avoidance, but unwillingness to take risk can create resistance to change, allowing competitors that leverage supplier ideas to tilt the competitive balance against you.

Whether supplier risks are tactical or strategic, they can dramatically change the competitive balance. Bankruptcies, plant explosions, computer viruses, and loss or misuse of intellectual property at critical nodes in the supply base can gradually (or quickly) erode competitive advantage. Balancing the advantage of managing supply risks with the cost of doing so becomes a key component of the "sustainable" in sustainable competitive advantage.

—Practitioner's Take—

Okay. All this theory about competitive advantage from suppliers seems fuzzy and even a bit scary. How does it apply to the real world of the practical supply professional?

The five concepts—sustainable competitive advantage, value, complexity, rapid change, and risk—are an environmental framework within which supply-based advantage is formed. The point is that the target, competitive advantage, is not stationary. It constantly moves, influenced by both external forces and internal perspectives.

Facts and science aren't the only components of supply-based advantage. Artful relationship building and dealing with unpredictable changes also make up this business imperative. If it were easy, everyone could do it and supply-based advantage would not be a way to win. The task is tough; now we will create a framework that outlines what it might entail.

Shooting at a moving target is achievable for an outstanding marksman, but when the movement is a sophisticated computer game with new targets leaping out everywhere and includes real-world consequences for losing, it means you need a plan. This book lays out the components of such a plan. Like a computer game whiz, getting to the top of the record score list entails skill and practice; likewise, truly gaining and holding supply-based advantage is not an overnight exercise, but rather a long-term program. Too many supply managers declare victory after some quick results, often just on cost, only to discover later that any advantage has slipped away.

Transformation Sounds Magical, but Is It Sustainable?

"Transformation" has become a buzzword in supply management, describing the shift from tactical buying to strategic sourcing. But that shift only addresses the beginning of supply-based advantage, initial achievement, not sustainability. Transformation gives the impression of a rapid, dramatic improvement. In theater it describes a miraculous change in appearance. Senior management loves its message of a "magical" overnight change to a new level of competitiveness. It is great marketing. The software and consulting industries use the term to explain what they can do for the "average or below-average" organization to suddenly remake them into a leading-edge player.

For the delivery of short-term results or as the first step toward leveraging supply in the business, indeed, transformation may be the right term. But the competitive advantage race is not a sprint, but, rather, a never-ending marathon requiring some parts to be run fast and others steadily. The results promised in the first six to twelve months of a transformation rarely "transform" the competitive landscape. Instead, they incrementally improve the existing situation, often simply reducing a competitive disadvantage.

A sustainable supply-based advantage program, capable of dealing with an ever-changing business environment, is not described by a marketing-friendly word like "transformation." Words like "journey" or "voyage" come to mind. Our choice is the analogy of constructing a building. This is about combining science in terms of the construction materials, civil engineering, and physics, plus art via design and style that provides strong attractiveness. Like construction work, this takes real effort, not a quick magic trick.

The architecture of supply-based advantage must align with company culture and integrate with strategy to balance short- and long-term outcomes. This requires a long-term architectural design, renewed with ongoing maintenance and remodeling.

Too often, "one size fits all" supply-based strategies masquerade as competitive advantage. Strategies like:

- ▶ Spend analysis to leverage volume for lower prices.
- ▶ Supply base rationalization.
- ▶ Mandated competition via auctions and bids.
- ▶ Supplier partnerships.
- ▶ Efficiency improvement via technology.

None are bad, each has its place, and some are vital at certain points in time. But a one-size-fits-all approach is like a cookie cutter housing development—the Levittown of supply—and rarely leads to sustainable competitive advantage.

Supply-Based Competitive Advantage: Architecture and Construction

Maintaining a winning supply base is part of a design-and-construct venture that will extend over a long period of time. Any initial transformation effort is just the first step of an ongoing plan that builds upon itself over time. Each part of the design and its implementation matters, much as a home construction project incorporates a series of building blocks, none of which can be omitted. Each aspect of the effort is covered in its own chapter.

1. *Architectural Drawings and Blueprints.* The architectural drawings represent the philosophical approach toward the supply base, including policies, principles, and ethical, legal, and corporate responsibility perspectives toward suppliers. The blueprint creates the framework for supply-based competitive advantage. It also creates the "customer persona" suppliers see when working with your company. (Chapter 4)

2. *Foundation.* Sourcing strategy is the supplier selection process that shapes the supply base, which is the foundation of any supply advantage. The sourcing strategy needs to integrate supplier competencies with the needs and strategy of the company. (Chapter 5)

3. *Walls.* Supplier relationships form the walls of the house. They, too, are critical to support the structure of competitive advantage. Corporate results often depend on suppliers, especially strategic ones. They are not just

the outcomes of a sourcing exercise. These relationships can become critical to future value creation. (Chapter 6)

4. *Roof.* The home's roof connects the walls and keeps out inclement weather. The supply chain/network connects multiple tiers of suppliers through to customers. Conventional wisdom is that companies compete as supply chains, not individual firms. The winner has a supply chain integrated with its business model and strategic direction. (Chapter 7)

5. *Rooms.* The first interior element of design, rooms create the home's living space and appeal. The analogy in supply base design and construction is internal organizational structure—how to configure the organization(s) that manage suppliers. This is more than "lines and boxes," also including organizational skill levels, rewards, measures, tasks, and decision processes. Each "one-size-fits-all" supply strategy mentioned above has its own set of capabilities and skills that become part of the organization's "room layout." As one is situationally (rather than universally) used, those capabilities and skills become part of the fundamental knowledge and skill set within the supply organization. (Chapter 8)

6. *Doors and Windows.* These are the passageways that integrate the home into a workable whole. Isolated rooms don't work, nor does a layout with bizarre or incomplete connections between rooms. Coordinated cross-functional communication and management of suppliers are the "doors and windows" of supply-based advantage. So is engaging senior management about the supply strategy such that supplier performance integrates with the customer imperatives from the other end of the supply chain. (Chapter 9)

7. *Utilities.* Timely delivery of fuel, light, communication, water, and air flow make a house livable. Supply's analogies are the flows of money, external information in, internal information out, talent, and knowledge. Competitive advantage comes from managing connective business flows across corporate boundaries from outside in, inside out, and across internal departments up and down the supply chain. Connections between information technology infrastructure and software, banking relationships and cash flow, employee recruiting and retention, and intellectual property with core competencies across the supply base all combine to create adaptive, dynamic business-focused supply strategies. (Chapter 10)

8. *Maintenance and Remodeling.* Continually adjusting to change is necessary in both homes and businesses. The decision to do this work yourself or hire external professionals is a pivotal choice. Outsourcing creates another set of suppliers that must be managed, often under complex circumstances. (Chapter 11)

9. *Home Insurance.* You also need to protect your home against risk of loss from fire, theft, and storm. Supply risk has expanded to include more than routine quality and delivery outages, also encompassing corporate reputation risk (when suppliers mistreat workers), price risk (when commodity prices fluctuate), disruption risk (weather, disasters), and regulatory risk (changing laws). Home and building insurance is a necessity in today's world, as is intelligent design (use earthquake construction codes in places where earthquakes are likely). The lack of such protections in supply base design will undermine your competitive edge. (Chapter 12)

—Practitioner's Take—

The pressures of day-to-day business and senior management mandates for quick cost reductions don't leave much time to do this kind of work. Right? Perhaps, but if sustainable competitive edge is the goal, then this kind of continuous progression is important. It is a process that takes years, not weeks or months, to implement and sustain.

Stop!!! Before reacting to this comment, take a moment and consider that each step of the construction project delivers results. This is a pay-as-you-go proposition—not a "wait-until-it-is-done-to-get-a-payoff" venture.

Broadly implementing sourcing strategy alone delivers significant savings. It also moves all the other elements to some degree, given the integrated nature of supplier management. In the early 1990s, the only part of this architecture P&G implemented broadly was sourcing strategy, yet our savings ran nine figures year after year. Additionally, we almost intuitively began developing supplier relationship methodologies and internal cross-functional partnerships that emerged as powerful value creators later.

The imperative in all this is value focus—and value inherently includes cost savings, avoidance, and control. Too many academics and alliance professionals criticize procurement for its focus on cost. Competitive cost is purchased value's price of entry and a critical organizational responsibility of purchasing. Few other functions see cost control as their primary goal (possible exception: finance). Gaining competitive advantage inherently includes controlling cost drivers. The trick is going beyond cost to include other value components as well.

Entrepreneurs understand the concept of getting their money's worth for every penny they spend. They also look to get more than their money's worth when they buy, always looking for collateral non-price value. Combining the advantages of large company leverage techniques with small company creative value acquisition is the essence of this competitive advantage construction project.

Notes

1. Vadim Kotelnikov, "Sustainable Competitive Advantage," www.1000 advices.com/guru/strategy, 10/31/2007.

2. Interview with Jim Dempsey, retired P&G Purchases Director, January 23, 2008.

3. Thomas L. Friedman, *The World is Flat* (New York: Farrar, Straus and Giroux, 2005), pp. 414–417.

4. Janet Adamy, "Half a Loaf: Interstate Bakeries Got Bread to Last but Didn't Rise," *Wall Street Journal*, September 23, 2004.

CHAPTER 2

Suppliers

The Forgotten Competitive Currency

> HISTORY: the branch of knowledge dealing with past acts, ideas, or events that will or can shape the course of the future.

Those who cannot learn from history are doomed to repeat it.
—George Santayana, philosopher

Suppliers represent an enormous percentage of any company's cost structure and, in many industries, provide significant impact on companies' ability to compete via speed to market and quality of products as well as customer experience, innovation, and operational execution. With the onset of outsourcing—whether offshore or nearby—for areas like information technology, human resources, marketing, and product delivery, this dependence on suppliers is growing rather than declining. Said another way, up to 70 percent of a company's real substance—products, service, and internal operations—is made up of goods and services that come from outside suppliers. What the customer sees is often as much based on supplier capability as the selling company's own skills.

While lots of supply studies and professional organizations trumpet the importance of suppliers and supplier management, they are largely preaching to the choir—their own members. The choir often does not include the CEO or senior management councils, who remain focused on customers, revenue, Wall Street/investors, and financial compliance. Supply is mouthed as vital, but it is top of mind for few leaders when they create strategy. Instead, it is an operational necessity and/or a place to extract cost savings, regardless of their implications longer term (although, sometimes cost extraction is exactly what must happen; the trick is knowing when and how to do it).

Exceptions to this tactical mindset exist. Current Wal-Mart CEO, Lee Scott, started in logistics. Indeed, logistics, supply chain, and global sourcing are integral to Wal-Mart's strategy and have driven its growth since Sam Walton founded the company. The approach has evolved from the superior quality/good price approach of its founder to the lowest possible cost/reasonable quality business model of today. But overall, supply was and still is critical to its success. Most corporate CEOs come out of marketing, sales, and finance with little or no experience in supply or supplier relations.

Much of what customers experience in their interfaces with a company—from websites designed by outside contractors and advertising messages crafted by ad agencies, to components of the products and services they sell—are the result of its supply base flowing through to the market. Despite the empirical and logical basis behind this observation, the management of suppliers is rarely viewed as a strategic element of company operations. Many managers don't think of their external auditor, advertising agency, or the Google search site that brings them customers as suppliers. Yet, that is exactly what they are—providers of services the company pays for.

In The Conference Board's 2004 CEO Challenge survey, which asked over 500 CEOs which of sixty-two possible challenges were most important and highest priority for their companies, only four challenges specifically mentioned suppliers or supply chain. Yet, the challenges of outsourcing, cost control, speed/flexibility/adaptability, and accessing innovation all made the top ten—without a clear connection to the fact that supplier performance is critical to each.[1] Management consultant McKinsey, in its 2007 assessment of the twenty-first-century purchasing organization, went further, saying that the last ten years of global competition have "opened the eyes of executives everywhere to the strategic benefits that can be achieved through the intelligent use of purchasing and supply management."[2] However, it goes on to say that this evolution in thinking has, in most companies, not translated into results and that the use of purchasing in the business has not evolved much beyond the function's traditional narrow tactical and transactional focus.

Supply Management: Unlikely to Make the Strategic Function List

As corporate structures evolved over the last 100 years or so, the importance of accessing goods and services slipped away. In part this was driven by vertical integration—the image of the Ford River Rouge plant taking ore at one end and spitting out cars at the other—but even as vertical integration lost its preferred strategy position over the last twenty years, supply and supplier management remained a backwater discipline, buried deep in the bowels of the organization's "backroom" operations. The management functions of marketing, finance and accounting, human resources, and even manufacturing (the transformation of inputs into the final product) became the basis of managerial science.

MBA programs did not, until recent years, generally spend much time on supply. It was typically the "given" in a case study, or simply not mentioned at all. Worse, the vocabulary of supply never standardized like that of marketing (4 Ps—product, price, place [distribution], promotion) or finance (debits, credits, return on investment, and other widely used CPA and financial analysis terms). Each of these functions also has well-understood subfunctional areas (advertising, brand management, financial analysis, accounting, mergers and acquisitions, treasury), all of which have common definitions across companies. A quick sampling of the titles that supply managers or their bosses hold emphasizes just how little commonality there is.[3]

Sampling of Supply Management Organization Names

Business Services	Procurement Services
Buying	Purchases
Commercial Outsourcing	Sourcing
Commodity Management	Raw Materials and Services
Contracts	Purchasing
Corporate Agreements	Strategic Sourcing
Early Supplier Involvement	Supplier Development
Global Sourcing	Supplier Involvement
Logistics	Supplier Partnering
Materials	Suppliers
Materials Management	Supply
Outsourcing	Supply Chain
Procurement	Supply Management

Even within the profession there is no common nomenclature. Take, for instance, the Institute for Supply Management (ISM), which is the largest and probably the premier professional purchasing and supply management organization in the world, despite its U.S. location and predominant membership population. In 2001, when the organization changed its name from NAPM (National Association of Purchasing Management) to ISM, each local chapter of the association voted on the name change. It was nowhere near unanimous, with cities like New York, Chicago, San Diego, and even my hometown of Cincinnati all declining to change their names despite the "parent" organization's decision.

Worse, the lack of academic and organizational alignment on vocabulary has led to definitional debates and conflicts between various professional organizations about which disciplines are included in broad names like supply chain or supply management. ISM has even included manufacturing supervision in its scope—probably not something the Manufacturer's Alliance/MAPI, the premier manufacturing professional association, appreciates. (Of course, MAPI has had a purchasing arm for years—professional associations compete too.) The problem is that terminology varies from company to company—supply chain in one place is about suppliers not internal manufacturing plants while at another company it is the outbound flow from the manufacturing location to the customer, with no supplier inclusion at all.

Logistics professionals and academics want to include procurement in their field and the reverse is true as well.[4] The problem becomes that, unlike marketing and sales or finance and accounting, where the related disciplines are clearly defined, there is no unifying framework of concepts, definitions, or even strategic components universally agreed upon across the professions competing for dominance in the management of corporate supply chains. The likelihood of a senior executive having had supply chain or supply management exposure in his or her academic background is between slim and none—and even if they did, it would not be consistent with similar exposure of another senior executive who graduated from a different university. (In some few industries, particularly automotive, however, career experience in supply is a distinct possibility due to the rotation of promising management talent through supply as a career-broadening experience.) This lack of common definition and exposure simply reinforces the lack of corporate leadership recognition of supply as a strategic player in setting corporate strategy or achieving competitive advantage.

For practitioners, two events took place in the early and mid 1990s that seemed to change this. The first was some high-profile coverage of supply in the popular business press, starting with stories coming out of the U.S. auto industry. A flamboyant Spanish Basque, J. Ignacio Lopez de Arriortua, took over as General Motors' head of global purchasing in early 1992 and began a brutal restructuring of their supply base that entailed ripping up all contracts and demanding double-digit price reductions. In an extremely short period of time (less than one year, from April 1992 to March 1993), his impact on GM's cost structure—and on purchasing leaders in other industries—was enormous.[5] At P&G we had spirited debates about the value of his philosophy, and truth be known, no small senior management pressure to duplicate his approach (which, generally speaking, we were able to resist).

The positive seemed to be that, regardless of his approach, Lopez changed the perception of management that purchasing was a non-value-added function. He also put suppliers on the management radar screen, if only as a place to squeeze out cost. Lopez reported directly to CEO Jack Smith and installed concepts like the QSP business award criteria (Quality, Service, and Price), commodity management, and advanced purchasing organizations to bring suppliers into new product platforms earlier.

The issue was that within GM's culture prior to his intervention, the engineering function that chose the suppliers and price was rarely a criterion they used to make those decisions. Hence, under Lopez the focus on price was overwhelming in the QSP trinity. (This will not be the last time we talk about corporate culture and its impact in shaping how concepts are actually executed.) He also did things like give proprietary supplier drawings to other manufacturers in order to get quotes without any R&D overhead costs. He then awarded business to those suppliers at the expense of the companies that had actually invented the technologies.

Ironically, almost simultaneously at Chrysler, the purchasing leader, Tom Stallkamp began an effort diametrically opposite from a philosophical standpoint. His program, called SCORE (Supplier Cost Reduction Effort), focused on collaborative relationships and savings sharing.[6] It too had enormous impact ($5 billion over about seven years). SCORE, a less controversial effort with fewer lurid details, was not picked up as rapidly by the business press as Lopez's slash-and-burn approach. It became more respected by procurement executives in other industries and, although it has rarely been duplicated, supplanted the Lopez approach in most circles. Later, it too became a darling of the press, but after a longer gestation period. Still, it was Lopez who elevated purchasing in the popular press for the first time—which says something about misconceptions in management toward supply and competitive advantage, since the damage done to GM's supplier relationships hampered its ability to access topnotch supplier innovation for years afterward, even as the press commented about the cost reductions Lopez quickly generated in the short term. (Interestingly, after he left GM for Volkswagen, he was replaced by current GM CEO, G. Richard Wagoner, Jr., who sought to rebuild some level of trust with what had become an alienated supply base.)

Then in early 1995, *Fortune* magazine actually put purchasing on its cover, declaring it was no longer a corporate backwater.[7] Surely, that meant the value of suppliers to corporate strategy would take off. The article linked the strategic value of purchasing with companies' ability to deliver profit and was peppered with a lot of truths. (The litany of what today, over twelve years later, are still leading concepts is almost endless: when the goal is boosting profits, look first at what you buy; tread the middle path between pressure and cooperation; lower the total cost, not just price; leverage your buying power by consolidating the number of suppliers for common items; commit to a handful of suppliers on which you can depend; look for sound finances, state-of-the art technology, and promised productivity improvement; contract long enough to demonstrate genuine commitment on both sides; work together to reduce costs; reduce administrative expenses; use part of the savings to make your end product a better value for your customer; schedule close-coupled deliveries carefully to reduce inventories, and so on).

The second event came out of the consulting industry.[8] While many consultancies had a purchasing practice, in about 1995, A. T. Kearney led the industry into strategic sourcing with what has become an icon: a seven-step process and a contingency fee–based business model driven by the delivery of purchasing/supply savings for their clients. The first client actually saved $500 million. Over the next ten years a large number of companies hired consultants to strategically source their purchases, but Kearney was clearly the groundbreaker. Many companies simply felt they did not have the expertise to effectively manage their supply bases—hence their use of consultants. The issue, of course, becomes whether these companies can sustain any sort of competitive edge when the consultant's outside expertise leaves and when the same approaches are commonly applied to other companies in the same industry.

So, did corporate management suddenly become believers? Guess again. The vast majority of companies continue to view purchasing as a "grimy, mundane" back office administrative function. Sure there were exceptions like Lou Gerstner's decision to import purchasing talent in the person of Gene Richter, then Hewlett Packard's award-winning procurement leader, into IBM. Richter's procurement group was a key component of IBM's turnaround.

Ironically, the rise of Wal-Mart and the big-box retailers like Best Buy, Staples, and Home Depot, all of which leveraged supply as a competitive advantage, resulted in much more focus by most of their suppliers (the goods manufacturers) on how to deal with the customer side of the supply chain. These retailers, and their relentless use of purchasing volume leverage and logistical agility to force change up their supply chains, defined competitive advantage in many people's minds as low price and consistent presence on the shelf. Their suppliers became more focused on how to sell to them than on extracting something special from their own suppliers. Yet, in so many businesses, cost alone is simply not a sustainable competitive edge and extracting too much cost from suppliers can result in a vulnerable, financially weakened supply base that is incapable of major breakthrough.

—Practitioner's Take—

Although some corporate leaders understand the power of strong supply management to the strategic business model of the company—Wal-Mart and Toyota quickly come to mind—most senior managers come out of the marketing or financial areas, where suppliers are the "givens" of the strategy discussion. Part of the issue is that the supply side of business varies significantly, unlike marketing, where academic study has somewhat standardized the key factors; or finance, where governmental accounting rules create common terminology around much of the world. Supply structure, key parameters, and even vocabulary can be quite dissimilar between companies.

Worse, most organizations seem to swing between the extremes of the pendulum—ruthless margin squeezing on one side and cozy "partnerships" that value continuity and friendship without accountability on the other. The quest for competitive advantage requires balance within that range (stopping the pendulum halfway), tough but fair expectations, and the use of competition to ensure cost effectiveness in the customer value equation. This kind of balance is very difficult to sustain. Big companies, in particular, struggle to do this—more often than not celebrating cost reduction more than any other metric. The functions that focus on suppliers are often so far removed from the real business of the company that their goals, while logical on the surface (like savings), are not well aligned with corporate strategic initiatives. The key is to clearly link the business model and the business strategy to supply in a way that integrates supply into its delivery and, more importantly, that takes supply into consideration in company strategy formulation. This will balance both parts of the value equation—performance *and* cost—which is vital to sustaining competitive advantage.

Has It Always Been This Way? Many Giants Knew Better When They Were Smaller

Companies have not always considered the supply side of the business a tactical back office function. Prior to 1900, almost no companies had separate purchasing organizations.[9] Purchasing as a function traces its roots to the American railroad industry, which held a semi-monopoly/oligopoly on that mode of transport. Given the railroads' dominance and limited number of competitors, the purchasing function became a more tactical operation geared toward keeping the trains running on time. However, if they were not particularly successful, there were no real alternatives with the same speed and capacity. It was the first step toward a nonstrategic existence in the bowels of a company.

However, in the more cutthroat competition of other hard goods, company founders and/or their close family members were in charge of supply, in part because it was their own money that was being spent; and how it was spent had a huge impact on the ability of the enterprise to grow and return a profit. For those that ultimately grew and prospered, in fact, it was often a differentiator that made their products unique or widely available, fueling their growth into major corporations today.

Sometimes value was defined as the availability, quality, and delivery cost of unique raw materials that enabled these entrepreneurs to fabricate and sell products that met their customers' needs far better than more commodity-like competitors. In his 2001 book, *The Purchasing Machine,* Dave Nelson, the well-known chief procurement officer at Honda, Deere & Company, and Delphi over a two-decade period, provided a classic example of this kind of competitive edge delivered on the supply side.[10] It relates how a blend of insight about customers with strategic sourcing of raw materials created the dominant farm equipment company, Deere & Company.

Founder John Deere, a Vermont blacksmith who moved to Grand Detour, Illinois, to escape bankruptcy, started his farm equipment company in 1837. At that time most plows were constructed out of wood or cast iron. The rich soil of the American Midwest created a huge problem for farmers of that era, as the soil stuck to the plow, resulting in numerous plowing interruptions as the farmers had to stop and scrape the heavy soil from the plow blade. Deere, using his blacksmith metals expertise, experimented with a number of alternative materials and found a type of steel that was only made in Great Britain. He began to import the material and developed a cast-steel plow that "self-scoured" the soil from the blade, eliminating manual scraping stops.

He parlayed that supply-based advantage with a new manufacturing business model—bringing in enough unique raw material to make plows ahead of orders and then holding them in inventory instead of the standard build-to-order model of the time. (In a strategic move, he shifted in the opposite direction of today's build-to-order best practice, which has become the mantra of the twenty-first-century high-tech supply chain.) Later, he also moved his factory to the current Deere headquarters in Moline, Illinois, to get better access to both inbound river transport of imported steel and outbound finished product transport via the railroads and the Mississippi River. The globally recognized bright green Deere agricultural equipment was founded on a supply-based advantage about 170 years ago by an entrepreneur who understood the connection between customers and supply.

Interestingly, just over half a century before in England, a similar story unfolded, only it "traveled" in the opposite direction. In 1775, during the American Revolution, another entrepreneur combined customer-focused business savvy with supply-based advantage to create another leading competitor—this time in the pottery business.[11,12] Wedgwood, England's finest china, began as a pottery company founded by Josiah Wedgwood in 1752. For centuries, superior porcelain was produced only in China, due to that country's deposits of top grade china clay. Wedgwood was making ornamental pottery, using the small amounts of china clay that were available. Most pottery at the time was crude, in part because the raw materials were inferior. His first use of strategic supply was to develop a substitute material (barium sulfate), source it, and work up a manufacturing process to use it, enabling him to produce higher grade products.

Wedgwood expanded his operation by importing china clay from the rebellious American colonies, where some deposits were discovered. It was hard to get and too expensive to allow volume manufacture. However, in 1768, a huge deposit of china clay was discovered in Cornwall, England, which opened the possibility of wide sale of porcelain dishes for more common people. Wedgwood realized that he needed to gain control over his raw material and also begin to manage its total cost of ownership (another modern idea that is not really so modern). He, along with partner Thomas Bentley, became merchant traders, not just manufacturers.

He took numerous trips to Cornwall to better create clay supplier relationships. His efforts didn't stop there. In the factory, he traditionally used wood to heat the ovens, which, when used to temper clay, became extremely expensive. His next supply effort was to replace the wood with coal, a much cheaper fuel. Finally, he realized that wagon travel over the primitive roads of the eighteenth century was both time consuming and an expensive proposition, so Wedgwood pioneered the use of water transport of the clay and coal to his factory to reduce cost and provide greater reliability. Thus, over a sixty-year time frame entrepreneurs on both sides of the Atlantic Ocean were creating competitive advantage by astutely linking strategic supply management with their business model and customer focus.

Unique Raw Materials Not the Only Advantage

Value comes in many forms, and in those forms, fuels competitive advantage. Today's procurement professionals, many of whom assume there is little strategic history in supplier or purchasing delivery of competitive advantage, believe many of today's leading-edge ideas were conceived in the late twentieth century. As we have already seen, concepts like material substitution (Deere) and total cost of ownership (Wedgwood) are not new.

However, one of the most secretive companies around, Mars, Incorporated, the candy industry leader, has known for a long time that supply is key to its competitive position.[13] While the company was started by Frank Mars in 1911, it was his son, Forest Mars Sr., who led its move to leadership in the chocolate industry. In 1932 Frank Mars fired his son, whose tyrannical approach to employees and the business did not match his father's more genteel style. However, after taking the rights to the Milky Way bar to Europe, where he started up a candy company, Forest Mars saw something that changed the Mars company's future.

During the Spanish Revolution, Mars observed a candy-covered chocolate product, which he would later introduce as the M&M. His company outgrew his father's, and three decades after Frank Mars died (in 1964 after Forest's stepmother passed), he took over the original company, firing his uncle and sister, who then owned it. (Interesting fact: Forest Mars was called the "original boss from hell" in his UK *Daily Mirror*'s obituary in 1999. While that may or may not be true, he was clearly driven, with little special regard for family members.) A key part of his business model was the recognition that the supply side of his business was as critical to competing as the marketing and product sides.[14]

Mars believed that inexpensive materials would be vital to the value his candies offered consumers, which led him to highly prize commercial supply deals. He created a Commercial Department, primarily made up of purchasing and logistics experts. Importantly, its mission was more than to just acquire materials and keep the manufacturing lines supplied. Commercial was charged with developing or discovering innovative ways to buy materials, which remains part of its role today, not just its heritage in the company. In the chocolate confectionary business, Mars was the first U.S. candy company to put people on the ground in source countries (in Africa and South America) to buy cocoa beans directly rather than through brokers.

These source country commercial experts implemented a cocoa pod counting system to estimate crop size and enable crop forecasts that beat the market being set by brokers. Mars's competitors, buying from these brokers, were one step removed from the market, with resulting slower reaction times. It was the beginning of commodity research and weather forecasting as part of commodity trading operations. This supply innovation did not stop with the candy business.

When Mars got into the pet food business, Commercial pioneered the purchase of meat offal and scraps to provide low-cost, yet safe, protein sources for the business. In the 1970s, Mars—through its Commercial Department—was one of a handful of companies that led the way in the use of commodity trading as a profit center in its food (largely grain) businesses and hedging currencies to help protect profits. Integrating supply skill with its marketing segmentation and manufacturing abilities created an integrated competitive position that allowed the company to become a leader in its industry.

Carpe Diem—Seize the Supply Opportunity

At other times, these entrepreneurial leaders leveraged supply when world or domestic events created an opportunity. My own company, 170-year old Procter and Gamble, is perhaps the premier example of opportunistic sourcing and management of their supply base during stressful times.[15] P&G was founded by two immigrants—Irishman James Gamble, a soap maker, and Englishman William Procter, a candle maker, who married a pair of American sisters in the city of Cincinnati. In 1837 they founded the company that bears their name today (coincidently, the same year John Deere began his firm in Illinois). They were one of eighteen soap and candle makers in Cincinnati alone. Competition for daily raw material supply became critical to survival, as the meat scraps and wood ashes necessary to make lye for the product had to be collected door to door from Ohio and nearby Indiana homes. Gamble, who ran buying, often found himself knocking on the back door of the same house while a competitor knocked at the front door. As time went on they evolved their products using then unique raw materials like red oil and palm oil imported from outside the United States.

Gamble used three key strategies, the first of which was a willingness to buy and store supply when it was available—tying up funds in return for secure supply to support growth. The second strategy was prompt payment and honoring contracts with suppliers despite tight finances. A newspaper article at the time stated that "suppliers of fats and oils could take an order from Messrs. Procter and Gamble and pass it along in lieu of cash." This made P&G the customer of choice. The third strategy was to locate near a canal to access cheaper transportation, much as Deere and Wedgwood did.

But the real impact of supply on the company's competitive advantage and market position came during the turbulent times of war, not once but twice. The first occurred as the American Civil War approached, when it became clear that supply planning would be needed, should war break out. Many of the ingredients, while likely to be short, were available in the north as well as the south. However, one item, rosin, came exclusively from the south, where New Orleans was the trading center for the entire country.

The partners, realizing the risk to their business, sent their two sons, William Alexander Procter and James Norris Gamble, on a rosin buying trip to visit the company's principle rosin supplier in New Orleans. (No short trip in those days!)

Upon arrival, they found a vast inventory available at $1 per barrel. On the spot, the young P&Gers made the decision to take an entire boatload—four years of supply! Their competitors back in Cincinnati laughed when they heard about it, expecting the cash outlay to bankrupt the company and/or require selling the rosin at a loss to those very competitors to raise cash. Three months later the Civil War began.

Union army procurement officers were looking for large quantities of soap—the rosin price, with southern sources unavailable due to the war, spiked to $8, then $15 per barrel. P&G got the army contract for all soap on the Western front. This selling breakthrough, enabled through supply, allowed P&G to became the premier soap maker in the Midwest, while its competitors struggled. Four years later, the rosin supply was finally running out when, luckily, the war ended. In the subsequent postwar years, the potential civilian demand for their soap increased. Because of the profits from four years of ultra-low-cost rosin supply, P&G had the cash to extend credit to brokers and merchants in the south after the war. Their business skyrocketed, expanding across the country.

The second war supply opportunity occurred about fifty years later in 1917. One of the founder's descendants, CEO William Cooper Procter, made a similar decision, buying a year's worth of raw materials during the height of World War I. German U-boats were sinking freighters, creating enormous demand for P&G products in Europe at the same time as the United States was experiencing increasingly severe raw material shortages. P&G saw the value of its raw material inventory increase by $8 million, a huge sum at the time. Once again, Procter made a marketing decision, fueled by astute procurement, to leverage that increased material value and sell products based on its competitively advantaged cost of goods rather than prevailing market prices driven by inflated raw material market values. Walking away from a major windfall profit (around 50 percent), P&G invested the outcome of its supply strategy into pricing for its products and delivered another volume increase both domestically and, importantly for its international presence, in Europe as well. These examples of supply-based advantage, at its best, tied the marketing and sourcing sides of the business together to create a competitive edge. They helped enable the expansion of one of the top consumer product companies in the world.

—Practitioner's Take—

A look at history shows that, in their early years, a number of today's major companies truly understood the importance of supply to their business strategy. Many of the concepts that modern supply managers think of as "new" were part of that thinking—material substitution, commodity market knowledge, hedging, total cost of ownership, supplier relationships—the list goes on. More important, the entrepreneurs who ran those companies saw the opportunity for competitive advantage in their supplier network as part of their business model and, importantly, saw supply as a key part of their work.

There is something about successful small companies that makes this connection between suppliers, deal making, and competitive advantage with customers. The key to unlocking what small companies do is to understand why men like Wedgwood, Deere, Mars, Procter, and Gamble were able to make that linkage and then leverage it—even when business pundits saw them more as marketers and sellers than buyers. These pioneers of industry intuitively understood how coordinated customer and supplier-facing interventions can create major marketplace success.

Will the majority of today's big companies get it? Perhaps. Just over twelve years after supply and purchasing made the cover of *Fortune* magazine, purchasing hit the front page of another leading business publication, the *Wall Street Journal*, on October 2, 2007.[16] The article relates the challenges of global sourcing for Manitowac, Co., one of the largest crane companies in the world, dealing with a worldwide shortage of construction cranes driven by an economic boom at the time in emerging market countries. It makes the point that purchasing can no longer be a corporate backwater (the exact same description *Fortune* used over a decade before in describing purchasing and supply!) because they must "navigate foreign cultures," manage complex relationships, and report to senior management. Manitowac's CEO, Glen Tellock, describes it well, "The thing you have to realize is that if you're going to buy so much from outside the company, you'd better be very good at it."

Manitowac's purchasing leader, Robert Ward, is dealing with Eastern European suppliers that are late on delivery, qualifying Chinese suppliers, getting raw materials (steel in this case) for his suppliers, and sourcing hard-to-find items like mobile crane tires from companies around the world. Purchasing is critical not only because of cost considerations but also because of supply assurance and dependability. Maybe this time the importance will stick when things become more stable. Who knows? It really didn't seem to in 1995.

Notes

1. Esther V. Rudis, *CEO Challenge 2004: Perspectives and Analysis,* The Conference Board, Inc., 2004.

2. Chip W. Hardt, Nicholas Reinecke, and Peter Spiller, "Inventing the 21st-century purchasing organization," *The McKinsey Quarterly*, November 2007.

3. Thomas E. Hendrick and Jeffrey Ogden, "Senior Purchasing and Supply Managers' (SPSMs') Compensation Benchmarks and Demographics: A 2001 Study," Department of Supply Chain Management, College of Business, Arizona State University CAPS Focus Study, www.capsresearch.org.

4. Ralph G. Kauffman, "Supply management: What's in a name? Or, do we

know who we are? A point of view," *Journal of Supply Chain Management*, September 22, 2002.

5. Robert B. Hanfield and Earnest L. Nichols, *Supply Chain Redesign: Transforming Supply Chains into Integrated Value Systems*, Chapter 10, "Managing Change in the Supply Chain" (Upper Saddle River, N.J.: FT Press, 2002).

6. Thomas T. Stallkamp, *SCORE! A Better Way to Do Busine$$, Moving from Conflict to Collaboration*, Chapter 7, "The Extended Enterprise Concept" (Philadelphia: Wharton School Publishing, 2005).

7. Shawn Tully with Ricardo Sookdeo, "Purchasing's New Muscle, What Used to Be a Corporate Backwater Is Becoming a Fast-Track Job as Purchasers Show They Can Add Millions to the Bottom Line," *Fortune* magazine, 2/20/1995.

8. Strategic Sourcing History, www.atkearney.com, 2005.

9. *The Encyclopedia of Management*, "Purchasing and Procurement Forum." Thomson Gale, 2006, www.gale.com.

10. Dave Nelson, Patricia E. Moody, and Jonathan Stegner, *The Purchasing Machine* (New York: The Free Press, 2001), p. 52.

11. John Lord, *Capital and Steam Power*, "Capital in Other Industries: Potteries and Wedgewood." London: P. S. King and Son, 1923; accessed at www.history.rochester.edu.

12. Historic Figures, Josiah Wedgewood; accessed at www.bbc.co.uk.

13. Sarah A. Klein, "The Black Sheep," *Crain's Chicago Business*, October 17, 2005.

14. Interview with former Mars Commercial Director Don Klock, currently head of Purchasing at Colgate, April 12, 2005.

15. Oscar Schisgall, *Eyes on Tomorrow, The Evolution of Procter and Gamble* (New York: Doubleday and Company, 1981).

16. Timothy Aeppel, "Global Scramble for Goods Gives Corporate Buyers a Lift: Purchasing Managers Are Prized Commodity; Mr. Ward's Tire Hunt," *Wall Street Journal*, October 2, 2007.

CHAPTER 3

Small Companies

Seeking Value to Offset Lack of Scale

> ENTREPRENEUR: a person who organizes and manages any en-
> terprise, especially a business, usually with considerable initia-
> tive and risk.

Running that first shop taught me business is not financial science;
it's about trading: buying and selling.

—Anita Roddick, founder of The Body Shop

Why does it seem that companies better understood how to link their business model with suppliers when they were smaller than when they became
much larger? Good question. Perhaps an exploration of some smaller companies' use of suppliers in their business strategy can shed some light on the
subject.

Entrepreneurs Use Suppliers When
They Set Up a Company

In 2004, *Money* magazine had a story of a young lawyer who left his corporate
attorney's position to open a one-man law firm.[1] The article described a list

of twenty-two start-up tasks that the lawyer, K. Clyde Vanel, needed to complete during the first month. Of them, an amazing 75 percent in some way involved working with, or purchasing something, from a supplier. (The other 25 percent included nailing down his first client retainer.) One of his selections—a mom-and-pop provider of letterhead and business cards—was a bad choice. Cards were promised in five days and the entire printing cost came to $1500. By the end of the thirty days—no cards, an unfriendly mom and pop, with $1500 spent and no value received.

The point here is that running a business requires setting up and sustaining its infrastructure. In today's world that includes Internet web hosting, office setup, communication, health insurance, computer support . . . the list is almost endless. When an entrepreneur starts up a business, much of the money is typically his/hers or requires signing away part of his/her life for seed money from an investor. When you spend your own money, the burn rate is personally important to you.

The giants we talked about in Chapter 2 (Deere, Wedgwood, Procter, Gamble, and Mars) all went through hard economic times and, in Deere's case, a bankruptcy. The first reason small companies seek value is that it is their money and the risk of failure is very personal. Many learn through mistakes that cost them money and self-esteem directly. That changes your attitude toward suppliers—due diligence and the ability to count on them become constant companions in the sourcing exercise, not just price. Okay, just spending money with other companies and individuals during the startup and investment stages of a business doesn't make the supply side strategic—but rather just an unavoidable necessity to get through quickly. Right?

We'll see. Let's see what supply-based competitive advantage might look like to a small company post startup. How do these companies and their principals see suppliers?

Business Model and Strategy Fit

On the surface, small companies face an enormous barrier to gaining competitive edge from suppliers—lack of meaningful volume. For the supplier, the monetary rewards of small business customers are modest, especially when the supplier is a large corporation. The phrase "necessity is the mother of invention," originally found in Plato's *The Republic* about 2400 years ago, probably best lays out the solution to this challenge. Many successful small companies place interest in their business near the top of the selection criteria for suppliers, way ahead of price. However, the real choice goes beyond that. It is about figuring out which outside suppliers will provide something—whether part of the product itself, or a service that allows successful operation of the business—that is essential to winning with customers. It is not uncommon for these small businesses to pair up with other small companies, where buyer/supplier reliance on each other is more balanced.

On the other hand, sometimes a very small company links up with a giant supplier in a way that makes the buyer's business model hum. Jim Lampman lives in Burlington, Vermont—known as the Queen City by its residents—where he was the first male in over 100 years to major in home economics at the University of Vermont.[2] Lampman became the owner of one of Burlington's top restaurants (The Ice House) and in 1983, routinely purchased boxes of gourmet chocolate as gifts for his staff. His pastry chef at the time was unimpressed, and challenged Lampman to do better. The result, developed by the chef, was a chocolate truffle that was spectacular, so much so that Lampman began giving them out as "the finisher" to patrons at his popular Sunday brunch. Soon he discovered that people were coming to the brunch as much to get the truffle as to eat a meal. This was the genesis of Lake Champlain Chocolates (LCC), the gourmet chocolate company that Lampman founded after selling the restaurant almost twenty-five years ago.[3]

In an industry where Hershey, Mars, Nestle, Cadbury, and a few other giant companies drive most of the volume, the key for LCC had to be quality and flavor. Lampman saw Belgian chocolate as the best in the world, firmly believing that this top-quality dark chocolate was key to hooking customers and consumers. Think of chocolate as a three-tiered industry—the first-tier companies go all the way back to the cocoa beans themselves, roasting and processing them into the building blocks of chocolate flavor and texture, cocoa mass, butter, and powder. Second-tier companies blend ingredients and then "conch" and temper them to change from a semiliquid state into a solid block. It sounds easy, but represents a delicate process that drives mouth feel, hardness, and many other attributes of great chocolate. Then the tier-three players take over and use these bricks of pure chocolate to make the confections most of us buy and enjoy—further tempering, formulating, molding, and packaging the treats we love to consume. LCC is a tier-three chocolate company, focused on the gourmet segment.

Ellen Lampman, the founder's daughter and head of Purchasing at LCC, relates the story of sourcing top-grade chocolate at the company's beginnings. Her father's convictions about Belgian chocolate led him to one of Europe's icons—Callebaut. Founded in the 1850s, the company began its chocolate business in 1911. Today, after merging with French chocolate leader Cocoa Barry in 1996, the company is known as Barry Callebaut, a Swiss-headquartered, CHF (Swiss Franc) 4.1 billion chocolate giant. Starting a relationship with a legendary large supplier when you were a new company in its infancy is no easy task. At the time, Callebaut sold very little in the United States and none directly.

Lampman traveled to New York City, where he found a distributor who handled some Callebaut imports. The quantities available were neither flexible nor easy to get. To access the quality he felt he needed required him to import a 40-thousand-pound container twice a year through the distributor—resulting in a six-month inventory. Ultimately, as Callebaut made the decision to expand into North America, Lampman made it his business to establish direct contact with them despite having bought through a distributor for the first ten years. Ellen Lampman is clear that her father "owns" the Callebaut relationship and has maintained contact with the people he met early on, even as they made the inevitable corporate pilgrimage from job to job, including the Barry merger.

Today, Callebaut has a small factory that provides two truckloads of chocolate pistoles (chocolate chips for processing into candy) to LCC every four weeks from a location thirty miles away in St. Albans, Vermont. Is it an alliance? Maybe, maybe not—but it certainly is strategic for LCC. Meanwhile, Callebaut gets insights into new products that, before they hit a grocery store with a major candy company's logo on it, are often proven out in the gourmet chocolate subcategory, where LCC continues to grow and thrive.

LCC's definition of value is not just about top quality. Innovation is a growing part of the chocolate industry and competition is intense. LCC, a tiny player, has been able to tap Callebaut's expertise to get access to trendy items like "origin chocolates" made from the beans of a particular country or organic chocolates well before competition, including the majors—many of whom also buy from Barry Callebaut. The relationship, like most of any duration, is not perfect and has its struggles at times, but in the end makes sense for both parties and is strategic for the Lampmans. During shortages, Callebaut has found ways to get product to LCC, even if it meant shipping across country from its California plant.

There are quarterly meetings between the companies, after one of which I happened to be in the plant (buying some great chocolates at the factory store) and overheard the Callebaut representative tell Jim Lampman, "I prefer working with a customer like you, who understands value and relationships, more than bigger accounts."

Ellen Lampman manages about 100 suppliers, some of whom are distributors for large corporations, but many of whom are fellow Vermont businesses (LCC buys over 350 tons of local ingredients, a number of which are organically grown). Only a select few of those suppliers are closely tied and help create the competitive positioning that LCC uses to drive its business. About a block up the street, a small fifty-year-old printer—Queen City Printers (QCP)—is one of those alliance partners. Gourmet chocolates are often packed in materials that simply are not that environmentally friendly—foils, plastic films, and fancy packages. As anyone who has been there knows, Vermont is a very "green" state—in more ways than just the Green Mountains that form its backbone. That is where QCP comes in. Whenever a new product is under development, QCP is part of the process, instrumental in coming up with environmentally friendly packaging and wrapper paper options, specifications that help communicate the product identity, and cost efficiencies that help make the product both profitable and hit target consumer price points to encourage sales.

The Lampmans have integrated supply into their business model and strategy—accessing the quality that gourmet chocolate requires from a global confectionary giant like Callebaut and the design and environmental positioning supporting that quality from a small local supplier like QCP. The result: Starting in 1989, six years after its founding, LCC has consistently won awards—sixteen of them to be exact—for its products, packaging, and sustainability efforts, and its business continues to expand by tying a customer-focused strategy with an important, enduring supply element.

Using Supply as an Integral Part of the Business Model

While the Lake Champlain Chocolate story illustrates the kind of value that suppliers can bring to a successful small business, sometimes value goes even farther. Suppliers can be critical in the formation of sustainable barriers to entry that keep competitors at bay. As the old adage goes, "Sometimes it is not what you know, but rather who you know that matters." Suppliers know people and that can make all the difference. Near another Queen City, 800 miles southwest of Burlington, just north of Cincinnati, Ohio, there is a small, successful spa called "Becoming Mom."[4]

Founder Dawn Bierschwal was a corporate type—one of my peers as a Purchases Director at Procter and Gamble. We go back a long way. I was one of the people who first interviewed her and extended an employment offer over twenty years ago. But she was, at heart, an entrepreneur who found big-company culture constraining, so after twenty years, she left to start a pregnancy spa and imaging center that offers pregnant moms, their husbands, and families a combination of spa services, 3D/4D ultrasound imaging, and maternity products and gifts. Quite a change from working in purchasing at a huge consumer goods company!

When you work for a large well-known company, you have three big supply management advantages—volume scale to drive supplier pricing down via production and market efficiencies; financial resources that make you a lower risk customer; and a corporate reputation that suppliers see as a benefit for use in gaining other customers.

During our interview, Bierschwal described the challenges of buying as a small business, "When you are a small startup company, you can't afford to just get what you ordered when you buy. You need to get more value than that by asking for things that the supplier can give and perhaps get something back for." Buying radio advertising illustrates the point. When Becoming Mom buys radio ads, Bierschwal insists on getting a promotion as part of the deal. Example: When she approached a local radio station to buy some advertising time, she negotiated a promotion in which callers described unexpected things that happened during their pregnancies. A Becoming Mom expert was available to address those situations. It turned out to be compelling advertising and something the station's listeners enjoyed as well: a win-win for both the buyer and the supplier.

Obviously, Bierschwal's knowledge of supply and suppliers shows up in her company's business model and how it is run. Superficially, the combination of massage and sonograms seems pretty straightforward. But Becoming Mom's business model is far deeper and more sophisticated than that. Pregnancy, while a special time for an expecting mother, can also bring with it physical stresses (the intense pain of sciatica, uncomfortable foot swelling, concerns about the health of the baby, etc.). The spa focuses on both physical well-being and the emotions of seeing the sonograms and, often for the first time, the gender of the child.

Elective ultrasound and massage for expectant mothers means that safety, not just the experience, must be part of the business model. Furthermore, when Becoming Mom started up, it was still the norm for many doctors to see elective sonograms as an "unprofessional" alternative and low-end competitor of sorts. Hence, Bierschwal's business model needed to stress safety, health, and medical credibility—which make it a leading-edge business in this space.

That's where suppliers came in. Bierschwal decided early on that her ultrasound equipment and its operators needed to be top notch, which led her to General Electric (GE) Medical's equipment. (Interestingly, her P&G experience included being the owner of the GE relationship for chemicals used in the beauty care—shampoos and deodorants—businesses. But, given GE's conglomerate structure, those contacts were of no use in establishing her GE Medical relationship.) As she worked with GE on her business concept, she recognized that she needed physicians to be supportive of the spa. Beyond the best imaging equipment in the field, part of the value GE provided included a contact with an OB/GYN specializing in perinatology (high-risk pregnancies).

As a result, a member of the medical establishment was supportive of the new business when asked about it. A major part of the business model incorporates building relationships with doctors. This includes regular communication with clients' doctors, hiring certified medical sonographers to run the equipment, and providing all results back to the new mom's physician. In fact, this has saved several babies' lives in the first three years of the business, giving Becoming Mom a great reputation for safety. Since its opening, lower cost, more "recreational" pregnancy spa/ultrasound shops have sought to enter the market, with little success. This medically professional approach is higher cost, but provides real value by erecting a barrier to entry for lower end competitors.

The second stage of the model involves the products sold in the shop. Two things shocked Bierschwal when she began to set up her specialty retail offerings. First, she found that many suppliers make it extremely difficult to make contact and buy products directly. Their distributors often were not particularly responsive and direct calls to the manufacturers didn't help much. It took real work to stock a good line of products. The second was how few clinically safe products are available for new mothers.

Her corporate experience with suppliers paid off in this part of the business strategy as well. Using suppliers to help develop ingredients and even products had been part of Bierschwal's job for most of her twenty-year corporate career. As Becoming Mom's owner and procurement guru, she found a supplier of a natural product line with protocols to deliver products both beneficial and safe for pregnant women. This company, Naturopathica, has the focused developmental capability that results in a spa "menu" of skin products certified for prenatal use—for skin, nails, hair, waxes, etc. Becoming Mom is, at the time of this writing, the only Naturopathica partner spa in the state of Ohio. Again, the use of supplier competencies enriched the spa's business model.

The final part of Bierschwal's business plan continues to evolve. Initially the plan was to franchise the operation, using another carefully selected skin product supplier relationship. One of Becoming Mom's skin product lines comes from a supplier named Mama Mio, whose products are designed especially for pregnant women with a key attribute in mind—skin elasticity. Bierschwal worked out a partnership with Mama Mio to lend its name (and thus stock its product line) to her franchised spas. Becoming Mom would remain Bierschwal's business, but any other franchises would be named Mama Mio. However, through the expertise of yet another supplier—her franchising lawyer—she discovered that many of the states that would be prime markets for her upscale business model had extremely complex and costly franchising laws. That ultimately killed the idea.

Instead, Bierschwal has a consulting business in which she helps people who would have been potential franchisees to start up similar businesses. One of the lines she strongly recommends to those clients is that of the supplier willing to help her expand the business when franchising was an option, Mama Mio.

—Practitioner's Take—

Small companies that successfully see the link between supply and their business model are experts in getting strategic value from those relationships. These entrepreneurs clearly understand that suppliers are important to them. They see supply as strategic because they are spending their own money and want the most value they can get for it. More important, small businesses are made up of people that see the entire span of the organization. Large corporations get so big that purchasing and supply people are far away from the customer, making the connection to business strategy harder. Instead, whatever management or the supply leader rewards becomes what supply should deliver. Too often that means metrics that are "generically good" like cost savings or departmental efficiency (order processing costs or headcounts)—not necessarily metrics that drive improvement of the overall business position. After all, who can argue with lower costs or delivering more with less?

The problem is that everyone seeks these things, so the likelihood that they will deliver competitive advantage is low—too many companies duplicating strategies provides nothing particularly unique. These efforts may help keep you competitive but often they do not let you break away.

Successful small companies, competing at the local level, may struggle to get the lowest price but they often get additional value tailored to

SMALL COMPANIES • 41

their specific needs. Those value components help them tip the balance in their favor with their customers. The lesson: Smart, successful small companies see suppliers as important. They understand that supply-based advantage is key to success. And they see the whole business, not just a single function or area.

Supply Matters in Emerging Markets, Too

Lest readers think that only businesses from developed countries understand the importance of supply to competitive advantage, a few examples from emerging markets may help defuse that misconception. This phenomenon is not just an American one. When P&G first entered China in the early 1990s, the Chinese government required foreign companies to enter joint ventures with local producers. In the laundry detergent business, P&G chose to ally with three regional detergent makers that had factories and local brand identities—one in Guangzhou (south), one in Beijing (north), and the last in Chengdu (west). Ron Juenger was sent to lead the local Chinese procurement organization as part of a key strategic decision to localize as many ingredients as possible, rather than importing them from the outside. He launched a strategy called "pan-China sourcing" that sought to link, under P&G purchasing leadership, the buying operations of P&G and its three joint venture partners. That strategy took a long time and much more effort to implement than most people expected.

Why was it so difficult? After all, the approach offered scale, savings, and potential competitive advantage. The logic and time-tested truth of the strategy seemed unassailable. Not to the Chinese, however. Many Chinese entrepreneurs were quite wary of outsiders spending their money. Juenger explained, at the time, that the owners of the companies typically were only willing to delegate purchasing to a trusted family member (perhaps like Jim Lampman's daughter Ellen at LCC? or maybe the sons of the founding Procter and Gamble during the Civil War?). As a result it took longer than expected to build enough trust to pull off pan-China sourcing. In other cases, extended family members ran companies that provided some of those purchased items, so the definition of "value" was not the same as it might be for a publicly traded corporation. (More on conflict of interest and supply-based advantage later.)

The point here is not about which approach, the multinational leveraging strategy or the local family-managed supplier relationships, was best. Rather, it is that these entrepreneurial companies, regardless of their nationality, frequently see suppliers as part of the holistic business proposition, often managed by someone they trust implicitly (especially a family member).

Using Technology to Reduce Cost in Emerging Markets

Historically, the ability of entrepreneurs to extract value from suppliers explodes when there is enormous change—often in terms of technology or innovation—that transforms the market. Today, some of the poorest places in the world are also where new businesses, whose owners are well aware of supply's impact on competitive edge, are starting to emerge. There are probably no more difficult and "emerging" markets than Africa or rural India. How do tiny local businesses there leverage the value of suppliers to deliver success in very rough-and-tumble environments?

In these places, unlike many of the stories I have related so far, cost control is a pivotal element in almost any winning strategy. Poverty is a great equalizer but also an incentive to innovate. Customers are never stupid—they know good value, especially when their resources are extremely limited.

One of the key technological breakthroughs in poor countries is the use of cell phones. This is not the expensive, "minute-intensive" use we see in developed economies, but quick, targeted use of communication to link customers and, importantly, suppliers to win against the competition. Many of these cell phones (and the towers they use) are very basic—a phone costing $20 that people living on $2 a day can use. A *Business Week* special report outlined the impact of cell phones on emerging economies[5]:

In the Kenyan village of Muruguru, a woman named Grace Wachira runs a sweater knitting business. The advent of cell phones, and the phone company as a key supplier, shifted her business model dramatically. What was once a several-hour walk or communal taxi ride to the nearest town to see a yarn vendor (who may or may not be there, and who may or may not have the stock she wanted) became a scheduled meeting, arranged by cell phone call. Her quote to *Business Week* (BW) was "I am saving time, I am saving money." This same phone supplier also enables her sell-side model as well—connecting to potential buyers without having to travel to the market.

Further east, in the poor Indian state of Kerala, the same BW article described how the use of phones enabled local fishermen to increase profits by using cell phone service to determine which coastal marketplaces offered the best (higher) prices for their catch because demand was strong enough to absorb the catch. Yet the buyers in these markets could price the fish lower to consumers because they had less waste. Their pre-communication with the fishermen (suppliers) allowed the fisherman to be more efficient because they eliminated stops at ports with low demand and went directly to appointments with interested buyers in more attractive ports. The result: supplier efficiency passed on to the buyer in terms of fresher fish (a commodity with high time-based perishablity), allowing lower buyer total costs because fewer fish are thrown away (and more sold) before they can spoil. Everyone's revenue goes up and costs down, creating value. The phone company, as a supplier to both sellers and buyers, makes that kind of difference.

Perhaps the most interesting part of using cell phone suppliers to change the game is the creativity with which the phones are used in these parts of the world. Entrepreneurs take out loans to buy telephony equipment and create "village phones," selling minutes to their neighbors. Others simply buy a portable memory chip—the SIM (subscriber identity module) card—and plug it into someone else's phone. Conversations are incredibly brief (both oral and text messaging) to reduce expenses. Some even use prearranged messages via ring number communications to tell others important information. This extension of developed economy teenagers' text message abbreviations further cuts cost and increases value from wireless communication service supply.

Value Beyond Cost, Even in Poor Countries

Even in Africa, however, value is not always about cost and efficiency. In another magazine article, author G. Pascal Zachary describes the amazing changes occurring in Rwanda, home of the chilling *Hotel Rwanda* genocide.[6] While the risk is high, a number of Americans are investing there with expectations of profitable business, and not always at the low-cost end of the market. One of the investments described seeks to leverage a growing upscale restaurant market for western aid workers in the capital of Kigali. There an American woman, Alissa Ruxin, whose husband is one of those aid workers, is starting up a restaurant, bar, and spa called the Heaven Café.

Her experience illustrates the small business owner's need to have a strategy and tie suppliers and supplies into that strategy. Seeing the entire business landscape and integrating its supply and demand sides becomes critical for supply-based advantage. In order to create the upscale restaurant atmosphere she envisions means incorporating buying savvy. The deck for her restaurant requires wood—but in Rwanda, interestingly enough, wood is not used as a building material (remember the movie—lots of concrete block not wood buildings). With no Home Depot around, she had to send a worker to the Congo to select individual trees for cutting and pay to have the logs milled and finished. Expensive—yes, but if the venture's strategy is to draw western aid workers, such extras can justify a restaurant that charges $20 a meal. (She also hires a guard—another supplier—to watch over her building material inventory and dole it out on a "just-in-time" basis to protect the investment.)

Will these businesses ultimately sustain a competitive edge or become failures due to the risks inherent in these regions? Will the edge created by cell phone use or a particular business model be too easily duplicated by hungry competitors? It is too soon to tell, but the use of supplier products and expertise to create these companies parallels history in more developed parts of the world.

—Practitioner's Take—

Supply-based advantage is not a single-culture phenomenon. Nor is it the sole purview of big companies reported in the business media. Its use by small businesses around the world is well documented. One of the advantages of being small is that the people who run these businesses inherently see the entire business and have quick, open, informed communication between the buying, selling, product design, and financial parts of the company. These entrepreneurs are not about documenting the whys and wherefores of linking supply into marketing to create a competitive advantage. They are too busy making those linkages intuitively based on accumulated experiential knowledge about the business and the local market in which it competes. "Small company magic" is often lost in big corporations when holistic business understanding is replaced by specialists in every function.

The other nagging question for both major companies and small businesses is that scale is still important. Imagine competing with another company that has a 20 percent cost advantage and is willing to use it to drive their business either through lower pricing or additional services funded from the savings. That is why value must include cost control. Supply goals must include cost savings, but not to the exclusion of other potential benefits that could lead to lasting competitive edge.

The challenge is to have a long enough vision to construct competitive advantage using the supply side, while managing the intense pressures of short-term results. The challenge is also to become small enough to capture the intuitive value linkage of a tiny company, while accessing the scale benefits of greater size. Managing the organizational complexity that comes with size requires a plan—especially on the supply side's linkage to demand-based customer preference.

Notes

1. Ellen McGirt, "30 Days," *Money*, April 2004.
2. Interview with Ellen Lampman, head of Purchasing at Lake Champlain Chocolates and founder Jim Lampman's daughter, June 8, 2007.
3. Sweet Profiles, Candy Wrapper, *Candy Industry*, September 2002.
4. Interview with Dawn Bierschwal, founder of Becoming Mom Pregnancy Spa and Imaging Center, November 12, 2007.
5. Jack Ewing, "Upwardly Mobile in Africa," *Business Week*, September 24, 2007.
6. G. Pascal Zachary, "Startup: Rwanda," *Business 2.0*, August 2007.

CHAPTER 4

Blueprint for Supply-Based Advantage

Plan Before Doing

> BLUEPRINT: a process of photographic printing, used chiefly in copying architectural and mechanical drawings, which produces a white line on a blue background.

It will not do to leave a live dragon out of your plans if you live near one.
—J. R. R. Tolkien, in *The Hobbit*

The challenge of combining the potential advantages of size, scale, and scope in large corporations with the agility and integrated business value understanding of small businesses is no simple task. Nor is it a short, instant gratification process. It takes constancy of purpose, a steady and sustained focus on building a business that wins over time.

Creating a supply-based advantage has to deal with this range of needs and, thus, is more like a construction project than a magical "transformation" event. The outcome, a beautiful home or an impressive building, captures the imagination when completed but is hard work along the way. Frequent design changes result in poorly laid-out living spaces that must be corrected later. Anticipating current and future requirements with a robust design creates something that will survive business cycles.

In my own experience, even P&G, with all its resources and scale, did not find it easy. When A. G. Lafley became CEO, he studied the company's history and found that over the past fifty years, P&G had never sustained growth for more than five consecutive years. In 2007, for the first time, P&G passed that hurdle under Lafley's leadership. It took constancy of purpose to do it. On the supply side, constancy of purpose is even more difficult because the *perception* of supplier importance to the business often varies considerably, depending on a company's current situation.

Barriers to staying focused in any company are embedded in the competitiveness of the markets, ever increasing expectations of customers, and human nature (pride and belief that when something is done, you move on to the next thing). The reasons also include continuing change in technology, product design, people, and economic cycles—all of which change the value equation. On the sales side, this shows up quickly in revenue figures and inventories. However, for supply—deep in the back office far upstream from the customer—the challenge becomes balancing a consistent overarching strategic message to suppliers with knee-jerk reactions to changes on the sales and profit side.

The typical supply management book jumps into the strategic sourcing process or just focuses on a single part—e-commerce or supplier management or those broad supplier selection approaches that "right-size" the supply base, saving lots of money immediately. However, if the goal is strategic advantage, you need to start first with the construction equivalent of planning. It comes in two steps—first at the corporate level, where supply fits into overall strategy (architectural drawings) and then at the supply management level, to lay out specific interactions internally and with the supply markets. The first plan provides a broad framework that integrates supply thinking into the business. The second provides direction on how to approach supply markets and individual suppliers to optimize their impact on current business situations. Managing suppliers requires the right mindset, not just performance of rote tasks. The corporate philosophy, principles, and policy that make up these "blueprints" set the tone for how supply will (or will not) be included in the quest for competitive edge.

Hot- and Cold-Running Direction Setting

How senior management thinks about suppliers, if and when they do, is critical to how the supply base will tie into the company's strategy. Unlike marketing and financials, the supply side of the business is often more like a hot- and cold-running faucet than a long-term link to strategy.

▸ When the business is weak and profits are at risk, supply often becomes "strategic" as a way to reduce supplier profits to help cover company shortfalls. Business recovery plans (and business press coverage of them) tout strategic supply actions that cut cost.

▸ During steady business periods, supply is a "given" in the business equation. Supplier relationships are assumed to be on maintenance, while the company focuses on more important elements elsewhere. Keeping things running within volume and budget forecasts is the mindset.

▸ When business is growing rapidly, supply becomes important again, but at a tactical level—just get the stuff to make growth feasible. If there are shortages, supply becomes strategic again, while in loose markets it becomes a given.

The chart below states this even more succinctly:

Business Climate	Management View of Suppliers	Goals
Business Downturn	Strategic to the business	Cost reduction
Steady Business	Just a given, expected to be there	Cost and delivery
Business Upturn	Tactical, deliver to support the plan	Supply availability

The expectations for each situation are vastly different. Suppliers and the internal organizations that manage them see this inconsistency over time. Every direction change sends different messages to suppliers about how they will be treated and what is important. Supply-based advantage recognizes that working with the supply base should not be a short-term intervention. I once heard Pierre Mitchell, director at The Hackett Group, say it best when he described the impact of procurement and supply management on company competitive advantage as "revolution through evolution." This effort takes time—often measured in years not months; and to stay on track requires a framework—the supply equivalent of architectural drawings and construction blueprints.

Architectural Drawings: The Company's Operating Framework

Nearly every major company, and lots of the good small ones, creates a set of principles and objectives that help define what the leadership seeks to achieve plus boundaries around how they will achieve it. This philosophy creates the "architectural plan" that defines the company approach to its employees, customers, suppliers, and other major stakeholders (shareholders, communities, governments, and so on).

In terms of supply-based advantage, this corporate philosophy sets the "atmosphere" within which supply and suppliers will operate. Think of it as the company philosophy and policy toward the outside world, and suppliers in particular. Simplistically, regarding supply, it is made up of just two components:

1. The company's overall values—legal, ethical, social. It is the description of how it will operate when it competes for business.
2. Management's view of what is important for its business, employees, and stakeholders, especially over the long term.

These components set the contextual framework within which supplier contribution to the business model and its operation will be measured. Employees who work with suppliers will approach the supply base with a bias created by this context. The challenge is to understand where supply fits into this framework, since many companies do not specifically mention it.

Supply's Applicability Varies with the Situation

Every company has its own unique situation. Some are dealing with falling sales or hemorrhaging cash. For them, competitive parity is first priority, not necessarily competitive advantage. Others, in tough, evenly matched competitive battles, are looking for something that will allow them to break away from the pack and help create a measure of sustainable advantage. Still others are the leaders. Already enjoying some level of competitive edge, for them, maintaining and growing that advantage, while searching for the next big opportunity, is the goal.

Each situation has different implications for how to deal with the supply base. Within a large company one of the big challenges is merging those implications across different business units with very different situations. An example from my own career took place in 1995 when the Mexican peso lost half its value relative to the U.S. dollar. My business unit, once fairly consistent between the United States and Mexico from competitive and market attractiveness standpoints, suddenly became very different.

In the United States, business was strong and shoppers were trading up to higher value products. In Mexico, the crushing devaluation of purchasing power led to a 40 percent demand contraction as consumers used less detergent per wash load and washed fewer and larger loads. Pricing issues were paramount because people could no longer afford high shelf outlays. The winning formula between these neighboring countries diverged. While some aspects remained the same (strong, trusted consumer brands), cost and price were dominant strategic issues in Mexico, while innovation and performance remained important in the United States. Global material sourcing strategies struggled to meet this need dichotomy and common suppliers (there were lots of them) received conflicting instructions from the businesses.

Corporate Values Applied to the Supply Base

The first piece of the framework sets overall boundaries. If you look for it, almost every major company has on its website a section that talks about its vision, mission, values, and purpose, along with some additional elaboration on its approach to its business. Think of it as a character description that, cynically, could be considered public relations eyewash, but, more genuinely, often does set the firm's operational compass.

These "soft" overarching principles define, in very general terms, target markets, approach to customer value, and how the company will compete and interact, both externally and inside. Sometimes, but rarely, suppliers make the document, but more often not. When they do, it's often because of an event in the company's relatively recent history that elevates supply management's position in the company's image. Example: In the 1990s Nike, the shoe and apparel industry leader, found itself in a public relations firestorm over labor practices in its factories.

All those factories were actually outsourced suppliers, most in low-wage countries. Nike's history had been somewhat cavalier about the issue prior to the 1990s.[1] In the 1970s when workers at Nike factories in Taiwan and South Korea proposed that a more fair wage needed to be paid, the company simply shifted production to another country. However, in a six-month period in 1996, all that changed. A June exposé, with pictures of child labor in Pakistan, was followed by reports of serious working conditions issues in Vietnam a few months later. The "sweatshop" scandal elevated supply to the level of corporate strategy and values.

Today, Nike's efforts represent some leading-edge social responsibility approaches, both within and outside its industry.[2] Nike has over 800,000 contract workers around the world. It has created almost incredible transparency about its factory conditions, shifting from reports that reactively answered criticism in 2001, to proactively listing publicly the name and location of each of the hundreds of contractor factories worldwide, along with assessments of their compliance status, in 2005. Supply bases are often "stealth" competitive weapons, so Nike's willingness to openly tell its competition every supplier name plus how Nike sees their social responsibility status is leading edge—driven by an event-triggered change in corporate values. Further, Nike opened its factories to ongoing independent outside monitoring, in addition to its large internal compliance staff.

More important, Nike's policies create serious implications for contractors that decide to break the rules.[3] In late 2006, the company terminated its relationship with one of its largest suppliers of soccer goods, Pakistani producer Saga Sports. It discovered that Saga had outsourced its Nike orders to people in their homes (thus avoiding labor conditions monitoring). After a six-month investigation and creation of a remediation plan covering a number of issues beyond home outsourcing, progress did not occur. While the outsourcing situation improved somewhat, other labor, environmental, and health violations did not. The real test, however, was that the decision to withdraw had serious implications for the business in terms of supply shortages of hand-stitched soccer balls in spring 2007, and the startup costs inherent in finding and qualifying replacement suppliers. A company's willingness to back its principles despite adverse short-term business impacts shows whether its commitment to values tests out in real situations. Nike continues to be criticized by some labor activists as too lenient despite these efforts, which is testimony to the difficulty of the task.

Nike did not stop with correcting contract labor abuses, but has also become a leader on the environmental side as well. Beyond the typical recycling efforts, illustrated by its Reuse a Shoe program that started in 1993 and by 2002 used over 50 percent of the rubber waste in 17 Chinese factories, this value leads to shoe innovation as well.[4] The classic Nike Air product used a blend of air and a potent greenhouse gas, sulfur hexafluoride (SF_6), to inflate the air pocket in each shoe's heel. When the greenhouse effect came to light, it triggered a fourteen-year research project (and tens of million of dollars) to come up with a viable replacement. The seemingly minor impact of shoe sole bubbles was the equivalent of 7 million tons of carbon dioxide (or the exhaust of 1 million cars).

In January 2006, the company launched nitrogen-containing shoe soles (Air Max 360s), which, by June of that year, had replaced SF_6 in over half the shoes it sold. While it sounds simple, the chemistry difference between the two molecules is significant—SF_6 is large while nitrogen is small and tends to leak out of the blow-molded bubbles embedded in the soles of the shoes.

The change required a shift from blow-molding to thermoforming the seals in the shoes, which entailed equipment changes across its broad supplier network—no small task. This effort, once the capital investment is paid back, represents a significant cost savings, provides an excellent running product, and was done quietly, without fanfare and without regulatory coercion (there were no rules forcing the change).

This effort has continued as Nike's design efforts led to another breakthrough green product, the Air Jordan XX3, which uses ingenious in-house design approaches and lean manufacturing techniques in its contractor plants to make a shoe that uses almost no chemical-based glues and an outer sole made of recycled material.[5] This strategy dovetails well with the company's labor practices work, by dramatically reducing the need to wear protective masks in its contract manufacturing plants because toxic chemicals are being designed out of the products.

The Legal and Ethical Side

The second "values" element involves the ethics of following the law. As any global sourcing practitioner knows, laws and regulations governing business practices across the world can vary substantially, and even contradict each other. Each company needs to set some overarching standards, based on its values and, in part, based on both its country of origin and the need to observe local laws around the world. At the local level, obeying the law is a must. The real question is which legal and regulatory areas are extended across the organization, regardless of permissive local laws. That's where values come in. For some companies, areas like product safety and the environment are primary; others ban any type of bribery or "introduction" fees paid to third parties, even where they are locally legal; still others abide by the financial reporting rules of their headquarters or stock-listing country.

There are two reasons why setting these value-based rules is particularly important on the supply side.

First, each day enormous amounts of money flow through supply, so the ethics of the organization must be impeccable. Crossing the line for personal gain, or to help a friend, violates the fiduciary responsibility that supply must enforce. Even the appearance of impropriety must be avoided, which in turn creates the second reason. The way a company lives its values drives the expectations it can anticipate successfully setting with its supply base. If the organization looks the other way when the rules are broken or gives the impression it can be "bought," it undermines its ability to set the expectation that the supply base needs to compete by bringing its best products and ideas to win business.

Similarly, managing the supply chain upstream from tier-one suppliers requires those suppliers to set expectations about how they will operate (witness Nike's labor efforts). A growing number of companies have concluded that their corporate reputation is an enormous asset with customers, regulatory agencies, NGOs (nongovernmental activist groups like the World Wildlife Federation or Sierra Club), and with their supply base. A strong reputation draws excellent suppliers and the value they bring to the company's business as well. Extend that thinking up the chain: those excellent suppliers will set consistent expectations with their suppliers and so on (just as poor suppliers will set weak expectations).

Unfortunately, each year, a number of probes come to light about governance and integrity issues—supplier kickbacks, accounting violations around supplier rebates, outright fraud diverting money to personal accounts, rigged contracts and inflated payments to suppliers, conflicts of interest, . . . the list goes on. Further, when legal and ethical supply issues arise, they can distract and preoccupy the company to the detriment of the business. The combination of increasing governmental regulation coupled with the advent of widespread global trade makes this area a potential minefield that must be navigated. Clear procedures and policies must be in place and enforced. These include policies and procedures addressing:

► Conflict of interest, including dealing with close friends and relatives, gift and entertainment policies.

► Antifraud controls including kickbacks and theft.

► Antitrust laws, including reciprocal dealing, illegal pricing, and dealing with competitors.

► Guidelines on gathering competitive intelligence.

► Handling confidential supplier information and intellectual property.

► International trade regulations, ranging from customs and antiterrorist rules to the use of bribes and following local and international labor laws.

► Appropriate accounting for purchase agreements with suppliers.

► Environmental regulations, including those that apply to supplier plants.

Sometimes, individuals who start out with high integrity have it erode away as supplier relationships cross the line from commercial to personal. Over the past several years government procurement, never lily-white across the world, has had more than its fair share of corruption cases. It is particularly sad when someone's good reputation is ruined by getting too close to suppliers.[6] Darleen Druyan was the number two U.S. Air Force acquisitions officer in 2002, with years of excellent performance. Yet, in an effort to help her daughter (and later her son-in-law) get a job from one of her suppliers (Boeing), she became ensnarled in a conflict-of-interest situation. Eventually, Boeing also hired her, even though she was negotiating contracts with them on several major programs. She confessed to the conflict-of-interest charges, including steering contracts to Boeing, and was sentenced to prison, as was the Boeing executive who recruited her.

According to the *Wall Street Journal,* Druyan's vulnerability was her family, both in terms of employment for her daughter and protecting her from investigation, and because her husband had health problems. The tragedy was that Druyan's intuitive integrity caused her to have second thoughts and call to cancel her request to Boeing for her daughter's employment. Too late—the process had already begun. The fallout from this case ultimately included outside reviews of the contracts in question, congressional scrutiny, and temporary transfer of acquisition authority from the Air Force to Pentagon procurement. A major Boeing contract for a new generation of air-to-air refueling tankers was taken away due to these irregularities and rebid. Boeing, too, had to deal with a number of issues stemming from this and several other military procurement scandals, culminating with new CEO Jim Mc-Nerney's decision in 2006 to negotiate a $615 million settlement in order to put the issue behind it, avoid criminal charges, and begin anew to recast its culture to preclude similar situations.

In other cases, powerful buyers simply go too far in their quest for value, allowing personal considerations to intrude on commercial negotiations. In the private sector (also in 2002), an unfortunate situation occurred in the sourcing of investment broker services at Fidelity.[7,8] One of the top mutual fund companies, Fidelity buys broker services to actually execute their stock and bond trades in the market. Under the leadership of Scott DeSano, head of stock trading, Fidelity was perhaps the best in its industry at extracting value from its brokerage suppliers.

Fidelity's value equation was well thought out, and DeSano expanded that thinking beyond simple cost, using a number of sourcing strategies, such as supply base rationalization to provide volume leverage for tough negotiations; strong persuasion that brokers commit their own capital to avoid mid-trade price risk during large trades; access to free research that included lower negotiated trading fees; adding trade speed and efficiency to the performance criteria for suppliers; and even pressing the New York Stock Exchange to move to more efficient electronic trading (instead of its slower floor trading). This value equation is vital to mutual fund performance, and Fidelity reduced its trading costs $2 billion, which flowed directly to its investors' bottom line returns by reducing its fund expenses (an estimated 0.2 to 0.3 percent improvement in fund returns—not insignificant in this business). This was a truly excellent sourcing strategy executed with precision.

Some brokers chose, in dealing with this powerful customer's services acquisition personnel, to add perks and gifts to their low-cost, efficient trading offerings. One, Jefferies Group, was accused of offering star traders at Fidelity junkets to Las Vegas, expensive wines, free trips to sporting events at Wimbledon and other hot spots, and golf at exclusive clubs. Ultimately, Jefferies negotiated a $10 million settlement and the trader seeking the business was fined.

On the surface, Fidelity came out okay, with no allegations that its fund investors lost anything—especially since fund expense monitoring expert Abel/Noser Corp. pegs Fidelity's costs at just half the industry average. But a deeper look shows disruption to Fidelity's trading operation, too. DeSano was transferred to another position, eight people left the trading desk and the company, Fidelity disciplined fourteen other people who remained with the company, and it rewrote its ethics policy and revamped enforcement—no minor disruption. DeSano left Fidelity in the summer of 2007.

The other aspect of these procurement scandals is that they never seem to go away. Amazingly, on two consecutive days in early March 2008 (more than five years later), both these stories hit the press again, causing embarrassment and disrupting business in Air Force procurement and Fidelity.[9] The defense procurement rebid was conducted and, in the political spotlight of a presidential election year, the contract was not awarded to the odds-on favorite, Boeing, but rather to a consortium led by U.S. supplier Northrup Grumman and European supplier EADS (European Aeronautic Defence & Space Co., the owner of Airbus). The debate between "buy American" and "buy the best qualified" broke out—often along party lines. As of this writing Boeing's formal appeal of the decision process was upheld and the Druyan case rehashed as background to the new story. Air Force procurement's capability has once again been called into question and the contract will be rebid yet again—seven years later!

The very next day, it was announced that the Securities and Exchange Commission settled a civil case with Fidelity Vice Chairman (and long-time manager of Fidelity's Magellan Fund) Peter Lynch,[10] who, during the DeSano years asked the trading desk to help him find some tickets to top events. His fine was the value of the tickets. More embarrassing were allegations that other key traders at the time (none of whom were still with Fidelity) took gifts of simply amazing value—from $145,000 to $450,000. Once again Fidelity was in the news over a misuse of buying power four years earlier.

—Practitioner's Take—

Ethics policies and values statements are givens in most companies, and, for the supply side, are almost universal. Except, sometimes they really aren't. To get the best from suppliers requires a tough but fair approach. As I mentioned above, if suppliers believe you can be bought, that becomes a cheaper, easier road for them than combining real commercial and technical capabilities with a sharp competitive cost position to get the business. Values need to be lived, not just posted on a website. While senior management support is important, it is not enough. The real challenge is to embed these values into the middle management supervisory levels and in the operating people where the real business unfolds. That requires a culture that supports values—and *that* is where senior leadership makes a difference, not in just communicating the policy.

Culture is critical. In examples where supply values are breached, cultural and market forces like Fidelity's enormous buying power can slowly overcome appropriate ethics policies, because the addition of personal perks begins an "everyone else does it" mentality and the company's continued success gives a "no harm, no foul" mindset that begins a slippery slope to favoritism. Policies must be enforced with real consequences and drummed into the organization—and into the new employee from the day he or she joins the company.

In governmental procurement examples, culture is also a major player but is compounded by a value equation that is not as simple as that of the private sector. Value expands to include elected officials' "value equations" with elements like supplier employment in their congressional districts (representing their constituents), politicization of appropriation processes (and accompanying press coverage), and separate, often competing, control entities managing budget versus policy versus expenses. Unlike a company, where eventually it all comes together, in government it is not that clear and the measure of success is not as simple as profit. That can lead to a culture in which every political intervention into the procurement process undermines what are, on paper, effective ethics policies. Conflict of interest is a significant risk.

To get the best from suppliers who will stand with you in tough times, living your values attracts suppliers who compete for the business because they believe they have a chance to get it. It also makes other values like product safety and environmental improvement transparent to the supply base so it can formulate solutions that meet those needs. In many companies, the sales side of the business has different rules around customer gift-giving and the offering of perks. Rather than getting caught up in those comparisons, the thrust for supply-based advantage requires that you make sure your company—across all functions that touch on supply—is not the one that makes a supplier's use of those tactics effective in acquiring contracts.

Another key positive enabler is to creatively approach values issues to couple them with typical business needs and results. In the Nike SF_6 replacement story, while the investment and human resources spent were enormous, the outcome incorporated major cost reduction, a performance improvement noticeable by consumers, and a "green" initiative pulled off without the pressure of specific regulation. The ability to improve the business as a part of enforcing values makes the ethical approach work extremely well.

Management View of Suppliers

The second part of the architectural drawing is what management sees as important to the business. Do suppliers fit in management's thinking? If so, how? Simplistically, there are three ways to think about it:

1. The first school of thought sees suppliers as a "cost pool" to be squeezed when things are tough. The idea is to extract and transfer value from supplier profit to the bottom line. When done to excess, it creates a "take no prisoners" mentality. The reverse auction craze of the late 1990s and early 2000s was a classic example. The tech bust and 9/11 hit profits hard. Management needed profit and if a supply manager could deliver cost savings quickly, rewards followed. Whether the tactics used to get those savings would impact future supplier interactions was not part of corporate thinking. Reverse auction savings rolled in during an oversupplied market, as

supplier margins transferred to the buying companies. The results included supplier bankruptcies, capability cutbacks, industry consolidation, and, sometimes, real efficiency improvement. (No tool is uniformly good or bad—the key is how it is used.) CEOs like GE's Jack Welch pushed for everything to go through auctions and after every CEO roundtable, conference, or benchmarking trip, other CEOs came back to ask why everything wasn't being auctioned in their companies as well.

2. The second school of thought sees suppliers as a source of value that compliments corporate competencies. This mindset sees suppliers more as members of the team competing together. The goal becomes balancing cost with various non-price elements, such as innovation, service, quality, speed, and the other value components. Trust is trumpeted as the source of advantage. The pitfall, often overlooked, is to make sure trust is earned and not just given, by setting high expectations and then measuring against them. Many huge outsourcing deals were driven by the misconception that a single supplier relationship would naturally create mutual dependence and great results. The information technology (IT) field, in particular, was littered with failed long-term outsourcing deals as a result. Still, few companies went back in-house because the outsourcing providers really did have competencies the buyers lacked. Regardless of outcome, this underlying management mindset sees suppliers holding different core competencies that can be combined with their own to deliver enhanced results.

3. The last school of thought is that there is no view. Supply is an "out of sight, out of mind" afterthought. Suppliers are invisible. They are expected to just deliver what they sell without problems (regardless of whether your company knows what it wants). Their job is to keep you running competitively by managing their own operations without taking much of your time and effort. Customer initiatives assume supply capability is there. This dream world is often shattered when a supply risk factor (remember the lead paint on Chinese toys and E. coli in salad greens?) explodes onto the scene.

Regardless of which school prevails, how suppliers are viewed gets incorporated into a company's strategy . . . and culture. When consciously combined with customer and internal strategies in mutually supportive ways, the odds of competitive advantage increase across a range of market conditions. Too often, some of the most creative supply changes are implemented by companies in deep trouble (necessity is the mother of invention, as pointed out earlier—and probably again, later). But without excellence at both the customer and supplier ends of the supply chain, competitive advantage is hard to build. Where great supply strategies do not deliver great business results due to flaws elsewhere, supplier contributions are often discounted.

A famous example of integrating supply into corporate turnaround strategy occurred when Lou Gerstner took over at IBM in the 1990s.[11] For every dollar of its computer equipment sales, IBM was spending forty-two cents while its competitors were only spending thirty-one. In addition to transforming IBM by making its services businesses larger than its traditional equipment revenues, supply-based advantage was a major component of Gerstner's strategy. Every plant and division of the company bought separately and often, the engineers and marketing people did the buying as a side task to their core work, while low-skilled procurement people just processed orders. Suppliers were blamed for problems that IBM created. Gerstner imported a purchasing icon, the late Gene Richter, from competitor Hewlett Packard (HP). Richter, who had won *Purchasing* magazine's Medal of Excellence twice before (at HP and Black & Decker), insisted on written sourcing strategies and centralized procurement. He upgraded the organization and, when Gerstner and the board mandated all spending had to go through his group, drove major improvements in cost, inventory, and quality as well as reductions in maverick spending (employee use of unauthorized suppliers).

IBM led the procurement industry move to the Internet by mandating supplier connectivity. It set up strategic relationships (interestingly, while banning any use of reverse auctions at the height of their popularity because Richter believed they would undermine the ability to leverage those supplier relationships). By the end of his tenure, Richter started up a procurement services organization—one of the first customers was United Technologies' indirect (non-product) purchases group. Purchasing and supply management's alignment with strategy was complete—supply contributed cost control, revenue, and, by the way, a Richter-led organization won an unprecedented third Medal of Excellence.

A less-well-known story played out at P&G in 2000, when current CEO A. G. Lafley took over. That company was in considerable disarray as well. Lafley began the turnaround effort by refocusing the organization on the "consumer as boss," emphasizing only those things that increased consumer satisfaction and shareholder value. The turnaround plan included focus on major customers, geographies/countries, and brands; internal collaboration rather than competition; hard work to delight consumers (people like you and me); and close collaboration with retail customers (like Tesco and Wal-Mart) to make selling P&G products attractive for them as well. So what did all that have to do with the supply base?

Lafley combined two levels of strategy—"where to play" that laid out the business priorities above, and "how to win," which concentrated on how to achieve the "where to play" objectives. Lafley had been a junior supply officer in the Navy in 1969, about eight years before joining P&G, and, in that role, learned about linking supply to what customers wanted.[12,13] While running the Navy Exchange in Atsugi, Japan, he set up "wives groups" to gather ideas about what they wanted to buy at the store (the customer side). He then became quite skilled at sourcing the things those military wives really wanted to buy—often from nontraditional suppliers (well, nontraditional for the Navy). Business boomed.

At P&G he included a "how to win" strategy to drive out all costs that did not deliver superior consumer or shareholder value. In it, Lafley formally called for a purchasing breakthrough companywide, across all expenditures. P&G leveraged more than volume across businesses, including supplier relationships and technology as part of the leverage equation. At one point, supplier executives were part of a P&G presentation to financial analysts, describing why P&G was a preferred customer.

As the company stabilized, Lafley set a goal that 50 percent of the new product pipeline come from outside the company—an "idea supply base" that included traditional suppliers as well as universities, inventors, and so forth. This open innovation approach, dubbed "connect and develop" (in contrast to "research and develop"), called on product development, purchasing, business development, and patent lawyers to bring outside supplier ideas and products into P&G—creating an idea "magnet." The massive Gillette acquisition integration also included a "scale strategy" to leverage both companies' purchasing and distribution capabilities. By 2007, both parts of value, performance and cost, included supply as an important strategy.

—Practitioner's Take—

If you are waiting for your company strategy to specifically say "supply is strategic," you may be in for a very long wait. The IBM and P&G stories, while not unique, are rare. The articulation of strategy by senior management is unlikely to include a discrete role for suppliers. Instead, it is up to supply-facing organizations to internalize that strategy and use deep understanding of both what suppliers can do and what the business needs to link the supply base to company strategy. Sometimes this requires selling back up the line where the connections are not as clear, as well as laterally to other functions. The responsibility for making the connection in a compelling way is what makes competitive advantage. It blends science (the connection to results) and art (articulating how to make those connections externally).

The tougher task is to integrate how management thinks about suppliers into an approach that works. For company leaders that "get" supply, there is little problem, but that is often not the case, as we described above. The pressure for short-term results, especially on cost, can lead to supply actions that preclude the long-term programs pivotal for sustainable competitive advantage. How management thinks about suppliers becomes engrained in the corporate culture—and therein lies the problem. A CEO who sees suppliers as competitors for his/her margin will clamor for intensely competitive supply strategies that can hinder other situational collaborative approaches.

Strong supply base leadership requires taking the risk to articulate an approach that may fly in the face of management's supply thought process. Knowing suppliers well and cultivating allies among other corporate functions is critical to making the case for change. Even when senior management buys in, most CEOs (unlike Gerstner) are unlikely to mandate supply involvement.

Then cross-functional influence becomes just as important as selling the senior folks. How often have you heard your counterparts in another discipline—manufacturing or engineering or marketing—reject early supply involvement in business strategy or deny access to their resources for supply strategy execution? The arguments are familiar: "Why do we need to help develop the supplier? We are paying them to know their business. Besides, if we teach them to be better, their other customers, including our competitors, will get benefit of our knowledge."

Or—"If we tell them too much, they will leak the information to the industry."

Or—"We're the customer. They need to do what we need. Isn't it their job to satisfy us and meet our needs?"

Or—"Why should I worry about whether they make a profit? That is their problem. They need to figure out how to make money at the price that wins the business."

Overcoming these mindsets is what influencing the company's competitive architecture to include supply is all about. Conceptually, the fundamental issues most companies face are quite similar, but each culture, and the people within it, is unique. Making suppliers a part of corporate strategy is about tailoring to company and industry culture in order to successfully execute. Companies that can do this gain supply-based advantage. The supply leadership's blueprint for action becomes the framework within which that plan will be executed.

Blueprints: What's the Plan?

In construction, once the architect is done, the building process begins. The translation from drawings to reality starts with another drawing, a precision drawing—a blueprint that subcontractors and construction workers can follow. The same is true for supply-based advantage—except that the blueprint remains more conceptual. Think of it as a combination of philosophy, approach, expectations-setting, and direction from leaders tasked with mining value from the supply base.

This blueprint has three important audiences:

1. Internal management: general management and key cross-functional leaders.
2. The supply base itself.
3. Supply personnel, who do the work of linking with suppliers.

This blueprint communicates the cultural and conceptual road map toward the supply base. Elements of this plan speak to each of the constituencies above.

Internal Management Communication

Senior management is most interested in four things:

1. Supplier fit to help make the company's strategy and business model work.
2. Supply's connection to company values and high-priority corporate responsibility programs.
3. The controls and compliance plan for expenditures.
4. Guiding principles for interactions with suppliers.

These elements create the case for supply's efforts to deliver competitive advantage and diagrams how that connection works. It also maps into corporate culture and seeks to influence leadership's mindset. This is the foundation of a business case for supply-based advantage.

When Mark Hurd became CEO of Hewlett Packard, part of his strategy, in addition to major changes in sales approach, was to better control the cost side of HP's value equation, where inability to capture synergies from the Compaq merger had been instrumental in his predecessor's departure. Supply leadership was able to map several programs into that cost structure strategy, both on the direct and indirect spending areas.[14]

At the "corporate values" level, another program that HP had invested in over the years also made the cut in the new priority-setting process.[15] In 1999, six years before Hurd's arrival, Bonnie Nixon-Gardiner, HP's Program Manager for Supply Chain Social & Environmental Responsibility, began a revolution in how HP managed the working conditions and environmental impacts of its high-tech contract manufacturing supply base. Nixon-Gardiner's passion and constancy of purpose rewrote HP's guidelines for suppliers and established a large internal auditing system after benchmarking other industries, including Nike and its apparel competitors.

HP's values translated to its supply base so effectively that Nixon-Gardiner was able to expand its reach beyond just HP when, in 2004, the Catholic Agency for Overseas Development published a report highly critical of working conditions in high-tech contract factories. She seized that opportunity to help create the EICC (Electronic Industry Code of Conduct) that sets out basic labor and environmental standards for the industry majors. Much of what was an HP initiative was transformed into an industry expectation of its suppliers—upgrading base expectations and leveling the competitive playing field at a more responsible plane. HP's social responsibility values integrated into its supply strategies without conflicting with their cost control imperatives.

Supply Base Communication

Supplier communication is more straightforward—even simple. Suppliers just want to know how to get business. However, that "how" often includes how the buying firm plans to interact with its suppliers along the way. In large companies with globally dispersed or business unit silo'd supply groups, it is not uncommon to find dissimilar principles and philosophies across the organization, which play out in distinctly different treatment of suppliers across the business for no good reason. When the same seller deals with multiple groups from the same buyer inconsistently, it raises two possibilities: the supplier becomes confused and frustrated or the supplier leverages the differences for itself and against the buyers. The goal is to avoid both negative outcomes and make it easy for the supplier to deliver value.

One way to see and contrast how companies think about suppliers is to peruse their supplier web pages. In addition to the typical supplier registration and entrance for supplier-specific shipment, invoicing, and performance measurements, these portals are also directed toward suppliers that are not currently doing business with the buyer. Usually the welcome page lays out an overview of the company's approach toward suppliers. The range of content is broad, but often reflects the "personality" of the buying company, stressing some elements more than others.

A quick look at ToyotaSupplier.com (Toyota's North American supplier website) is a particularly impressive example.[16] Toyota has long integrated its supply base into its sales, design, and famous Toyota production system, turning it all into a compelling business model that has steadily built a competitive advantage over most developed country automakers. In support of its objective of "Seeking the best Suppliers in the World," the site announces Toyota's basic supply principles:

- ► Fair competition based on an open door policy (suppliers of any nationality with or without prior Toyota business).
- ► Mutual benefit based on mutual trust (long-term relationships that require close and wide-ranging communication).
- ► Contribution to local economies, good corporate citizenship.

The website also contains a section on how Toyota helps suppliers compete. This includes its purchasing policy (clear expectations on quality, delivery, cost, and, in North America, a "values" component around supplier diversity), and a section on supplier support systems through which Toyota will dispatch experts to suppliers that ask for assistance in development or improvement of their operations.

Finally, and perhaps most impressively, the next two sections go beyond the normal list of items the auto giant buys and specific requirements to be a Toyota supplier, to help define what supplier value really means for Toyota. It explains what supply value entails at Toyota. The "products needed" section includes value components for both parts and capital equipment. Value elements like *cost performance* (individual parts and total cost including assembly, installation, logistics, etc.); *future needs* such as low environmental impact, safety (vehicular, passenger, production); and *amenity/utility* (comfort, ergonomics, fashion) come across as the real "products" Toyota wants to buy.

The "supplier standards" section simply reinforces this value message while further clarifying its definition. Toyota explains that value includes *quality* (built in), *cost* (conservation of material, low price from genuine cost competitiveness rather than margin cutting, unceasing effort on cost-effective performance), *delivery* (reliable and flexible), and *technological capability* (value add, sophisticated, ahead of competition, speed to market, dramatic cost reduction).

An example of the supply-based advantage stemming from the execution of these principles is Toyota's production factories. When compared to many of its competitors, the automaker's plants show how its capital equipment suppliers have internalized its direction relative to its value equation. Those suppliers' equipment design efforts have resulted in "lighter, shorter assembly lines that can be readily reconfigured as market demands change. The upshot? Nearly 30% in savings on the cost of building a new plant."[17]

Supply Personnel Communication

For the organization, this is a key direction-setting document. It sets the boundaries, expectations, and principles for crossing the company's external boundary into supply markets. It also lays out the organization's purpose, principles, and work-process ownership responsibilities, all tied back to company strategy and priorities. The principles, processes, and skills show employees the framework for both *what* is important as well as *how* to approach those "whats."

This blueprint provides the internal wiring diagram that brings it all together for the people doing the work. What they are doing is linked to why it is being done at the corporate level, both in terms of company values as well as strategy. How they interact with suppliers (e.g., is the thrust to predominantly use competition to select suppliers and, if so, how does collaboration fit into that philosophy?) and internal customers (cross-functional teaming), is tied to the skills they must acquire and the care with which those skills are used (controls, stewardship, and compliance). All of this together weaves a philosophy toward suppliers and their contribution to business success.

This high-level stuff is sometimes dismissed as "fluff" or "eyewash" that does not matter—until, that is, a company faces very different philosophies across its internal business or geographical boundaries. These conflicts can unwind competitive advantage opportunities because the disagreements can quickly expand to poison internal alignment. In 2000, Bertelsmann AG's Gruner + Jahr's publishing business aggressively changed its strategy and brought in a new American management team in an effort to enter the top tier of the U.S. market.[18] By 2005, the company sold off its properties after twenty-seven years in the U.S. market. Surely, supply strategy alone did not cause this decline. Disasters like the implosion of entertainer Rosie O'Donnell's career, inflated circulation numbers of her magazine *Rosie,* and its resulting demise all added to corporate culture incompatibility between the Germans and the Americans to deliver corporate failure. Diametrically opposed approaches to their supply base played a role in the trans-Atlantic strife that tore the company's strategy apart and undermined its ability to gain any supply advantage relative to its competition.

Gruner + Jahr was, in part, vertically integrated, owning a printing company, rather than outsourcing all its production. The German managers set an expectation that all magazine units would use the internal printer. The American side vehemently disagreed; claiming that outside suppliers had superior capabilities, especially in printing periodicals with large circulation. During a bidding process in 2001, the European leadership ordered the U.S. subsidiary to extend a bid period and provide its competitors' bid prices to the internal printing company.

The Americans reacted negatively, expressing significant ethical disagreement with sharing prices. On the other hand, the Germans saw no problem and ultimately forced the price disclosure. The industry quickly learned that Gruner + Jahr shared the bidding information with its sister company. The depth of feeling around this philosophical difference fed the culture clash emerging over a number of other business approaches.

The lesson: simply crafting the message is not enough. Supply leadership needs to spend enough time debating the principles and aligning on the implications of the approach that is decided upon.

—Practitioner's Take—

Too often, companies think the blueprint for supply-based advantage is a series of top-down procurement strategies like supplier rationalization, volume leverage through spend analysis across the company, or standardization of technical specifications or part utilization. While those strategies may look like a blueprint, they are actually generic strategies of limited duration, not always applicable to every commodity or business situation. (More on that in Chapters 5 and 13.) The "drawings and blueprints" we are talking about go beyond a particular broad procurement strategy. They are about how supply influences and supports the company's business and what philosophy and skills will be applied to the supply base in search of value.

The blueprint, at a minimum, should include:

- Clear connection to company strategy and its business model.
- Connection to corporate values, including legal, ethical, and social areas.
- The supply organization's purpose, mission, and supply-process ownership responsibilities—linked to both corporate needs and the skills supply people will acquire and employ with suppliers.
- Operating principles toward the supply base. These are best prepared in a way that can be shown to suppliers as well as internal stakeholders.
- The legal and financial authority, controls, and compliance approach toward the firm's supply side.

Like so many other policies, the real impact is the result of embedding this blueprint into the psyche of the organization so that its use becomes second nature. That is driven by leadership "walking the talk," middle management accountability to instill it into work processes, and strong "policy training" modules that make competitive supply value and ethical and responsible behavior part of the culture. One warning—don't expect that embedding these supply values into your organization within the larger corporation will transfer to your cross-functional counterparts. It is not that simple. Engaging employees from other functions in ways that integrate suppliers into their effectiveness in doing their work is far more compelling.

One last consideration—periodically renew the blueprint.

In a 2005 renewal of an earlier version, P&G CPO Rick Hughes and his leadership team clearly communicated how that firm will integrate supply into its business model. The supply organization's mission "Outside In, Best Value—Always!" is supported by the following organizational imperatives:

- *Linking and Leveraging Is Our Business* (linking suppliers to business needs, leveraging across corporate boundaries, delivering business value).

- *Strategic Management of External Suppliers* (long-term view, grow top suppliers and eliminate poor performers, supplier relationship management).

- *Commercialize 360-Degree Innovation* (collaborate, link commercial strategy and technology platforms, leverage commercial relationships for new ideas).

- *Organizational Excellence Throughout* (clear, aligned principles, top talent, skill mastery, diverse global community, always do what is right).

If done well, a supply policy blueprint should last for several years, but changes in the business environment, in technology, company direction and ownership, and value migration over time all conspire to make other parts of the philosophical baseline obsolete. Renewal of these messages to keep them relevant and consistent is an imperative.

Once the blueprint is clear and the message makes sense, the construction of competitive advantage from the supply base can begin.

Notes

1. Michelle Amey, Tom Brazel, Che Chorley, and Thomas Stead, "Nike: Leading the Corporate Responsibility Movement?," 2002; accessed at: www .ssn.flinders.edu.au/global/glob1002/2002book/globalisation%20website/ conve rted/whatsit.html.

2. Associated Press, "Nike Cites Efforts to Promote Labor, Environmental Issues," *Wall Street Journal,* June 1, 2007.

3. Stephanie Kang, "Nike Cuts Ties With Pakistani Firm," *Wall Street Journal,* November 21, 2006.

4. Stanley Holmes, "Nike Goes for the Green," *Business Week,* September 25, 2006.

5. Nicholas Casey, "New Nike Sneaker Targets Jocks, Greens, Wall Street," *Wall Street Journal,* February 15, 2008.

6. Andy Pasztor and Jonathan Karp, "Career Crash: How an Air Force Official's Help for a Daughter Led to Disgrace," *Wall Street Journal,* December 9, 2004.

7. Kate Kelly and John Hechinger, "Tough Customer: How Fidelity's Trading Chief Pinches Pennies on Wall Street," *Wall Street Journal,* October 12, 2004.

8. Susanne Craig and John Hechinger, "Entertaining Excess: Fishing for Fidelity Business, One Firm Employed Lavish Bait," *Wall Street Journal*, August 11, 2005.

9. Daniel Michaels and August Cole, "Pentagon Embattled Over Tanker Decision: Air Force to Defend Choice of Team Led by Northrup-EADS," *Wall Street Journal*, March 5, 2008.

10. Kara Scannell, Suzanne Craig, and Jennifer Levitz, "'Gifts' Case Nabs a Star," *Wall Street Journal*, March 6, 2008.

11. Douglas A. Smock, Robert A. Rudzki, and Stephen C. Rogers, *On Demand Supply Management: World Class Strategies, Practices and Technology* (Conyers, Ga.: J. Ross Publishing, 2007, pp. 169–183).

12. Alex Markels, "Turning the Tide at P&G," *US News and World Report*, October 22, 2006.

13. Sarah Ellison, "Focus Group: P&G Chief's Turnaround Recipe: Find Out What Women Want," *Wall Street Journal*, June 1, 2005.

14. Smock, Rudzki, and Rogers, pp. 93–94.

15. Peter Burrows, "Stalking High-Tech Sweatshops," *Business Week*, June 19, 2006.

16. www.toyotasupplier.com/sup_guide/sup_principles.asp.

17. Philip L. Carter, Joseph R. Carter, Robert M. Monczka, John D. Blascovich, Thomas H. Slaight, and William J. Markham, *Succeeding in a Dynamic World: Supply Management in the Decade Ahead, a Joint Research Initiative of CAPS Research, Institute of Supply Management* (A.T. Kearney, Inc.; copyright Institute for Supply Management and W.P. Carey School of Business at Arizona State University, 2007, p. 29).

18. James Bandler and Matthew Karnitschnig, "Lost in Translation: European Giant in Magazines Finds U.S. a Tough Read," *Wall Street Journal*, August 19, 2004.

CHAPTER 5

Sourcing Strategy

Foundation of Advantage

> FOUNDATION: the natural or prepared ground or base on which a structure rests.

You've got to think past your nose.

—Elia Rogers, the author's mother

The strength of any building is based on its foundation. A weak foundation will lead to cracks in the walls, shifts in the roof, leaks when it rains, and, ultimately, the need to reconstruct it—a cumbersome, tedious, and expensive proposition. The foundation is rarely what drew the homeowner to the house he or she purchased. It's not part of the aesthetics or, in many cases, even visible from the outside. When building a supply-based competitive advantage, sourcing strategy plays the same role. It is rarely visible from outside the company until after it begins visibly playing out in the marketplace. Then, like so many other types of strategy (military, political, or business), it looks so obvious that no one could overlook it . . . in hindsight. But foresight is a far harder proposition. The skills of the workers make all the difference in the final quality of the structure, be it a supply chain or a house or a skyscraper.

The word "strategy" is highly overused. Nobody wants to be doing "tactical" when "strategic" sounds so much more important. But tactical tasks are *not* unimportant—in fact, nothing could be further from the truth. In setting up their supply networks, strategy is a particularly garbled concept, with way too many meanings espoused by consultants, software suppliers, supply executives, and conflicting descriptions of supply base strategy in the business press.

Some familiar examples include confusing "strategic sourcing" with "sourcing strategy." They are more than a semantic shift of two words. Strategic sourcing incorporates both the supplier selection and supplier management tasks—think of it as an "umbrella process" that encompasses the complete interface with the supply base, often including "process leadership" hand-offs to multiple functions within the company as the focus shifts from market analysis to supplier selection to contracting to performance management. It is a combination of sourcing strategy and supplier relationship management. (By the way, senior management could care less about this semantic debate—they want results.)

Worse, some companies are so intent on getting results quickly that the method with which they go to market—reverse auctions, traditional request for quotation, or old-fashioned company-to-company negotiation (not the euphemistic "negotiation" term that many software suppliers have renamed bidding)—is thought to be the strategy. They are, rather, simply tactics that play out the strategy's intent. (Senior management's desire for results can reinforce this confusion.)

In other cases, especially for those just beginning to seek some sort of advantage on the supply side, sourcing strategy becomes a "top-down" broad strategy that is applied uniformly across the various spend "categories" or "pools" within the company. There are a number of widely publicized examples:

- ► Supplier rationalization—reduce the number of suppliers to leverage volume in price negotiations.
- ► Global sourcing—look beyond the local market for potential suppliers.
- ► Low-cost country sourcing (LCCS)—play the labor arbitrage game by hopscotching from country to country seeking low labor rates.
- ► E-sourcing—run everything through electronic supplier selection tools.
- ► Specification simplification and standardization—rationalize the number of parts or specs so that volume leverage or part reapplication is easier, especially in decentralized businesses.

While all these are legitimate strategies, they are not the means to true competitive advantage because they are generic. Remember, competitive advantage needs a degree of uniqueness to sustain itself.

Finally, many companies that recognize the difference between various spend categories and commodities go no further than the use of the iconic Kraljic four-quadrant matrix. It was conceived in 1983 (yes, it's that old) by Peter Kraljic, an ex-basketball player, metallurgist, and McKinsey consultant, during an engagement with German chemical giant BASF. The newly appointed BASF purchasing manager, a recent transfer from sales, was stunned to discover that procurement had no strategic tools to guide its activities, unlike the sales function from which he came.[1] He asked McKinsey for help and Kraljic developed the model that today shows up almost constantly in supply management product sales brochures, academic texts, and magazine articles (normally with no mention of its creator).

The point of the matrix, which compares business impact/risk on the Y-axis and supplier market complexity on the X-axis, is that the items a company buys—whether goods or services—fall into distinct groupings, each with a generic "strategy." The bottom left (low-impact low-complexity) with a generic noncritical "automate or outsource" strategy; bottom right (low-impact high-complexity) with a generic risk management strategy due to the complexity; upper left (high-impact low-complexity) with its leverage competition strategy—where reverse auctions took hold around 2000; and upper right (high-impact high-complexity) with an alliance or close integration strategy.

All of this is good stuff, but to gain sustainable advantage, relying on such a widely used basic model alone is also too generic. Think of it as the first step of genuine supply strategy. But strategy is not a one-step process.

Strong Analogy to Corporate Strategy

So, what is sourcing strategy and how do you formulate it? Sourcing strategy is amazingly like corporate strategy and, like corporate strategic planning, almost all strategy tools and models created for that discipline will translate to supply. The goals are the same—competitive advantage and winning in the market. The mental shift is to apply the tools using a "mirror image" where the supply base is the subject, not your own firm. Example: Michael Porter's Five Forces strategy template that explores the impact of an industry's internal rivalry, its suppliers' power, its customers' power, potential substitution options that could replace its products, and potential new entrants into the industry, is equally applicable to supply by moving the focus of the analysis one step back in the supply chain. That is, the supplier's industry rivalry becomes the center, with their industry's suppliers, customers, potential substitute products, and new entrants making up the analysis.

Other tools include standbys like the resource-based view of strategy that assesses the strength or weakness of a set of "capitals" (resources) within a company—financial, physical (plants, equipment, offices, etc.), human (talent, operational expertise), intellectual (patent, trade secrets, etc.), and social (ability to deal externally with stakeholders like governments, customers, and suppliers). Another is SWOT analysis—four quadrants that match up internal capability across the top (S = Strengths and W = Weaknesses) with external factors (O = Opportunities and T = Threats). This tool essentially feeds the outcomes of the resource-based view of strategy (which is largely focused on internal resources) into the top of the model (S and W) and Porter's five forces (which are largely focused on the external market) into the bottom (O and T) as a means of sifting the data and developing potential strategies.

Sourcing strategy uses these and other tools to develop the same kind of sophisticated strategy toward suppliers and supply markets that the company does toward its customers and the competitive market for its products. In fact, with the advent of global sourcing, the breadth of tools has expanded to consider external environmental forces such as those in PEST analysis (yet another four-quadrant matrix—P for political, E for economic, S for social, and T for technological factors).[2] In a magazine interview in late 2006, Willis Pugh, executive director for Honeywell Aerospace sourcing, described his first use of this tool while with the Fleetguard division of Cummins Engine. When Fleetguard chose to increase its offshore sourcing, it needed a tool to help its people think about the risks of doing business with suppliers from different parts of the world. PEST provides a good framework to do so. The point here is that all these tools are ways to structure your ability to think— they do not just spit out the answer, nor are they a replacement for thinking.

A Sourcing Strategy Process

In most firms the purchasing side of the business is just not seen as an area with rich strategic potential. There, sourcing strategy is nothing more than the plan to pick suppliers (which it is, but with potential for so much more). Yet, in the same companies, if you talk with the sales and marketing disciplines, you will see a lot of strategizing about how to get customers to buy what they sell. Those customers, especially in business-to-business commerce, are the purchasing side of strategy. The same richness of opportunity and threat exists on both sides of the table. The trick is spending the time and building the skill to see it.

Unlike the top-down generic strategies mentioned above, getting real strategic advantage requires a bottom-up approach that seeks to optimize each spend category via its own strategy. In some categories, supplier rationalization might be the answer, while simultaneously, for another purchase, expanding the number of suppliers is right. There are a number of sourcing strategy processes that can do this—some with as few as four or five steps and others with up to fifteen. One that I have found to be particularly helpful over the years includes eight steps:

Step 1: Assessment of Business Needs and Capabilities

What are the needs of the business? The depth at which this is considered is what drives competitive advantage, because it forces more direct thinking about company business models, strategies, and, importantly, its ability to effectively interact with the supply base across internal functions.

Step 2: Assessment of Supplier Industry, Specific Potential Suppliers, and the Industry's End-User Market

This is where all these strategy tools come in. This step also includes assessment of individual suppliers and a view of those suppliers' customer base that goes beyond the buying company's industry. Example: As Boeing began construction of the 787 Dreamliner aircraft, other users of the composite materials replacing metal in the hull faced enormous changes in their sourcing strategy. Hockey stick producers simply did not have the amount of buying leverage once a giant like Boeing entered the market.

Step 3: Macroeconomic Analysis

This is where PEST comes in, along with traditional macroeconomic indicators—expansion or recession, industry forecasts of supply and demand, currency impacts, etc. It also includes cost structure analysis, risk analysis, and other macro factors.

Step 4: Establish Desired Results

Once internal needs and capabilities are linked to what is going on in external markets and economies, the results needed from the strategy need to be established, both in the near term (say six months) and longer term (three-plus years). This forces thinking about both short-term absolute goals (e.g., specific savings, time to market, and innovation levels) and longer-term relative goals (competition, the market, etc.) that can be updated as time goes on. These goals need to be measurable, time bounded, and reasonable yet stretching.

Step 5: Strategy Development

This is the creative part of the process. It takes all the analysis in the first three steps, the desired results from the fourth step, and synthesizes potential strategies that could be applied. This is often as much art as science, so judgment, experience, and skill need to be applied to the facts. It also must be forward looking, so the facts—which come from the past—are not enough. Forecasting potential futures is as much part of this step as analyzing current or historical facts and data.

Step 6: Strategy Alignment

Just articulating the strategy is not enough. This step also needs to include a broad cost-benefit analysis since few game-changing interventions can be done without cross-functional and, sometimes, supplier involvement. This is about making choices. It is too easy to decide to do everything—with the result that nothing gets accomplished.

Step 7: Tactical Planning and Execution

Getting it done. Mapping responsibilities, selecting the sourcing tools and approaches to be used, setting time lines and interim measurement points—all the elements of project management going forward in a cross-functional action plan. This is where the "go to market" tool (bidding, negotiation, choosing to make not buy, etc.) is chosen and then used. In the end, executing strategy and tactics means actually doing it, not talking about it.

Step 8: Documentation and Renewal

A two-pronged step, this both captures the strategy and its rationale for reference and direction setting. It also creates a framework to review progress and make adjustments.

As you review the eight steps, it will become apparent that parts of the sourcing strategy process apply to and even originate from other parts of the supply-based advantage "construction process" described in Chapter 1. For example, supplier relationship management, supply chain design, and make vs. buy outsourcing analysis all might fall into sourcing strategy consideration. While each of these (and others) will be discussed sequentially in this book, it is important to note that the real world is much more fluid than theory, so using suppliers to build competitive advantage requires integrating parts of many steps along the way.

—Practitioner's Take—

All of this looks straightforward until you actually try to do it. In some markets, getting the data you need for the right analysis is a challenge while, due to the Internet, in many others the problem is that there is too much data, causing people to get lost in the details. After leading this kind of work for over ten years, here are some real pitfalls I have seen:

- Lack of organizational time and discipline to do the work. It is not like all the other work goes away or that you can afford extra staff just for this effort. In addition, the staff needs to have some skill, since these markets are not simple and creativity is key to advantage. Leaders must insist on written strategies (a hallmark of Gene Richter's tenure at all three of his award-winning organizations mentioned in Chapter 4), which don't have to be elaborate (a short memo or a few PowerPoint slides will do nicely), and, before approving tactical plans, must insist on confirming the consistency of these plans with the agreed-upon strategy. This discipline is not easy to sustain when the pressure for results rewards doing instead of thinking.

- That leads to the second pitfall: skipping strategy and tactically reacting to changes in the market. It happens more than you might think and is always a temptation because, in the short term, logical actions do indeed look "logical." But supply markets are dynamic, with any firm's actions capable of triggering a rebalancing reaction in sometimes unpredictable ways—e.g., the loser of one of your bids cuts a great deal with your competitor to fill its factories and order book. Your advantage is gone in an instant.

- At the other extreme are companies that really get into the strategy side and go "model crazy." In one consulting engagement, I found a client using as many as seven models—all very pretty—but never reaching a common conclusion that would create action plans. Analysis paralysis (don't you love that phrase?) took over. Always remember, the goal is to take actions that let you win, not have an intellectual debate while your competitors bypass you in the real world.

- Finally, strategy is about making choices. If you try to do everything, not much will happen because there is no focus. Strategies must include more than just the "go to market" element (bid the business, negotiate the deal, write the contract, etc.). Think of a strategy as a platform with several "planks"—each plank is a strategic element that, together with the others, creates a sophisticated set of interventions, both external and often internal, that change the game. The problem is that too many interventions lead to a splintered focus. During my career I told my people that strategies should target three or four planks and when I got one with more than five or six, I did not approve it.

Analysis Must Lead to Intervention

In 1990 a European Union regulation changed the game for winemakers across the continent and, especially, for those that make champagne.[3] Industry leader LVMH (Moet Hennessy Louis Vuitton), in the wake of that rule change, created a long-term sourcing strategy for grapes that has strengthened its market position via a unique supply-based advantage. Champagne can only be made from grapes grown in the Champagne region of France, which naturally limits the supply of this key raw material. Prior to 1990, the region's grape price was fixed by the Comité Interprofessionnel du Vin de Champagne (CIVC), the ruling body for champagne. The EU dissolved that approach, mandating that champagne producers negotiate directly with each individual farmer over the price.

Initially, farmers who had long histories with particular vintners suddenly had the opportunity to sell to the highest bidders. Jacques Peters, the chief of grape procurement for one of LVMH's labels—Veuve Clicquot—saw his brand lose 15 percent of its suppliers when he relied on "relationship loyalty" and a bid of only a few pennies higher than past prices. In 1990 the price of champagne grapes increased 31 percent. Peters reassessed LVMH's sourcing strategy.

Inevitably, laws of supply and demand continued to operate and, three years later, a 15 percent drop in worldwide champagne sales (in part due to higher prices) resulted in grape prices just above where they began when the EU changed the game. Nervous farmers were looking for assurance that future crops would sell and the Veuve Clicquot label's strategy was to lock in the low prices for long-term contracts—six years instead of the normal three. That, however, was only the beginning of the sourcing strategy shift. Given that the capacity to make champagne is limited by the geographical boundaries of the Champagne region, simple opportunistic buying at the bottom of the cycle would not provide sustainable competitive advantage.

LVMH's industry analysis (Step 2 above) of grape growing in the Champagne region showed that the dynamics of the market were changing because large farms were being left to the children of the original owners, resulting in smaller tracts and an increase in absentee or part-time owners with little farming expertise. Peters extended the strategy by creating a "relationship unit" that provided both technical support (consulting on fertilizer, crop disease treatment, etc.) at no cost. The next step in the strategy was to expand relationship unit operations to include field support services (trained workers to actually do the manual labor in the fields) at a reasonable cost. The value equation for small owners was enormous—availability of trained workers doing the work at reasonable cost. The quid pro quo was, of course, an LVMH position as a preferred buyer for the resulting crops.

About eight years into this "relationship strategy," as other competitors installed similar programs, the head start that LVMH had established allowed it to lead the market. Thus it could afford to make huge changes to the contracting process with lengths as long as twenty-five years and a signing bonus at the beginning, thus assuring supply in a naturally constrained geography, while using its expertise to increase yields, maintain supply, and sustain competitive costs. Even though France will probably expand the champagne-growing region, it takes up to fifteen years to get newly planted champagne vines to yield—so a few years before then, maybe the strategy will need another major renewal.

LVMH chose a relationship intervention as the centerpiece of its grape sourcing strategy. Fundamentally, there are about seven interventions that can flow from sourcing strategy. The important proviso is that too many interventions dilute execution, while the right number creates synergy. These strategic interventions include:

1. *Market Interventions.* These define choices that occur in the commercial marketplace—bidding, supplier rationalization, global vs. regional vs. local sourcing, make vs. buy, competitive vs. collaborative negotiation, involvement in feedstock procurement, upstream inputs, supplier capacity planning, etc.—all of which typically impact price and availability.

2. *Technical Interventions.* These involve simplifying and standardizing specs, rebalancing product formulas, innovation, electronic/information technology applications, intellectual property agreements, etc.

3. *Cost Structure Interventions.* This is where lean, six sigma, yield improvement, tariff reduction, value analysis, etc., fit. The goal is to eliminate waste and variability in supply products and processes.

4. *Supplier Relationship Interventions.* This category covers leveraging or building on existing relationships, structuring new relationships, shifting the nature of the relationship, etc. This type of intervention is rarely accomplished in a short period of time.

5. *Work Process Intervention.* This is about changing how the business is accomplished. The Internet was probably the biggest change in history, with software applications and real-time communication making a huge difference. It also includes installing work and thought processes like strategic sourcing and supply chain management.

6. *Supply Chain Interventions.* These interventions involve redesigning the supply chain to eliminate or add steps, tailoring the chain's flow to different customers and channels, adding flexibility (e.g., multisourcing, backup supply points), incorporating control points along the chain, etc.

7. *Cross-Strategy Leverage Interventions.* These interventions link across spend categories to create new connections between normally independent sourcing efforts or suppliers, adding services to goods, assembling system solutions that span multiple suppliers up and down the chain or across separate chains, flexible substitution designs across commodities, etc.

LVMH's strategy, while predominantly a relationship effort, also had elements of work process intervention by becoming an "employment agency" for farm workers, technical/cost structure interventions via the fertilization and yield improvement aspects of its relationship approach, and long-term contracting on the commercial side.

Important Steps in Sourcing Strategy

Sourcing strategy spans the entire range of business planning, from determining needs to analysis and strategy development, on to the tactical implementation. The reason it includes implementation is that too many strategies never happen because they are just documents that get filed away. Instead, they need to be a stimulus for actually doing something.

Looking over the sourcing strategy process, most practitioners would gravitate to the market analysis (Step 2) and actual "go to market" actions (see Step 7) as the most important, because they provide the intelligence to select those suppliers who potentially can do the job and they guide the actions that ultimately do the selection. Indeed, they are important steps, without which, the odds of supplier selection delivering strong results drop significantly or even move in the wrong direction. Still, as a foundation for competitive advantage three other steps are vital.

Those three are: assessment of needs and capabilities (Step 1), desired results (Step 4), and renewal (Step 8). The first—assessing internal needs and capabilities—is not as easy as it sounds. When sourcing strategies have to deal with multiple business units or customer markets, understanding the needs of the business—especially strategic needs—and then integrating them is an enormous task. This is where supply and business strategy must come together, driven by the business, not by some reward system that uses functional or more tactical measures. There needs to be a level of sophistication in thinking that probes the supply market both broadly and deeply. Sometimes the right sourcing strategy is not global or enterprise-wide in scope because there is not enough commonality between markets or business units.

In my own experience, P&G's entry into Russia and China in the 1990s coincided with a push for global material supply strategies. Early on, several materials in both markets were priced well below prevailing world market levels for the same or similar items outside those two largely isolated markets. Once the price levels were communicated within the company, every country general manager instructed his or her purchasing people to get some of this low-cost material. The challenge became managing what could easily have become the buying equivalent of a gold rush.

These former USSR and Chinese suppliers were not stupid. Once they realized the local market was well below external price levels, it would only be a matter of time before prices rose, regardless of the destination of the goods. We crafted a "separate but linked" strategy that kept local Chinese and Russian organizations in charge of those markets to maintain competitive prices for our local finished goods. At the same time, representatives from these geographies were added to the global sourcing teams and decisions were made on how much and where to ship some of this artificially low-cost material—but not enough to encourage price increases. The receiving destination was typically driven by either desperate needs of another business unit for cost reduction to compete in hotly contested low-cost markets or by the ability to use low-cost imports to influence price levels in other local markets.

The strategy only lasted about two years (inevitably, suppliers recognized the price differentials and dramatically reduced them), but during that time, our head start in both global sourcing strategy from these low-cost regions and in internal collaboration across business units to allocate material where it did the most good gave us an advantage. Assessing business needs was the foundation of that allocation process and therefore critical to seizing the opportunity. That plus the capability to work across business units enabled the internal negotiations that protected local material prices in strategically important fledgling emerging market business units while sending some low-cost material to help more deep-pocketed sister organizations. (The metric was not maximum cost savings but rather competitive business situation and competitive leverage.)

Business need focus is what differentiates sourcing strategies in a bottom-up, category-by-category strategy approach. Common generic strategies will not deliver competitive advantage. Perhaps this is best illustrated in the apparel business, with its wide range of segments and clothing price points that generate dramatically different supply approaches. In late 2007, a *Wall Street Journal* article did a great job of illustrating supply differences between two black mock turtleneck sweaters.[4] The author explored the different global supply chains between a $99.50 Land's End and a $950 Brunello Chucinelli black cashmere sweater.

The lower-cost product was made in China. The fabric came from yarn spun from long-haired Mongolian goats. The supplying factory provided "full service"—that is, the factory that made the sweater also bought the yarn and provided the finished goods to meet Land's End sweater specs. Yarn sourcing was part of the larger sweater manufacturing service, not something actually done by Land's End.

In contrast, the more expensive product was produced in Italy. Brunello Chucinelli bought the yarn itself, using Italian luxury thread supplier, Cariaggi, who sourced the goat hair fiber in bales from Mongolia. This sweater incorporated more handwork.

In both cases, "good quality" was measured, although by different standards—neither inherently right nor wrong. Company business models and value equations were different because their target consumers were also different. The results were good supply strategies tailored for very different outcomes.

The majority of the apparel industry moved to more supply-based competitive models years ago, with nominal price point items having long migrated to LCCS strategies that hopscotch between low-wage locations. Luxury producers only recently have begun looking to low-cost countries for manufacturing savings without destroying their reputations. The extremes of the industry represent vastly different supply strategies tailored to the business model and strategy of each market segment.

Take the mall-based clothing chain, Steve and Barry's.[5] Named after founders Steve Shore and Barry Prevor, its value proposition for consumers was about basic clothes at low prices (mostly under $10). Its business strategy dictated that this not be a fashion knockoff operation like Zara, but rather basic jeans, T-shirt, and university logo product sales with steady demand. Constant focus on cost to meet low price points led a supply strategy that "fills base capacity" for its suppliers, whether they were the landlords that rent store space or the factories that sew the clothes. By locating its stores mainly in malls, a channel that has lost its leading-edge position among retailing venues, Steve and Barry's was able to negotiate lower rents and higher interior building allowances than many big-box competitors. This half of the business model looked to hire contractors to do the interior work substantially under the allowance amounts—delivering the bulk of the profit versus the near breakeven clothing sales price points. This part of the model had less long-term staying power and the supplier interfaces worked less impressively than the garment sourcing strategy.

As for the more effective clothes sourcing strategy, basic garments not linked to fickle fashion changes allowed the chain to buy its finished goods by "base loading" factories with steady, predictable (nonseasonal) production that paid the suppliers' bills during fashion's off-season. They also were willing to trade some inventory en route from the factory for these lower prices. Unlike many apparel supply chains that stress rapid delivery, Steve and Barry's looked to source low cost—even if lead-times were longer. Therefore, more of its suppliers were in low-cost Africa than its competitors (who use China). The African connection also avoided duty and quota issues because the United States does not impose them on African countries—another cost avoidance. We will revisit Steve and Barry's in Chapter 13, because their garment sourcing strategy alone did not sustain advantage.

Compare this "barebones" sourcing strategy with high fashion's Loro Piana SpA label.[6] This company sells the fabric for some of the most exclusive clothing in the world, like $23,000 vicuña wool suits and $16,000 overcoats. The key to its ability to demand such high prices lies in its sourcing strategy for the fiber it uses to make its wool. The company, originally a major cashmere fabric producer, was becoming commoditized as Chinese producers got into the cashmere garment business.

In its search for a more exclusive product, Loro Piana found vicuña wool, spun from the fleece of a Peruvian relative of the llama. Vicuñas are rare (they were almost hunted into extinction in the 1960s before the Peruvian government banned the trade of vicuña fleece) and expensive to raise because the animals take a lot of space and can only be sheered once every two years.

Pier Luigi Loro Piana, co-owner of the family-owned Italian company, formulated a brilliant sourcing strategy that provided real competitive advantage for his firm. While highly profitable, vicuña wool fabric makes up less than one percent of the company's business. However, the strategy's value proposition includes an impact on the company's reputation for high expertise and superb quality among its luxury goods customers and consumers, for whom reputation and image are everything. His strategy, over a twelve-year period, has incorporated six "planks" in its competitive advantage platform:

1. Loro Piana leveraged the Peruvian government's interest in using vicuña fleece as a means to improve the situation for peasant farmers and its concern about avoiding the hunting and poaching that had almost killed off the animal. In 1994, he offered an exclusive ten-year supply contract for 100 percent of the fleece at $400/kg. It offered the government a level of market control and an incentive to guard the herds from poachers.

2. He entered into a "supply chain consortium," which included his fabric company, a Peruvian textile company, and an Italian knitwear company, to produce and market vicuña wool products. (Linking the supply and the customer sides of the business model—sound familiar?)

3. The consortium launched a breeding and conservation effort for its fleece herder supply base (remind you of LVMH's grapes?).

4. Loro Piana put significant effort into lobbying for the fiber, which was limited in its distribution in some countries, including the

    United States, because it was from an endangered species. The conservation effort rebuilt the herd and the lobbying got out the word.

5.   Now that the ten-year exclusivity deal expired and Loro Piana's portion of the vicuña supply market dropped to between 60 and 70 percent, the company has begun to try to expand the herd outside Peru, in neighboring Andean countries.

6.   Meanwhile, they search for a new exclusive fiber, which could possibly be what they call "baby cashmere," from the coat of infant goats in Mongolia and China.

These strategies are targeted at the business models and strategies of the companies that have implemented them. They are about bottom-up, commodity-by-commodity development of supply and suppliers that will integrate into the business. None are inherently better or worse than another, but Steve and Barry's cost focus would certainly never work for Brunello Cucinelli garments. And that is the point. Competitive advantage requires creativity and uniqueness to endure.

—Practitioner's Take—

The other two steps in the strategy process I want to spotlight best fit here, in the practitioner's section. The first is to establish desired results (Step 4). It may strike some as curious that this is not part of the first step, simply replicating the business needs into measurable goals. One of the toughest elements of supply-based strategy is that it is a linkage between needs and what the market can realistically do. Many supply executives do their firms a disservice by simply accepting needs without question. While it is a highly unpopular action, pushing back on senior management when its goals are unrealistic is paramount in delivering competitive advantage. Why? Because it forces either a much more sophisticated approach to supply or it influences the company strategy due to the realities of the market.

    I have seen purchasing executives become heroes by always promising two-digit cost indices year on year (i.e., never 100 + percent, always less). This becomes a problem when it is simply not feasible. Any steelmaker whose purchasing organization promised cost reduction on iron ore (which has increased in price 300 percent from 2003 to 2008) has set its company up for failure, especially if such promises are embedded in finished goods pricing and business strategy. The reason the desired results are not determined until after completing the market, supplier, and economic assessments is that result commitments need to flow from the combination of needs and market capabilities, not just from the need side. The watch-out is to stay aggressive without fantasizing. That is part of the art of sourcing strategy development.

The other step to highlight is renewal (Step 8). Strategies must inherently take a longer view than tactics—strategies need to look at least three years out. That means a strategy that will only work in a near-term buyer's market is probably more tactical than strategic. Importantly, in cross-functional execution processes, it is incredibly frustrating and disruptive to constantly change strategies. The sourcing strategy needs enough stability to provide direction in both tight and loose markets, hence the use of several planks in a strategic platform rather than declaring the go-to-market tool, alone, as the strategy.

(I recently read a report that three- to five-year time frames are not enough and ten years would become the norm. Interesting perspective, but in a market where innovation meets the laws of supply and demand, I believe a ten-year horizon will lead to such generic strategies that they will have to be reformulated as change occurs.)

Having said this, things change, and change is seldom predictable. Sourcing strategy needs an ongoing check and balance. In part, the measures of strategy outcomes—did cost drop? is there enough supply? did quality improve? did we beat competition to market with new products incorporating supplier innovations?—provide this check. But even more important is to build renewal into the ongoing standard strategy process.

Remember, if a strategy is not working there are three possible reasons:

1. The strategy is flawed.
2. The strategy execution is not well done.
3. The circumstances have changed, requiring either tactical or strategic change.

One last point—every sourcing strategy should include a cost-benefit analysis for each potential strategy plank. Degree of difficulty and size of return are key considerations. Inherent in strategy is the allocation of today's resources in anticipation of a return tomorrow. Sometimes a great idea is simply too hard or takes too long to execute, resulting in an inordinate expenditure of resources for the return on that investment. When that kind of problem can be anticipated, it serves as a basis to reject that strategy and seek a different intervention that is more likely to succeed, but still provide potentially game-changing results.

As you think about some of the sourcing strategy examples in this chapter, it should be apparent that the blockbusters go beyond simple supplier selection interventions in the market. Once a strategy is executed and suppliers selected, the game is just beginning. Managing those suppliers in a way that continues to deliver competitive value, despite competitive environment changes, is mandatory for sustained advantage.

Notes

1. Johan Beer, "To make or to buy—that is (still) the question," *Efficient Purchasing*, 1:2, pp. 26–35, 2006.
2. Jill Schildhouse, "An interview with Willis D. Pugh," *Journal of Supply Chain Management*, 42:1, pp. 2–3, Winter 2006.
3. Christina Passariello, "To Rule Champagne Market, LVMH Courts Grape Growers," *Wall Street Journal*, January 2, 2008.
4. Christina Binkley, "Style Showdown: $1000 Sweater Faces $100 Rival," *Wall Street Journal*, November 29, 2007.
5. Robert Berner, "Steve and Barry's Rules the Mall," *Business Week*, April 10, 2006.
6. Stacy Meichtry, "Golden Fleece: Seeking Edge, Fashion Firm Bets on Rare, Furry Animals," *Wall Street Journal*, February 21, 2007.

CHAPTER 6

Supplier Relationships

Erecting Support for Advantage

> **WALL:** any of various permanent upright constructions having a length much greater than the thickness and presenting a continuous surface except where pierced by doors, windows, etc.: used for shelter, protection, or privacy.

Business is not just doing deals; business is having great products, doing great engineering, and providing tremendous service to customers. Finally, business is a cobweb of human relationships.

—H. Ross Perot, industrialist

The topic of supplier relationships is extensive. These relationships are decisive in the pursuit of competitive advantage because they are established with the people in those companies. It is those people who make decisions or operate systems to deliver value to the buying company—or don't. Therefore, entire books have been dedicated to supplier relationship management, exploring tactical approaches and strategic plans to operational and personal interaction.

Relationships: The Walls That Support the Business

After a devastating natural disaster, the videos of the destruction show what happens when building walls are not strong enough to withstand events. While the foundation remains intact, the house is gone when the walls crumble. Weight-bearing walls are particularly important, but non-weight-bearing walls also provide structure and some protection. As more and more of a firm's products and internal processes are accomplished through services and components from suppliers, the ability to integrate those suppliers of components into corporate strategy becomes a key means to put competitive distance between the firm and its competitors. They are the supply analogy to the walls that support a house. Those that may not be as skilled in supplier management will find competitors that better use suppliers forging ahead in the market.

Consider supplier management icon, Toyota. Creating the kind of competitive advantage Toyota's supply base provides takes time. A company that announces a new program or "sudden" change of heart to encourage deep supplier collaboration is in for a surprise. True progress in this area takes effort, consistency, and strong expectations—both of the suppliers and internally. It starts with picking the right suppliers to begin with (using sourcing strategy—Chapter 5), and continues through the interactions after the award of business. The real strength of a supplier relationship is not clear until times get tough—dating and honeymoons are fun, marriage is hard work on both sides.

With this perspective in mind, think about supplier relationships in four phases:

- ▶ Supplier analysis
- ▶ Supplier segmentation
- ▶ Supplier performance management
- ▶ Supplier relationship management

While we have separated supplier relationships from sourcing strategy in this book, like the connection between the foundation and the strength of load-bearing walls, the two are intertwined. Thus including supplier analysis and performance management in sourcing strategy is as important as conducting ongoing supplier analysis and performance management after the business is placed.

The Day Toyota's Supply Base Made All the Difference

The fire broke out at 4:18 A.M. By midmorning it had destroyed both proportioning valve (p-valve) lines in Aisin Seiki's plant in Kariya, Japan. It was February 1, 1997, and for the first time, it looked like Toyota would pay a high price for its just-in-time, close supplier relationships. The automaker's approximately 15,000-car-per-day production operation depended on Aisin for this part, vital to the brake system.[1] Contrary to Western business mythology, Toyota does not rely on sole source suppliers to support its production lines. While Americans were being told to single-source by Dr. W. Edwards Deming, who was one of the fathers of Japanese manufacturing's revival after World War II and the namesake of Japan's Deming Prize, Toyota was following the more pragmatic advice of fishbone diagram creator, Kaoru Ishikawa, whose philosophy included a directive to always have at least two sources—in order to anticipate the unforeseen.

Hence, Toyota uses what is called "parallel sourcing," calling on more than one supplier to ensure uninterrupted supply in the event of a catastrophe. Of the over 6000 parts in their cars, as luck would have it, however, the p-valve was one of a handful that only had one source. Aisin Seiki was one of Toyota's most trusted and oldest suppliers—found to be superior in p-valve quality and reliability at an extremely competitive price, which justified a 100 percent award of business.

Now, in a matter of three to four hours, it appeared that this reliance on a single source, regardless of how trustworthy, might have been misplaced.

As Toyota purchasing and engineering people scrambled into action, the ripples from the fire were quickly felt as all its Japanese plants, including those at assembly subcontractors, were shut down within three days. The fire had destroyed not only the production capability but also the machine tools necessary to restart once the plant could be repaired. Its competitors saw a huge opportunity! Toyota's plants were expected to be down for several weeks at a minimum.

Toyota's supply base rose to the challenge in one of history's most amazing examples of a supply organization's ability to harness and leverage supplier relationships. By February 4, the first few "alternative" p-valves arrived at Toyota from a company called Koritsu Sangyo (an Aisin supplier). By February 6, two Toyota plants were up and running and by February 10, just nine days after the fire, all its assembly lines were back in operation. A supplier failure that could have brought the Japanese market leader to its knees instead was an example of what sustained, extended supplier relationships can do when the suppliers seek to support their customer!

Behind the scenes, the story was even more impressive; it included the efforts of over 200 companies, ranging from Toyota itself (who fabricated some alternative p-valves) to a small six-person sewing machine company that delivered a few each week. While Toyota orchestrated the overall effort, dispatching engineers, fabricating equipment, and communicating priorities, its suppliers jumped into the battle and, using enormous self-direction, established a supply chain for not only the p-valves but also for replacement machine tools to manufacture them. The emergency supply chain was impressive.

For the p-valves themselves, it included Toyota, Aisin, twenty-two of Aisin's primary suppliers (including Koritsu Sangyo), thirty-six of Toyota's other tier-one suppliers (including some industry giants), and four suppliers that were not regular participants in any related supply base. The supply infrastructure assembled to enable that group was even more elaborate—150 other companies that made raw materials and equipment, including seventy machine tool makers. They accomplished tasks from reproducing blueprints for the tooling from valve drawings, to setting up makeshift production lines, to installing quality control systems. Aisin used a second plant as part of the backup supply capability, but in all, over fifty lines scattered across several suppliers pitched in to make the difference.

Afterward, Toyota reimbursed every single supplier for their efforts on its behalf. Supplier relationship management is a term that has many meanings—ranging from software modules, performance measurement systems, strategic supplier management, and interpersonal interactions—so many, in fact, that it has become a phrase that brings with it a modicum of hype and overpromise. Yet, this story exemplifies the meaning of supplier relationships to the building and, in this case, sustaining of competitive advantage. The picture of about 220 companies mounting a "rescue mission" that reestablished a shattered supply base in less than two weeks illustrates the importance of supplier relationships.

—Practitioner's Take—

I was speaking to a procurement executive from one of the American auto companies. His comment about the Aisin fire story was that it does not apply to non-Japanese companies because Toyota holds equity stakes in its supply base—the keiretsu. (A keiretsu is à Japanese management concept that is a grouping or family of affiliated companies that form a tight-knit alliance to work toward each other's mutual success.)

Such defensive, closed-minded reactions are not the way to supply-based competitive advantage. While it is true that Toyota does hold stakes in many suppliers, the point is to create the kind of loyalty and response that saves your business, not use cultural differences to justify why you are unable to do so. The point is finding shared business interest that creates supportive interactions, regardless of the means behind that shared interest.

In Jefferey Liker and Thomas Choi's *Harvard Business Review* article about the Toyota and Honda supplier networks in the United States,[2] they describe how Toyota expanded its car seat supply base at its huge George-town, Kentucky, plant from one to two suppliers. The initial supplier was not a Japanese keiretsu member, but rather an American company, Johnson Controls (JCI). When the capacity of the Lexington plant exceeded JCI's seat-making capability, the supplier wanted to invest large amounts of capital to build a second plant, which would have significantly reduced its profits. Toyota said no, opting instead to send lean production experts to increase the existing plant capacity.

Six years later, when the size of Toyota's business made it seek a second seat supplier, it approached JCI and suggested a keiretsu-like arrangement. JCI entered into a joint venture with Araco, Toyota's Japanese car seat manufacturer, who was planning to enter the U.S. market in competition with domestic seat manufacturers. The resulting joint venture, Trim Masters, is jointly held by JCI (40 percent), Araco (40 percent), and Toyota (20 percent). It is JCI's main competitor for Toyota's business but the Japanese connection did not mean it became the dominant player as its keiretsu status might have led people to expect. JCI holds two thirds of the business, and, as a shareholder in Trim Master, it gains benefits from that company's profitablility. Meanwhile, Toyota has a competitive supply situation that encourages continuous improvement and sharp competitive costing.

My former firm, P&G, does not practice keiretsu investing. Yet, when Hurricane Katrina knocked out P&G's Folgers' New Orleans coffee plant, the coffee business's supply base rallied around Folgers in a manner reminiscent of Toyota's Aisin fire years before.[3] Besides having a competitor offer (for a price of course) to roast and pack Folgers coffee using its suppliers' metal cans (instead of the unique plastic "can" that was Folgers' store shelf package), P&G and its plastic can supplier jointly worked to restart a new can plant in record time.

More impressive was the raw (called "green") coffee supply network's support for Folgers' business. For years prior to Katrina, Folgers had invested enormous amounts of personal capital in developing strong relationships with its entire coffee supply chain from source country through the transport and warehousing operations of many firms. Even before the hurricane, P&G's coffee purchasing leaders made a conscious decision to forego a legalistic approach to relationships, preferring to build trust throughout the chain. As a result, few suppliers declared force majeure during the Katrina chaos. (Force majeure, which means "greater force" in English, is a contract term that excuses a company from performance under a contract when an unforseeable outside force—such as weather or another disaster—makes it impossible.) When the port of New Orleans was effectively eliminated by the storm, coffee suppliers, ocean carriers, local warehouses, and truckers all chipped in to change the outcome for Folgers.

Coffee destined for New Orleans ended up in ports from Jamaica and Houston to as far away as California. Suppliers stepped in to help by absorbing the cost to transship the coffee to the contract manufacturing locations without cost to Folgers. At the same time, ocean carriers agreed to waive container demurrage charges (a seven-figure cost) during the chaotic disruption of the supply chain, even though they were without these valuable ocean containers for a long period of time. Local truckers and warehouses (including one that had lost a major piece of the Folgers business a few years before) that had withstood the flooding stepped in to provide access to coffee inventory and finished product shipment from New Orleans once the P&G plant was back in operation. (The Folgers plant was the first manufacturing operation to start up in the weeks after the storm—and without an amazing effort by the coffee supply chain to overcome massive physical barriers to delivery, the plant startup would have meant little to the business.)

P&G did not have a keiretsu—instead they had enduring relationships that included graceful exits and ongoing principled relationships rather than strictly interpreted legal contracts. It was not about equity stakes or contract clauses, but rather about how relationships were nurtured over time. As one major Brazilian supplier said later, no other coffee company would have survived the disaster. Folgers was able to draw on relationships built over decades to emerge from Katrina with a viable business.

Supplier Analysis—Understanding Suppliers as "Individuals"

Supplier analysis can be thought of as a combination of three analytical efforts—spend analysis, supplier assessment, and supplier analysis. The first two are often part of the selection process, but all three should be thought of as ongoing processes that extend through selection into ongoing management. The first, spend analysis, has become a "holy grail" for sourcing strategy by amassing all of the spending on a particular item across a company and leveraging that volume by rationalizing the number of suppliers to take advantage of economies of scale.

However, another aspect of spend analysis is that you understand the amount of spending you do with a particular supplier across all its divisions and subsidiaries. For years Dun and Bradstreet has called this kind of analysis "parent-child analysis" (named to describe how the children—subsidiaries and divisions—relate to the parent company). It allows the buying company to understand clearly what it purchases from a supplier across all the seller's divisions, along with who the various entities are within the buyer that buy from the supplier's entities. The resulting maps of touch points across both companies' businesses help dimensionalize the impact of a supplier on the corporation. Think of it as an "importance meter."

This is particularly important when dealing with suppliers that provide a wide range of products—like the information technology industry with hardware, software, outsourcing services, and consulting; like conglomerates similar to General Electric with goods, financial services, and entertainment; like chemical companies with commodity chemicals, specialty chemicals, toll processing operations, and feedstocks for other chemicals purchased from other suppliers. Parent-child analysis provides visibility into, among other things:

- ► Volume across all purchases (money and units).
- ► Where that volume is coming from within the buying company.
- ► How important the buyer is to the supplier (compare the size of your buy versus their entire sales; then do it again by supplier division or business category).
- ► The level of risk due to a supplier's financial condition (combine your spend with externally generated supplier financial information [e.g., D&B reports].

> ► Which suppliers are also customers and should be co-managed by sales and procurement (combine customer revenue and supplier spend analysis).

> ► Legal risk (combine spend information by item bought with public information on intellectual property—patents and copyrights—and pending court cases—liens, lawsuits, and regulatory infractions).

This analysis goes beyond sourcing to help identify large, strategic, or risky suppliers by mapping the business they do with your company and, sometimes, the fact that you also sell to them as a customer. The result is a diagram of the relationship's business impact. It is an early step in executing the supplier relationship element of supply-based advantage—hence an importance meter.

Supplier Assessment—Can They Do It?

Supplier assessment has been around for a long time, starting years ago as the "grading sheet" inspectors carried with them when auditing a potential supplier plant before any qualification business was placed. The idea is to make sure the supplier has the capability—at least from an inspection perspective—to handle the business. Supplier audit visits are an expensive way to assess capability, so some companies are beginning to use sophisticated software products with questionnaires, key stroke analysis, and question response analysis to provide a first cut at capability.

Traditionally, this analysis focuses more on the organization that will deliver the actual product—a plant or an office, rather than the entire supplier company. A fairly common set of criteria include:

> ► Quality control processes

> ► Operations or manufacturing reliability

> ► Cost management and financial management

> ► Information systems including electronic purchase to payment

> ► Business management including social responsibility, employee relations, and management approaches

> ► Environmental, labor, and safety practices at the plant level

Despite being somewhat tactical, this is an important analysis. Successfully completing it should be the price of entrance for any supplier—to be followed by production or product usage trials and repeatability verification. However, alone, it is not sufficient to award business and can change over time.

Supplier Analysis: Thinking About "Fit"

Robert Lynch, the alliance consultant I mentioned in the Foreword, has a Three-Dimensional Fit model (3D Fit) that explores three types of fit—strategic, operational, and "chemistry."[4] *Strategic fit* is about the reason doing business with this supplier makes sense—what does each company get from the other? For the buying company it is, at a minimum, the product involved; while for the supplier, the minimum is the revenue from the sale. But strategic fit can go much further to include acquiring a set of core competencies that compliment those of the buying firm going forward, not just in the current transactions. It is the value proposition for the business relationship.

Operational fit is about whether the two companies can actually make the strategic fit happen in the real world. Can the two companies interact effectively to get the work done? It includes things like planning, technical systems, project management, and the interface of the order placement and payment systems on the buying side and the order fulfillment and invoicing systems on the supplier side. The supplier assessment criteria become important here.

Chemistry fit comes in two "flavors." The first is "interpersonal fit"—do the people get along or are there personality issues at key interface points? This can range from whether senior managers trust each other to the compatibility of personal values between people who work together. The second is "institutional fit"—and relates back to the supply advantage architectural drawings we talked about in Chapter 4. Is there a cultural fit between how these companies see suppliers and customers, respectively? While interpersonal chemistry is important, it will seldom be enough. If, in the course of routine business, the myriad interactions create enormous friction, a close relationship will be difficult to sustain. On the other hand, for a simple buy/sell relationship on a standard item, cultural fit is far less important. Chemistry fit is all about the "soft skills" in the relationship and increases with purchased item importance and complexity.

The three-fit model helps explain why this element of supply-based advantage is much harder to achieve than sourcing strategy, and takes longer to develop. The intersection of hard criteria in strategic and operational fit elements must be matched with the soft chemistry criteria of relationships and interactions. The first step in assessing these three "fits" is an ongoing comprehensive supplier analysis.

Think of supplier analysis as the supply equivalent of an investment analyst's research on the supplying company. It is an ongoing process and, when the desired outcome is competitive advantage, must create a perspective on how each supplier stacks up within its industry. Business environments change and if your suppliers are passed by, your ability to compete will be adversely impacted. There are many check lists and approaches to supplier analysis, but one that uses an acronym to promote ease of recall has been most helpful to me. It is called the SOCCER model, with each letter representing a facet of the supplier that needs to be researched (see Figure 6.1).

S—Strategy

This element goes beyond the supplier's business strategy to include the makeup of its management team, company structure including both business unit and functional layouts, how major decisions are made within the businesses, and the corporate social responsibility approach. It also includes key alliance relationships on the marketing and development sides. How does the intersection between a supplier's leadership, business strategy, and internal resourcing priorities match up with the buying company's needs?

O—Operational Capability

This component includes the supplier's ability to make and deliver its products—production capacity, quality control, information systems, work processes, logistical and distribution capabilities, and, importantly, its human resource quality—how good are its people? Does it have the infrastructure and capital assets to deliver?

C—Customer Approach

Is this supplier the market leader? Does it lead pricing in the industry or follow? This factor looks at the supplier's approach toward customers in the broadest sense of the word—customer service, relationship management, market share, and commercial approach. Becoming a preferred customer is an important factor in gaining competitive edge—especially for those goods and services that are strategic to your business. What does it take to be preferred by this supplier?

Figure 6.1 Supplier Analysis

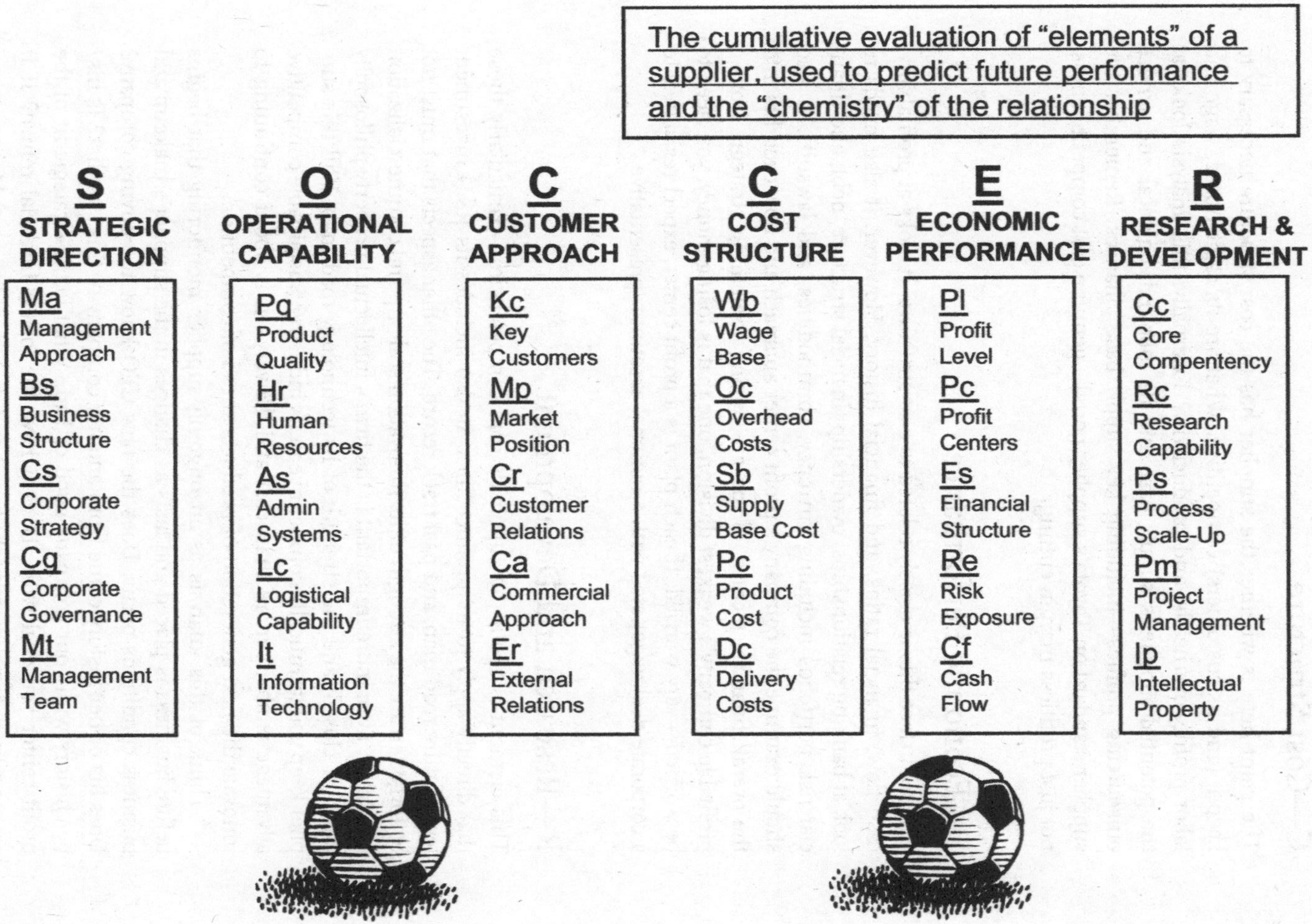

The cumulative evaluation of "elements" of a supplier, used to predict future performance and the "chemistry" of the relationship

S STRATEGIC DIRECTION	O OPERATIONAL CAPABILITY	C CUSTOMER APPROACH	C COST STRUCTURE	E ECONOMIC PERFORMANCE	R RESEARCH & DEVELOPMENT
Ma Management Approach	Pq Product Quality	Kc Key Customers	Wb Wage Base	Pl Profit Level	Cc Core Competency
Bs Business Structure	Hr Human Resources	Mp Market Position	Oc Overhead Costs	Pc Profit Centers	Rc Research Capability
Cs Corporate Strategy	As Admin Systems	Cr Customer Relations	Sb Supply Base Cost	Fs Financial Structure	Ps Process Scale-Up
Cg Corporate Governance	Lc Logistical Capability	Ca Commercial Approach	Pc Product Cost	Re Risk Exposure	Pm Project Management
Mt Management Team	It Information Technology	Er External Relations	Dc Delivery Costs	Cf Cash Flow	Ip Intellectual Property

C—Cost Structure

The point here is whether the supplier has the cost structure necessary to keep it (and its customers) competitive. What are its capital base, wage and labor profile, overheads, and productivity? Externally, this analysis looks at the potential supplier's supply base and its inbound logistical and service outsourcing profiles—including key supply base alliances. Remember the supplier standard on Toyota's supplier portal—genuine cost competitiveness, not just profitless margin cutting.

E—Economic Performance

On the surface this is closely related to cost structure. It looks at profitability, cash flow, financial ratios, and financial history. However, it also needs to look at banking relationships, ownership financial structure, debt, and financial risk portfolios including currency, commodities, and lawsuits. It also should examine the company's profit center approach and how each fits into the overall financial picture. If you are buying something strategic from a profitable company's weakest division, one that is losing money, you need to be worried—very worried. If each plant is a profit center, expect resistance to a corporate deal negotiated with a national account representative.

R—Research and Development

This element is about the supplier's core competencies—particularly those that directly apply to its product lines. It also includes its R&D investment level, future road map, and past track record. The other aspects that must not be forgotten are the strength of its innovation scale-up and commercialization capability. Even more important is the firm's intellectual property philosophy (open or closed) and the strength of its technology road map. Will this supplier keep you technically competitive in its industry? Sustainable competitive advantage is about more than cost and delivery—it is about continuing to innovate the next generation of products ahead of competition.

Think of this analysis as an ongoing supplier monitoring that begins before business is placed and lasts as changes in the supplier's makeup and business conditions occur. Does the new CEO know the buying company? Does his or her history come from another company or this supplier? Is his/her history with your company good or bad? What is the strategic fit of the profit center you deal with? Does it have the lowest financial return? If it seems nonstrategic, who might buy it and do they "like" you? Many companies found that suppliers owned by private equity investors made very different decisions than their publicly held predecessors—with major price increases that "fix" low-profit businesses regardless of the impact on its customers.

—Practitioners Take—

Change is constant. Dun and Bradstreet stresses that somewhere a supplier declares bankruptcy every eight minutes, ceases operations every three minutes, and changes its CEO every one minute. Hence, analyzing suppliers is a vital part of using them to support your business, as well as to create competitive advantage. The intersection between the 3D-Fit model, parent-child analysis, supplier assessment, and more strategic supplier analysis can create real advantage if it is an ongoing exercise, not a one-time event. You never know what changes will occur—Enron was touted as the best company in the United States just a year before it became a bankrupt pariah.

In the late 1970s and early 1980s disposable diapers moved to elastic as a way to improve performance. Prior to that, diapers used only tape and pad size to control fit (no doubt only readers with gray hair will remember those products). P&G was a leader in the elasticized diaper transition, but sourcing the elastic was a challenge. Initially, we approached the garment industry, making the conceptual connection between underwear elastic and diapers. A division of then apparel giant J. P. Stevens became the development supplier. A few years into the elasticized diaper change, it became apparent that we would need more than one supplier for what was becoming an important material.

The search turned up a company, Fulflex, headquartered in Ireland, operating in the heart of U.S. apparel country. Fulflex's material was more expensive, but seemed to run better on our equipment. As we pondered fostering a major increase in supply, we decided to visit both potential suppliers. Fulflex was culturally secretive about their production lines then, so when we visited their operation in the United States we were denied entry to the production area—meeting instead in a conference room. We laid out our plans for the business but made the point that we needed to see Fulflex's capabilities firsthand to assess their long-term capability. They relented, and as we toured the facility, we realized that the golf ball elastic industry, where Fulflex was the leader, ran at speeds and requirements more similar to our applications. In a way, diapers were more like a golf ball than underwear. The plant was well set up to meet the kinds of demands we would put on an elastic supplier, plus Fulflex's research efforts seemed better suited to our future needs.

The die was cast and Fulflex became the dominant producer despite the price difference. Later, when P&G (also highly secretive about manufacturing processes) finally let Fulflex into our plants, their first reaction at seeing our lines and hearing about our elastic productivity challenges (and its higher total cost of ownership) was to utter the words "golf balls!" They told our plant people about elastic handling approaches used in high-speed golf ball facilities to handle elastic and these approaches became solutions to some of our issues. Elastic total cost of ownership dropped and elasticized diaper plant capacity increased almost without capital investment. Total value equated to a market advantage that lasted for a few years, until the rest of the industry fully reacted and technology moved to the next level—elasticized synthetic films. By the way, hitching our wagon to the golf ball industry proved to be far more sustainable than the U.S. textile industry, as by the late 1980s J. P. Stevens, once in the top 125 Fortune 500 companies, no longer existed as a stand-alone textile operation.

The Power Equation

Another aspect of supplier relationship analysis on competitive edge is the concept of power, who holds it, and how they choose to use it. Power is driven by lots of things: volume and size, supply market conditions (loose or tight), company reputation, patents or brand names, even regulatory limits on competition. Andrew Cox is a British academic and consultant who made the study of power a primary focus for understanding how supply relationships work. Developing yet another four-quadrant model (the Business Power Matrix), he has described a range of potential power structures and then applied them to both buyer/seller relationships and supply chains.[5] His point is that the company with the power has greater latitude to extract the lion's share of the supply chain's profits. Often this leads to adversarial relationships, but not always. The model's quadrants, set by buyer and seller power relative to each other, help identify where a potential relationship's balance of power lies:

- ▶ Buyer dominance (buyer extracts the most value).
- ▶ Seller dominance (seller extracts the most value).
- ▶ Independent (neither has power so the market rules—typically in the buyer's favor due to multiple, interchangeable supply options).
- ▶ Interdependent (both have power, leading to balanced negotiation).

The other point Cox makes is that both buyers and sellers seek to shift their position over time in this model, that is, it is a dynamic not a static world and optimizing your company's part of the pie is part of the motivation rewarded by investors.

Apple, in the last several years, has dramatically increased its power in the market. Interestingly, unlike Wal-Mart, IBM, or HP, this is not volume driven. Apple's design and leading-edge product reputation draws top suppliers to it. This is coupled with an intense sourcing strategy effort to find unique materials and supplies to marry with top designs. Apple's supplier relationships are shaped by the power it holds due to its outstanding product and trend-setting reputation.[6]

Apple's suppliers must accept its rules of engagement—excellence, secrecy, "need to know" communication protocols, immediate root cause analysis of problems, heavy reliance on oral communications rather than on drawings (no paper trail to leak), and no supplier ever sees the whole picture. Its business model—make the best product—requires it to seek out the best suppliers. Even in markets where device makers are usually the supplier, Apple has changed the game. Phone companies typically pick the phone hardware, but for iPhone's introduction, it was more like Apple picked AT&T as its phone's service supplier—and was paid well for the choice.

Apple seeks out what it uniquely needs.[7] Apple chose German phone component maker Balda to make small-format displays for the iPhone, according to *Business Week* magazine. While the supplier typically makes plastic phone shells, it made a deal with a Chinese touchscreen producer to get access to technology that expanded its product line to include glass-surfaced screens. Its screens are harder and scratch/smudge resistant with a thin single-unit housing and can sense several human digits simultaneously (in contrast to the older touchscreen technology, which can be confused by multiple fingers). The result is a great fit with Apple's image and revolutionary design.

Not every supplier always wins, however. Apple's power allows it to drop suppliers (one chipmaker that spent a year developing a chip was dropped—crushing its stock and leading to its takeover by a competitor), yet continue to be courted by other players. It can be quite demanding because its power allows it to be. The key is sustained innovation and product wins that draw suppliers to Apple.

Supplier Segmentation

The idea of supplier segmentation is pretty simple—grouping suppliers in a supply base by their impact on the business. There are a number of segmentation methodologies out there, most of which divide into two categories. One uses business impact to segment groups (think about Kraljic's model in Chapter 5, with purchased items in noncritical, bottleneck, leverage, and strategic quadrants translating into supplier categories of the same names), while the other uses the nature of the relationship as the segmentation criterion (alliance, preferred supplier, vendor). These models tend to blend sourcing approach and relationship approach. For example, the "leverage" quadrant or the "vendor" segment implies intensely competitive supplier management while the "strategic" quadrant and "alliance" segment implies a more collaborative approach.

When the goal is competitive advantage, the segmentation approach needs to look at two types of segmentation. The first addresses the entire supply base, while the second looks more closely at the suppliers that will make the most difference. Both are necessary.

The first helps define the nature of the relationships relative to the buying company's business and the management of its entire supply base. In my experience, a five-level set of segmenting criteria gives the most benefit when accompanied by some guidance on how to manage each type of interaction. The five segments are:

> *Alliances.* These are major suppliers with whom the 3D-fit dynamics are all generally positive and the impact on the business is large. Alliances take resources and normally involve the transfer of highly proprietary information (business plans, new product road maps, joint development efforts). Both business impact and corporate fit matter if the relationship is to be a real alliance. Managing the relationship is a cross-functional, carefully orchestrated process with governance, measurement, and joint business processes to manage conflict, innovation, and ongoing results.

> *Essential Suppliers with Experience-Driven Relationships.* These are the major suppliers that have consistently delivered value over the years.

They typically provide meaningful supply categories to the buying firm, but not necessarily the most strategic ones. In fact, if the items being supplied were more strategically important, the relationship would probably be an alliance. The levels of trust, communication quality, and performance metrics are relatively aligned and effective. Because of this and the slightly less important nature of what they supply, these relationships can operate with less extensive governance and a lower resource infrastructure.

▶ *Essential Suppliers with Market-Driven Importance.* These are suppliers where the relationships are troublesome, but absolutely necessary, because the buyer needs what they make. It is not an alliance because the relationship does not have enough openness or trust. However, these suppliers are important to the business and must be dealt with. In a way, they require as much, or more, effort than alliances because they are vital to the organization but difficult to manage. This means dedicated resources and deep analysis about why the supplier finds the business of interest. Often these are supplier-dominant power relationships with significant accompanying risk. You need the supplier badly. Exit barriers are high. These companies must be very carefully managed.

▶ *Competitively Based Incumbents.* These are the bulk of the supply base, handling somewhat less important items that are typically "won" from other suppliers due to a better value proposal. They have a history with the buying firm, so the relationship is somewhat predictable but typically not strategic. Routine supply processes should work well with these relationships—get the results without having to invest inordinate resource levels to achieve them. Multiple suppliers are available, and where they are not, substitutes can replace the item in question.

▶ *New Suppliers.* These are suppliers with little or no history with the buyer that have recently won business. The fact that the supplier is new means the relationship has really not developed. This lack of experience can lead to miscommunication as the parties have little experience working together. For potentially strategic items, this requires extensive and precise communication (with checks to ensure that understanding is clear) as well as early resource commitment, often with the goal of establishing a higher level cooperative relationship over time. For nonstrategic items, clear communication ensures needs are met without too much resource investment.

—Practitioner's Take—

Supplier segmentation is a standard best practice in supply management. However, when the goal is more than just prioritization of effort, it becomes a more complex decision. Many companies simply categorize the supplier and move to a relationship management technique generic to that type of relationship. Over the years I have seen this rote approach lead to some major mistakes.

1. Companies assign a "type name" to the relationship and manage accordingly, even though they have little experience with the supplier. This has been especially true in low-cost country sourcing (LCCS) efforts that play the labor arbitrage game with new suppliers. In my career, I came to understand first that trust needs to be earned not just given. Until the supplier proves its ability to deliver value over time and interact in ways that are cooperative and predictable, trust given too soon can lead to unpleasant surprises. Second, a relationship is never really tested until it goes through hard times. One enzyme supplier relationship, an alliance, went through a couple years during which any outsider parachuting in would have concluded it was the antithesis of an alliance. Yet it came through the trial and this supplier has delivered enormous value. It saw my company as one of its best customers. The test of a relationship is its ability to deal with major conflict. If it comes through the trials, and the parties understand how each other will approach issues, the relationship emerges stronger. Unfortunately, sometimes you don't find out whether the supplier will stay with you until after the disagreement.

2. A second issue is "relationship before strategy." Beware choosing a relationship before the sourcing strategy is clear. More important, if the strategy changes, recognize that the relationship needs to change, too. One of the toughest shifts is when a supplier transitions from highly strategic to one of the lesser segments. In one case, changing needs and the shift from new product launch to ongoing production deemphasized a particular material supplied by one chemical company. Its top management had frequent access to senior business unit leaders at P&G during the develop-

ment and rollout of the new product platform, but when things changed, the need for such top-to-top meetings declined. When we sought to reduce/eliminate that access, it actually caused significant friction that had to be smoothed with expectations realignment—several sessions with their senior people to explain our changing focus and their continuing place in our business. The supplier remained a source of value but more as an ongoing rather than a developmental source.

3. Supplier segmentation groupings often become the basis for resource allocation. This leads to a potential miscue. Not every function within the corporation sees the supplier in the same light. The engineering or product development groups can see a supplier as highly strategic while the new product is under development, but when it goes to market and the next generation's key component is not from that supplier's capability portfolio, interest quickly wanes. This is just about the time that the operational importance at a plant or internal customer's organization surges. While a procurement or enterprise-wide supplier management group may see the whole value and competitive position picture, that doesn't mean other groups will agree. Internal resourcing of the relationship must deal with such shifts in interest because disinterested relationship managers can do enormous damage. One best practice is to use different criteria for segmentation depending on the spend category (e.g., information technology suppliers should be segmented on very different criteria than product raw or packaging material suppliers).

4. Deciding which suppliers to make top priority is not just about whether they are an alliance or preferred supplier. Rather, when competitive advantage is the goal, importance to the business regardless of the nature of the relationship should be the selection criterion. Importance can be measured in many ways, but some norms to consider are:

- Financial importance—size of spend and its impact on the product or budget economics.

- Business product performance importance—does this supplier provide an element of your product or your operational capability that is integral to the ability to service customers and drive sales volume?

- Innovation importance—sometimes suppliers with whom you have little business (or experience) are the ones coming up with the next big idea (e.g., next-generation materials or components for new products) or have a new business model with greater value potential (initially, outsourcing suppliers in India and China fell in this camp before they became commonplace).
- Operational importance—this is where chronic supply problems or disruptions drive importance. Supply chain risk is especially significant.

5. Finally, some suppliers provide many items of differing importance to the same buying firm. These "umbrella" relationships can be tricky to manage. A mistake I have personally made is to use one "relationship approach" across several independent interfaces—typically gravitating to the most important relationship to set the overall tone. Hence, a supplier of both innovation and commodity goods is treated as an alliance across both areas. The situational nature of competitive advantage and value extends to each spend category. When a "one-size-fits-all" relationship approach applies to very different commodities, value and thus competitive edge can be compromised. This is either by supplier design (i.e., leveraging the importance of one item to gain concessions on another) or by inadvertent buyer behavior (psychological relationship exit barriers within the buying organization). Yet, it is necessary to be cognizant of the full range of items a particular supplier provides and the range of needs they fill, because on the supplier side the relationship is ultimately run by people who also see the whole picture—or don't. One of the myths of spend management is that knowing what is spent always leads to buying leverage. Suppliers do not always agree, and that "sword" can have sharp edges on both sides. Understanding the nature of each subrelationship and setting the right expectation with supplier management is an important element in managing umbrella relationships.

Supplier Performance: Managing Outcomes

All of this upfront analysis and relationship segmenting is of little value (and thus competitive edge) if performance is not measured, managed, communicated, and improved continuously over time. Supplier scorecarding is a technique that is pivotal to managing performance. A discussion of supplier performance measurement and how it delivers value is essential to using suppliers to develop competitive advantage.

Supplier scorecards have been talked about for years, yet, perhaps surprisingly, most companies struggle to implement the kinds of comprehensive measurement systems described in academic and software company literature. One industry, however, that seems to be a leader in this arena is retail. The Wal-Marts, Targets, and Home Depots of the world have strong result measurement systems. Home Depot, while dealing with serious housing industry economic issues and store management problems that threaten its claim to competitive advantage, still remains a good example of a supplier performance management system that delivers fundamental value.

While Robert Nardelli was heavily criticized as CEO of Home Depot, one positive he implemented was a significant level of process discipline.[8] When a company has thousands of suppliers to measure and manage, such discipline is critical. When Nardelli arrived there were numerous standalone measurement systems and no single communication center for the company's 10,000-plus suppliers with global scope from China to Brazil. Home Depot's approach to improved supplier performance measurement is instructive.

The company combined process rigor with information system improvements, supplier scorecards, supply base communication methods, and clear, comprehensive performance categories and goals. Expectations were set for performance improvement going forward across three areas—operational (cost, quality, innovation, delivery, availability), supply chain (integration, time, standardization), and behavior (social and environmental responsibility).

Enabling this transition was a revamped information technology platform with a supplier center for communications, a Web-based result scorecard system with graphs and thirteen-month trend data, links to other systems (warehouse, purchase orders, invoices, etc.), and a documentation system to reconcile information from multiple internal sources.

All this was coupled with internal efforts to calibrate results expectations and metrics internally across stores; perform six sigma measurement analyses to increase the accuracy and credibility of the data; and initiate a cross-functional, integrated "voice of the supplier" effort to incorporate supplier input across the organization. Simultaneously, the performance management structure incorporated supplier workshops on how to work with Home Depot—including on-site sessions in source countries like China—and a council of fifteen strategic suppliers that works on specific initiatives.

On the behavior side, Home Depot is another company that has integrated its corporate values into its supplier performance system.[9] In addition to a supplier diversity program that seeks to have its supply base reflect the demographic makeup of its customer base, Home Depot has aggressively attacked environmental areas. The firm has chosen to help protect natural forests across the world through expectations setting and business placement with its lumber suppliers. The company's environmental global project manager has the authority to sever logging contracts and, in fact, did so in Indonesia where slash-and-burn logging is a huge problem, and in Gabon where the same technique endangered the lowland gorilla's natural habitat. Home Depot has mediated environmental group interactions with timber suppliers in Chile (Home Depot buys 10 percent of Chile's wood exports) and has joined with competitor Lowe's to lobby Canada to protect parts of the Great Bear Rainforest in British Colombia.

Home Depot has an impressive supplier measurement infrastructure and, in its vernacular, a socially responsible "supplier behavior" expectation. Like those of many major retailers, it is based on a strong power position in addition to good design and information technology investment.

—Practitioner's Take—

The combination of credible data, willingness to invest in information technology on the supply side of the business, and result reporting that is shared with suppliers are what make a supplier performance management system work. Amazingly, discussions with many companies show that most organizations know supplier scorecards are valuable, but few do it well. The presentations in conferences and the popular press often discuss pilot programs with a handful of suppliers in glowing terms, but few are systemically applied across the supply base. Most of these systems measure the basics (delivery and quality) for only the largest suppliers.

The issues include information systems that cannot integrate and aggregate across the many functions and locations that measure suppliers. The data exists, but the ability to report it and then drill down into it depends on strong software products and, even more importantly, close internal collaboration across organizational boundaries. Worse, an Aberdeen Research study noted that only a third of companies share the scorecard metrics with suppliers.[10] Instead, they use them internally to weed out the supply base. How can you gain real improvement and create the dialogue to find competitive advantage if you do not share the report card with the student?

Another aspect of performance management is contracting. The reader will note that contracts and legally holding suppliers to them has not been a big part of this chapter. (We will talk about contracts more in Chapter 12.) The reason is *not* that contracts are unimportant. They create a framework for the relationship. However, the shifting components of competitive advantage and unforeseen business changes will inevitably make the assumptions in place at contract signing obsolete. Jointly, these changes conspire to make rigid, legalistic contract management a weak supplier management option when it is the only aspect of the governance mechanism. Relationships that create supply-based advantage need to go beyond the contract.

Interestingly, when talking with an executive formerly with one of Home Depot's suppliers (who asked to remain anonymous), her immediate reaction was mixed. She agreed with the assessment that the scorecard system is excellent. However, it was clearly linked to a feeling that some of the tactical negotiation approaches that accompanied it were less loyalty-inducing for the suppliers. This complaint has long been whispered about the dominant retailers and "category killer" stores by suppliers that do not want to publicly criticize their powerful customers.

These types of techniques (not specifically practiced by Home Depot or any other particular retailer) include tactics like constantly rebidding in markets where innovation does not steadily reduce pipeline inventory value (contrast plumbing supplies with electronic components). Other approaches include creating onerous price increase justification forms in deals that allow cost pass-through and stretching out the process using formatting and the review process as a means to avoid the increase (while the supplier's margin disappears); having suppliers include freight in the price and then deduct from the invoice based on a lower freight rate that "should have" been used—although the carrier with that rate is seldom capable of meeting the load requirement; stopping orders regardless of lead-time agreements and then restarting them after supplier crews have downsized, causing training costs and emergency shipment costs suppliers then must absorb; releveling inventory, especially after holidays (in retail) and preearnings reporting (in non-retail).

Seasoned supply people are probably sheepishly smiling now—we've all seen these approaches and probably even been rewarded or recognized for the results they deliver. They are part of the game. The question is whether the emotions they raise at suppliers—and in many cases the similar petty responses they elicit from the supply base (this is by no means a one-way street!!) are the means to tapping supplier knowledge to achieve competitive advantage or something only a tiny minority of high-power buyers can use. Reapplying the scorecarding skills of retailers like Home Depot is part of the supplier performance effort, but it is not an independent effort. Negotiation tactics are inevitably coupled with these scorecards. Think about the value a supplier offers beyond today's negotiation when selecting negotiating tactics—and always consider your supply principles as well. Undermining the philosophy built in Chapter 4 is a high price to pay for short-term cost avoidance when the goal is sustainable competitive advantage, not hitting this quarter's purchase price variance goal.

Supplier Relationship Management—It's About People, Stupid!!!

The term "supplier relationship management" (SRM) has many definitions, but in this case it is about actually having a relationship with the supplier's key contacts and the supplier doing the same with the buying company. Sounds like double-talk, right? "SRM is about actually having a relationship with a supplier." Yet, that is just what it is about, and people can forget that.

The problem is that the combination of supplier segmentation, sophisticated software products that allow "collaboration" electronically rather than directly, and international supply lines that often preclude face-to-face interaction, all combine to give the illusion that relationships don't matter any more. Nothing could be further from the truth. Supplier decisions to support a customer—which include questions of how, how much, where, why, what's in it for us (the supplier)—are made by people. So are the daily choices that create operational fit.

Corporate relationship management is a combination of personal and institutional relations. To gain a supply-based competitive advantage and then hold on to it requires deep supplier understanding, access to the right contacts, and good overall "cultural compatibility" in day-to-day interactions. This is particularly true for the most strategic suppliers, but also applies to more routine relationships.

Building these associations takes planning and effort. You will need to:

▶ *Have a profound knowledge of the supplier and its key people.* Analyze the nature of the current relationship—is it adversarial or cooperative? Why? Are the strategic directions of both parties consistent (not necessarily the same but at least compatible)? Perhaps most important is understanding how the supplier's reward systems and decision processes work. The decision processes tell you who to know and the reward system tells you what they care about (both personally and as a business). Knowledge of these elements is not superficial—hence the phrase "profound knowledge."

▶ *Map the key players on both sides.* This requires internal stakeholder recruitment and involvement at the corporate boundary. It also requires supplier willingness to invest similarly on the other side. (Sometimes buyers assume the supplier is prepared to match their efforts when that is simply not the case.) These people become the "governance" organization that manages the relationship's ups and downs. The Hackett Group's report on competitive advantage and procurement (December 2007)[11] dimensionalized how challenging this is. Cross-functional teams and high levels of involvement are an established best practice in sourcing strategy and execution efforts (over 70 percent of best in class companies do so). Everybody wants a vote on who supplies them. The problem is that the real work takes place after that, when dynamic business conditions require ongoing adjustment. Even among Hackett's best in class group, only 18 percent have cross-functional teams that stay together to manage ongoing relationships (for the "normal" company the number is just 8 percent). This is a critical differentiator with regard to competitive advantage because flexibility, adjustment to changing market conditions, and knowing when to hold and when to shift are what sustained advantage is all about. When cross-functional involvement is not there to help define and align on those direction changes, competitive edge is at risk.

▶ *Keep the relationship's direction and the sourcing strategy in sync.* That includes making sure the strategy is in sync with the business model and needs as they change.

▶ *Develop the right contacts at the supplier.* This means *personal* contacts, not an e-mail address. Periodic face-to-face meetings, especially early in the relationship, are part of this investment. If the first time a supplier executive talks to your company is during a problem, the outcome is highly uncertain. Trust, and even just predictability, takes time to establish. Either one is enough to manage the relationship. (Trust is typically better, but the nature of the relationship may preclude it. Predictability can sustain a productive relationship for years when trust is too difficult for the parties. Alliance theorists hate to hear that, but in the real world it frequently works that way.)

▶ *Build an institutional relationship.* Set the internal expectations on how suppliers are treated in general (remember those architectural drawings from Chapter 4), and *this* supplier in particular. Have sensing systems that highlight when the personal relationship vision of senior leaders does not match the day-to-day feel of the interactions. This key alert exposes the potential for serious problems, and should trigger efforts to solve the problem.

▶ *Set and update expectations.* This must be two-sided. Focusing only on your company's expectations of the supplier, without factoring in their expectations of your company, is a recipe for later conflict. Managing expectations and especially *balancing* those two sets of expectations are critical skills in gaining competitive advantage from suppliers.

▶ *Build trust over time.* As we mentioned before, trust is earned not given, and any relationship that has not gone through hard times is suspect. Conflict and taking the other side for granted are common pitfalls that must be avoided. Building trust and relationship duration requires that both parties possess the following ingredients:

- A track record of achieving results, early communicating of misses, providing straight feedback, and demanding accountability.

- Integrity—living up to operating principles established between the companies.

- Empathy—showing concern even when business circumstances do not allow action.

- A level of behavioral and operational predictablity that allows reasonable anticipation of individual or corporate reaction to a situation.

All of this represents the "soft side" of business. It is the soft side that can make all the difference because business decisions are typically made without all the facts, which are frequently not available. So judgment, the ability to "read" peers in other companies and your own feel for the business, become deal makers and breakers, especially for things like supplier innovation or supply chain redesign efforts.

The Use of Soft Skills Is Not About Group Hugs

A major risk in all this is that the soft side comes to mean comfortable interactions and close personal relationships that overcome the hard business choices that sometimes have to be made. As any marriage counselor will tell you, respect, honesty, and willingness to work through conflict are key skills in relationships. Delivering bad news and demanding accountability is part of the job.

Let's go back one more time to Toyota.[12] While the company consistently gets the highest relationship marks in the auto industry from its suppliers, those same suppliers do not say Toyota is easy to deal with. Quite the opposite, they claim—Toyota is amazingly demanding, expecting the most from suppliers, and unafraid to raise the bar should business needs require it—yet always in a reasoning manner. Toyota exerts a great deal of control over its supply base—in Andrew Cox's "power model" they want to be in the buyer-dominant quadrant.

In 1998 a competitor mentioned in a private conversation with Toyota executives that they were paying too much for parts from their trusted suppliers. Toyota strongly believed it had an insurmountable cost advantage and was insulted by the comment—so much so that they set out to disprove it. Current CEO Katsuaki Watanabe, who was then the head of Toyota's purchasing organization (remember the comment earlier that some companies actually do "get" the importance of supply?), undertook the effort to disprove this criticism.

The company's thorough, months-long study unearthed the fact that in about half its purchases the competitor's comment was, indeed, correct. This humiliating outcome led Watanabe to launch the CCC21 program (Construction of Cost Competitiveness for the 21st Century) to change the way parts were designed and fabricated without affecting quality in any negative way. The goal was a trillion yen cost reduction (30 percent or $8.7 billion) over five years from 2000 through 2004. Suppliers were presented with this "demand" but also were in a joint effort to accomplish it—not the typical "cut the cost and mail in the check" approach of many companies. Part of the project included changes in Toyota's specifications and explored capital equipment supplier development efforts that dramatically improved internal plant flexibility and capital cost structure. CCC21 was successful as the suppliers of 173 components and subsystems reconceived the products and processes to lower cost and deliver reliable quality.

The demand for a 30 percent cost reduction from what its suppliers felt were already excellent results is not a "group hug." Toyota's sense of urgency, clear expectations, and willingness to pitch in and work with the suppliers were the basis for its success and reestablishment of competitive advantage. It also reinforced a sense of humility, which can be one of the most important elements in sustaining competitive advantage through suppliers. Too much praise can blind a company to its competitor's improvements—especially on the supply side, which is often invisible or incompletely transparent outside the company—unlike many marketing or customer initiatives that are far more visible.

—Practitioner's Take—

All of this stuff sounds great, but achieving it is extremely difficult. In my own experience, I was not always able to sustain it. The biggest challenges that must be overcome are allowing the time and having the skill to manage these relationships.

Supplier segmentation sets priorities—the problem is that it inevitably misses important supplier contributions because there are not enough people to chase them all, nor hours in the day to deliver them. Prioritization is step one. Just as important is to build into the middle and lower levels of supply-facing organizations a series of operational mindsets that enable the discovery and elevation of supply advantage. We will talk about these skills in more depth later, but want to briefly touch on a few here. You will need to:

- *Manage and invest the appropriate resources.* If your company is unwilling to invest on the supplier side of the business, competitive advantage becomes an underfunded internal program. No company has a monopoly on good ideas, so limiting yourself to your own ideas is a dangerous strategy. One of the most important investment vehicles is people's time to work on the supplier side of the enterprise.
- *Make transparent choices.* The decision to interact with suppliers and differentiate within umbrella relationships requires clear choices and transparent communication of those choices both internally and sometimes externally.

- *Make conflict resolution your top priority.* Conflict, which is inevitable, is also a key catalyst for improvement if it can be channeled constructively. During my career, one supplier relationship was with a packaging supplier that provided extraordinary value by taking P&G from a traditional package to one with better consumer safety, performance, and cost structure. This began a decades-long relationship in which one of the success measures was low conflict. Unfortunately, our relationship lacked the spark of conflict and our competition in this product category evolved to new suppliers with new technology that gave them a major cost advantage. This enabled them to aggressively invest in products that hurt our market share. When conflict finally did arise, it was so alien to the relationship that we were unable to use it to influence the supplier to change its approach, resulting in a painful but necessary "divorce." But this occurred only after our cost disadvantage and our competitor's product expertise combined to put it into a hard-fought market standoff that was less profitable and higher risk than the leadership position we had long held. We had let supply-based advantage slip away because we erroneously saw *conflict* as a symptom of a bad relationship, rather than seeing *managed conflict* as an element of a healthy one. Peace at any price does not deliver competitive advantage.

Limited Resources

Besides an adversarial mindset, perhaps the biggest barrier to using supplier relationships as part of a firm's competitive battle plan is lack of resources. While linking with the few top-tier suppliers is something many companies manage to do, few go much further. Overlooked is the significant potential of the "middle ground" suppliers—the 15 to 20 percent of the supply base that fall between the top 5 percent's strategic differentiators and the bottom 75 percent's routine commodities. The problem is you won't have the time to work in depth with this middle tier of suppliers.

The skills needed to draw non-price value from suppliers take time to develop. That's where delegating responsibilities and coaching relationship skills into the middle and even lower levels of supply and internal customer organizations can make a difference. The important midrange supplier relationships that matter, but do not make the cut for formal relationship efforts, are seldom completely ignored either. Instead, midlevel supply managers and their internal customers frequently interact with them. Value and, ultimately, competitive advantage from this category of suppliers can be mined by instituting more basic and fewer resource-intensive relationship approaches modeled on the ones discussed earlier for strategic suppliers.

In particular, establishing contacts up every supplier's management chain rather than just at the local sales representative or Internet ordering site level will encourage better understanding of the supplier's view of the relationship. Similarly, leveraging interested internal customer knowledge about total cost of ownership and supplier responsiveness metrics can help the buyer understand where hidden value might lie. Equally important, creating informal internal supplier management liaisons can transfer information—and understanding of what your business needs from that supplier—collaboratively across functional silos. Coupling this scaled-down approach with periodic management reviews and coaching will groom the next generation of supplier relationship owners for strategic suppliers by letting them "practice" optimizing value from important midrange suppliers.

A problem with creating these personal relationships is that personnel turnover on both sides—the buyer and the seller—is the norm. This results in a lack of institutional memory about the relationship over time. Embedding the philosophy (Chapter 4), sourcing strategy (Chapter 5), and cross-functional, multilevel internal supplier management methodologies (this chapter) into the organization's normal operating approaches can help to overcome this obstacle—but probably not completely. History matters in these relationships. It is unlikely that a supplier who has seen a customer move from collaborative to adversarial and back again will fully trust that any change is predictably in place for the long haul. Management changes, strategy changes, and acquisition or divestiture activity on both sides can create huge shifts in the overarching philosophy toward the relationship.

The odyssey of Chrysler over the past ten years is a classic example. As a U.S. company, Chrysler launched and embedded the SCORE program (Supplier COst REduction) that Tom Stallkamp put in place. It was extremely collaborative, with benefit sharing, and delivered $5 billion over six years (1991–1997). After buying Chrysler, German automaker Daimler dismantled the program with a philosophy of intense supplier competition replacing savings sharing. (The name SCORE lived on for a while but the approach was not the same.) Today, private equity ownership, with its premium on financial measures and cash flow, has articulated a blend of the two philosophies but, so far, we see more of the later than the former. (We will talk more about that below.) Suppliers remember, even when the managers who experienced a buyer's inconsistent messages have moved on, it becomes part of the internal "lore" of the company.

Interestingly, this does not mean suppliers don't come back after being "mistreated." However, the return engagement is often more cautious and contract driven. In the auto industry, large numbers of suppliers have sought other customer industries to lessen their involvement with the car firms, with some simply exiting the auto business, but it takes time to wean away from historical economic dependencies. Example: Delphi was aggressively diversifying its customer base but ran out of time as General Motors' (GM) business fell faster than the new customer ramp up, ultimately resulting in a lengthy and difficult bankruptcy.

—Practitioner's Take—

One of the most important skills in using supplier relationships for competitive advantage is the "graceful exit." In addition to maintaining a reasonable reputation in supplier industries, the concept behind a graceful exit is to sustain the ability to come back if need be. Predicting the future is by no means foolproof, so just because a supplier is not needed today does not preclude intense need at another time. This is a fundamental difference between suppliers as competitive advantage enhancers and suppliers as cost savings pools. Those only looking for cost reduction simply move the business with little concern for the nature of the split. Those that have woven the supplier into their business model and, due to changes in the competitive environment, now need to replace them, recognize the value in being able to call upon a one-time ally in the future without fear of reprisal.

The graceful exit strategy falls into two categories: reduction of importance and severing a commercial relationship. A major challenge of supply chain relationships is that they tend to be more open ended than other marketing or codevelopment efforts. It is common for a relationship to continue after the strategic alliance aspect is gone. Ongoing supply needs remain even when the innovation or service aspects of the business change the buyer's focus to other suppliers. This de-emphasis of the relationship normally results in less access to the buyer's senior management, a change that must be managed.

The second type of exit is business termination. This is often far more difficult because it creates a hole in the supplier's revenue forecast that, for large strategic accounts, is extremely difficult to refill.

The way in which buyers deal with both these situations is crucial to the ability to count on this supplier again in the future, should the need arise. In my experience, graceful exits require:

- Investment in the relationship while it is healthy so that the players know each other and frank communication is possible.

- Early warning—even if it is just a hint—to executives with whom trust has been established. The key is to avoid a supplier pullout when the exit decision is not firm yet. Knowing the supplier's leadership is critical in order to provide a warning without triggering a panic.

- Be able to explain the circumstances behind the change. The ability to describe the need for change and the rationale behind it (performance shortcomings, product redesign or obsolesce, cost economics, etc.) is pivotal. It is also important that if performance or high cost are the reasons, it does not come as a total surprise. Ongoing feedback systems can avoid this.

- Once exit is decided, empathy becomes an important skill. Business circumstances may not allow the current (or any) relationship to continue, but showing a level of understanding and emotional support is important to sustaining some level of personal and institutional chemistry fit.

- If possible, negotiate a mitigation plan that allows the supplier's business reduction to be a phased approach. This could include adequate lead-time, partial award reductions over time, or willingness to provide a reference (where performance supports it) for other customers. If this is not feasible, working through the possibility of smaller awards in areas where the supplier can be competitively justified or a financial settlement are other possibilities. Through it all, empathy coupled with firmness on the execution of the decision are essential.

- Once a decision is made and communicated to the losing supplier (and the winner) a reversal undermines the buyer's future position—alienating the winning supplier who now loses and causing the losing supplier to think winning can be bought psychologically, without having to deliver real results. Sticking with a tough decision is vital to maintaining integrity in the relationship, even if it is ending.

Exits Are Not Always Graceful

The lack of a graceful exit can enormously impact the buying firm's reputation despite executive statements that seek to justify the termination. A classic example is Chrysler's 2008 "divorce" from molded products supplier Plastech Engineered Products.[13-18] Plastech was a woman-owned, minority (Asian) supplier that made molded parts (door panels, floor consoles, engine covers, etc.) for several major automakers including GM, Ford, Toyota, tier-one auto supplier Johnson Controls, and Chrysler. Development of supplier diversity had been a major initiative in the auto industry for years, and Plastech, a $1.3 billion revenue company with thirty-five plants, was one of the results of that effort, starting up twenty years earlier in 1988 and representing the largest minority supplier in the auto supply chain.

Plastech, like many auto suppliers, had been squeezed for years but somehow found ways to survive and dodge the economic crises that struck many of its peers. However, by early 2008, it found itself on the edge financially as auto sales fell during the housing credit crisis in the United States. During 2007, several of its customers, including Chrysler, provided both a $46 million bailout and, in January 2008, accelerated payments on $40 million to help cash flow. A frequent U.S. auto company approach toward such troubled suppliers is to align procurement groups to support the supplier. In Plastech's case, its largest customer, Johnson Controls, was leading another such effort when Chrysler pulled out on February 1, 2008. This action came just two months after CEO Robert Nardelli (remember Home Depot's extensive supplier management program) announced during internal meetings that he wanted to work more constructively with Chrysler's supply base.

Chrysler declared its intent to pull its business, reallocating it to other suppliers, and wanted to remove the tooling to make about 500 parts going into all its models from Plastech's plants. According to bankruptcy court records, this action was due to a significant Plastech price increase (probably triggered by surging raw material costs and economic-slowdown-induced lower Chrysler order volumes) and some quality problems. (At the time, industry analysts estimated that Chrysler would incur a price increase with the new suppliers as well, but would avoid cost over the long run. It had hired PriceWaterHouseCoopers LLP [PWC] to analyze the finances and operations of its suppliers, and notified suppliers that it expected them to let PWC into their plants and provide them information.) Nardelli, drawn into the supplier dispute, explained that if suppliers increased prices, Chrysler had no choice but to respond in kind.

Unfortunately, the plan did not go as planned. Plastech declared bankruptcy, claiming Chrysler pushed this minority, woman-owned supplier over the edge. The bankruptcy also was a means to protect Plastech's possession of the Chrysler tooling (to which Chrysler had legal rights) from seizure. Parts shipments to Chrysler stopped. Within a day, four Chrysler plants shut down (along with its tier-one supplier, Dana Corp.) and the national media was all over the story. None of Plastech's other auto customers had any disruption at all. (Chrysler was 15 percent of Plastech's business—the other 85 percent continued to be produced.)

After agreeing to a two-week interim supply plan, Chrysler and Plastech headed to bankruptcy court to battle over the all-important tooling. Chrysler had new suppliers lined up and planned to shut its lines down for up to a week while the tools were moved and started up in new supplier factories.

But like so many court cases, the legal system's outcomes are not always predictable. Despite contractual rights to the tools (and even the support of Plastech's other customers that Chrysler should have access to them), the bankruptcy judge found for Plastech, saying that pulling the tooling so quickly would undermine any reorganization effort under the bankruptcy. Therefore Chrysler had to keep buying from Plastech and the other suppliers did not start up.

Was Chrysler wrong to exit Plastech? Perhaps not, given significant cash inflows to support the supplier ($7 million of the $46 million bailout came from Chrysler, according to the press), possible quality problems, and whatever the PWC study told them. Private conversations with other auto industry people and a quick scan of the auto and purchasing blog world provide decidedly mixed points of view on this particular supplier. However, the point was that the exit was messy rather than graceful on so many levels:

➤ A public relations nightmare for Chrysler, having cut off a minority, woman-owned supplier and opening itself up for public second-guessing.

➤ A court case that did not result in clear victory.

➤ Plant shutdowns.

➤ An exit plan without a low-risk backup supply plan (which leads to questions about the strength of the original sourcing strategy and the level of planning Chrysler did before reacting to a price increase).

➤ Chrysler choosing to walk out on its industry in the midst of joint problem-solving efforts. (These efforts supposedly helped automakers survive similar situations with Collins and Aikman [C&A]

and Tower Automotive—two other financially weakened suppliers—although Chrysler said they got no parts from their C&A effort.)

- ► Notice to suppliers that the previously predictable behavior of Chrysler, the publicly held company, would be less predictable as a privately held firm.

Chrysler's decision may ultimately lead to a stronger supply base, but the nature of its exit from Plastech will likely make efforts to gain the trust of at least some other suppliers more difficult.

(Ultimately, Plastech ceased to exist. Its bankruptcy reorganization became a self-liquidation exercise in which it sold itself to two other major auto suppliers—interior products to Johnson Controls and exterior products to Magna.)

Without trust, any company's chances of getting first crack at unique supplier value propositions that lead to competitive advantage will certainly be more difficult. Graceful exits generate trust and the reputation for smart supplier management. Messy exits do not, even when they are justified.

Sometimes graceful exits are simply not possible, despite intense buyer efforts. A different kind of vehicle manufacturer (who shall remain anonymous) faced a very difficult exit situation. A key supplier, almost 80 percent of whose business was with this manufacturer, had, over time, become uncompetitive relative to other sources. The components were highly important to the buyer's cost structure and products, leading to a multimonth effort to convince the privately held supplier to launch a cost elimination program. The owner refused.

This triggered a supplier assessment effort that found suppliers capable of delivering the components at lower cost with comparable quality. The buyer approached the supplier again and advised that there would be a re-sourcing effort. The supplier did not change its commercial position in the bidding/negotiation process—and lost the business. The buyer began discussions with the supplier's financial officer on a transition plan that would phase out the production over several months (allowing the supplier to try to fill some of the capacity) and sustain the portions of the relationship that were not involved in the re-sourcing effort (around a quarter of the company's volume with the buyer, much of which was already multisourced).

However, when the owner discovered he had lost the business, he instructed that all shipments of product to the buyer be stopped. In addition to the legal due diligence such cutoffs prompt to make sure everything is done appropriately, the buyer's CPO once again reached out to the supplier's chief financial executive, traveled to the supplier, and reworked the exit plan and remaining business allocation. Shipments resumed for a couple weeks. Then the owner cut them off again.

In the end the buyer had to scramble to cover its production needs. Some plant shutdowns occurred, but none longer than about a week as the new suppliers were well into their qualification when all this happened. All business was pulled from the supplier, who suffered a major business crisis (and is still in existence as of this writing, but greatly downsized). From the outside, this exit looks anything but graceful, yet the buyer did everything possible to make it so. Grace requires two sides—and in this case, one side's efforts were simply not enough. But those who know the story, including the new suppliers, still hold the buyer's commercial reputation as a customer in good esteem.

Notes

1. Toshiro Nishiguchi and Alexandre Beaudet, *Self Organization and Clustered Control in the Toyota Group: Lessons from the Aisin Fire*. MIT International Motor Vehicle Program, copyright 1997 Nishiguchi & Beaudet.

2. Jeffrey K. Liker and Thomas Y. Choi, *What Westerners Don't Know About Keiretsu*, (Cambridge, Mass.: Harvard Business School Working Knowledge, May 9, 2005).

3. Interview with Gregory White, former Purchases Director in charge of coffee trading at Folgers coffee, February 24, 2008.

4. Robert Porter Lynch, *Business Alliances Guide: The Hidden Competitive Weapon* (New York: John Wiley & Sons, Inc., 1993), p. 54.

5. Andrew Cox, Joe Sanderson, and Glyn Watson, *Power Regimes: Mapping the DNA of Business and Supply Chain Relationships* (Warwickshire, UK: Earlsgate Press, 2000), p. 18.

6. Peter Burrows, "Welcome to Apple World," *Business Week*, p. 89, July 9 and 16, 2007.

7. Jack Ewing and Arik Hesseldahl, "The iPhone's German Accent," *Business Week*, April 16, 2007.

8. Robert J. Bowman, "Home Depot Turns Its Attention to Supplier Performance Management," *Global Logistics & Supply Chain Strategies*, June 2006.

9. Jim Carlton, "Once Targeted by Protestors, Home Depot Plays Green Role," *Wall Street Journal*, August 6, 2004.

10. Beth Enslow, *Supplier Performance Management: What Leaders Do Differently—A Benchmark Report on How Companies Manage Supplier Performance and Supply Disruptions*, Aberdeen Research, September 2004.

11. Pierre Mitchell, "How Procurement and Supply Management Drive Com-

petitive Advantage," The Hackett Group, December 2007 presentation with *Supply Chain Management Review* magazine.

12. Norihiko Shirouzu, "Paranoid Tendency: As Rivals Catch Up, Toyota CEO Spurs Big Efficiency Drive," *Wall Street Journal*, December 9 and 10, 2006.

13. Jeffrey McCracken, "Car-Industry Woes Push Key Supplier to Financial Brink," *Wall Street Journal*, January 31, 2008.

14. Neal E. Boudette, Jeff Bennett, and Jeffrey McCracken, "Chrysler Shuts Down Four Plants," *Wall Street Journal*, February 5, 2008.

15. David Bailey, "Chrysler CEO: Plastech tried to raise prices," Reuters News Service, February 5, 2008.

16. Robert Sherefkin, "Plastech not the only troubled supplier," Crain News Service, February 11, 2008.

17. Jewel Gopwani, "Chrysler cites questions about quality in Plastech court hearing," *Detroit Free Press*, February 13, 2008.

18. David Bailey and Kevin Krolicki, "U.S. judge rules against Chrysler in Plastech fight," Reuters News Service, February 19, 2008.

CHAPTER 7

Supply Chain Management

Connecting Across and Between Companies

ROOF: the external upper covering of a house or other building.

A chain is no stronger than its weakest link, and life is after all a chain.
—William James, psychologist and philosopher

A house without a roof makes no sense. It is the roof that keeps out the rain or snow. When it leaks, the result is structural damage inside the home. The roof, covered with shingles or tile to withstand water, is what ties the structure together, connecting with the walls and capping the foundation. Roof styles range from flat to steeped, depending on the building style, providing a distinct look for the home.

The supply chain plays a similar role in the construction of supply-based advantage. It weaves together a range of external parties that extend from the customer to upstream suppliers, internal infrastructure, and the connections between these internal and external parties so that, hopefully, the right hand knows what the left is doing. Going back to the basis of supply's contribution to competitive advantage in Chapter 1, the operational lines between the customer and suppliers are the direct connection of supply into the business model and operating strategy of a company.

Supply chains exist regardless of the nature of the company. In the production of goods, the chain is obvious as a product moves through a manufacturing and distribution system. But virtual supply chains exist as well—take the Internet delivery of software products from companies like Intuit or Symantec to a personal computer, or the software packages preloaded on cell phones and "smart phones." The days of having to buy a CD to load the product are gone. The electronic delivery of software to a computer desktop is as much a supply chain—made up of servers and security systems—as the physical chain that sends program CDs to store shelves. In fact, these software providers, while pushing people to the Internet, still today have to manage a dual electronic and physical chain.

The concept of a chain is, of course, a simplification. Almost every company actually has multiple chains made up of many suppliers, distribution points, channels, and customers. Hence the use of words such as "network" or "web" to describe these multiple chains. This image of a networked web completes the analogy to the roof of a house, where the gaps in trusses and beams are filled in by planking, insulation, and shingles—a web of material that gives the house functionality.

Supply Chains: Where Real Customers Meet Supply Chain Designs

The traditional view of supply chains deals with the flow of products (physical or virtual/services) from suppliers to the customer. A closer examination of the flows in question, however, raises deeper thoughts. The buying firm's business model is impacted by five flows along the chain from upstream suppliers to the customers of its customers.

1. *Relationship Supply Chain.* The series of relationships various players have in the chain with their supply chain members.

2. *Idea Supply Chain.* The flow of knowledge, innovation, intellectual property, and new concepts through the chain.

3. *Information Supply Chain.* Aggregating operational data across the chain, inventory, capacity, demand, time, etc. into forecasts and communication.

4. *Financial Supply Chain.* The money flow from order to invoice to payment, including cash flow and credit.

5. *Product Supply Chain.* The flow of goods or services from suppliers to customers.

The last three flows drive actual business results—customer purchases that turn into cash and profit. The interface of sophisticated computer software and data management techniques in those last three flows have, as most practitioners well know, allowed information to replace inventory and working capital, resulting in a leaner supply chain.

Still, the globalization of many supply chains makes these "routine" flows a challenge. In late 2005, the Massachusetts Institute of Technology's Center for Transportation and Logistics' newsletter *Supply Chain Strategy* outlined the everyday problems in Hitachi High Technology's supply chain and how that company took steps to manage them.[1] The article described a series of issues at one extreme, often small connection points deep in the operational details of the chain, and more conceptual issues like cultural differences between countries in a worldwide supply network at the other end. Hitachi Hi-Tech makes etching equipment for semiconductor manufacturing and only produces its product at one plant in Japan. Its supply base is global, ranging from local Japanese suppliers to far-flung supply and warehousing points in the United States, Ireland, and Israel. Its customers, semiconductor manufacturers, have contracts with financial penalties for late delivery, so reliability is an important measure.

To manage this, Hitachi must manage customs rules, transportation (including expediting shipments to avoid those penalties), special packaging supplies, and shipment consolidators as part of the supply chain. The use of rolling forecasts with its suppliers, flexible transportation approaches, and appropriate buffer inventories help, but the fact that lead times for Hitachi's incoming components range from two to six months, while the typical lead time from customers can be as short as eight days, illustrates the challenge. Creating a supply network that can anticipate and react to these kinds of inconsistencies has led Hitachi to redesign its physical chain to move some subassemblies from Japan closer to the final customer and its information chain to enable better inventory visibility and supplier production schedule options. This is the norm of supply chain operations, supported by even more elaborate "cross flow" interrelations, with the ability to influence the chain to deliver higher profits and more preferred supplier status.

When the Flows Come Together

J. K. Rowling's Harry Potter book series was an incredible phenomenon, selling tens of million copies worldwide. By the last volume, *Harry Potter and the Deathly Hollows*, the publisher, Scholastic, faced a daunting supply chain challenge.[2] Avid fans were camped out in front of bookstores across the country, while the suspense about which characters would live and die (including rumors that Harry was a dead duck) made nightly news programs and websites everywhere. The game for Scholastic became to synchronize its supply chain so that the books all showed up no more than a day before the official release date at 12:01 A.M. on June 21, 2007 (to avoid having a spoiler expose the ending on the Internet before readers had a chance to experience it themselves). At the same time, the publishing run was 12 million books—a huge financial investment—no one wanted lying around longer than necessary.

All five flows came into play. Obviously, the product and financial flows occurred as suppliers shipped, customers received, and invoices were issued and paid. A *Business Week* article made the point that the line of trucks involved in delivering the books in the United States alone would have been fifteen miles long. The information flow became critical given the need for speed, security (no delivery truck drivers giving their kids an advance copy), and timeliness on the physical side of the flow. Demand management required intense planning for several months before any books were printed. The chain spanned the publisher's printing suppliers (R.R. Donnelley and Sons and Quebecor World), their material suppliers (paper, binding, ink, printing cylinders/artwork, corrugated cases, pallets, etc.), logistics and transportation service suppliers (Yellow Transportation and J.B. Hunt Transport Services), to customers—both stores (Barnes and Nobles, Borders, etc.) and websites like Amazon.com.

These customers engaged in the process, making decisions on their shipment supply chain—using the U.S. Postal Service and UPS to deliver almost simultaneously across the country. Trucks were fitted with global positioning satellite (GPS) devices to follow every truck's route. Amazingly, the ending did not get leaked and the success rate on deliveries was about 99 percent. Without tight relationships across the planning network, such results would not have translated into real-world activities.

From a Chain to a Network

Describing the supply chain represents the first step in harnessing it to fuel your business. Supply networks and value networks are what practitioners working to gain an advantage picture in their minds. However, the complexity and details of these webs make analyzing them a time-consuming and easily siloed task, with each product, function, and spend category focusing on only their part—and suboptimizing the whole. To help uncover where competitive advantage might lurk and what interfaces might need to link throughout the company's supply and customer bases, the following conceptual process aids thinking about the many supply chains a typical company must manage. See Figure 7.1 for a diagram of steps 2 through 8, discussed below.

Step 1—Lay out a traditional (simplistic) linear supply and value chain of basic business activities at the conceptual level for the company.

Step 2—Wrap the chain into a circle that both starts and ends with the external customer and at least those customers' customers. At P&G, that meant considering both the retailer and the consumer. For an auto company it would include dealers and drivers, for their tier-one suppliers it would include the car companies (OEMs—original equipment manufacturers) and the dealers, and so forth—you get the idea.

Why do that? Simple—the customer represents the end of the process where products are purchased, but also the beginning of the process, where new products are designed from customer needs and wants. The rest of this conceptual process takes the product design and commercialization event sequence and examines the supply chains that support each phase. Defining and describing each of the events in this sequence represents a step in the conceptual process. Importantly—the nature of the company's business determines where each supply chain fits in each company. For example, in a manufacturing company computers and servers are part of corporate infrastructure. For a bank it is a part of transformation/service formation (Step 5 below).

Step 3—Identify the firms and connections that make up the product development "idea supply chain." It includes suppliers that contribute to new products, which range from the next generation of products from current component suppliers to support services for labs, research relationships with inventors and universities seeking intellectual property, and contract design firms.

Step 4—Identify the firms and connections that make up the ingredient and component inbound physical supply chains for goods or the service providers that make up more "virtual" products, including subcontracts for intellectual products incorporated into a final service offering (e.g., subprograms incorporated in software, temporary

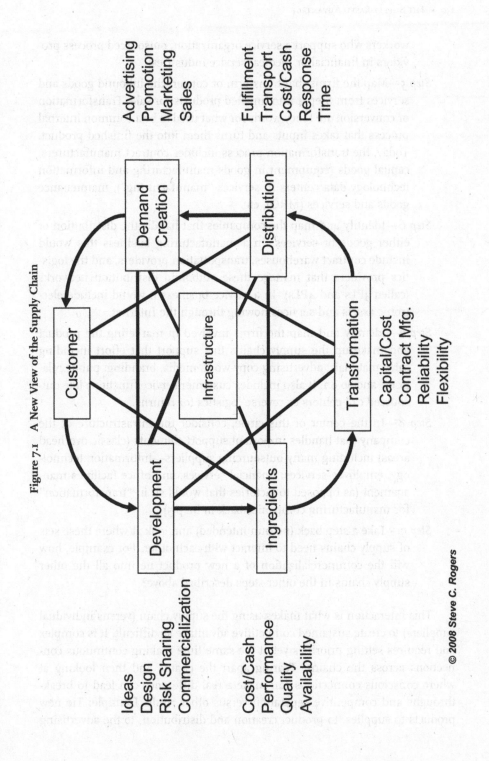

Figure 7.1 A New View of the Supply Chain

Advertising
Promotion
Marketing
Sales

Fulfillment
Transport
Cost/Cash
Response
Time

Demand
Creation

Distribution

Customer

Infrastructure

Transformation

Capital/Cost
Contract Mfg.
Reliability
Flexibility

Development

Ingredients

Ideas
Design
Risk Sharing
Commercialization

Cost/Cash
Performance
Quality
Availability

workers who support a service organization, outsourced process providers in financial or medical service industries).

Step 5—Map the firms that transform or convert the inbound goods and services from Step 4 into finished products for sale. Transformation or conversion are fancy words for what used to be a common internal process that takes inputs and turns them into the finished product. Today, the transformation process includes contract manufacturers, capital goods (equipment in goods manufacturing and information technology data centers in services "manufacturing"), maintenance goods and services (MRO), etc.

Step 6—Identify and map the companies that handle the distribution of either goods or services. In a manufacturing business this would include contract warehouses, transportation providers, and the logistics providers that manage these outbound distribution networks (called 3PLs and 4PLs). In a service business it would include electronic assets and services flowing through the Internet.

Step 7—Identify and map the firms involved in marketing the product and make up the supply chains that support that effort including sales materials, advertising copy work, media, branding, public relations, and so on. It also includes customer service functions like outsourced call centers or reverse logistics for returns.

Step 8—In the center of this circle, consider the infrastructure of the company that handles important support elements (classic overhead areas) including many outsourcing suppliers—information technology, employee services, financial services, and office facilities management (as opposed to factories that would sit in "transformation" for manufacturing companies back in Step 5).

Step 9—Take a step back (no pun intended) and look at where these sets of supply chains need to interact with each other. For example, how will the commercialization of a new product tie into all the other supply chains in the other steps described above?

This interaction is what makes using the supply chain (versus individual suppliers) to create sustained competitive advantage so difficult. It is complex and requires setting priorities yet at the same time making continuous connections across the chains. Tearing apart the chains and then looking at where conscious connections can make a real difference can lead to breakthroughs and competitive separation versus other rivals. Example: Tie new products to supplies, to product creation and distribution, to the advertising message, and, finally, tie the financial systems to billing and to call centers for customer service response.

—Practitioner's Take—

It is all well and good to set the stage using a lot of theory about types of flows. Dissecting value networks and supply webs into components to better see the players and where they can add value helps find competitive advantage. But theory is not necessarily how the real world works. Two widely embraced supply chain perspectives have become quite popular in the last few years—first, that supply chains are what competes rather than companies and, second, that collaboration is the only factor that makes one company's supply chain better than another's. Both have elements of real truth, but both also oversimplify and, sometimes, are just flat wrong. Sounds like heresy (and maybe it is) but before deciding, let's look at a couple of real supply chains.

Supply Chain Power

In the last chapter, we talked about Andrew Cox and his perspectives on power in purchaser/supplier relationships. His power concepts are even more relevant to an alternative perspective on supply chains and value networks. Having grown up in a consumer packaged goods company, over my thirty years in the industry I watched the balance of power shift through the supply chain more than once. Short-term shifts were often market driven (e.g., supply/demand fluctuation). A longer-term force was the consolidation of the retail trade and emergence of "big-box" and megaretailers like Wal-Mart, Tesco, and Target. This changed the balance of power from front-line manufacturers (like P&G, Kimberly Clark, Unilever, Kao, Colgate, and Henkel) to the retailers.

In his book, *The Wal-Mart Effect,* Charles Fishman describes how powerful this giant has become. In it he relates a story about Snapper lawnmowers and the decision of former Snapper CEO, Jim Wier, to walk away from the Wal-Mart business.[3] His company, Simplicity, bought Snapper in late 2002, at which time it was already supplying Wal-Mart with mowers. Snapper sold the bulk of its product as a premium product through independent lawn equipment dealers. However, trying to meet Wal-Mart's price points put pressure on product design and margins. This reduced the profit necessary for R&D and to cover raw material (steel, for example) price spikes. It also caused enormous friction with its larger established dealer network. After his decision to walk away from Wal-Mart, Snapper's volume dropped almost 20 percent. Wier admits that he may have made the wrong choice, given the amount of volume he chose not to pursue, but the story demonstrates just how tough a bargain the big retailer's low-price strategies can drive back into their supply chain.

I saw that difference while at P&G. One of the key principles in our purchasing approach was that of incumbency—that the existing supplier got the benefit of the doubt. Early in my career, when the product manufacturers held the balance of power in retail, we would often agree to pay a short-term premium for a portion of our business with an incumbent whose pricing "missed the market." This was done with the expectation that they would need to be more aggressive next time and that their overall value (quality, service, etc.) remained strong and justified the decision. If, after such an award, a supplier was not able to compete, they would ultimately lose our business. This incumbency approach supported supplier R&D for our business and provided a level of security against supply chain disruptions, while maintaining long-term competitive cost structures (although not necessarily lowest cost in the short term).

As the balance of power in the supply chain shifted to retailers—especially those that communicated shelf price as the predominant element of value—the ability to pay a premium to keep a supplier was reduced. The size of the premium became smaller and the need to understand real value, both in terms of cost (not just price) and non-cost components (service, risk mitigation, etc.) became even more critical.

Cox's view is that the company with the most power in the chain is able to extract the most value. In recent years, no industry has exemplified how power rules better than iron ore.[4-11] For years, the steel industry and several of its customers like auto, construction, and appliances, had the power in the supply chain. Iron ore comes in three forms—fines, lump ore, and pellets. For over twenty-five years the mining industry was not particularly profitable, with fines prices ranging from the low $20s to the low $30s per ton (in only four of the twenty-six years from 1976 and 2002 were the prices over $30).

Over time the iron industry consolidated, and as it did the balance of power moved upstream in the auto/steel/iron supply chain. By late 2003, three major mining companies, two Australian (BHP Billiton and Rio Tinto) and a Brazilian (Cia Vale do Rio Doce, now called Vale), were the dominant players, representing over two thirds of industry capacity. At the same time, steel demand began to escalate, especially driven by construction booms in China, India, and other emerging economies. All those years of narrow iron ore margins and low power were suddenly gone.

The result has been one of the most amazing exhibitions of supply chain power in recent times, if only because a number of companies that normally hold power suddenly lost it for several years. The game began in 2003, when the iron companies got a 10 percent price increase. That was just the beginning. In 2004, Brazilian Vale started the real escalation, announcing a 71.5 percent price increase after negotiating with Japanese steelmakers. That set the tone, despite public declarations of disagreement from other large steel companies. Yet, by later that year most had caved.

In early 2005, with Vale demanding a 90 percent increase from Arcelor (before its acquisition by Mittal partially in response to the shifting power structures in the chain), the final capitulation occurred. By March 2005, just ten days after saying the 71.5 percent Japanese increase should not be an industry benchmark, Arcelor accepted the same price. The next year the big three announced a 20 percent increase on top of the previous years' whoppers. Then the big gorilla of steel buyers stepped in—China consolidated all its purchases and sent Baosteel into negotiations to stop the price increases. It slowed the rise for a year to 9.5 percent, but did not stop them. Within days of the Chinese agreement, Japanese and South Korean steelmakers followed suit. All announced that they would pass the costs on to their customers.

At that point, the auto industry, especially in Europe, began to push back on the steel companies (it did not work). By 2008, the Chinese steelmakers announced they would follow a 65 percent iron increase agreed to by Japanese and South Korean negotiators. By early 2008 the iron ore fines price was 265 percent more than in 2003. The iron ore industry showed little restraint, choosing to price what the market would bear, despite attempts by traditionally high-power buyers to stop the increases. Steel manufacturers' business strategy was shifted by this adversarial use of supply base power (the miners also sell coking coal and leveraged their power against the steel companies there as well). Mittal-Arcelor's combined size was an attempt to create more buying leverage (along with Mittal's vertical integration into the iron ore business as the fifth largest iron ore miner). Iron ore escalation even rippled into the scrap steel market, causing Nucor, the U.S. steel leader that only uses scrap not iron ore, to vertically integrate into the scrap metal business.

—Practitioner's Take—

Unbridled power at any position in the supply chain can change the dynamics throughout the chain. Actions like this fly in the face of many supply chain collaboration theories. The point of this discussion is not to disagree with collaboration, but rather to recognize that companies are independent entities and, depending on their market view, strategic collaboration may or may not be possible. If it is impossible, that does not eliminate the need to find a competitive edge even in the most trying supply situations.

At the day-to-day tactical operations level, there needs to be enough collaboration to allow effective flow, even if the more strategic price negotiations or intellectual property interactions are adversarial. Going back to the five-flow model, the last three—products, finances, and demand information—need to be aligned. The basis for doing business is getting what you need when you need it, and that requires working together, not adversarial conflict. Even the mining companies were working diligently to deliver against orders despite, during the commercial conflict, a series of extremely difficult supply chain challenges like floods in Australia, rail and port congestion, labor shortages, and rapidly escalating shipping costs/ship limitations. These tactical flows still have strategic implications for buyers to gain competitive separation from competing users when they allow the buying company to deliver its products more reliably or faster than competition during a shortage market. Speed and delivery become more strategic than cost in the short to medium term.

However, the top two flows—ideas and relationships—set a strategic tone and can be undone between industries by ongoing adversarial commerce. At this level, "collaboration" can be a more difficult proposition. It is still the ideal, and in many cases possible. However, the degree of difficultly increases geometrically as the number of tiers in the chain expands. Why? Because each company in the chain has its own personality and approach to its supply base. These idiosyncrasies make full alignment difficult. Mistakes on the tactical flows can generate distrust in the strategic ones. Even the passing of demand information back through the tiers of the supply chain is hard. In addition, when a supplier combines your volume with that of other customers whose willingness to give information varies from yours, the resulting aggregate demand volatility can impact your business, even when you are trying to be transparent.

The Federation Concept in Supply Chains

In 2001, consultant Booz Allen Hamilton, in talking about the promise of e-commerce for the supply chain, predicted that it would be a long hard slog to transmit alignment through the chain.[12] They suggested that from a planning perspective, the supply chain is more like a federation than a centrally planned economy. In other words, the members of the supply chain have more in common with the independent, self-motivated entities in a federation than they do with a single, "owned" supply chain. Concepts of harmonious unified networks that share the economic benefits of the chain miss the competitive pressures for performance within each entity. These pressures shape the interactions from tier to tier in the chain as much as individual relationships shape the interface between two single companies. Worse— they are much more opaque when viewed from more than one tier away.

This federation concept is actually quite descriptive of supply chains in many ways beyond the planning area that the Booz Allen Hamilton article described. The pressures are driven by four elements:

1. The business results of each member of the supply chain come from the three tactical flows (product, money, and information), whose outcomes are measured by profit, cash flow, and margin. The firms are externally judged by measures like stock market capitalization for public companies, and return on investment or cash dividends for private equity owners. These relative measurement systems drive each company to maximize its return and seek to be "better" economically than its industry peers. Each industry's normal profit margin drives how investors react, not some theoretically equal split of the supply chain's profit.

2. Supply chains are rarely made up of unique members anymore. There is enormous overlap, with one company supplying several customers, all of whom have that player in their supply chains (often with differing commercial terms). How the suppliers see that overlap from their perspective matters enormously in the transparency of strategic supply chain flows like those for relationships, ideas, and longer term information sharing. Again, relative margins and cash matter, but more importantly in these longer range flows, so do growth potential and market breadth (new product areas). Suppliers inhabit many supply chains where each player is independent yet connected. Each wants to maximize its position and understand its tradeoffs.

3. The factors of supply and demand also create change in the supply chain. Michael Porter's strategy model calls out some of these forces—new entrants (new suppliers), new customers in different industries, substitutes that replace items with lower cost value equations, and the basic economics of supply and demand changes that trigger price increases and decreases.

4. Lastly, the constant churn in company leadership and strategy, driven by the first three factors, makes stability across multiple tiers in a supply chain difficult to maintain, and sometimes perhaps not even the right thing to attempt. Supply chains rarely keep all the same suppliers (or supply locations when a supplier does stay) for long periods of time

The Shangri-La vision of a single leader, a benevolent dictator that directs the chain's activities, is often unrealistic. Occasionally the power dynamics and the company's long-term collaborative culture allow the combination of power and concern for the other members of the chain to exist, but not often.

—Practitioner's Take—

Sound pretty discouraging? Don't despair. The difficulty of achieving the ideal state is, in fact, the doorway to competitive advantage. If it were an easy task, duplicating it would also be easy and would rob any sustainable competitive advantage from the proposition. Competitive advantage is measured in relative terms more than absolute. Doing better than the competition is what matters—not being a perfect ideal model. Information technology tools help in this regard (more on that in a later chapter) because they greatly increase the transparency for those companies having the internal culture to allow it.

Building a chain that supports competitive advantage (or neutralizes a disadvantage) creates a hierarchy of actions:

- Strive for perfection in the tactical supply chain's flows. Orders, costs, shipping, delivery, billing accuracy, and quality are the price of admission to the competitive advantage game.
- Strategically prioritize along the chain's tiers. Understand where the highest potential for value lies and insert your limited resources there. This building block also includes the need to reprioritize as business needs, models, and strategies change.

- Map the chain and look for places where common suppliers show up in multiple tiers. Strong relationships with some of these companies can make a huge difference. A quick example—in the late 1990s the supplier of a key ingredient in Tide with Bleach learned from its supplier's supplier that a sourcing initiative two tiers back in the chain moved to a single source to save money. When the resulting supplier had a shortfall and prioritized its customers, our supplier's supplier's supplier (yes, three tiers back, four if you count P&G) did not get its needs fully met, leading to supply shortage. As we got engaged we found that the other viable material supplier (which was dropped by the supplier's supplier) was also one of our tier-one suppliers for another major component of Tide with Bleach. Using that contact enabled us to reestablish supply even though the two materials were from different divisions of that company. In fact, our first request was rejected at the divisional level but was honored at the next higher level because those senior managers saw the full impact on the supplier—loss of direct P&G business on one material because a sister division refused to supply another material further upstream in P&G's supply chain.

- Make the tough calls on how to allocate resources to do this work. The likely situation is that existing work has already stretched the organization. Those that gain strategic advantage for the longer term are able to free up some people to focus on the strategic elements of the supply network. The resources may include internal people and information technology investments, delegation to key suppliers that devote resources to your business, or outsourcing with good governance. Intelligent supply chain architecture finds value in the chain and harnesses it to do better than competition can.

Supply chain design is the outcome of these actions. It is a daunting task because most chains already exist and have evolved without any or perhaps only some conscious design. Very few companies have the luxury of launching a completely new supply chain. Therefore the majority of changes are adjustments to the current state and require alterations in sourcing strategy and supplier relationships that match supply chain shifts. As with supplier relationships and sourcing strategy, linkage to the business model, strategy, and customers is the starting point.

Supply Chain Design: A More Detailed Process

Companies with multiple product lines have multiple supply networks. For each line, the supply chain design process begins with a single question. How does our product compete? Supply chain design thinking must begin there in order to connect with the business model—an imperative for competitive advantage. The thought process progresses through eight steps:

1. *Product and Business Competitive Linkage.* What is your product's competitive strategy vis-à-vis its competition and how does its supply chain play into that strategy? Essentially, you are building a supply chain strategy based on the product's business strategy—a parallel effort to that described for sourcing strategy. Supply chains need to be tailored to the company and its products. (For years Dell and Hewlett Packard had different personal computer supply chains based on different product strategies.)

   Across industries these changes can be even more varied. Consider cell phones, where the business needs, technology maps, and customer value components lead to extremely rapid industry development and the need for an adaptive, innovative, fast supply chain with global scope. Contrast that with utilities, where the time frame is slower and customer value is about cost and delivery reliability and availability, with local competitive scope and much less flexible delivery channels. A leading-edge high-tech cell phone supply chain, while containing some elements of excellence reapplicable to a gas and electric utility like wireless meter reading, would not be the best overall model for that utility supply chain.

   Yet each company could have a world-class supply chain—in its industry. Again, the question is how the product competes at the customer level. The task becomes working backward from the customer to determine supply chain strategy that will underpin the corporate business strategy.

2. *Strategic Activity Identification.* This step starts with supply chain mapping to create a high-level view of the flows. Then it targets those elements and activities that, for a particular company, make a difference.

   For the utility it could include energy sourcing, power generation, environmental compliance, distribution lines, billing, safety, and, in many places in the world, energy regulatory influence. For the cell phone company it could include hardware components, software, service network capability and reliability, technological innovation speed, contract manufacturing flexibility, global trade management (transport, logistics, planning, and tariff/security regulations), technology convergence skills (merging voice, Internet, video, audio, gaming, etc. into its competitive strategy), and communication regulatory influence skills. Some elements are common to both industries, but not all.

3. *Value Capture Analysis.* This step seeks to understand where the value lies in this supply chain and improve the odds of capturing enough of it to provide both a return and an advantage. It entails power analysis, market analysis (supply/demand including trend analysis and the impact of demand balance shifts), proprietary position analysis (intellectual property, regulatory analysis), and complimentary markets (co-products, changes elsewhere in the chain—think the arrival of Internet distribution of software instead of CDs on a shelf).

From your company's position in the chain, what is the realistic likelihood that you will be able to capture enough of the chain's value to meet your investment return requirements? At one point, then CEO of Motorola Ed Zander was widely criticized for a negative comment about his customers in a front-page *Wall Street Journal* article ("I love my job. I hate my customers.").[13] While probably not the smartest comment, it represents the fact that U.S. phone service carriers seek to control access to consumers through restrictive service contracts and careful control of software and hardware options. The providers use subsidized phone prices on the models they choose to sell, in an effort to capture more profit by selling their services rather allowing other service providers to access their customers via the phone.

Why do they do that? A little historical research quickly shows why. These same phone companies became the "dumb pipe" low-margin losers in the Internet revolution. Telephone dial-up was the entry point but content providers AOL, Yahoo!, e-Bay, and Google made the money. A generation of executives learned a tough lesson about value capture analysis that influences their approach to the growth of cell phone services—they want control and are looking to create the power to sustain it at the expense of their suppliers (Apple's iPhone represented an early dent in that control).

4. *Supply Capability Determination.* This is a combination of traditional insourcing–outsourcing analysis (more on that in a later chapter)

extended up and down the supply chain, plus gap analysis between the ideal chain and a more realistic alternative. The mind-shift is to think beyond your own company to understand what suppliers and customers are likely doing with their chains. It requires thinking along three dimensions:

- Capacity at each critical node in the chain—is there enough and will there continue to be enough?

- Knowledge and innovation at each critical node—where are these businesses going technologically and do you know enough about the intellectual property and skills of your suppliers and their up-tier suppliers?

- Cost through the chain—what are the cost and market drivers in these chains, how will they impact your business, and what are companies in each tier doing about them (managing them or leveraging them to raise prices downstream)?

This high-level review of these business flows provides both a conceptual "ideal" chain and a view of the real constraints that stand in the way of that ideal chain—leading to a more pragmatic option. The gaps between today's chain, the ideal, and a constraint-tempered pragmatic option create the design template for supply chain modifications going forward.

5. *Customer Requirements Assessment.* What do customers expect from their suppliers' supply chains? In most chains the customer's ability to sell its product to the ultimate consumer or user is what makes profit and cash flow. Customers translate what is needed for them to win into demands upon their supply chains that blend six areas: innovation, responsiveness, cost efficiency (including pricing and system cost), reliability, safety, and corporate reputation. These elements, coupled with their ability to extract value for themselves, become the goals of supply chain design outcomes. The ultimate user has the last say in all this.

Recently I was talking with the vice president of electronics vendor management at a well-known U.S. retailer, whose "take" on changes in user involvement in his industry was that it dramatically reshaped supply chains for his company, its suppliers, and their suppliers. As he put it, "Today, the consumer edits the assortment in our stores instead of us. Because of Internet blogs and product assessment sites, the buzz in the industry will kill or create demand regardless of our plans or those of electronics hardware marketers. This revises our forecasts before we can, creating holes in the several-week-long supply pipeline from Asia. That forces our suppliers to air-ship in order to draw forward the inventory in the chain. Or, on the other side, it creates unsold inventory that will either have to be marked down or returned to the manufacturer for distress sale." Understanding the implications of this customer demand change, as it gained strength after the tech bust of 2000, required huge changes in electronics supply chain design to grapple with the ultimate customer's growing Internet-based power. It also created supply chain success measures that cascade back into supplier measures for reliability, flexibility, and commercial agreements consistent with consumer-driven product assortments.

6. *Tier Design*. This step uses the analytical elements above to provide a supply chain design plan going forward—looking at all five flows (products, money, information, ideas/innovation, and relationships). It creates the overarching logic and "policies" that the company will use to manage its chain and deal with others' management logic for their chains. Then it tests that policy to determine how/if it works in the real world, including who does what and how far upstream the company should extend its influence upstream into the physical supply chains of its suppliers, especially to impact economics and intellectual property.

   Remember that each supply chain tier's members are seeking to improve their situation, which creates complexity and uncertainty that makes long-range predictability somewhat unlikely.

   Another complication is that companies must run the existing chain while simultaneously retrofitting it. It is not like you can call "time out" and stop the commercial action.

7. *Change Contingency Planning*. Flowing naturally from the uncertainty inherent in the previous step, a supply chain contingency plan needs to incorporate potential forces imposed from up- or downstream into the design. This takes analysis and ongoing, regularly scheduled renewal of the chain's design, even when things seem okay, in order to highlight potential vulnerabilities—such as where internal operations are inflexible or external entities have power or leverage over you.

8. *Cross-Chain Linkage.* This last step returns to the "circular chain" model to coordinate how and where the various chains within the company must mesh to create a difficult-to-duplicate competitive advantage. For instance, the product development and marketing chains need to mesh on product quality, advertising claims, and customer requirements while the product assembly and distribution channel flows must link to marketing so sales promotions and product distribution mesh. And of course central financial and information infrastructure supply chains must match and transact the business flows. Constant changes in business forces today require multiple value chains to be connected into value networks that are reconnected when obsolete "junctions" are eliminated and new ones generated.

—Practitioner's Take—

A couple thoughts born from some practitioner mistakes on all this high-level design stuff:

- Design from the outside in, starting with the customer. Too many companies design their supply chains from the inside out, focusing on what they want and are capable of doing rather than what other players in the chain require, want, and will maneuver to get.

- Search for the inflexible tiers. Sometimes these are based on physical assets such as plant locations, but often they are based on an emotional attachment to outmoded supply logic or policies that do not work well when the market has evolved, neutralizing past competitive advantage.

    Sometimes these market changes go further, turning competitive advantages into disadvantages. It is particularly important for successful companies to test where core competencies have become core rigidities (outmoded competencies that tie the corporate paradigm into past success models like Dell's stumble when its Internet customer–directed product design was overcome by growing user interest in more hands-on and physically aesthetic designs.) For years IBM's internal hardware design/production supply chain strategies gave its computers competitive advantage, but with the advent of power shifts to software supplier Microsoft and microprocessor supplier Intel, clinging to vertically integrated hardware production led to business distress. Today, IBM continually shifts its value equation to create exit and adjustment strategies as part of a business design to avoid its past core rigidity mistakes.

- One other thought on supply chain design—do not expect management to always see the supply chain implications of its business strategy. While senior management talks about supply importance, too often the actions they demand from their supply organizations are based on what some other CEO said to them at a conference or high-level networking session. What makes sense for that CEO's company and business model may not fully apply in your situation (or may be exactly what you must do!). While a delicate task, providing senior management a more workable design based on deep understanding of your firm's business and its linkage to suppliers is imperative to successful supply chains— which are made up of 90 percent suppliers, not customers.

Design Is Great but Implementation Is What Matters

All this design theory is great, but putting it into practice is much more what gaining competitive advantage is all about. For example, the logistics systems that work in the developed world often will not meet emerging market needs of other geographies. Kraft Foods' Chinese operations, as discussed in the *Wall Street Journal,* are a case in point.[14] An "old China hand," Kraft has been making and selling there since the mid-1980s (via joint ventures). They learned that logistics supply chains in China are very different than those in the United States or Europe. Yet Kraft has one of the better, more streamlined ones in China. They have five regional distribution centers run by suppliers— third-party logistics providers (3PLs)—each of which feeds a web of networks into nearby provinces. Kraft hired midsized 3PLs, not the big boys, because of the stature its business gives within their customer lists. High priority as a customer means you get transportation vehicles when other customers don't. In China, that priority is the difference between average and top-tier delivery performance. It also plays out into better truckload configurations.

To avoid theft of high-value goods on rail shipments—a chronic problem in China—Kraft uses container load configurations that place high-value cases in the center of the rail container near the bottom, where it is harder for thieves to find and remove. The *Wall Street Journal* story included an anecdote about one Kraft warehouse manager who took day laborer jobs in local logistics companies to see how they ran the warehouse—providing important firsthand input for sourcing from these midsized, local companies pivotal to Kraft's Chinese product distribution.

When products require refrigerated supply lines, the obstacles are even greater. Anyone who has been to China, seen the open-air meat and perishable markets, and seen consumers carry items home on foot or by bicycle (as I have), has some concept of the difficulties involved. "Cold chain," the access to refrigerated trucks and warehouses, is vital to distributing meat, vaccines, and other spoilable products over longer distances.[15] About 30 percent of China's meat and produce is lost on the way to market due to inadequate cold chain.

In order to create this supply chain competence, some U.S. producers (like Hormel or local company Henan Luohe Shineway Industry Group Co., controlled by Goldman Sachs investment) chose to have internal cold chain capacity to ensure safety and reliability, rather than using contract logistics companies. This effort is slowly building a more sophisticated Chinese supply chain capability. But today it remains something done best in-house most of the time—a difference in supply chain design relative to developed countries.

Conceptual supply chain and supply base strategies often look good on paper. Simple reapplication from a similar but different industry seems quite doable. But within supply networks the devil is in the details. That is why managing execution is the real skill necessary for complex supply chain management. When Boeing announced its tiered supply chain approach to its 787 Dreamliner commercial jet construction, as a supply practitioner I was excited. The previous aircraft generations experienced delays (the 747 had a three-month delay) and huge cost overruns (the 777 budget ballooned from $6 billion to $12 billion) when designed and produced in Boeing's own plants several years earlier. Given that history, a reapplication of the auto industry's tier-one integrator strategy made all the sense in the world.[16,17] Boeing's 767 planes took about a month to assemble, while the 787 plan called for about three days, sort of like assembling a giant plastic plane.

Boeing's supply chain strategy was elegantly simple—create risk-sharing commercial agreements with a number of tier-one contractors to create major subassemblies. Pick well-known and capable suppliers dispersed around the world to integrate with the global sales strategy. Maintain oversight as those companies manage the flow of materials and software into the project and look to them to manage their subcontractors while providing some level of transparency to Boeing. The supply chain structure for the Dreamliner took best in class supply chain thinking and applied it from the design phase through to production. That kind of leading-edge work requires "extreme" supply chain management. There's the rub—the scale and scope of the task was enormous when considering the sheer number of parts, amount of innovation, number of subcontracting tiers, and geographical dispersion of the contractors. No company ever managed such a project before.

By mid-2007 news stories began to appear that hinted at delays in the delivery of Dreamliners due to supply chain management issues. Perhaps the difficulties should have been expected when one realized that the company had to reconfigure three of its largest existing planes into massive large cargo air freighters capable of carrying three times the cargo of a normal 747 in order to transport 787 subassemblies to their final assembly location.[18] Add to that the multitiered supplier management leap Boeing expected to make from the auto industry model—a car has between 6,000 and 10,000 parts—to an airplane with a few million parts subassembled in multiple countries due to the international and often political nature of the airplane sales market.

Finally, Dreamliner's level of revolutionary material innovation is massive.[19] The airliner uses sophisticated carbon-reinforced composite materials (all sourced from one supplier—Toray) in place of aluminum, requiring different types of fasteners (nuts and bolts) than older designs. This composite technology takes an enormous number of lines running at relatively slow speeds to produce parts, requiring lots of subcontractors and thus, greater oversight both at the subassembly and component stages. The composite aspect alone required the following breakthough manufacturing techniques—all done by suppliers:

▶ Mass production of very large carbon-reinforced plastic structures on relatively slow processing equipment.

▶ Developmental tooling to produce the parts, coming from the machine tool and yacht industries.

▶ Development of new coatings to prevent cracking.

> ➤ Development of new mechanisms to deal with electrical shorts in this composite environment (versus traditional aluminum environments).

In addition, the plane includes innovative materials—the aircraft industry's first use of thermally conductive thermoplastics as plastic heat sinks, an advanced titanium alloy, and an emerging aluminum-lithium alloy.

The first problems turned up in June 2007 when a shortage of the unique coated titanium fasteners, produced by Alcoa, resulted from a consolidation in the fastener industry caused by the 9/11 terrorist attack's impact on the industry.[20] That was just the beginning. When the first plane was to be assembled in October 2007, instead of finished subassemblies, some crates included boxes of loose parts. Analysis of the supply chain turned up a number of delays in the upstream supplier network, some of which should have been obvious and others simply a function of the complexity of the task.[21-25] Examples:

> ➤ Italian subcontractor, Alenia Aeronautica, chose a 300-year-old olive grove in Grottoglie, Italy, as its new plant site. This led to intense wrangling with local authorities. The result was a delay in construction as the company had to replant the trees elsewhere.
>
> ➤ Software suppliers Honeywell, Smiths Aerospace, and Rockwell Collins had to scramble intensely to complete their coding and then make the code talk across supplier boundaries. The problem was exacerbated by the fact that the three companies were serious competitors, not used to working with each other.
>
> ➤ Vought Aircraft Industries' new plant in South Carolina hired a number of inexperienced laborers, which slowed production.
>
> ➤ Quality problems emerged (probably predictable in a new process) during the baking of the plastic composite tape for the fuselage, requiring molding tool mandrel replacement.

At the time of this writing, Boeing was still throwing people, technical support, and money at the problems that have resulted in a delay of over a year in the first 787 deliveries. Already the longest in Boeing history, the delay is rumored to be extended again. Time will tell.

Was Boeing's strategy flawed? Probably not. The risk-sharing and subcontracting arrangements enabled a revolutionary aircraft in terms of price/performance ratio (remember that value equation). Order levels for the plane continue to be unprecedented. However, the time lines, given the level of innovation and complexity, were too aggressive. Worse, once a supply chain redesign is as far along as the Dreamliner's, the game becomes fighting through it. The learnings will be enormous, but likely, so will the pain (Boeing faces some stiff delay penalties if the time lines extend too far, but the airline route "downsizing" precipitated by high jet fuel costs provides a moderating influence on jet demand). Changes in the project leader and a more intense supplier support and monitoring system were put in place and progress appears to be occurring. Still, based on personal experience, once you get behind the curve it is very hard to catch up when starting up a radically new supply chain.

—Practitioner's Take—

Therein lies the lesson from Boeing's 787 story. An elegant supply chain strategy is not enough. Intense supplier governance, including reviews that extend many tiers back into the chain for high-risk components, are critical to success. So are realistic time lines, the recognition that there are never enough resources to manage it all, and, even if there could be, the cost of management would destroy the value equation. The key is to manage what counts and find ways to extend resources through the use of suppliers. This is easier said than done since many tier-two and tier-three suppliers have allegiance to the tier-one supplier, not the company that is buying the chain's combined output. Why? Because the relationship is typically tier to tier, not across multiple tiers.

That is where the previous supply-based advantage element, supplier relationship management (Chapter 6), comes into play. The relationship supply chain flow becomes the means to manage such complexity. In the late 1990s Harley Davidson was a charter member of NISCI (the National Initiative for Supply Chain Integration), which was a small consortium of nine leading-edge companies attempting to link more than two tiers of the supply chain. In 1997, Harley was working a project to manage the "jewelry" on its bikes (jewelry is the chrome-plated parts that give the Harley part of its iconic look).

This supply chain, made up of Harley, its parts makers, metal suppliers, and metal finishing houses, was dealing with a high-cost, competitively differentiating element of the bike, which had, for years, struggled with quality issues. The NISCI project, which was experimenting with "deep collaboration" across multiple supply tiers, was the forum to improve that process. The companies created five "mandate" teams—design, production, cost, sales, and support—with technical, conversion, and cost linkages.

NISCI failed. It was absorbed by the Institute for Supply Management (ISM) and ultimately faded away.

However, Harley's project did not.[26] Seven years later, after some personnel and supplier changes, the motorcycle company presented the successful completion of its "jewelry" project in 2004. Harley oversaw the series of projects across several motorcycle models, but delegated supply chain responsibility to each of two supplier companies to manage the extended chain beyond the three companies. Interestingly, each managed the other in some situations and they faced the same "competitor must collaborate" mindset shift that the Boeing software suppliers were grappling with. In this case Harley forced (not "requested") them to collaborate. It took two years to work through the issues involved before there was much proficiency. (Boeing has quite a journey ahead of it.)

Harley explained that its sourcing strategies drove the relationships. Its supplier capability assessments determined which supplier would lead a particular chain based on that supplier's importance to the product and skill levels in production, supply chain management, and relationship management. The reward system called for shared investment and return on sales. It also required the members of the chain to share best practices, even with competitors, and work out a "no fault" scrap agreement when defects occurred—the die casting supplier eats the die cost and the plating supplier eats metal plating costs.

One supplier had to manage the continuity planning when a competitor's plant burned down, impacting Harley's material availability. If a particular part or process does not fit the lead supplier, that company is responsible to find a competitor for whom the part is a better fit. Suppliers described it as being tier one and a half—sometimes a tier one, and sometimes a tier two. Harley Davidson pays both suppliers directly (rather than each paying the other). Since the project, one of the lead suppliers has extended this approach to the supply chains of five other customers. It is a means to overcome the resource limitations in managing complex multitiered chains, but is highly dependent on the relationship supply chain's health. Harley Davidson had long-term, collaborative relationships with its supply base, clear sourcing strategies, and, in this area, took the final step to develop supply chain strategies and joint Harley/supplier-led collaborative supply chain implementations.

Risk: The Final Watch-Out

We will spend more time on risk in a later chapter, but no supply chain discussion can be complete without mention of supply chain risk. The fragility of most modern supply chains, especially complex global ones, is frightening, as toys with lead paint, tainted pet food, contaminated bagged salad, massive meat recalls, and counterfeit drug instances over the past five years have proven. More and more products and services depend on a series of suppliers and distribution middlemen that make risk management down the supply chain and across multiple supply networks amazingly difficult. For now, we will examine the degree of difficulty supply chain risk management entails. The advent of outsourcing has, in many cases, led to cases of "chain blindness" in which the contracting company, in the name of focus on core competencies, has delegated upstream supply network supervision to the outsourcer (much like Boeing did with some of its components) only to be surprised later.

One European supplier (a wholesaler) of luxury-style watches had a well-designed supply chain and maintained a level of penetration into that chain that enabled a profitable business.[27] The first tier was dual-sourced through a reseller in Hong Kong and an Egyptian supplier of watches and parts. They were managed out of Austria and Switzerland, respectively. The shipments were accompanied by sets of written documentation and metal plates for labeling that provided specific instructions so as to ensure quality. These suppliers managed a broader network of subtier suppliers in China, Korea, Japan, and Hong Kong. The gold cases and wristbands came from northern Italy. The finished goods shipped from Austria over the road to Italy for sale by the buyer. (Later, as the business grew, the company opened an assembly operation in central Italy.) The financial supply chain that paralleled this flow moved from Italy to Switzerland to New York to Hong Kong. The final aspect of the business was the startup of a luxury watch repair service leveraging the component supply chains of the primary suppliers.

The problem? This was the supply chain of a luxury watch counterfeiting operation, established by a former store owner and global businessman. The supply chain was pieced together from European court documents by the *Wall Street Journal*. In a world where outsourced manufacturing has spread brand assembly via low-cost country sourcing, counterfeiting is just one of the risks of an opaque supply chain. As economic sanctions are imposed by governments on other governments, a combination of organized crime, terrorist organizations, and rogue governments raise money through the counterfeiting industry. In the name of profit they have recruited manufacturing and distribution companies that specialize in counterfeit goods. This "shadow" supply chain has members that can disappear and reorganize to reenter the chain. This is business and these operations, because of the unique risks in their business model, manage their sourcing, supplier relationships, and global supply chain operations with a unique blend of opaqueness yet transparency compared to legitimate companies. As supply chain risks to profit, safety, and corporate reputation increase, legitimate companies may need comparable care in knowing the details of their far-flung supply webs.

When asked by the *Financial Times* about its products and IT infrastructure hardware containing refined tin, Microsoft was forthcoming in saying that they "do not have visibility into the activities of commodity suppliers at the beginning of the hardware supply chain."[28] Very few companies do—certainly none of the companies FT asked. In this case the question was triggered by the takeover of the largest tin mine in the Congo by a renegade brigade of the Congolese army. The brigade is using the proceeds from the sale of cassiterite ore mined by children to traders and road toll collections along the ore transport route to fund its operations. The traders, in turn, sell to middlemen who sell to exporters and international traders that sell, in turn, to smelters that purchase ore on the open market. At the smelters it is blended with all the other purchased tin and sold through the international metal exchanges for use in electronic hardware.

In the pharmaceutical industry the combination of active ingredient sourcing out of China and counterfeit products can be tragic.[29] In a well-publicized example in 2006, the Panamanian government bought and distributed prescription syrup that was manufactured at a Chinese factory, sold by a broker owned by the Chinese government to another layer of brokers in Spain, and shipped to Panama, where the mislabeled material was bought and distributed by the government there. It contained antifreeze (diethylene glycol). More than 110 people died. More than 170 were poisoned. All this stemmed from forty-six barrels of syrup that moved through a supply chain that was not managed well.

These stories illustrate the risk and difficulty in managing supply chains that are geographically broad, operationally remote, and commercially complex. A growing number of legitimate industries are moving to establish and enforce standards, while some governments are increasing supply chain monitoring agencies, whether to avert terrorist threats or tainted product risks. These efforts will help with the illegitimate chains described here, but even legitimate businesses must grapple with the problem. Software systems and more penetrating supplier management are part of the answer. The risk to a competitively advantaged business of an emerging risk deep in the supply chain can be significant.

While toymaker Mattel appears to have weathered its product design (small magnets in toys that can be swallowed) and lead paint product recalls, its stock fell 25 percent from its peak.[30] The lead-tainted toy supplier closed, and its owner committed suicide because one of its suppliers further up-chain substituted cheaper lead paint to increase margins without telling anyone. Preventing situations like that is the challenge. Value can be devoured quickly when "chain blindness" occurs.

Notes

1. Loren Gary, "The Everyday Problems of Global Sourcing," *Supply Chain Strategy* (Cambridge, Mass.: Harvard Business School Publishing and The MIT Center for Transportation and Logistics, October 2005).

2. Dean Foust, "Harry Potter and the Logistical Nightmare," *Business Week*, August 6, 2007.

3. Charles Fishman, *The Wal-Mart Effect* (New York: Penguin Books, 2006), p. iii.

4. Geraldo Samor and Paul Glader, "CVRD Gets 71.5% Price Rise For Iron Ore in Japanese Deal," *Wall Street Journal*, February 23, 2004.

5. Paul Glader and Geraldo Samor, "Steelmaker Accepts Big Price Increase From Its Supplier," *Wall Street Journal*, March 4, 2005.

6. Patrick Barta, Geraldo Samor, and Paul Glader, "China Steelmakers Take Lead in Ore-Price Talks," *Wall Street Journal*, March 3, 2006.

7. Rogerio Jemayer, "Iron-Ore Prices Get Boost from Asia," *Wall Street Journal*, December 28, 2006.

8. Alex Wilson, "Rio Tinto Signals Ore Premium," *Wall Street Journal*, October 1, 2007.

9. Robert Guy Matthews, "Automakers Weigh In on Steel," *Wall Street Journal*, October 9, 2007.

10. Robert Guy Matthews, "Arcelor Mittal to Raise Prices as Cost of Iron Ore Increases," *Wall Street Journal*, November 20, 2007.

11. Patrick Barta and Sebastian Moffett, "Miners Win 65% Jump in Iron-Ore Prices," *Wall Street Journal*, February 19, 2008

12. Keith Oliver, Anne Chung, and Nick Smanich, "Beyond Utopia," *Special Report, Strategy and Business Issue 23*, Booz Allen Hamilton, April 1, 2001.

13. Dana Cimilluca, "Customer Is Pauper in Eyes of Motorola's Zander," Blog: Deal Journal, April 27, 2007.

14. Ben Dolven, "Kraft Foods Works on Improving Its Recipe for Logistics in China," *Wall Street Journal*, August 30, 2004.

15. Jane Lanhee Lee, "China Hurdle: Lack of Refrigeration," *Wall Street Journal*, August 30, 2007.

16. Daniel Michaels and J. Lynn Lunsford, "Streamlined Plane Making," *Wall Street Journal*, April 1, 2005.

17. Jena McGregor, "Most Innovative Companies," *Business Week*, May 14, 2007.

18. J. Lynn Lunsford, "Ugly in the Air: Boeing's New Plane Gets Gawks, Stares," *Wall Street Journal*, January 8, 2007.

19. Doug Smock, "Boeing 787 Dreamliner Represents Composites Revolution," *Design News*, June 4, 2007.

20. J. Lynn Lunsford and Paul Glader, "Boeing's Nuts-And-Bolts Problem," *Wall Street Journal*, June 19, 2007.

21. Stanley Holmes, "The 787 Encounters Turbulence," *Business Week*, June 19, 2006.

22. J. Lynn Lunsford, "Boeing Scrambles To Fix Problems With New 787," *Wall Street Journal*, December 7, 2007.

23. J. Lynn Lunsford, "Boeing Delays 787 by Six Months As Suppliers in New Role Fall Behind," *Wall Street Journal*, October 11, 2007.

24. J. Lynn Lunsford, "Boeing's 787 Faces Less Room for Error," *Wall Street Journal*, September 6, 2007.

25. James Wallace, "Boeing executive faults some 787 suppliers," *Seattle Post-Intelligencer*, November 1, 2007.

26. Kevin Martin, James E. Forrest, and Philip A. Gould, "Integrated Plating Services (IPS) Collaboration: Harley Davidson, Leggett & Platt and Southwest Metal Finishing," presentation at the University of San Diego Strategic Supply Chain Management Forum, September 29, 2004.

27. Alessandra Galloni, "Faked Out: As Luxury Industry Goes Global, Knock-Off Merchants Follow," *Wall Street Journal*, January 31, 2006.

28. Nicholas Garrett and Harrison Mitchell, "Electronics groups alarmed after renegade troops take over Congo tin mine," *Financial Times*, March 6, 2008.

29. Walt Bogdanich, "Panama Releases Report on '06 Poisoning," *New York Times*, February 14, 2008.

30. "Does Your Supply Chain Deliver Shareholder Value?," *Supply Chain Strategy* (Cambridge, Mass.: Harvard Business School Publishing and The MIT Center for Transportation and Logistics, February 2008).

CHAPTER 8

Floor Plan for Supply Advantage

Organizing People, Skills, and Tasks

ROOM: a portion of space within a building or other structure, separated by walls or partitions from other parts.

The things we fear most in organizations—fluctuations, disturbances, imbalances—are the primary sources of creativity.

—Margaret Wheatley, organizational behavior consultant and author

Until now we have focused on the exterior of the "supply advantage house," the commercial structure including its foundation (sourcing strategy), walls (supplier relationships), and roof (supply chain). We started with an "outside-in" view, looking for supply-based sustainable advantage. This helps create a mindset that is open to external contribution to business strategy. However, as everyone knows, the exterior of a house is just a shell. It is the interior that personalizes the house into a home with internal uniqueness fashioned from "chemistry" fit's important philosophy and cultural linkages (Chapter 6).

Now it is time to work on the interior, after the external framework and mindset toward suppliers define its perimeter. Too often companies focus mainly on their own internal structure, without considering their suppliers' structures and how they interconnect with their own. The supply-based advantage home floor plan must be more than an organization chart's lines and boxes, including:

- ► Organizational design
- ► Organizational skill requirements
- ► Organizational health measures
- ► Organizational resource and budget planning

Organizational Design: More Than Just Structure

For years the structural design debate about supply-facing organizations has swung between centralized and decentralized. Tradeoffs between the two have always been clear—centralization allows greater volume leverage, market power concentration, methodology efficiency/standardization/cross-fertilization, and common management of people and skill development. Decentralization gives tighter business connection, much the way entrepreneurial small company environments (Chapter 2) lead to a better understanding of value, and can enable enhanced "line of sight" between suppliers and customers, without the organizational obstruction of internal staff hierarchy.

The advent of "spend management" software, and the sourcing and supplier management activities it spawns, drove the pendulum toward centralization. In 2003, before his death, IBM's Gene Richter wrote an article in *Purchasing* magazine entitled "Centralize!"[1] He pointed out that centralized procurement can lower acquisition costs between 15 and 20 percent more than in firms where procurement is decentralized. Yet, the shift to centralization was gradual, not immediate and massive. Many companies stayed decentralized across scattered, highly diverse businesses because procurement was patterned after customer management approaches that prized customization on the sales side.

Richter also stressed that simply establishing the position of chief procurement officer (CPO) without real internal authority over the supply base would fail. Instead, he emphasized the importance of convincing the CEO, creating real belief (not just "support") in centralized supplier management's inherent advantages, translated into a supplier governance structure. IBM did centralize. It also sought decentralization advantages by building linkages with its myriad businesses through connections to its sourcing teams.

Since then, this central approach evolved into the popular "center-led" procurement design, that is, having centralized supplier selection and commercial management using cross-functional sourcing teams including business unit representatives, plus dedicated, ongoing, "co-located" supplier management groups in the businesses. This design, including a company-wide CPO position, is widely perceived as best in class structure at the time of this writing. Some consultant studies reinforce this view.

Accenture Consulting, in late 2007, studied the linkage of high-performance procurement to value and competitive advantage in 225 companies.[2] The results fell into master, midrange, and low performers, with 100 percent of "masters" using a center-led structure to deliver 30 percent higher cost savings with 50 percent lower operational costs than low performers and a ratio of savings equal to 10 times the procurement department budget cost (versus a ratio of 4 for low performers). A 2007 Deloitte Consulting study also concluded that top performers consistently use center-led sourcing to develop better sourcing strategies (see Chapter 5) that are the key determinant of better performance.[3]

Yet, at about the same time, A.T. Kearney and the Institute for Supply Management (ISM) issued a study entitled "Succeeding in a Dynamic World: Supply Management in the Decade Ahead."[4] They highlighted that to deal with local talent recruiting and development challenges in the coming decade, global companies will need to move away from center-led models to more locally led, yet cross-geographically networked, approaches. McKinsey Consulting's late 2007 purchasing assessment did not specifically endorse any structure.[5] Instead, it emphasized connecting purchasing to the business—a trait of more decentralized organizations. Net: The pendulum continues to swing, both among experts and in the real world. There is no universal, static vision of a perfect structure.

—Practitioner's Take—

Unfortunately, many companies jump to redrawing organization chart lines and boxes, with little thought about how the operation actually works. It is no surprise that there is not consensus, even among experts, on one "right" supply organizational structure. Reality is that supply structure coexists with corporate structure and culture, whether decentralized or centralized. That doesn't mean it must match corporate structure, but rather that supply must operate within the context of that corporate "layout."

Structure is overrated. To manage increasingly global supplier commerce for competitive advantage requires business and supply base linkage across geographical distances. This requires looking at the supply base from three different angles when designing the organization:

1. Commodity or spend category
2. Business unit
3. Geography (Is the scope of the supply base global, regional, national, or, in large countries, local or regional within the country?)

The commodity axis is fairly straightforward, with commonalities of work, suppliers, feedstocks, patterns of supply and demand, etc. Business unit and geographical elements require more tailoring for competitive advantage because they have more potential combinations—different business units need different things from suppliers, and the geography of the supply base can easily be a combination of global and local. Yet the lure of volume leverage leads many supply organizations to formalize spend category structure and try to matrix geography and business unit. However, supply management often can do little without internal customer support—technical and operational across the company's geographical span. Given different cultures and leadership, two companies with similar situations can easily arrive at different organizational designs—each with successful results.

Nokia began its transition from very decentralized purchasing to a strong center-led supply setup in 2000.[6] It took six years. Nokia's business was (and still is) global with significant (but not complete) technological overlap along with some business and regional variation. Its supply design goal was to blend close business strategy linkage (which the decentralized model already delivered) with better supply management coordination through reporting lines to central executives. The resulting design was relatively centralized with very strong regional matrix linkages. It was implemented in steps—and exceeded its goals of €300 million savings and increased internal integration between supplier management and business unit supply chain groups.

In the early 1990s P&G also had a decentralized purchasing organization. Our business was (and still is) global, with some overlap in requirements but very localized products and packaging. The design goal, similar to Nokia's, was to get $300 million savings via centrally leveraged global sourcing across decentralized, semi-independent geographical regions and businesses. Unlike Nokia, the choice was to focus the organizational design around business units and geographic regions. The spend category axis became the "informal" one—hardwired within the business unit but optional across business units. This choice was driven by a culture of strong regional business unit control and, in part, on personal relationships in the purchasing function. About fifteen years earlier, several international managers rotated into Cincinnati for temporary headquarters assignments. Eventually, they became the international leaders, retaining relationships with former U.S. peers who were running U.S. purchasing. Informal, personality-driven spend category links—albeit not without intense rivalry over approaches and skill levels—sustained the effort. Where technical and operational support were critical (in specific businesses and regions), the structure was more formal.

Two companies from different industries and cultures. Startlingly similar goals and outcomes. Yet, two different organizational structures. The point?

The point is that there is no one "right" supply structure. "Right" depends on corporate culture and business needs, leadership personalities/trust levels, and tolerance for the inevitable conflict that working across profit centers can provoke. The internal politics of operating a global supply network in a multibusiness firm can be brutal! Access to scarce resources and thirst for influence and power often pit internal functions against each other. What needs to be right are the enabling processes for broad sourcing efforts capable of addressing often different, sometimes conflicting, profit center business needs and value definitions suppliers must meet.

The "Ideal" Organization?

Even though there is no one right supply structure, a theoretical look at what one might be can help your design effort. Any design effort targeting competitive advantage must start with business perspective, not the supply function. That means engaging senior management to connect the importance of suppliers to their business goals. A good way to start is by asking senior management four basic questions:

1. What percentage of company expense is paid to suppliers? Typical answer: between 30 and 80 percent (averaging 50+ percent) and,

given increases in infrastructural outsourcing (e.g., IT, health care, personnel administration, etc.) and marketing (advertising, call center management, etc.), 30 percent is becoming more rare. Many senior managers might get this one right.

2. Which suppliers are paid the most and what percentage of the supply base do they make up? Fewer senior managers will be able to name their top twenty suppliers, nor will they get the percentage correct (typically under 5 percent).

3. How much do suppliers contribute to company capability? If honest, manufacturing companies answer "a lot." Service companies might be surprised how much suppliers contribute to their business, given dramatic increases in services outsourcing (software, IT, communications, and advertising).

4. Should an area that receives over 50 percent of the money spent by a company be considered tactical or an investment in a strategic asset?

The answers might spark a different conversation and some investment in organizational capability to gain the maximum return possible on that spending. Ideally this might lead, in turn, to a seat at the business strategy development table and encourage penetration of the functional skill sets needed to manage such a large asset base across both direct and indirect supply chains.

Direct Material Chain

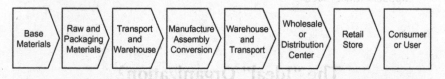

Managing an asset as broad as the direct material supply base would entail a range of skills, including commercial disciplines (sourcing or procurement), product/component technology (quality assurance, R&D), financial (finance and accounting, accounts payable, cost engineering), communication and data access (IT), logistics (transportation, contract warehousing, inbound supply planning), legal, and production (contract manufacturing). This results in a supplier account team, analogous to more commonly used multifunctional customer account teams. Frequently, the organizational barrier is that, relative to customers, supplier management is fragmented, utiltizing many part-time resources buried in several functions deep in the organization.

Indirect Goods and Services Chain

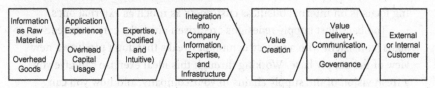

The indirect supply base relates to overhead goods (e.g., computers, leased buildings, etc.) and support services (e.g., outsourcing part or all of advertising, IT, maintenance, etc.). This chain has some challenging differences when compared to direct goods and services because the integration step (comparable to the manufacturing step in direct chains) is more subjective for services. Specifications can defy quantitative measurement, so the resulting reliance on personal relationships and experience often leads to high emotions and psychological exit barriers, making some of these relationships resistant to competition. These exit barriers can increase supplier post-contract power if and when internal knowledge of the area declines.

The belief that these suppliers can be managed by detailed contracts or personal relationships has consistently been proven wrong. Application of professional purchasing, competition, relationship governance approaches, detailed cost driver/structure analysis, waste elimination (Lean and Six Sigma), and specification reviews result in significant savings and cost avoidance. Comparable to the direct material supply chain, managing these suppliers requires a comparable range of skill sets; commercial management, service area operations and R&D, cost analysis, information technology, and financial measurement expertise all apply here as well.

—Practitioner's Take—

If you can't create an ideally designed supply chain, how does an ideal design exercise help get competitive advantage from suppliers? Why bother with such a theoretical exercise?

Simple: It conceptualizes the connections necessary across functional boundaries to mimic the "ideal" structure. It makes you think about supply as a "business unit organizational design" that can replicate entrepreneurial small company end-to-end connection between suppliers, customers, and company leadership. It is about holistically applying a wide range of skills against a huge set of external physical and intellectual assets—essentially a supply-facing business microcosm whose sales and marketing focus is on internal business customers as much as external ones.

Too bad most supply redesigns are driven either by corporate redesigns (consistent with a new structure) or tweaks that don't produce a new view of the supply base. Working through this ideal exercise can give you a fresh vision of the supply chains in your company, and how you can enhance their ability to give your firm a supply-based competitive advantage. It dimensionalizes the range of skills that must be aligned across the company and applied to the supply base to achieve the advantage you seek.

Organizational Design "for Real"

David Hanna was a human resources expert at P&G when, in 1988, he wrote the book, *Design Organizations for High Performance,*[7] which included an Organizational Performance Model (OPM) to help internal organizations link their structure and organization to business needs. This model ties business strategy, situation, and results with the firm's people side (culture in particular). Its focus is internal organizational design.

However, when applied to a boundary function like supply management, the design must be two-sided[8]; if not, what makes sense internally may be disruptive or confusing to an outside supplier. On the flip side, integrating consciousness of suppliers' organization structures into the internal design allows supply managers to more effectively target their influence within the suppliers' organizations. Supply "faces both ways" with different environments on either side of the corporate boundary, including language and norms.

Hanna's OPM assesses six design elements that are then integrated to judge whether the design is workable. Structure—the lines and boxes—should be the last element finalized, only after the other five are understood.

> *Tasks.* What work needs to be done on both sides of the boundary? This element includes external tasks like soliciting bids, negotiating with suppliers, connecting to markets, and measuring supplier re-

sults; plus internal tasks like cost and availability planning, financial reporting, cross-functional alignment, project management, and personnel duties.

▶ *People*. This goes beyond individual aptitudes, skill levels, and the processes to acquire, train, develop, and retain people. This element aggregates them into an organizational view of overall capability, resources, and critical mass to handle the tasks. Externally, connecting to the "right" people at suppliers (that is, people with comparable aptitudes, knowledge, and skills) falls here.

▶ *Information*. Information is the "raw material" of supplier and market analysis, hence assessing the supply group's access to internal, market, and supplier information and metrics is vital. Real competitive advantage takes information to a new level, including intellectual property management considerations and personal relationship knowledge on both sides.

▶ *Decision Making*. Who makes important calls on issues? Internally, this includes the supply and, often more importantly, cross-functional and senior management decision processes that enable true collaboration to implement supply opportunities. Understanding supplier decision processes/makers focuses influence toward mining strategic supplier value.

▶ *Rewards*. What makes the organization and the people within it tick? Reward systems drive action based on the "what's in it for me" axiom, but each individual's extrinsic and intrinsic motivators are unique—internally and at suppliers too. They make or break the success equation and must be carefully linked to "what's in it for the business"? Organizational rewards also matter (functional pride, recognition). All the nuances of internal rewards exist at suppliers as well, so understanding what makes key supplier representatives and business entities tick is part of this element.

▶ *Structure*. Finally, here are the lines and boxes for roles, responsibilities, and authority. Simply redistributing responsibilities and reporting lines will not change outcomes. Implicit power (people respected in the organization regardless of level) has to be overlaid on the formal structure as part of a "sanity check" that connects the new structure to the other five elements and to company culture. Then hooking into a supply base, with its myriad unique structures on the outside, must be considered as well.

—Practitioner's Take—

This theory really works. I have personally used it many times to renew existing organizations and design new ones. I've also seen the pitfalls of ignoring such a holistic model or, in supply management situations, only applying it on the internal side. While it sounds simple in the abstract, real application, like most people-related theory, is far less easy.

The trick for supply-side organizations is the complicating factor of linking to outside markets. In the late 1980s P&G launched simultaneous reorganizations to finished product categories (laundry detergents, disposable diapers, shampoos) and integrated product supply chains (combining purchasing, manufacturing, plant design/engineeering, customer service, and logistics for each product category). Manufacturing leadership was put in charge of most of these new supply chain groups—at that time production was viewed as strategic and management of large numbers of people and implementation of high-performing blue-collar work systems (in factories) were considered important leadership qualifications.

Within plants, manufacturing structure mirrored businesses—e.g., shampoo lines were separate from deodorant lines. This internal mindset drove use of the OPM in the new design, leading to a highly decentralized procurement group. Almost overnight a largely spend-centric U.S. procurement organization was splintered into a series of small, business unit–specific purchasing groups. A couple of business units kept procurement and inbound supply fairly centralized in the unit but many others decentralized down to the product level (shampoo or coffee) and, in the case of two, all the way to the brand level in order to align a "buyer" with each manufacturing department and marketing group.

The results were catastrophic. By focusing only on the internal side of the design, the firm virtually eliminated its buying scale. Within two years what had been a strong sourcing organization was largely in shambles. Benchmarks showed a cost structure higher than the competition's. Supply chain measures prioritized manufacturing operational cost and reliability (not total product cost), creating enormous disincentives for supplier change regardless of price and delivered cost premiums relative to the market. Psychological barriers to supply competition and supplier change created "mini-monopolies" that led to higher costs built into finished product pricing. Consumer value and product sales fell.

Internally, the impact was even more disturbing. Relatively efficient spend category organizations were ripped apart and redeposited in many supply organizations. (One strategic spend, plastic bottles, went from a small eight- or nine-person cadre with deep industry knowledge, to thirty-three bottle buyers in the United States alone.)

Besides confusing suppliers with the complexity of the structure and sheer number of people to talk to, the design made transferring supplier ideas from one business to another virtually impossible. Suppliers quickly discovered we were suddenly vulnerable to "reverse leveraging" with the weakest, most inexperienced members of the "herd" taken advantage of due to their low volume and relative isolation. Worse, the skill erosion was rapid and intense. Few of the thirty-three bottle buyers only bought those containers, while most were spread across many spend categories, leading to weak industry expertise and, when those who had some expertise moved to new jobs, there was no experience elsewhere in the fractured organizations to train their replacements. The result: major commercial expertise "brain drain."

The business crisis caused the organization to rethink decentralization and supply. Experienced purchasing leaders, who had transferred to manufacturing to advance their careers, were transferred back with the task to re-create a capable commercial sourcing group. This time the OPM model was viewed through a broader, balanced internal/external lens. A series of restructures emerged that recentralized within broad business units (rather than brands or individual product lines), creating a springboard for the early global and low cost country sourcing efforts of the mid-1990s.

Within that broader view, the OPM also allowed business-specific designs where they made sense—separate groups to work with R&D on innovation and unique business-specific supply groups like coffee's combination of futures and cash market trading, quality control, blending, and logistics into one organizational structure.

Still, culture does not change quickly. Despite ten years of successful, more central designs, the "c-word" (central) remained vehemently opposed by many manufacturing-bred supply chain leaders. In order to move to global cross-business spend category sourcing groups, the recommendation was not called "center-led." Instead it was termed "externalization," sold on the merits of more effective external supplier interfaces patterned after the company's external connect-and-develop innovation strategy. "Externalization" was saleable where centralization was not.

Supplier management, like information technology and sales, gains substantial leverage from more central designs. The risk is that without tight connections to the business, supply strategies can miss substantial value. On the flip side, even highly decentralized companies with tight business connections can benefit from some center-led supply coordination. One of the most fiercely decentralized cultures in business, with over 200 operating companies, is that of health care leader, Johnson & Johnson (J&J).[9]

J&J recognized that its independent operating practices, while enhancing business alignment, generated redundancies and inefficiencies—especially in the supply chain. Using Six Sigma and a design method similar to Hanna's, this one a five-element model created by Jay Galbraith (structure, processes, lateral capability, people, and rewards), J&J began a redesign on the customer end of its chain. The model facilitated the combination of three redesigns—business, technical, and organizational—into a virtual organization that improved order management, warehousing, outbound transportation, and accounts receivable. The model forced process redesigns ahead of structural changes by incorporating cross-business, cross-functional, and leadership enrollment. The new design was credited with a receivables days' outstanding reduction equal to several million dollars a day. Again, a holistic, culturally sensitive, broad design view was far more effective than a semi-independent single function effort.

Skills: Doing the Work Means Knowing How to Do It

So far this book has focused on processes important for the creation of supply-based advantage. Now let's talk about the skills that must be embedded into people to make these processes work. Competitive advantage requires managing the broad supply base, not just a few strategic suppliers. This requires a range of skills used in the right situation or market condition with the right type of supplier relationship. Mature supply organizations that develop advantaged positions have to (a) manage the range of the supply base and (b) do it situationally—knowing when to change approaches and tools.

As Pierre Mitchell, director of the Hackett Group, said in his December 2007 presentation about driving competitive advantage via procurement and supply management, the sheer number and breadth of suppliers most companies deal with makes procurement complex.[10] Consequently, the number of tools supply organizations use can be overwhelming—different types of supplier relationships or levels of supply chain tiering involve either dissimilar tools, or the same tools applied very differently, resulting in skill complexity. Without the knowledge and experience (even intuition) to use the right tool at the right time, serious mistakes can happen.

—Practitioner's Take—

The skill nomenclature discussed below is a little unusual, but the idea is to follow the progression to draw ever increasing and more unique value out of suppliers throughout the supply base. The four commercial skill sets are additive, with basic skills continuing to be a vital part of the repertoire, even as more advanced skills are learned and applied to higher level supplier relationships or more complex industries and markets.

Like organizational structures, a discussion of an ideal set of skills is helpful in describing the range of skill applications to various supplier relationships and supply market conditions that a procurement or supply management organization will contend with across the various spends the firm must source. The skill sets discussed below contain a lot of skills, so as a former practitioner, I want to provide a practical caution.

Most organizations, especially those seeking to initiate a skill program, are not prepared to try to install many skills. Worse, trying to put as many as ten in place at one time can overwhelm the organization and cause the skill system to collapse under its own weight. A better approach is, after assessing all the skill areas that could potentially be put in place, to pick no more than half a dozen that really matter and focus there.

Now, let's move on to the ideal state. Each skill incorporates tools, the rationale for tool use, and the implications of using a particular tool or tool set—on suppliers as well as on the buying company. For example, the comprehensive skill of competitive bidding incorporates all types of bidding tools (reverse auctions, requests for information, proposals, and quotes), deciding when to use bidding, which tool to use, which suppliers to invite to bid, and formulating pre-/post-bid communication messages. The four sets of tools include analysis, "synergesis," genesis, and "systemesis" skills. Let's take a look at each in some detail.

Analysis Skills

These are the base skills used in strategic sourcing. They are vital to smart, timely supplier selection and optimizing cost reduction parts of value that occur in supplier selection processes. Often acquisition of these skills is trumpeted during "transformations" from tactical to strategic procurement. However, they are foundational to "first stage" supply expertise not advanced, sophisticated value creation, and capture. The ten analysis skills include:

1. *Linking.* This requires the ability to connect with internal customers and business needs to craft strategies that align desired results with business needs, not just with functional supply goals.

2. *Leveraging.* This involves the ability to work laterally across the company to leverage aggregated demand volume, supplier relationships across commodities and businesses, skills across organizational boundaries, etc. Spend analysis is core to this skill.

3. *Industry Analysis.* This assesses the competitive structure of industries including all of Michael Porter's five forces (mentioned in Chapter 5)—rivalry, supplier power (in this case your supplier's suppliers), buyer power (looking at all the industry's customers not just your industry), new entrants, and substitutes.

4. *Competitive Analysis.* This skill assesses the sourcing approach of your competition including how and when they go to market, who their key suppliers are, and how they structure their supply functions. This also includes reverse engineering competitive specifications and products to understand their value equation (cost and performance).

5. *Market Analysis.* This requires a combination of supply/demand analysis for the sourced item and economic analysis to understand the impact of macro- and microeconomic factors (economic cycles [recession versus boom], currency, local labor markets, etc.).

6. *Supplier Analysis.* This skill involves ongoing analysis of specific suppliers using the SOCCER model (Strategy, Operational Capability, Customer Approach, Cost Structure, Economics, R&D—see Chapter 5) and supplier assessment tools. Assessment includes verifying that a supplier can do the work (often with technical function support).

7. *Cost Analysis.* This uses the total cost of ownership analysis (we talked about this earlier).

8. *Sourcing Strategy Development/Execution.* This skill uses the process discussed in Chapter 4 to drive supplier selection.

9. *Competitive Bidding*—utilizing competitive bidding tools (example above), including supplier prework necessary to ensure successful tool application.

10. *Deal Negotiation*—negotiating the details of the deal itself, not just the price. Basic contract negotiation starts here.

"Synergesis" Skills

Synergesis skills create supplier relationships, take advantage of synergies between the two companies, and leverage differentials in core competencies. These skills are vital when managing strategic suppliers, complex service providers, and long-term supplier relationships. They take over the supply relationships that the analysis skills, just enumerated, deliver. There are also ten synergesis skills:

1. *Supplier Relationship Management.* This involves managing the three "fits" (strategic, operational, and chemistry, discussed in Chapter 5), using a triage process to identify and prioritize strategic suppliers, and managing "umbrella" relationships, where one supplier provides several items requiring different relationships (e.g., commodity and specialty items from the same company; see Chapter 6).

2. *SOW (Statement of Work) Development.* This consists of "specification writing" that defines outcomes and requirements without forcing the buyer's work processes on the supplier. This skill is particularly important in services relationships.

3. *Contract Management.* This skill includes drafting, negotiation, and especially, subsequent management of supplier contracts, including service level agreements (SLAs). Contract management expands on the deal negotiation skill (analysis skill #10), above.

4. *Forecasting.* This involves integrating internal knowledge from the linking skill with external knowledge (industry, market, cost, and supplier analysis) and supplier relationship contacts to forecast future cost and availability of supply. Demand management is the internal side of this skill.

5. *Relationship Governance.* This skill involves governance structure design, results measurement systems (scorecards), and conflict resolution processes (see Chapter 11).

6. *Hedging.* This skill involves using financial instruments (or physical inventory) to manage cost volatility. It includes establishing a market view, risk exposure analysis, hedging strategy development, hedge accounting, and hedging instrument use and analysis (see Chapter 12).

7. *Waste Elimination.* This uses Six Sigma, Lean, and Total Quality Management tools to improve supplier operations and reduce variation to increase efficiency of joint supplier/buyer work processes and product delivery.

8. *Supplier Development.* Skilled internal resources must be allocated toward supplier operations to improve results. This includes waste elimination, but also supplier improvement plan development, technical and commercial training for suppliers, and joint supplier/customer value improvement teams.

9. *Supply Risk Management.* This includes assessment, mitigation, and management of supply risk—physical supply, reputation, fraud, electronic, financial, and regulatory—beyond the first tier. This skill includes working with suppliers to identify and manage risk in their suppliers and influence upstream tiers that may not be direct business relationships (see Chapter 12).

10. *Relationship Negotiation.* This involves working through how changes in business situations impact the commercial supplier relationship. Different than deal negotiation above, this refers to negotiations within an existing contract or across two independent contracts.

Genesis Skills

Genesis skills encourage innovation from the broad supply base by managing the risks of innovation, an inherently uncertain process (you don't know in advance if a new idea will work). This skill set deals with how to increase the odds of success while managing the possibility of failure with suppliers. More subtle than earlier skill sets, these ten skills are more closely aligned with competitive advantage's need to adapt to business climate changes.

1. *Nurturing Supplier Relationships.* This means establishing relationships that can withstand development failures and market uncertainties. Relationships must be sustained through tough times using communication and trust building. This skill includes understanding both the supplier's dependence on your projects and your dependence on the supplier—and managing those vulnerabilities.

2. *Intellectual Property.* This skill requires close alignment with patent lawyers to develop intellectual property ownership frameworks with suppliers. It includes managing commercial implications of innovation projects including exclusivity, open innovation (licensing), sup-

plier talent assignment, and commercial success criteria on both sides.

3. *Developmental Supply Agreements.* These are contracts that commercialize new products from suppliers (R&D services, construction of manufacturing lines or plants), including investment economics volume contingency implications, scale-up economics, and new-material transition to ongoing status.

4. *Commercialization Risk Management.* This deals with decision making about continuing or killing supplier projects during the commercialization process. Incorporates success criteria–driven "gate management" systems that move suppliers and projects along a launch path while identifying, understanding, and consciously managing risks along the way and synchronizing investment commitments on both sides to avoid unexpected overcommitments. This skill relies heavily on the synergesis relationship nurturing skills.

5. *Project Management.* Traditional individual project management skills need to be applied across corporate boundaries so that supplier efforts are part of the management process.

6. *Supplier Portfolio Management.* The project management concept must be expanded to look across all the projects a particular supplier has with a firm and establishing project resource priorities. This skill requires knowing the extent of a supplier's capability to manage multiple projects and managing the "too many eggs in one basket" risk of concentrating too much with a single supplier.

7. *Project Portfolio Management.* This extends the project management concept across suppliers and projects to manage how long-term supplier commitments overlap with new product platforms that may make those investments obsolete.

8. *Target Costing/Should Costing.* This involves cross-functional reverse engineering of the costs of developing new products to make them economically viable. It includes working with technical organizations to create design flexibility; with suppliers on cost-effective product delivery methods; and with manufacturing or logistics on assembly and/or distribution costs. Target cost determines what new products must cost to hit customer-preferred price points and producer profit margins. Should cost looks at each component in a product, determines a best cost, and assembles individual component best costs into an ideal cost structure against which to compare supplier pro-

posals. Sometimes should cost models include in-depth cost analysis of each step in the supply chain.

9. *Design Value Analysis.* This skill flows out of target costing and applies cost analysis to performance requirements and specification design to enable a better value equation and/or set up flexibility in the product design to deal with potential cost driver changes.

10. *Co-Creative Negotiation.* Co-creative negotiation seeks to create gain by using approaches that develop a "bigger pie" and determining how that extra value should be shared—easy to say but often hard to do. It also tries to find ways to avoid or minimize shared pain when things go badly.

"Systemesis" Skills

An integration skill set that helps direct the use of the other three sets, these are systemic supply base management skills that integrate the overall membership of the supply base into a competitive web of supply capability applied against the business's value equation. Managing suppliers beyond just financial and operational assessment, these skills allow a firm to see its suppliers as an extended workforce to be managed for value and a source of sustainable competitive advantage. Supply leadership must be adept at using these ten skills.

1. *Supply Principles/Policy Application.* These skills embed corporate values and supplier management principles into the fabric of the work, as discussed in Chapter 3.

2. *Leadership.* A classic internal management skill, leadership expands to incorporate leading multiple suppliers toward your firm's goals (sometimes like herding cats). Supply leadership encompasses "network delegation"—the ability to realistically determine when leadership should be delegated to a supplier or another internal function and what degree of leadership is feasible given a supply network's power structure.

3. *Influencing.* This critical ability is necessary to convince suppliers to make you a preferred customer, allocate resources where you need them, and make commercial decisions (often about pricing) that advantage your firm. Few companies have the power to truly control their suppliers, so influencing becomes a key differentiating skill.

Internal influence with senior leaders and other functions is also part of this skill.

4. *Expectations Management.* This is another skill used both internally and externally. The internal side ensures that senior management understands and incorporates supply's likely results, risks, and market climate changes into company strategic and tactical plans. Externally, it explores up- and downside business scenarios with suppliers to anticipate potential outcomes and proactively avoid surprises that undermine relationships. It is a means to shift future supplier direction.

5. *Collaborative Communications.* The skill of giving suppliers information needed to deliver value is vital (too often suppliers miss the mark through lack of information—no one pointed out the target). Simplistically, this means working well across both internal and external boundaries.

6. *Conflict Management.* It's important to be able to turn conflict into a constructive force to drive differentials in thinking. Part of the value of suppliers lies in their differences from the buying firm. These differentials in thinking have the potential to add valuable and unique perspectives to problem solving or innovation efforts. The skill manages conflict away from destructive outcomes by reducing and channeling the impact of emotion.

7. *Change Management.* Supply requires this classic skill to excess. Internally, few companies see supply as a strategic differentiator, so selling the concept invites substantial change. Externally, change management is even more important, as it involves grappling with the constant change inherent in competitive markets, people, and organizations outside your own. It requires managing business direction–triggered changes with supplier decision makers. "Downward" changes are especially delicate to manage.

8. *Trust Building.* Increasing mutual trust, widely acknowledged as vital to strategic supplier relationships, is necessary throughout the supply base. An important element of the skill is empathy, which can provide intangible value to sustain strategic relationships through hard times. Call it an old-fashioned sense of honor.

9. *Supply Financial Portfolio Management.* The first of two supply base–wide skill sets manages broad supply base financial impact on the firm (much as an investor balances a portfolio of stocks and bonds). As individual markets go up and down, some supplier or commodity

costs will as well. This skill—particularly necessary for senior supply leaders—delivers supply financial goals by cross-roughing gains against losses, minimizing downside and driving upside value opportunities, incorporating and accelerating cost project time lines, and delaying or minimizing supplier price increases and maximizing decreases relative to competition.

10. *Supply Network Orchestration.* This second holistic supply base management skill builds flexibility to deal with volatility and change into the supply base. Apparel supply chain leaders like Li & Fung (see Chapter 14) describe it best as the ability to see the supply base as a global network that must be coordinated to deal with the unforeseen. It encourages cost-effective supply agility through intelligent anticipatory chain design and responsive near-term operation—containing a blend of strategic and operational activities. This is where links between the direct and indirect supply chains keep product supply in harmony with marketing and infrastructural supply, orchestrating suppliers while maintaining relationships that weather shifting market needs for flexibility, agility, cost, and speed. This is the capstone skill in a multidimensional chess game. Few corporations have it, but those that do usually overwhelm their competition.

—Practitioner's Take—

"Four areas with ten skills in each? Ridiculous!" you're thinking. "Isn't that overkill?" I warned you. Early on we said building sustainable supply-based advantage is not a short "transformation," but rather a long-range competitive strategy marathon requiring continuing organizational maturity. I was lucky enough to spend more than thirty years with a company that, a majority of the time (but not always), saw it that way and also saw ongoing evolution of skill as a means to do it.

In order to be practical about such an overwhelming list of skills, two things are worth discussing briefly—one positive, the other, not so much. First, inspection across the skill sets reveals many interconnections that build on each other. They model the maturity curve an organization must travel—sourcing followed by true relationship management, followed by innovative value mining, and culminated by holistic, networkwide supply base design, management, and leadership. A couple of illustrations might help make skill integration more visible and thus more manageable.

- *Contracts:* Contract management (synergesis skill set), intellectual property and developmental supply agreements (genesis), and deal negotiation (analysis) all build legal awareness from basic to more advanced knowledge.
- *Negotiation:* Relationship negotiation (synergesis) and co-creative negotiation (genesis) are extensions of deal negotiation (analysis) into more complex and mature situations.

The progression is logical as well. The first skill set (analysis) focuses on individual suppliers and commodities, the next two (synergesis and genesis) blend individual and connected supply base skills—e.g., supplier relationship management (synergesis) adds umbrella supplier management to narrower scope relationship management. Supplier portfolio management and project portfolio management (genesis) look beyond a single project or supplier. Finally, the last set (systemesis) is about breadth of perspective from supply principles/policy application to supply financial portfolio management capped by supply network orchestration.

The second practical discussion point is the gap between listing a bunch of skills on paper and the task of growing and embedding them into people and organizations. It is more than just training. Embedding skills means:

- Defining the skills both conceptually and behaviorally (what is actually done) as well as identifying tools used within each skill.
- Developing training content to illustrate the skills and tools. Then providing opportunities to use the skills by setting the expectation for actual skill use to deliver results. This is not about regurgitating information, but rather, using it. Line managers must be integrated into the training system as instructors and "skill usage expectations setters" on the job.
- Defining skill proficiency levels that progress with experience and aptitude across a range of assignments. These kinds of skills are not mastered in one assignment. To become expert in their use entails application in multiple industries, markets, and business situations. Part of this requires incorporating skill mastery into career progression so that concrete business results from the mastery of several skills is a criterion for promotion and assignment selection.

- Identifying senior managers who are the best in each skill and making them that skill's owner. Why? Skills evolve and change over time. Example: The advent of reverse auctions changed competitive bidding, adding a tool requiring different techniques for success than traditional request for proposal systems. The skill owner had to learn when and how to use it with suppliers and integrate it into the overall bidding skill context. (Small organizations have to prioritize the number of skills to feasibly balance senior resources with skill potential for advantage.)

- Building and maintaining a skill system that incorporates career-long learning. This includes building the more advanced skills on the foundation of basic sourcing and relationship skills, teaching the policies and principles early in people's careers, and establishing a cadre of central "masters" who, in cooperation with line leaders, appropriately balance skill standardization, situational application, and calibration (i.e., avoid having one leader's "great" be another's "average").

In my experience, this was an incredibly difficult task—a systemic effort superimposed on intense day-to-day business pressures that nearly crowded it out. Successfully sustaining a deep skill system is more evolutionary than revolutionary—trying to simultaneously become expert at too many things leads to expertise in nothing. Our skill system was established during supply's capability crisis in the early 1990s, when we had to reverse a deep skill erosion.

The first step was identifying fundamental skills we felt were most important (mostly "analysis" skills with a couple "synergesis" and "systemesis" included for context and direction setting). In the late 1990s I attended a benchmarking session and watched a major pharmaceutical company describe its skill system using almost the same language and skill progression as ours. We had never talked to them. Clearly, experienced supply veterans "get" what matters—the trick is systematizing it.

Over the succeeding years the skills were expanded, mostly in recognition that sourcing alone is not enough to deliver competitive advantage. Training in more advanced skills, extending from the foundational set, was targeted toward people who would use them most. Calibration across our large supply leadership and middle management layers was even more of a challenge and remained imprecise.

Organizational Health: Skills Are Not Enough

Building, using, and embedding skills into the operation is good, but not enough. Metrics drive action and too often, supply is not measured in a balanced way—cost reduction is the sole barometer of success or failure (plus a base level of quality and delivery considered "givens," not goals). Worse, while companies use balanced scorecards, supply gets stereotyped by senior management for its financial impact alone. This creates a self-fulfilling prophecy that makes supply leaders measure the same way.

This, in turn, elevates the cost half of the value equation into the driver's seat, pushing performance value to the rear. Drs. Robert Kaplan and David Norton, in *The Balanced Scorecard: Translating Strategy into Action*, popularized a four-quadrant metric approach: financials, customers, internal business processes, and learning/growth of the organization.[11] Accessing suppliers to generate competitive edge is more than a financial game. Balanced scorecard supply metrics better underpin competitive advantage and value. (This scorecard approach is also valuable in holistically measuring individual strategic suppliers too.) Supply's version looks at the four quadrants as follows:

1. *Financial.* Measurement of both cost (total cost of ownership) and cash flow implications of suppliers on corporate financials (payment terms, inbound inventory turns), plus systemic financial process health (accounts payable and internal controls effectiveness).

2. *Business Processes.* Measurement of supplier process outcomes relative to the firm's business—things like quality, delivery, invoice accuracy, submission (and relevance) of improvement ideas, etc. Some are basics (quality/delivery); others leverage those basic capabilities even further (e.g., supplier innovation, improved reliability/risk mitigation, technical support, agility, etc.).

3. *Customer.* Deals with three distinct "customers": the firm's customer (real customers); internal supply customers (functions that use supplier products); and suppliers themselves (as stakeholders of the firm and customers of the supply organization's work).

4. *Organization Learning/Growth.* Addresses the health of the supply organization: skill levels, talent (recruiting, retention), morale, maturity, etc.

The first two areas—financials and the non-financial business process results—are traditional. They need to be penetrated: What is the cost trend?

What are the quality levels and how do they translate into customer-perceived quality? How do supplier-caused outages impact customer satisfaction and sales? What percentage of company innovation comes from outside?

The second two areas, more "soft side," give both quantitative and qualitative perspective. The customer measure, besides numerical customer requirements, indirectly tracks internal and external influence (can the supply organization get internal cooperation or supplier resources and support dedicated where the firm wants/needs it?). The organization measure, besides tracking retention or headcount productivity numbers, indirectly determines whether supply is positioned well for the future to deliver on its promises. Contrary to short-term thinking, the latter two best differentiate the firm from its competitors, creating the difference between good results and sustainable competitive advantage. They deliver the first two measures. Figure 8.1 provides a useful starting point to develop a supply balanced scorecard tailored for your own company.

—Practitioner's Take—

Easier said than done. Off-the-record discussions with experienced supply executives often reveal measurement mistakes—yet "you are what you measure." Measures drive the organization and, in supply, also drive supplier actions. Superficial measures can lead to unintended results—too great a focus on cost leads to service and quality erosion; too much Lean results in outages from fragile supply chains; too much relationship loyalty creates blindness to breakthough ideas elsewhere. The list is endless. This is about balance—cost and performance.

Common mistakes (I've made several of them) include:

- *Failure to Balance the Soft Measures with Hard Results Orientation.* The balanced scorecard is about (what else?) balance. The easy-to-measure metrics in the first two quadrants, where most companies focus, are not holistic enough. The second two, which include some subjective elements, are much harder to measure effectively and take time to digest. But they are the ones that spawn competitive advantage, which is ultimately the subject of this book. Advantage puts a high premium on both these sets of metrics. The dynamic market for your products means application of organizational competencies—built on work processes and skills—and

Figure 8.1   Supply's Balanced Scorecard

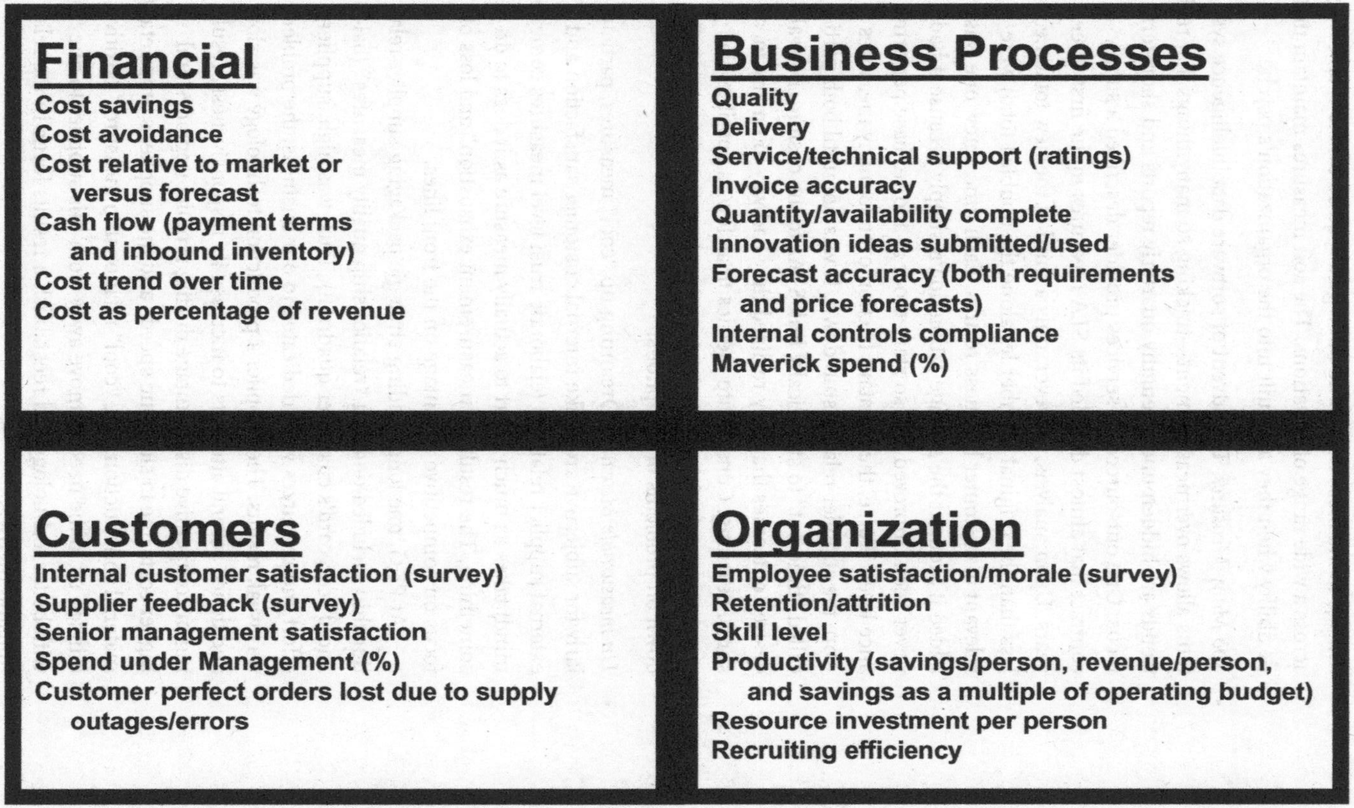

Financial
Cost savings
Cost avoidance
Cost relative to market or versus forecast
Cash flow (payment terms and inbound inventory)
Cost trend over time
Cost as percentage of revenue

Business Processes
Quality
Delivery
Service/technical support (ratings)
Invoice accuracy
Quantity/availability complete
Innovation ideas submitted/used
Forecast accuracy (both requirements and price forecasts)
Internal controls compliance
Maverick spend (%)

Customers
Internal customer satisfaction (survey)
Supplier feedback (survey)
Senior management satisfaction
Spend under Management (%)
Customer perfect orders lost due to supply outages/errors

Organization
Employee satisfaction/morale (survey)
Retention/attrition
Skill level
Productivity (savings/person, revenue/person, and savings as a multiple of operating budget)
Resource investment per person
Recruiting efficiency

linkage to business needs and strategies require constant tailoring across a wide range of situations. The soft measures maintain that flexibility when they are built into the organization's psyche.

- *Too Many Measures.* The advent of software data intelligence systems allows overmeasurement—tracking so many things that real trends are hidden under lengthy quarterly reports and short-term focus. One outsourced IT services provider described a supply contract that almost doubled its SLA measures in the first three years. Upon analysis, however, only a third of the new total (i.e., less than the original number let alone the doubled total) were relevant to customer business results. Each time a new one was added it brought the average rating down simply because it had never been improved and so started out at a lower base performance level. Worse, the constant friction over so many measures wore the supplier relationship down. It was not until both parties called "time out" to statistically link SLAs to the customer's real desired outcomes that they realized they had way too many measures. Learning: Consolidate metrics to as few as possible, tie them to meaningful results, and use the remaining data to drill down on problems or exceptions.

- *Un-measurable Measures.* Dreaming up "cool" measures, particularly for subjective areas like internal customer satisfaction and external supplier relations (elaborate trust level measures come to mind) takes as much effort to actually measure as it does to do something. The result is "measurement exhaustion" and loss of focus on competitive advantage on the front lines.

  At P&G, one longstanding strategic packaging supplier relationship included ongoing "relationship quality measures" (balanced scorecard's customer quadrant). Trust was high, supplier effort and resources were dedicated to our business; the problem was weak results. The supplier's production technology was slow and defied several attempts to increase its responsiveness, resulting in competitive disadvantage during product upgrades and higher costs due to slow line speeds and the supplier's proprietary material construction. The "cool" relationship measures' positives blinded us to the need to move away from this supplier to one with better technology and reestablish a results focus in the relationship metrics.

- *Misleading Average Measures.* Experienced supply professionals know how misleading averages can be. However, statistics and numbers can be correct and still lie. Don't be fooled into citing high average delivery numbers only to be confronted with real business shortfalls. Supply delivers results when everything is at the right place, at the right time, in the right quantity, at the right quality, at a competitive cost. That means that one outage makes perfection elsewhere irrelevant. Nominally high numbers like 98 percent availability need to be looked at from the down side (the number of misses the 2 percent represents). Organizational metrics that look great on the surface because the law of averages makes them look good can hide serious problems. Ultimately the business outcomes, not functional averages, count. (That's where Six Sigma's detail mentality has real merit.) Value is always in the eyes of the customer, not in a set of internal numerical metrics. Customers are not "averages." Taking the time to periodically correlate metrics to real-world results as customers see them is well worth the effort.

- *Poorly Thought-Through Metric Outcomes.* Metrics can be insidious because they drive behavior. What on the surface seems a simple result metric pushes a company away from its customers. A "low-cost producer" or "high-reliability provider" focus can single-mindedly drive the metric in question to the exclusion of the rest of the value equation. More subtly, single-dimension focus leads to a "metric at any cost" mentality and short-term heroes who sacrifice medium- and long-term outcomes. Ask the U.S. auto industry what years of cost pressure have done to its supply base as they reluctantly "donate" money to keep afloat suppliers they had squeezed mercilessly. While writing this chapter I read with interest that General Motors, in an effort to resolve a key supplier labor dispute at American Axle (a supplier with an excellent track record until a divisive labor dispute in early 2008 caused shutdowns and production slowdowns at thirty GM plants), offered $200 million to help fund American Axle employee early retirements to break the negotiation impasse.[12] Not the first time an automaker had to inject cash into a supplier to keep it running.

Early in my career, I had fixed price contracts in a market much like today's (soaring commodity prices for an unexpectedly long time). Suppliers asked for price relief as they lost money. For a while we declined the requests, per our contracts, but as the preponderance of evidence showed supply base damage, we chose to relent. We approached each supplier and offered a tailored level of relief (not always the full market value) despite our contract language. Without internal discussion at the highest levels this would have been folly in that cost-charged atmosphere. Response from that supply base to our business needs over the next couple years was amazing.

By the way, our business kept growing because when our competition faced the same cost pressures, they apparently did not handle the inevitable outcome with as much mutuality of approach and faced supplier backlash when things turned around. The intervention, early in the cost cycle before too much damage to the supply base, gave a different outcome than the U.S. auto industry's dilemma today. It still comes down to balance and the creation of a measurement system that encourages thinking about the right balance at a particular point in time, not just about maximizing a single dimension like cost reduction.

The most frustrating area I have faced is the mindless mantra of many supply professionals that the only cost metric that matters is year-on-year "real" cost reduction. That simplistic approach is great in loose or even balanced markets or when the firm is at a cost disadvantage versus competition, but it is a one-trick pony. At the time of this writing, commodity and energy prices were at record levels for food, fuel, metals, established low-cost country wages, and much more. Year-on-year cost reductions evaporated across many industries mid-decade (2004–08). Does that mean that the supply executives of those companies were all incompetent? Hardly. Since retiring I have had the chance to attend luncheons with financial analysts following P&G (a luxury unavailable when working full time). Analysts look hard at how cost movements (up or down) and cost trends (both raw material and overhead accounts) compare across competitors. The game is a combination of absolute cost, cost relative to customer expectations and budget constraints, cost direction and velocity, and, importantly, cost relative to competition.

Savings Measurement—Not Simple

A seemingly simple task, measuring supply cost, can erupt into arguments across companies and even within a single firm. The almost universal use of cost metrics to reward (and punish) procurement and supply management executives makes a deeper look worth our while. One major decentralized manufacturing company commissioned a study across nine independent business units to compare cost savings calculation rules. Leadership was surprised by the variation, ranging from differences in how savings were calculated (forecasted volume × price differential versus actual volume × price differential); recognition timing (driven by inventory, contract timing, and fiscal year calendar—annualized versus fiscal year versus cumulative); handling of cost avoidance, cost reduction, and cost increases; who got credit (whether savings from design modifications counted for technical groups or procurement; whether downward commodity market counted or upward moves should offset savings reported).

It took several months to work out a common system because finance in each business unit, as the final auditor of savings validity, often designed that unit's approach. The down side to cross-functional involvement was the addition of a second opinionated group to the savings calculation debate.

Market conditions drive how cost plays out—a fact forgotten during the loose supply of the 1990s and early 2000s. Cost metrics must be relevant to the firm's business and financial needs, and must work whether markets are escalating or de-escalating. This leads to using a series of metrics, not just one.

Year-on-Year Cost Reduction

While the volume figure in the "price difference × volume" equation is debatable, this is the "gold standard" because it tracks real money that shows up in the profit line (if not spent elsewhere). Close collaboration between supply and finance are critical to clarifying the volume part of the calculation. More sophisticated companies embed supply price reductions into profit forecast and business budget processes item by item. In overhead budgets, where line item management is less common, finance (not supply!) needs to lead the process to communicate supplier cost reductions to general management for conscious decisions about whether to "invest" those savings elsewhere in the overhead department or take them to the bottom line.

Marketing services spend reductions are a particularly good example. Is the right decision to save the money (profit) or to invest it in additional marketing events/programs (revenue, hopefully with profit)? This is a management decision, but supply and finance together need to highlight incremental funds, recognize the supply base as their source, and introduce the discussion. Regardless of whether the cost reduction flows directly to the profit line, they do represent how suppliers enhance business value.

Cost Relative to Market/Cost Avoidance

This much-maligned measure is the basis for cost avoidance, a "credibility eroder" for many supply organizations. If supply delays or reduces cost increases in an escalating market, the reported "savings" will not show up in company financials. Ludicrous "theoretical" savings numbers that overshadow the company's real costs and camouflage increases destroy supply's ability to gain cross-functional and management support for supplier initiatives. Having said all that, cost avoidance and controlling cost escalations below market levels (and de-escalations at above market levels) are valid and important measures. They just aren't "savings"—and shouldn't be counted as such.

For ongoing purchases, understanding where you are relative to the market provides valuable perspective for the company's overall business value proposition. The absolute dollar difference versus market is not the point. Very few market indices or public prices are accurate. Your value proposition is trend related. It is built in part on the cost denominator of value (see Chapter 1). As cost increases or decreases, the value equation shifts. Understanding how you move relative to the market and your competitors is vital to understanding your value's competitive standing.

For new products, negotiation, value analysis, and material-efficient design take cost out before launch. That, too, will never show up as cost reduction in the income statement, yet it makes far more sense than to launch at a higher cost, incur premiums, only to get credit for "real" savings later.

Two provisos about cost avoidance are:

1. Describe it as avoidance not savings/reduction to avoid management cynicism.
2. Finance must endorse the measure and provide oversight to verify that avoidance "start points" are not artificially high, which will make supply look good internally but will disadvantage the corporation in the real business environment.

Cost Relative to Competition

While important, this is also the toughest to measure (face it, competitors won't tell you their cost so you can benchmark against it). Like target and should cost analysis, this effort requires extensive cross-functional or external expert support. Product design reverse-engineers competitive products to understand ingredient or component differences. Finance provides insight from competitor financial reports on cost of goods sold/external overhead trends, and supply professionals add commercial input about the identity of competitors' suppliers and design of competitor's supply chains, often drawing information from their own suppliers about those suppliers' competitors.

External consultants and industry intelligence firms can provide great intelligence (e.g., iSuppi Corp. in electronics; CMAI in chemicals and energy, the *Journal of Commerce* for import price records). Many services and industry-specific consultants can be engaged—for a fee. For particularly strategic markets and major competitors, willingness to invest can help to build savvy about competitors.

However, many companies won't or can't devote resources to this. In such cases, my suggestion is that you always assume competitors are at least as competent as you are, maybe more so. A major mistake is assuming your volume has inherent advantage or that only you are talented enough to cut a great deal. Neither is a bankable assumption. Procurement organizations with less scale are likely to shop harder for extra value and/or select suppliers that match their operations well. Underestimating competitors without compelling confirmatory data to support that assumption is a grave error.

—Practitioner's Take—

The cost measurement lessons to keep in mind are:

1. Alignment with finance is critical both to audit results and communicate with one voice to senior management.
2. Balance the three cost measures, (1) year-on-year actuals, (2) cost avoidance relative to market indices or initial suppplier proposals, and (3) cost relative to competition. In buyers' markets year-on-year real reduction matters most, both in the absolute and relative to competition. Avoidance and measures relative to forecasted costs, market, and competitors are important in understanding differential versus competitors, why they exist, and what you are doing right. In a sellers' market, beating the market via a below-market increase, especially relative to competition, directly impacts your business value proposition. The absolute dollar increases give cost push input to pricing decisions for your products as well as targets for cross-functional value analysis, product design, and Lean and Six Sigma efforts with suppliers.

3. Define the difference between cost savings and cost avoidance. Then be rigorous in following and communicating those differences correctly.

4. Finally, cost management targets are "minimum goals." In other words, if you hit the targets, don't stop there. The difference between a mindset of doing the best possible and just hitting the target is the difference between an "okay" supply organization and one that gets competitive advantage.

This chapter talked a lot about supply organization skill and health. While important, supply alone is insufficient to gain competitive advantage. Too often the goal is a world-class supply management function. That is not enough. It does provide a focal point for viewing the supply base strategically, a reservoir of supplier management skills, and ownership for the mindset that suppliers matter. However, to harness suppliers for competitive advantage requires more than expertise in supply management skills. It also relies on functional expertise from other areas.

Notes

1. Gene Richter, "Centralize!," *Purchasing*, February 6, 2003.

2. Greg Spray, "High Performance Through Procurement: Accenture Research and Insights into Procurement Performance Mastery," presentation of September 2007 Accenture Survey at the NAPP Conference, February 11, 2008.

3. Deloitte Consulting, "Effective Commodity Management: A Source of Competitive Advantage," October 2007.

4. Philip L. Carter, Joseph R. Carter, Robert M. Monczka, John D. Blascovich, Thomas H. Slaight, and William J. Markham, "Succeeding in a Dynamic World: Supply Management in the Decade Ahead," a joint research initiative of CAPS Research, Institute of Supply Management, and A. T. Kearney, Inc; copyright Institute for Supply Management and W. P. Carey School of Business at Arizona State University, 2007.

6. Tim Minihan, "Nokia: Journey to a Center-Led Supply Organization." Supply Excellence Blog, November 28, 2006.

7. David P. Hanna, *Designing Organizations for High Performance* (Addison-Wesley OD Series) (Englewood Cliffs, N.J.: Prentice-Hall, 1988).

8. Steve Rogers, "Supply Management: Six Elements of Superior Design," *Supply Chain Management Review*, April 2004.

9. Lizbeth Yacovone, "Organizational Design for a Supply Chain Transformation: Best Practice at Johnson & Johnson Health Care Systems, Inc.," *Organization Development Journal,* Fall 2007.

10. Pierre Mitchell, "How Procurement and Supply Management Drive Competitive Advantage," presentation with *Supply Chain Management Review,* webcast December 21, 2007.

11. Robert S. Kaplan and David P. Norton, *The Balanced Scorecard: Translating Strategy into Action* (Cambridge, Mass.: Harvard Business School Press, 1996).

12. Terry Kosdrosky and Bhattiprolu Murti, "GM Offers $200 Million to End Supplier Strike," *Wall Street Journal,* May 9, 2008.

CHAPTER 9

Cross-Functional Collaboration

The Door to the Ultimate Differentiator

> DOOR: a movable, usually solid, barrier for opening and closing an entranceway.
>
> WINDOW: an opening in the wall of a building for the admission of air or light, or both.

No employer today is independent of those about him. He cannot succeed alone, no matter how great his ability or capital. Business today is more than ever a question of cooperation.

—Orison Swett Marden, American author and founder of *Success* magazine

This chapter may be the most important one in this entire book. Companies that delegate their supplier interactions solely to one or two functions to manage are unlikely to use suppliers to sustain their competitive position over time. They can have periods of good, even excellent, performance, but, as we have tried to explain, that's different than having a competitive position that is renewed and sustained by proactive supplier management.

Just as the design of a house or an office building includes areas that enable movement, logical flow between specific rooms, entrance and exit capability, and the ability to see the environment outside the structure, a supply-based advantage strategy needs comparable capability. The mindset of the organization needs to embrace suppliers as a way to beat competition and delight customers. To do that requires cross-functional belief in the premise that suppliers can make a difference. The access to that cross-functional belief parallels the inclusion of doors, windows, hallways, atriums, and foyers/waiting rooms in a building. The ability to flow the right cross-functional expertise into the supplier interface with an aligned view toward its value potential is the differentiator. Famous architects craft transition areas, windows, and doors into their design such that they differentiate the resulting building.

Note that I did not use the terms "cross-functional team" or "cross-functional involvement." The concept here is stronger. It's about cross-functional *belief* that drives inclusive planning, action, internal collaboration, and external engagement. As mentioned before, cross-functional teams often form to pick suppliers but seldom live beyond the selection process. The groups that truly manage the supply base are typically the procurement, contract management, and, at a very tactical/transaction level, the internal recipient of the suppliers' products. While better than organizations in which the supply deal makers toss the contract over the wall to those who must actually live it, such an event-based cross-functional involvement is not enough to sustain advantage. Corporate teams are too often temporary and supply is a far more permanent business process.

Having an aligned corporate mindset that embraces suppliers as part of a business solution for customers allows far more latitude for the use of supplier capability. While it's still important to have a group that views managing the external supplier interface as its reason for being, such organizations are often relatively small given the natural leverage that volume aggregation and supplier consolidation provide. Such an outnumbered cadre in a company where the view toward suppliers is that of a necessary evil, or a convenient excuse for performance outages, makes supply-based competitive advantage hard to attain systemically. More often, integrating supplier and internal skills is an exception in a specific, narrow application area. Having said all that, the challenge is to change the corporate cultural mindset to see suppliers as a strategic business intervention.

Start at the Top

Virtually every supply management article or book urges creation of a business case for use in selling strategic sourcing to senior management. As stated in Chapter 4, C-level executives often set the tone for how firms see suppliers and their level of strategic importance during varying business conditions. In a presentation about the economic importance of supply chain outcomes to business success, Office Max's Executive Vice President of Supply Chain, Reuben Stone, made an important point—that the importance of supply must be continuously justified to the CEO.[1]

Why? In part, because the supply side of the business involves operational details that require cross-functional integration at the working levels, a view of the company that most CEOs seldom get, given their position and other responsibilities. Another reason is that supply vocabulary often does not match the language of senior management and needs translation into terms (both financial and strategic) that "click" with upper-level concerns. Too often words like "savings" do not translate into the financial statements directly and supply goals focus on the obvious functional role of cost or price management.

Other functions like marketing and customer service focus more on the "performance" side of value. It is this side of the business model that drives growth, and growth is the success mantra for investors. The ability to create C-level executive commitment lies beyond doing the expected (cost management) and, instead, allying with other functions to deliver what, for supply management, is considered the unexpected (revenue improvement, innovation, customer delight, enhanced corporate reputation).

Bob Rudzki, former CPO at Bayer Chemical and Bethlehem Steel and currently president of Greybeard Advisors, LLC, has studied the interface between suppliers and business success at length. He repeatedly makes the point that selling supply management's business value to senior management is critical. He views a key component of supply leadership as the ability to communicate supply's compelling business case to the firm as a strategic asset.[2]

To do this requires understanding what CEOs must accomplish to get high ratings in their jobs. Senior executives get to stay employed when they:

1. Meet or exceed growth and earnings expectations of investors and product expectations of customers.

2. Deliver sustained growth in volume and earnings year over year.

3. Navigate business risks in ways that avoid negative outcomes and keep stakeholders (not just shareholders) satisfied.

4. Evolve company business models to stay ahead of competition.

5.   Improve capital productivity and return on invested capital.

6.   Lead the formulation and execution of a business growth strategy.

Supply's task is to persuasively make the case that suppliers are part of what makes *all* those outcomes possible, not just one or two. Unfortunately, most CEOs see supply as a role player in the first, third, and maybe even the fifth items above; not one of the starting team and certainly not a star player.

That's where Rudzki's argument comes in. Focus on the obvious "role player" opportunity of supply management—cost management—and then communicate results in CEO/CFO financial language that lays out the strategic implications of cost management.

The key financial outcomes include earnings per share, free cash flow, and return on invested capital. A firm's financial performance is the great enabler, allowing investment in marketing, new products, and acquisitions when it's good and the great disabler when it's bad. Just before declaring bankruptcy retailer Linens 'n Things had to use its cash to prepay suppliers in order to keep its shelves stocked. Within a month, bankruptcy was filed because miracles seldom happen. Store improvements and merchandise upgrades require cash and credit access, something Linens just did not have. When the suppliers desert their customers by refusing to offer credit, the end is near.[3]

The ability to link supplier-driven results to strategic financial measures gets the supply organization a seat at the table as a strategic contributor. It gains supply management two vital perks from senior leadership—legitimacy and resources. Legitimacy in terms of organizational importance to provide the political power that allows internal influence. (Be careful how that power is used—more on that at the end of this chapter.) Resources in terms of having supply priorities get past the early budget triage so they are actually debated at the real approval level.

—Practitioner's Take—

As we said already, this kind of business case creation is discussed in every book, article, and presentation about making supply management strategic. However, single-minded focus on financials is still not enough. In fact, it can create the price = value pitfall we discussed in Chapter 1. Furthermore, cost reduction is not an eternal benefit. The law of diminishing returns eventually sets in. So do the laws of supply and demand—low prices eventually beget high prices and high prices eventually beget low prices. The cycle time is typically the great unknown. Taking an ineffective and inefficient supply base to a better place will deliver financial results even in tough markets like those we are seeing in the mid-first decade of this century.

That is why the financial case is not enough and often will not sustain a supply organization's legitimacy over the long run, which is the basis for sustained competitive advantage. It is valuable in the initial "transformation" from a niche function with a tactical, "we provide service not business perspective" organization to one that "gets" the business connection to suppliers. But the quick alchemy of transformation is not enough. Markets turn and the true value of supply to top management had better be more than just cost based.

Two lessons flow from this discussion relative to gaining senior management support.

1. Results are worth more than promises in a business case.
2. Stage two of the journey goes beyond cost.

Lead with Results

Supply can be elevated in companies in a number of ways: senior leaders that "get it" and expect it; a crisis that requires suppliers to help and thus creates visibility; and markets that create windows of strategic importance that are seized before they are closed by market equilibrium. All those have senior leadership "pull." Many organizations don't have that luxury. It is about supply "push." If the internal politics and senior leadership mindset are just not there, business results need to lead. Track record becomes the resumé for supply organizations that want to be "hired" into the strategic leadership circle.

In the early 1990s at P&G, procurement was buried in a manufacturing-dominated supply chain organization with the result that the suppliers had no presence at the business strategy level. Manufacturing-bred supply chain leaders spoke about supply base issues (often in generalities or as an assumed "given") in business planning discussions. Senior management seldom interfaced with supply management.

A cadre of purchasing leaders across business units and geographies met to try to change that. These leaders believed that sourcing globally across independent business units would deliver huge results. The supply chain leaders saw it as something that couldn't hurt but was not as critical as manufacturing reliability. And so "global sourcing" made it into supply chain strategy. General management bought the theory but opposed having their resources work on somebody else's business. Net, as long as purchasing could guarantee no one else's priorities would be adversely impacted, it was an okay thing to do but probably not a game changer. The savings that were promised were huge—the goal was to use global sourcing as a driver to deliver dramatic economic business results (nine-figure cost reduction per year for at least three consecutive years) but the expectations about delivery were moderate (a project with high return but high degree of difficulty).

Within two years the financial results began to hit the radar screen in finance, manufacturing, and general management. The cost reductions and supplier responsiveness improvements began to dwarf other supply chain initiatives initially believed to be far more important. That sparked senior level interest in supplier management.

The supply management leadership conducted frequent sourcing strategy reviews and cross-business unit phone discussions that evolved the plan. The strategy that emerged looked like the following:

1. *Create Organizational Capability.* This involved procurement leadership alignment, skill definition and training, and dedicating strong players to the effort despite the organizational pain that entailed

2. *Partially Align with the Existing Organizational Structure.* We chose to "go global" by business across the world so there was a basic alignment at the market and supplier level with the businesses, even though regional and country profit centers were independent and there was no formal mandate from senior management for their people to cooperate.

3. *Seek Cross-Functional Allies.* In this case they were (1) an "orphan" group within the product development (R&D) organization called "technical buying services" that maintained quality, qualified new suppliers, and managed/rationalized specifications; and (2) supply chain finance, which was asked to audit the results for credibility purposes (they were surprised and happy to be asked) and who, given their function, cared about cost reduction.

4. *Deliver Results and Worry about Senior Management Recognition Later.* Recognition for those actually leading the work could come

from purchasing leadership—it did not formally come from other organizations for almost two years.

5. *Use the Delivery of Financial Results to Seek a Seat at Leadership's Business Strategy Table.* Interestingly, at first we thought this meant being formally made part of the strategic leadership team, which would have flown in the face of the supply chain organization structure in the business units. General managers resisted making their leadership teams bigger—they saw that precedent as dangerous to decision-making processes and leadership team size/effectiveness. What we learned was that access to the table is not about formal lines and boxes; it is about getting the call and having management's ear for input and information. Some businesses made procurement a member of the team and others didn't. The key was that suppliers and external supply strategy became part of the business strategy discussion and was handled by the market experts, not a hierarchical leader one level removed from the suppliers.

While this overall strategy has learnings—including the importance of talent, aligning with business structures to avoid unnecessary conflict, and getting internal allies that matter—the major point is that the fourth strategy (get results) had to precede the fifth (get management's ear).

Look Beyond Financial Results

Once supply makes the strategic function list, it opens itself to a new, significant risk. Once the "easy" low-hanging fruit have been picked, sustaining cost reduction is very difficult, especially when markets turn against you. If supply is completely defined as the cost reduction function, eventually significant additional supplier value will be lost and supply leadership will be at risk.

Additionally, even in buyers' markets, once senior management "gets" the value of suppliers, cost reduction becomes the base expectation, and the question becomes what else can be done? To sustain the long run, supply needs to add non-financial measures to the scorecard:

- Leveraging supplier capabilities that improve corporate effectiveness, not just efficiency, particularly via outsourcing as a means to move to a new level of performance, not just as a cost savings.

- Gaining unique access to supplier innovation skills, intellectual property, external contacts, and new product roadmaps.

- Enhancing risk management, both in terms of supply continuity and corporate reputation (i.e., product safety, green-climate change and environmental impact, labor standards, etc. in the supply base).

- Ensuring supply market input into business plans/strategy. Every time I see a corporate leader say that commodity or purchased material/service "headwinds" erased expected cost savings and led to an earnings expectation miss, I lay the blame at the feet of his/her supply leader. Companies that consistently deal with adverse supply markets have integrated supply market forecasts into their business plans—witness repeated jet fuel hedging coups by Southwest Airlines or the increased profitability of General Mills in early 2008 despite record grain price levels and its ability to explain reduced profits later in the same year to analysts as markets dropped lower than its hedged price levels. Those CEOs were in touch with supply markets—and their supply leaders were proactive in communicating potential market moves early enough to be incorporated in the business plan and stock analyst communications.

- Leveraging supplier presence in new geographies to support and advise on geographical expansions, regulatory issues, and competitive analysis. Provide senior management a window on market conditions via contact with senior supplier management.

- Incorporating supply strategy and preferred supplier relationships into the business plan to ensure supply availability during shortage markets.

Net, managing suppliers as an asset portfolio in addition to a cost portfolio broadens supply's business impact and expectations with senior management.

Top Is Not Enough

Support and legitimacy from senior management is, unfortunately, not enough at most companies. CEOs want their business and functional leaders to manage their businesses for results. If those executives are not convinced that suppliers can deliver strategic advantage, even senior management support will not force them to engage suppliers beyond the traditional approaches and, therefore, competitive advantage from the supply base will never hit the radar screen.

Supply executives often try to take over the supplier relationship activities and competitively bid the contracts of longstanding suppliers that other functions see as important. Such frontal assaults rarely work. The logic that "professional procurement" will bring value versus the "amateurs" that manage suppliers in their spare time is not persuasive to peer organizations, which see those same suppliers as trusted partners or as possessing unique technical or operational capabilities. Spends like senior level consulting, marketing agencies, software and hardware technology providers, legal services, financial auditors, and banks are frequently selected and managed by the internal customers of their services. These people are fiercely loyal to long-term suppliers they trust, and understand how these suppliers interface with their work.

Interestingly, integrating suppliers into the business is a function of three fundamental things:

1. Knowing how to apply supply skills.
2. Knowing your business and the supplier's business and understanding how the supplier's business impacts your own.
3. Knowing the supplier and its people well.

These internal functions possess the latter two of these three attributes, so seeking to wrest control away from them and give it to supply skill experts with no deep appreciation of the other two areas is often a formula for failure. Instead, the strategy should be to leverage what the internal customers already have while injecting some of what they lack. Create an alliance for value rather than a struggle for control.

The goal is to make the entire company, not just the disciplines that manage supply, a means to deliver competitive advantage through their interactions with suppliers. This is about culture and mindset change. Not-invented-here thinking across non-supply disciplines is the biggest barrier to supply-based advantage once the supply organization has reached a basic level of competence. Overcoming it requires a combination of the four supply skill sets from Chapter 8 (Analysis, Synergysis, Genesis, and Systemesis) applied internally.

Analysis—Segment the Internal Landscape

Because supply is a small function relative to others in most companies, marshaling and deploying resources is critical. The first step is to triage the internal organization's ability to manage supplier-provided value. Typically, where the internal customer has little or no skill, problems arise, either in terms of performance issues, cost overruns, or internal control gaps. Functions with a basic commonsense understanding of how to work with outside companies typically get value—maybe not the maximum but value nonetheless.

Several years ago I was talking with a supply executive from Kraft Foods at a purchasing conference. She explained their triage system for assigning scarce supply resources to spend areas they had traditionally not been involved with. It made sense. Based on supplier performance (both relative to objective measures and subjective user opinions), cost management (relative to budget/profit pressures), and control (internal auditing results), the internal organizations fell into four camps. The procurement organization used these groupings to "touch" all suppliers, by tailoring how the supply group interfaced with those internal customers' needs for help. Using a golfing analogy, the groupings were:

Group 1—Consistently in the fairway. These internal customers were effectively managing their supply base and naturally understood the balance between competition and collaboration as mechanisms to get value. The supply approach was to praise the work, seek to learn from it, stay in contact, and add value if asked. In a nutshell—recognize good work and use it to create an internal ally.

Group 2—Generally around the fairway or in light rough. These disciplines generally delivered acceptable value. They were less skilled in supply selection and management, but had good suppliers and elevated performance over personal relationships when managing supplier outcomes. They understood when they were okay and when they were in over their heads. The supply approach was consulting to help solve problems or make supply base changes. In a nutshell—supply on-the-job training for the users when requested. In a crisis, supply was often asked into the business to help.

Group 3—In the rough, at the edge of the trees or in a sand trap. These disciplines were struggling. Often what had worked in the past was no longer acceptable due to business changes, supplier leadership/ownership changes, or an erosion of supplier capability. Value was deteriorating to levels below those necessary to effectively or efficiently do the work. The supply approach was close coaching, sometimes even "player coach" status. This involved a more significant resource allocation, but more in a teaching mode to develop the internal customer's skills to deal with change and problems. In a nutshell—help the customer do the work better through coaching and oversight, pitching in when needed. Again, in a crisis supply people were fully engaged.

Group 4—Lost ball in high weeds or deep woods. These folks were in trouble. Sometimes they knew it (due to poor supplier results) but often they were clueless because long-term personal relationships or tradition rather than real business needs were driving interactions, and performance expectations were colored by those friendships or traditional inertia. Here was where supply needed to insert itself proactively. For those who knew they were in trouble this was quite workable—supply looked like help. For the clueless, this is the frontal assault and is best handled in concert with other internal allies (more on that later). Sorry, no nutshell here.

Synergesis: Helping the Customer Leverage Supplier Competencies Better

The first two triage groups often fall here. This is an organizational "court-ship" process in which supply strives to look like help not interference, builds the customer's self-sufficiency in a way that keeps contact strong going forward, uses resources efficiently, and leverages customer ownership for the supplier relationship to improve supply-based value for the business. Often one of the key value levers supply can provide is linkage with other functions/ business units that use the same supplier. This creates volume leverage, cross-business cooperation or cross-fertilization opportunities, and higher level supplier management access.

Supply needs to live up to any promises/commitments made, report back on outcomes, help the customer look good, provide some education or training to help the customer improve its supplier management, help the customer know when to call in experts (you), and help the customer better utilize the knowledge it already has (the technical or operational aspects of the supplier's work and how it applies to the business).

Where supply involvement needs to be more ongoing, the sales pitch is freeing internal customer time to focus on their core competency without trying to limit or stop their ability to work closely on the business with key suppliers.

Genesis: Create New Beginnings for Supplier Management and Value

This skill application is about innovation regarding how an internal function changes its approach to its supply base. It typically happens where supplier performance is in question (typically groups 3 and 4 above) and the genesis involves more direct supply involvement in the other function's business. It means dedicating supply resources, building internal customer expertise so they remain engaged but at a higher skill level, and sometimes investing in new supplier relationships (sourcing new suppliers) or intense supplier governance interventions. At times this requires leveraging senior management support or enlisting allies within the function in question or from other influential power functions within the company (like finance, legal, or marketing).

Systemesis: Broad Internal Mindset That Sees Suppliers as Value

This is the most important element of evangelizing supply-based advantage across the firm. The skills learned here are necessary to make interconnections across functions and businesses internally. Its absence is what makes frontal assaults rarely work. Making a peer function lose face is not the way to establish a strong cross-functional understanding that will endure. Instead, it leaves a strong motive for revenge when, inevitably, the ebb and flow of corporate politics raises them and lowers you in the eyes of senior management.

The internal customer often sees realities that the procurement or supply management organization misses. Seeking a combination of both supply and users makes far more sense. Help users save face and get credit for good supplier involvement in their business while staying engaged with them as an ally.

—Practitioner's Take—

Leveraging opportunities to help solve peer organizations' supplier problems is the first step to creating joint situational decision-making processes that get the most out of suppliers. One supply management executive (who has asked to remain anonymous) tells a story at his company that involves one of those politically charged spends that supply typically has to fight to be involved with: the printing of the annual report. At this firm, the finance and external relations organizations owned this process, using the same supplier for years.

Gradually the supplier's costs climbed and its dedication to capital and information technology changes in the custom printing industry fell. One day the supply executive's phone rang with a request for help.

The people managing this supplier were frustrated. Their management was unhappy with the supplier's recent cost submission and the prior year's experience had been difficult due to last-minute changes to the report's content. The call came at a typical time—well after supplier selection and a couple weeks before the work process of design and layout was to begin. It was clear from the body language in the meeting that engaging supply was a last resort on their part. They feared that procurement would step in, choose a different supplier at the last minute, and create chaos.

The supply executive, rather than confronting their mistakes, spent the time exploring what value looked like and how they felt the supplier fit into that value proposition. He also suggested that they continue handling the supplier relationship but with coaching from him. After a supplier performance review (done by external relations and finance but planned by the supply executive) the supplier returned with a 20 percent lower cost and some suggestions for better response. Customer management was quite happy, but the supply executive explained that the response left a lot of value on the table and that if the internal customers wanted to tap it next year they needed to start earlier. The project ended and the supply leader went back to his very full plate.

Six months later the phone rang again. The internal customer asked if they were early enough. They had found the prior year's experience using the supply organization not only painless, but one for which their management gave them praise. A sourcing strategy and supplier relationship plan were established (including a discussion with the owner of the supplier who was unaware of the customer's discontent; and exploration of annual report printers, which supplied other companies with comparable reports that senior management and investor relations saw as excellent). Costs collapsed another 60 percent (six figures), the incumbent supplier invested in more up-to-date technology and agreed to collaborate with one of the other printers on the technological end. Within another year, supply had embedded a person in the customer organization, at its request, to work on much larger spends. Moral of the story—honey draws more bees than vinegar and putting yourself in the shoes of your customers creates the honey.

Companies do not stand still. Neither do functions within them.

Sometimes the supply organization's skills erode and the prior investment in peer functions' cross-functional commercial skill can make a difference. Talent loss or leadership changes can result in almost unconscious expertise loss. A good friend represents a supplier that makes an energy efficiency product that, given the new reality in energy prices, makes real sense for many companies. He approached a casual restaurant chain with which he had extensive experience. The restaurant company had recently brought in a new senior procurement executive from the outside whose definition of value was clearly price. The reaction was "lower the price 20 percent and maybe we'll talk." Anyone familiar with restaurant operations understands the impact of high energy costs on the business. Food and labor costs get the headlines, but a way to use less energy and extend the life of restaurant appliances provides a cost infrastructure advantage that is invisible to competition and thus contributes to market advantage.

The procurement executive would not even return calls and, through his secretary, refused to grant an appointment. In frustration, the seller called two peer executives—the CFO (to whom the purchasing VP reported) and the CLO (Chief Legal Officer) to explain the opportunity. They connected internally with restaurant operations leadership, who quickly recognized the total cost of ownership potential. Within a week the purchasing VP granted the appointment and within a month a pilot test was underway. Most procurement executives call this "backdoor selling" (which it is) and fight it tooth and nail. However, in this case the previous supply executive had invested in peer organizations to develop a commercial sense for supplier value. It was this cross-functional expertise that allowed an opportunity to get past the "price = value" barrier. Hopefully the new VP will learn from this and seek to better integrate his people and supplier ideas into the value proposition of the business. If not, maybe this was a hiring mistake that needs correction. Short-term thinking simply allows survival, not growth.

Backdoor selling is the risk that comes with engaging in cross-functional supplier management that extends beyond the selection process. When it occurs it is important to understand why. In the case above, the procurement leader brought it on himself by not understanding value. Another source is a supply management organization that wants to control supplier contact with the company but does not have the resources to respond to internal customers in a timely fashion. Other functions have their work to do and suppliers often represent a key ingredient in that process. They will do what needs to be done if the supply organization itself becomes the bottleneck for workload or procedural reasons.

In other cases, it is a carefully crafted supplier sales strategy to avoid the commercial and economic considerations of the selection and management process and make "windfall" profit off a customer. Sometimes it is a mix of both. Creating the ongoing internal dialogue to determine the difference between internal customer "wants" and "needs" is critical to addressing backdoor selling.

Innovation Is a Cross-Functional Process

Innovation is the lifeblood of competitive advantage. A company that stands still in a competitive marketplace is probably moving backward. Engaging suppliers in value creation for the next idea, not just the current business, is part of what separates good use of suppliers from competitively advantaged use of suppliers. For direct spends this typically means working with product design and development.

Traditional supply management priorities (e.g., low-cost focus and control of supplier interfaces) are the predominant reasons product design/development (PD—also called engineering or R&D) often works around supply. Understanding what drives those organizations (new products that deliver more revenue from customers) means recognizing that the sourcing and supply management processes must integrate cost consciousness with vision about customer need and willingness to pay for value. Tapping suppliers can dramatically increase smart innovation.

In companies that do this well, procurement consistently makes the painful decision to carve off a few highly skilled resources from the current business supply organization and fully dedicate them to innovation work with PD. Why? Because the emergencies of the ongoing day to day—supply outages, cost pressures, quality issues—typically create urgency that causes the innovation work to move to the back of the queue, thus creating the environment for backdoor selling. Numerous studies over the last fifteen years make the same point. Eighty percent of a product's cost is designed into it on the front end. For this reason many procurement experts call innovation sourcing "early involvement." Buying innovation requires measures like cost avoidance and recognition that supply's role is broader than being a cost watchdog inside PD. Rather, it is to enable new product customer value (performance divided by cost) through use of suppliers at the right time in the product development cycle. Investment in real cross-functionality of mindset with R&D toward suppliers pays incredible dividends.

Ken Buell was one of P&G's top scientists, and was awarded Victor Mills Society recognition for his career development of baby care patents and product inventions. He often worked directly with suppliers, but his timing about bringing purchasing into a project was absolutely impeccable! He understood when to combine commercial and technical expertise and that early consideration of potential suppliers can allow more supplier options longer in the development process.

Invariably, Ken's call to say, "Steve, I am working on such-and-so. I think there are three or four technologies that might work and want to go check out the suppliers with you in the next couple weeks," was timed perfectly— sooner would have wasted my time and later destroyed commercial leverage. Ken "got it." His sixth sense for combining technical and commercial negotiations is the kind of understanding and skill, when positioned outside the supply function, that triggers competitive advantage.

One last thought—innovation is not just applicable to direct spends. Tapping into suppliers of infrastructure (IT, energy conservation), knowledge (market research, call centers, sales support), and surge capacity (temporary labor or outsourced service providers) all provide an opportunity to source innovation. The concept is the same—dedicate some resources that work with the internal customer's next-generation designers to provide a commercial and relationship framework for improved supplier access, commercial work processes, and the use of knowledge across the company (not just for new products). For example, new-generation servers and data center designs are of vital importance in lowering the cost of computing. Combining IT operational skills and savvy commercial negotiation can make a difference in the overhead costs of data management.

Three Internal Allies as Game Changers

Too often, the objective of the supply organization is to penetrate internal functions just to manage the money they spend with suppliers. Instead, consider the possibility that working closely with internal peer organizations can enhance the firm's ability to tap into suppliers. When other disciplines are enrolled in supply efforts elsewhere in the company, their openness to collaborate on their own budgetary spend is greater.

Three functions of particular importance on this front are finance, legal, and IT. In many firms the relationship between these three and supply leadership is strained at best. A firm's supplier interface often does not get any priority relative to internal and finished product customer-facing organizations. Changing that can have a powerful effect on the bottom line.

Finance: Collaborating Across the Full Function

For two functions that supposedly keep score in monetary terms and have the same goal (lower cost and increase profit), finance and supplier management have certainly had their differences. The rivalry is based on a few major conflict points:

> *Credibility.* The flow of actual costs through financial reports can result in very different savings claims. Procurement has a tendency to multiply price differences by forecasted volume and trumpet an immediate cost reduction. In fact, most firms leak some of the savings due to unexpected total cost of ownership problems, slow new supplier qualifications, and underlying commodity market moves that erase savings and replace them with cost avoidance. Then, forecasted volume and product mix rarely match reality—worse, for indirect spends, budget owners in every department can choose to spend purchased service savings on other items as long as the budget is met. Finance looks at fiscal years (not annualized) and finished goods inventory adjusted cost impacts (e.g., if there is sixty-day inventory of finished goods the reduced costs of raw materials will not show up in cost of goods sold actuals for two months). The result is constant haggling over the "real" savings in a world where the identified, implemented, and booked cost reductions are rarely the same number.

> *Policing.* In most companies, finance is charged with tracking the money and rewarded for either finding some or, at a minimum, identifying who should be finding it. Financial analysts map funds flow and identify gaps versus competition or best in class benchmarks. That puts supply organizations on the defensive with senior management—justifying why the circumstances in their company are not quite the same as in others. Given the cross-functional nature of most supplier-impacted business processes, sometimes benchmark gaps are as much the result of another function's approach to suppliers as it is what procurement or supply chain does. Add to that finance's internal controls responsibility to audit and insist on

improvements that, when applied to supply, raises all procurement's blemishes to the attention of the CFO.

Net, it is no surprise that a late 2007 Aberdeen Research study stated that fewer than 20 percent of CFOs view procurement as having a very positive influence on company competitiveness and 37 percent view procurement's impact as neutral to negative.[4] Given that about 30 percent of procurement organizations actually report to finance and about half the CPOs in the United States have finance experience, the pent-up frustration that such a result implies is shocking. Despite three fourths of the CFOs saying that supply management is strategic, only 6 percent dedicate a financial resource to supplier management, which represents well over half the money that flows out of the company. The logic and operational disconnects that this study expose make creating an internal alliance with finance vital to gaining competitive advantage from the supply base.

—Practitioner's Take—

My experience with finance is no different from the Aberdeen report. The relationship is often thorny, and requires constant maintenance to sustain productively. Yet, when done well, it is an enormous entrée to improved results. One way we approached this relationship was to dedicate a purchases director to be a contact point for the finance organization. The idea was to understand where the conflict points were and how to resolve them, as well as to get to know and cooperate with the leaders of the various financial subfunctions.

Three approaches gave the most payback. First was to request financial support in verifying all savings and, more importantly, cost avoidance numbers in every business unit. This is common among well-run procurement groups. The initiative grew into a collaboration to help gain financial support for supply management investments (software, headcount, budget) and the assignment of dedicated finance people to help with supplier management.

The second was to approach internal controls (IC) and request both an audit and their help with resolving any gaps the audit uncovered. The IC relationship had been rocky for years and their response to the request was surprise. As we corrected many of the outages and showed interest in elevating IC in our organizational measurement system, IC became an ally in helping to bring professional supplier management to many indirect spends that had fought procurement involvement. When an internal audit of an organization turned up a weakly managed "maverick spend," part of the recommended action plan proposed by IC was to connect with procurement and improve the supplier selection and management processes.

The last step in the process was to be responsive to requests for help from finance. When Sarbanes Oxley legislation was passed in 2002, the accounting organization asked for help with supplier commitment reporting. Links with treasury led to protocols to deal with currency devaluations and, later, to a joint treasury/procurement commodity hedging program. Line business financial analysts looking for help in their profit forecasting had access to commodity managers and were asked to help with supplier negotiations, especially when they involved underwriting or guaranteeing unique supplier capital investments. The tax organization sought help when acquisitions led to new corporate entities that had to be incorporated into supply agreements for tax reasons. The supply director responsible for the finance liaison was instrumental in addressing these requests and, with each response, the finance relationship became more solid.

Not every relationship was without conflict, but the joint involvement increased dramatically. Eventually, we incorporated a "finance for supply" course in our supply training program that was taught by finance and reciprocated with a supply/supplier risk management course in the finance functional college.

One key watch-out, however! This is not a maintenance-free process. Assuming that things are fine is a mistake. Financial pressures require the kind of gap analysis that can spark defensiveness on both sides. IC must call out issues, regardless of whether cooperation exists or not. In addition, personnel turnover often means the relationships have to be constantly rebuilt. If someone on either side fails to do so, the interface can quickly regress into conflict. Initiatives can rapidly erode and disappear as the individuals who perform the tasks are transferred and the responsibility to work internal bridges is not transferred to the new player. The issue lies on both sides of the functional boundary and must be mutually addressed at more senior levels.

Working well with finance involves much more than just speaking their language. It requires investing time and effort—focused on the business, not just the function. The results, both in terms of business results and internal image, are worth the effort.

Legal: The Contracting Alliance

"Contract management" has become a popular buzz phrase among supply professionals and internal controls/compliance auditors. It focuses on the delivery of the negotiated terms of a supply agreement to the bottom line and delivering against the business need that the buying company engaged the supplier to accomplish. The foundation of contract management is a strong relationship between supply and the legal organization. Unfortunately, legal and supply management are often not on the same page.

One (legal) is rewarded for reducing company risk in terms of strict interpretation of contracts and the ability to take that contract language into a courtroom or arbitration hearing and get a "win" under the law. The other (supply) is rewarded for getting the deal that delivers from suppliers what the company needs to compete, regardless of its power position relative to the supplier or market conditions at the time. Blending these two points of view through internal relationships and education is critical to establishing effective contracts with suppliers. The key is the definition of "effective"—is it about protection against supplier performance failure? Or is it about the flexibility to deal with business changes without major renegotiation? Both? In a conversation with Tim Cummins, President and CEO of IACCM (International Association for Contract & Commercial Management), he commented that IACCM studies have confirmed that the relationship between supply and legal is frequently strained.

Too often supply management practitioners see lawyers as a barrier to timely action in the market and the authors of language that is so confusing that the "normal" people that administer and "live" the contract are unable to understand it. On the other hand, the lawyers see supply using shoddy contract language with key risks and provisions omitted—often through ignorance. A situation in which the company has no recourse in tough circumstances results in management questions about where the legal people were during the negotiation.

Establishing an ongoing supply contract center of excellence by linking legal and supply experts is how a number of companies (including IBM, Steelcase, and P&G) have chosen to address this issue. This is no small task, for, just as different supply executives have different market views and philosophies toward supplier management, so too, individual lawyers often have strongly held interpretations of the law. Add to that the wide variation in local laws in a global marketplace and you have the makings of internal gridlock, where what one country's supply/legal team thinks is okay simply does not work for another country's team—all within the same firm.

Dedicating experienced and internally respected resources to the supply side of the value chain is only the first step in creating a legal/supply alliance that can get the best out of suppliers. Within that "center of excellence" there must be:

▶ *Commercially savvy approaches to the business—both sides have to be tied to the business need, strategy, and business model.* The point is to acquire what the business needs. Lack of availability means an operational breakdown.

▶ *Educated understanding of each other's work processes and how they play out in dynamic markets that change supplier leverage positions over time.* The best in class create both a dialogue between legal and supply as well as a training program that provides in-depth knowledge of various contract clauses—the what, why, and how of their workings for commodity managers.

▶ *Joint agreement on how flexible the company wants to be on certain legal clauses and issues.* Each company has its own risk appetite for the terms and conditions that can be compromised in a tough negotiation with a supplier who has the "power" in the relationship. For some firms, warranties and supplier quality guarantees are most important. For others in rapidly changing businesses, the ability to exit the contract may be vital. In yet other cases the legal jurisdiction or intellectual property definition/rights are most vital. These "must have" clauses are part of the company's culture and risk tolerance. Legal needs to take the lead here.

▶ *Commercial flexibility, which may be the most important part of the legal/supply interface.* Creating this flexibility includes putting clauses into easily understood "non-legalese," determining backup negotiating positions for each clause, and being clear on the legal boundaries beyond which the company will not go without very senior management review and concurrence—all this in terms of personal conduct and specific clauses. The global realities of various countries' legal systems must be mapped into a contract "library," and both functions' practitioners across the world must buy in to the internal agreements that have been forged.

▶ *An efficient process to work contract creation and approval.* If it doesn't already exist, it must be developed. While software has become an important tool in this effort, the work process that identifies when supply should draw legal into negotiations is even more valuable.

For a large company there are probably not enough lawyers to negotiate every contract. So, the delegation of authority to create and modify contracts before legal review must occur is a critical aspect of supply's use of contracts.

—Practitioner's Take—

A quick note from personal experience—while my lawyer friends may not appreciate this observation, I must say that the most troublesome and inflexible contracts I have had to deal with over my career were often those drafted by the attorneys rather than the business people. Besides being incomprehensible, they simply did not match the market conditions and changing value propositions of the business for either the supplier or my organization. They were probably great in a courtroom or for a particular point in time, but not in a dynamic commercial situation.

Interestingly, more than half the time the problem was with the supplier—it was their sales or sales contract management organization that was not empowered to do the deal. Provisions agreed upon at relatively high levels in negotiations were overruled by the supplier's legal organization. The impact on trust levels (belief that legal intervention was always part of the other side's negotiation strategy to extract still more concessions) and the pure workability of the contract were quite negative.

Getting clear on how legal's contract review authority connects with supply's (or sales') negotiation authority is a big part of enrolling legal into the search for competitive advantage from the supply base. Some companies are such powerful buyers that they can simply demand that suppliers sign their contract terms. Most firms do not have that luxury all the time. Allowing for give and take in the deal negotiation is critical to value creation. Deciding how much latitude is smart and when too much becomes risky and stupid is the crux of the legal/supply alliance's value proposition for the company.

Information Technology: Working Together to Use Information

In today's often virtual world, information and the ability to mine it, bundle it and use it are a big part of competitive advantage. This is especially true when dealing with external companies like suppliers and customers. Yet, the organization tasked with managing the flow of information, IT, often has a highly adversarial relationship with those looking to access supplier value. Why?

> *Partly Because of Vocabulary.* Having sat on the supply side of this relationship for years, the jargon of information technology is almost too hard to overcome. Plus it changes all the time as the technology rapidly evolves. Then the supply guys start using *their* jargon and the whole conversation becomes incomprehensible.

> *Partly Because of Perspective.* Much of what has been discussed on the supply side has put a premium on uniquely creating the right supplier connection to deliver value. This is not about standardization or simplification of the supplier interface. Instead, it is about customization and uniqueness on the most complex side of the supply chain (multiple tiers and a range of supply industries). When it comes to computers, software and data management infrastructure cries out for standardization. IT looks to make work processes conform to software rather than the other way around.

> *Partly Because of Rewards and Management Expectations.* IT is about information access, certainty, and predictability. The uptime of the computer system needs to be 100 percent. Management expectations are that cost needs to be low and reliability high—sort of like a utility, except one that has its "power plants" constantly changing design due to new inventions. A tough chore. Meanwhile, supply lives with uncertainty. Markets, suppliers, and supply/demand balances are not certain nor, in some cases, even predictable. Management expects cost reduction but also great flexibility. Supply's desire for ultimate information flexibility adversely impacts IT's cost control and reliability. IT's simplification and control adversely impacts supply's ability to get the information quickly enough and in the multiple formats needed to remain flexible and respond to real-world changes.

> *Partly Because of Priority Setting.* First call on information system capability in most companies is either internal (financials and human resources) or customer-focused users. That is why ERP (Enterprise Resource Planning—Oracle and SAP) systems were the first big software implementations for major corporations and why CRM software (Customer Relationship Management) led the development of

SRM systems by years rather than months. In the budget battle for information technology investment, the internal and customer sides of the business supply chain typically get the attention, while the supplier side languishes. In recent years on-demand "software as a service" that uses software provider server capacity has emerged as a partial answer to this problem. Still, transferring the data from these solutions into corporate systems takes some integration work and many IT departments are not prepared to support that resource investment—leading to conflict with supply management.

Yet, when these two functions choose to cooperate, the payback for the company and its ability to implement its business model are enormous. Joe Robinson is the Director of Central Operations at Fifth Third Bank. In a bank, operations have everything to do with information technology in terms of accurate processing of deposit, loan, lease, and debit/credit accounts. Prior to joining Fifth Third, Robinson spent several years with General Electric. He tells a story about his early career and the impact he, as an IT analyst, had on a GE business.[5]

He was asked by the procurement people at his location to undertake a data mining project to get some insight into what GE was buying from several suppliers—think of it as the early internal predecessor to spend analysis software products available today. One day he was asked to attend a meeting between GE's senior buyer and the president of a company named Champion Bolt. Bolts were one of the simple products that his data mining project addressed, finding significant volume across multiple sites. GE's procurement group used that information to gain a much improved agreement with Champion.

Over lunch, the GE buyer mentioned how happy he was with the data mining tool that Robinson had developed. He mentioned that it allowed GE to see all the business it was doing with Champion and consolidate its bolt contracts into a higher volume/lower cost set of agreements. Robinson recalls that the supplier's president glared at him without a word, "If looks could kill, I would have been dead! The project led to a big leverage shift and a major cost reduction." He remembers it as one of the most significant personal impacts he had on GE's business over the first eight years of his career.

The moral of the story? IT is core to the business in today's world and, when combined with smart supply strategies, can dramatically impact a firm's bottom line. That means finding a way through the differing perspectives of the two functions in order to move the business ahead. Sadly, many procurement groups are so focused on trying to take over control of sourcing

IT's supply base that they forget to use the knowledge and perspective they gain about IT's cost structural challenges and organizational priorities in the internal negotiation for IT resources and support.

—Practitioner's Take—

Throughout this chapter, the approach toward cross-functional alignment probably looks kind of "soft"—seeking to understand peer organization goals and then helping them achieve those targets through suppliers, without overtly trying to wrest control of the supplier interface away from the other function. That is not the theoretical textbook approach, which is more apt to move supply management control to the procurement or supply specialists, often via attempted mandates or political maneuvers.

My own experience with the "frontal assault" and "backroom political" approaches has not been good. If the goal is *business advantage*, not just a positive functional benchmark against other firms' supply functions, cross-functional peer organizations have to see suppliers as strategic success components for their success and strategic weapons for company success. The hurt feelings from internal control battles undermine the belief that supply and suppliers need to be incorporated into the corporate strategy. Instead they create tactical rivalry that is more about who is in charge than what can be gained more broadly.

Orchestrating such cross-functional alignment and belief is extremely difficult, even when it's the announced goal. Late in my career I was asked to lead a contract management software project. Procurement leadership had decided such a software tool was vital to our ability to improve our global supplier management and favorable contract negotiation capability. Finance also wanted the system as part of the corporate response to Sarbanes Oxley controls legislation in the United States. They saw a single repository of contracts as the best way to understand the impact of supplier commitments on the company's financials. The CLO was also in the boat—personally stressing the need and offering the support of his organization for the project. Sounds great, doesn't it?

However, the IT organization was embroiled in another major corporate initiative, to make our supply chain more consumer- and customer-driven—no small or unimportant task for a global company. The software budget process was set up so that functions (in this case procurement) submitted proposals—ours for the contract management project—and IT approved them (which was the case on this item). Importantly, IT owned the authority over the budget money, i.e., it was in the IT organization's budget not the procurement organization's and, while local mid-level IT people were in the loop, senior, global-level IT was not.

By the time we selected the software supplier we felt was best (jointly with local IT), we were several months into the budget year. Global IT leadership was not committed to the contract management project and, in the ensuing political squabble for resources, was outgunned by the other functions, whose involvement I solicited. Rather than meet to discuss the issues, the parties were driven by the urgency to get going as quickly as possible and a time limit on the supplier's software proposal, which we saw as very attractive. The project was funded over IT management's disagreement. In hindsight this "victory" was a mistake. Senior IT was never passionate about making the project work. Technical relationships with the supplier were strained. (I recall disagreements about the type of server that should hold the application—we used what we wanted, of course.)

Three years later (after I had left the company) my successor concluded the software was a failure, largely due to poor user interface. Was the problem the supplier/product procurement selected, the lack of true support from IT, or just insufficient project management skill? I will probably never know. But what this experience did teach me was clear. Taking the time to engage senior IT management and link the interested functions into a united front would have better managed both the supplier and the project. The aligned vetting of the application would have eliminated a lot of internal distrust that made supplier management more difficult and would have smoked out the real issues much sooner.

Internal battles provide the winners a short-term high, but the scars can be painful. That is not the road to competitive advantage. We might have been better off postponing the project until the next budget year, enlisting all interested functions, continuing to use the "acceptable but not great" approach we had in place (which we had to do anyway), and even getting the benefit of another several months of software evolution in the rapidly changing contract management space.

This lesson made an impression. Interested functions must want to work with suppliers to improve the business. The supply/procurement function's people cannot legislate that desire. Instead, they need to tap into it and help shape the supplier selection process to ensure good choices. The resulting suppliers' value has to be apparent and of enough importance to overcome subjective functional preferences. The best way to do that is find a way for all the functions to get a benefit rather than fight a battle that creates winners and losers. Sometimes, a conflict is unavoidable, but that needs to be the rare exception.

At the beginning of this chapter, a hypothesis was made that cross-functional belief in the supply base as a means to competitive edge may be the most important concept in this book. Creating such belief takes time, effort, and a willingness to see the other organization's perspective. All are very difficult to do. But if it were easy, everyone would be able to do it and cross-functional alignment toward suppliers would not be a means to competitive advantage.

The challenge is to understand what makes various functions tick and how suppliers can improve their performance. This kind of internal cross-functional integration in large companies mirrors the operations of small companies, where managers often wear multiple hats. This creates a better understanding of how the business operates and how suppliers can make a difference. Early in the book the idea was espoused that small companies understand that suppliers need to sell value beyond simple cost reduction. This cross-functional "multi-hatting" is part of what enables that. Deep internal understanding of other functions by the procurement or supply organization and understanding of how supplier management allows suppliers to provide better value in user and key support functions is the best way to approximate the small company experience on the supply side.

Notes

1. Reuben Stone, "Are You the Weakest Link in Your Supply Chain?," presentation at the Institute for Supply Management's 93rd International Supply Management Conference and Educational Exhibit, St. Louis, Mo., May 7, 2008.

2. Robert A. Rudzki, "The Gold Medal: Transforming Supply Management into a World Class Driver of Corporate Performance," presentation at the Institute for Supply Management's 93rd International Supply Management Conference and Educational Exhibit, St. Louis, Mo., May 5, 2008.

3. Jeffery McCracken, "Home Retailer Expected to File for Bankruptcy," Wall Street Journal, April 11, 2008.

4. Andrew Bartolini, "The CFO's View of Procurement: Same Page, Different Language," study by Aberdeen Group, November, 2007.
5. Joe Robinson, keynote speech at the Xavier University Management/ Human Resources Student Professional Society fall dinner, November 14, 2007.

CHAPTER 10

Market Flows

Monitor and Manage the Forces That Shape Performance

UTILITY: a public service, as a telephone or electric-light system.

The architect should strive continually to simplify; the ensemble of the rooms should then be carefully considered that comfort and utility may go hand in hand with beauty.

—Frank Lloyd Wright, architect

Running a business and managing a supply base are about work, not just theory, architecture, and design. The building of a home is no different. Part of the architecture and design has to include how the building will operate to enable it to be a livable structure. That's where utilities, and the appliances they hook into, fit into our supply-based advantage construction project. It's no wonder that real estate and home building companies repeatedly make the point that kitchens, bathrooms, and the overall heating and air-conditioning systems are what enhance the resale value of a home.

Utilities enable critical flows to enter, be utilized (hence the name utilities), and exit the building. The table below captures the five most critical flows in a home and how they match up with the five most critical supply chain/supply management flows in a company. Just like in a house, the efficiency, effectiveness, and aesthetics of the supply utility network make a huge difference in the value of the overall business.

Building Utilities	Supply Flows
Air and ventilation	Talent
Electricity/light	Data and information
Fuel/furnace	Money
Water/plumbing	Knowledge
Communication/entertainment	Analysis/interaction/work flow

One of the mantras of business success that is consistently stated by software companies and consultants selling their products is that excellent operations consist of three elements: people, processes, and technology (by "technology" they typically mean information technology and software). They always caution that technology is just a tool, making the people and processes primary—then the technology sales pitch begins. It will provide work process structure and enhance the effectiveness and efficiency of the organization, and indeed, it may. But too many companies forget the early cautionary disclaimer, and begin to believe that mastery of the tools equates to supply advantage. The three elements can quickly blur.

The bulk of this book has been spent on processes and the skills that the people who manage those processes ought to have, plus the structures that house them. Now it's time to examine the dynamic movement of a supply base within a company's business market. That is where the other two elements—people and technology—come in. In Chapter 7 we talked about types of supply chains and networks—physical, financial, informational, ideas/innovation, and relationships. They flow along the processes and within the structures we put in place (sourcing strategy, relationship management, supply chains/networks, organizational structures, and across boundaries [both internal and external]). To monitor them in a fast-moving global business context means using people and technology.

The five flows above are highly intertwined and should not be viewed independently if your goal is to create a competitive weapon that extends advantage, rather than just good execution that delivers steady results. These supply "utilities" use and build on each other as they meet and run various supply "appliances." Just as electricity and other fuels are important to delivering all utilities in a home: electric lights, communication (phones, Internet, television, computers, etc.), furnaces, air conditioners, hot water heaters, and stoves; people and technology drive the supply utilities' ability to deliver value. People flows include talent and knowledge; technology enables financial and information flows that support the physical business; and the combination of the two drives the analytical, communication, and connectivity flows that result in actions to deliver competitive edge.

The Talent Flow: Key to All the Rest

Corporations like to say "People are our most important asset." Talent is an asset—human capital. It is not a flow, right? Guess again. Just as "working capital" is a label for what has become a monetary and physical flow of receivables, payables, and inventory, talent has become a flow of people—a flow that, unlike working capital, companies try to slow down and hold on to. Perhaps twenty-five years ago, talent was a fixed asset, but the huge upheavals of the late 1980s and early 1990s changed all that. Loyalty on both sides of the employment table transitioned—employees found companies less loyal as downsizing and layoffs became common. On the other hand, employees viewed the concept of staying at a single company for a career as passé—the "free agent" era dawned. The winning career path became one of job-hopping. Talent truly became a flow.

The challenge is to acquire, develop, retain, and occasionally cull this flow. The transformation of talent into results is driven by:

> *Ability.* The underlying capability of individuals. Are they inherently smart, collaborative, decisive, analytical, or creative? Do they show any evidence they can lead, influence, and effectively follow? (Yes, good "followership" is a vital art.)

> *Capability.* The application of ability to the supply arena. Are these individuals able to work across boundaries, balance the use of competition with collaboration, understand and use sourcing and supply tools to deliver what the business needs? Do the individuals build into an effective organization?

> *Interest.* The most intangible of the three. Are they interested in the supply side of the business (often not the way to general management), do they have passion for both deal making and the resulting governance that delivers real results, or, more simply, do they like

the work and are they comfortable with the firm's ethical principles toward the supply base?

Nearly every future-focused study on supply management has identified talent as a crucial issue. There are simply not enough skilled procurement people to go around, so let's start with recruiting. Every firm has its own approach to recruiting new employees. Within that approach, they recruit candidates into supplier management and selection organizations—some from colleges and universities, some from other internal functions, some from other companies.

A growing number of universities have incorporated supply chain management into their curriculum and companies have been drawn to these graduates, looking for people who are already familiar with supplier management. Then college recruiting looks more like an extension of the other two talent pools—internal functions, other companies (including consultants who are often engaged to do the work of supply leadership and/or supply operations)—all three of these deliver people who have experience working on the supply side in one aspect of their career or another.

That's great if your goal is to build a strong supply management organization. However, if the goal is competitive advantage, this experience is often a "nice to have," unless your organization simply does not, today, have even a vision of supply as a competitive force. Then importing the vision through people with experience is probably a key first step. However, the real criteria to look for lies in the "ability" description above, not in a university major or previous job experience. Recruiting a commodity category expert every time your company needs to source a new item gives instant experience but not much flexibility. The test of competitive advantage is flexibility to expand market knowledge in the existing organization as needed.

Are the people you are hiring, regardless at what level, commercially savvy—that is, do they like doing commerce, from both analytical and interpersonal standpoints, and are they able to influence others, either as leaders or peers? Those are the qualities to look for, not just a supply management degree. Today many young people have informally experienced the sourcing process tactically, due to frequent Internet buying experiences as consumers including: checking multiple vendors, comparing design/functionality differences, price and warranty shopping, seller quality and trustworthiness rating sites, secure payment processes, and so forth,. The difference between this and strategic sourcing is the ongoing nature of the business and the changes in circumstances ongoing business entails.

—Practitioner's Take—

My experience is somewhat unique because I spent my career with a company that largely promotes from within—an increasingly rare phenomenon. Still, our experience in the purchasing recruiting arena might be of value. For years we recruited people off campus (or sometimes from the military) into entry-level positions in procurement and supply. The function did a good job of training these people, but retention was an ongoing issue. By the 1990s the dot.com boom and strong investment banking/consulting markets made recruiting competition tough for a bricks-and-mortar company, especially for supply rather than marketing and finance positions. A growing percentage of the people we lost after two years were headed for then popular e-marketplaces, auction software, and e-consulting outfits.

Those trends caused us to begin recruiting young people who were leaving their first job at another company and, thus, still willing to accept an entry-level position at a well-known firm. We also accepted (even recruited) people from other functions into procurement (not always into entry-level slots, but also seldom into senior levels), which was unusual in what was then a very functionally driven company. As the North American purchasing leadership began to debate how to counteract our attrition problem (face it, when a promote-from-within company loses most of its recruits after a couple years, it's a serious long-term problem), we reviewed the function's hiring records, performance trends, and exit interviews. Two interesting conclusions rose to the surface:

1. Over a five-year period the attrition of new hires straight from college was over 75 percent, while attrition of hires who had worked at another company—regardless of function—was half that number.
2. Cross-functional transfers, many of whom were rated "very good but not great" by other functions, seemed to have found their groove in supplier management and sourcing. It was as though their unique aptitudes were better suited to the "commercial/analytical/social" blend of supply management.

The outcome was a conscious choice to recruit a blend of 20 percent college graduates, 40 percent people with prior work experience, and 40 percent cross-functional transfers (some at entry level and others at middle levels). The other outcome was confirmation that degree did not matter—strong training to create a common process and mindset was what counted, as did the general criteria of "commercial savvy"—being smart and collaborative and having leadership, influence, creativity, and analytical skills. We also found that the Internet was far more effective at drawing in strong candidates, especially those with some prior experience, than on-campus efforts.

Obviously, if your company is recruiting senior supply leaders in order to change the organization, track record at other employers is crucial in your recruits because vision, change management, and proven achievement are vital. You are looking for talent magnets to both draw aptitude from outside and find/elevate underutilized talent internally.

One last thought—if your organization operates in multiple regions of the world, part of the talent flow must include recognizing that the hiring process and approaches to retaining those hires can vary significantly across geographies. In one manufacturing company's Swiss business center, where the procurement organization was relocated for tax reasons (several European companies have made this move over the years), the eyeopener became the governmental approvals to obtain documentation for new hires and transfers from other Western European countries. When an employee chose to leave, the lead-time to refill the slot was largely driven by these approvals, not the time to find and hire a candidate.

In the early years (the 1990s) of recruiting college graduates in China, good relations with the Chinese government Ministry of Education were critical. It made all the difference in attracting the top candidates. While this remains somewhat important, so does understanding which of China's many universities are first tier and creating either Web-based or on-campus ways to interact with and explain talent expectations/job expectations to students—more like traditional Western approaches.

Once talent is acquired, the key to retaining it is to grow and develop it. Too many companies make two fundamental mistakes in this area. First, they count on direct supervisors to be responsible for their employees' development, which injects enormous variability into the process. A number of studies over the last several years have consistently reported that almost 70 percent of people leave the company they work for because of their boss, not for better opportunities, more money, or to enter another field. Those things matter, of course, but the primary reason is the boss. Further, one of the big complaints about those bosses is that they don't coach employees enough, and with increasingly lean management ranks, time to coach is scarcer than ever, leading to a negative cause-and-effect spiral.

Second, for those who understand the importance of a system to grow talent, "system" means training. But while very important, training is not enough. Growing skilled people needs to incorporate career and skill planning that "roll up" the individuals into an overall organization. This is particularly important for supply management, where people are constantly interacting with other companies and can inadvertently create a corporate reputation based on how they perform. Net: Giving responsibility to interact with suppliers—often with levels that are higher than the buying employee—while growing well-rounded skill sets and market experience that are relevant to the business balances the benefit of supplier management experience with the risk of a relationship mistake. Err on the side of the risk taking.

PNM Resources is a utility located in the southwest United States with a range of fuel sources and a good performance record. Its somewhat traditional supply organization needed to evolve to the next level, bringing in new leadership from other utilities and industries. One of the first moves was to conduct a skills assessment/inventory. Step 1 was to do an "as-is" versus "to be" organizational skill comparison looking forward, which identified a skills gap at the more senior commodity management and strategic sourcing levels—both in terms of headcount as well as particular skill sets. This helped set the staffing plan necessary to move the organization to the next performance level. The study became part of the business case.

Step 2 was to chart each supply employee against their level of expertise across thirty-nine skills (maybe Chapter 8's forty skills is closer to what's needed than most would think!) and each position's required skill set. This provided a detailed map of where the organization needed to focus both its training and its hiring over the next few years and how much of each skill level was actually necessary. This kind of skill inventory can underlie any organizational improvement plan.

Supply management is a family of complex processes that include an amazing number of tools and skills in order to span the range necessary to manage the full supply base. This is an organizational challenge that limits the number of companies that can truly extract longstanding competitive advantage from the supply base. Pierre Mitchell, director of The Hackett Group, sees the process family as including sourcing, supplier management, supply operations, demand management/compliance, and supply functional management. It consists of, as Mitchell puts it, "a sea of best practices" and many tools to support each. The organization's ability to digest the sheer number of techniques necessary to deal with the supply base is part of why this effort takes time and is a journey, not an instant "transformation."

The second organizational analysis needs to look at the people and the commodities in order to sketch out the types of experience necessary to develop the market and business savvy required to enable flexibility, performance rigor, and change response. The approach first takes the firm's spend categories and assesses them to judge which are most strategic, dependent on deep spend market knowledge, internal user application knowledge (i.e., cross-functional technical knowledge), and close supplier personal contacts. Next are those spends that could be somewhat amenable to supply management personnel turnover without major disruption and those that could be outsourced, delegated to users, or automated.

In parallel, current leadership must broadly look forward to create a future leadership talent pipeline. This analysis integrates the need to staff some spend categories with more continuity (at P&G, surfactants, or cleaning agents, was one such category). At the same time, firms need to develop a series of leaders who have experienced different markets (seller's versus buyer's versus balanced), limited supply (sole source) versus multiple sources, entrepreneurial suppliers versus large multinationals, suppliers from different countries/cultures, different internal businesses and user groups, and vastly different spend categories (services versus capital versus direct materials). The goal is to build a flexible talent development program that balances supply base management continuity and a growing, well-rounded experience base that is prepared to step into leadership roles.

This kind of talent planning must take place in an environment where turnover is a given, attrition is expected, and performance can be rewarded so that enough good people stay, while the less talented are more likely to go. Managing the talent flow is one of the toughest aspects of getting the most from suppliers, especially when you remember that suppliers are doing the same thing with their people, making relationship management even more demanding.

If your organization becomes successful at gaining supply-based advantage, expect high attrition. Why? Because companies less advanced than you will want what you have. Low turnover and a highly skilled supply management group are rare. Twenty years ago when purchasing was a backwater, most companies with skilled procurement were unlikely to get raided. It was like a stealth bomber, able to fly undetected and deliver its payload. Today, supply's growing visibility makes hoarding talent impossible. The "free agent employee" culture makes it so. Interestingly, many of the companies that hire these people away are simply looking for cost reduction or competency in supply, not competitive advantage. The only way to counteract this threat is to nurture a strong supply culture that develops talent at an exportable level—to either be exported to other parts of the firm or to be "poached" by other companies.

As VP Supply Management, Kent Brittan was the architect of United Technologies' (UTC) well-regarded supply management organization.[2] In 1997 he was tasked with vastly improving the supply capability of UTC's wide range of autonomous business units including Carrier heating and air conditioning, Hamilton Sundstrand aerospace systems, Pratt & Whitney engines, Otis elevators, Sikorsky helicopters, UTC Power fuel cells, and UTC Fire & Security alert systems. UTC's senior management had the vision that supply needed to be a major value contributor and encouraged Brittan to bring together a strong mixture of leaders and skill sets, recruited from across the various UTC business units. Brittan's group was empowered and rewarded to take risks, learn from mistakes, share knowledge, and encourage continuing supply education. UTC was an early user of sourcing consultants (A. T. Kearney), e-tools (FreeMarkets, now part of Ariba, and Open Ratings, now part of D&B), and procurement outsourcing (IBM Services).

Brittan, a twenty-year finance executive, saw supply management from non-supply eyes and set out to build it into a value-creating powerhouse. Ultimately, he was named Chairman of UTC's International Operations after eight years leading the supply management organization. As UTC grew its sourcing and supply talent base, it also discovered that even the best lose people—it comes with the territory. By the time Brittan retired in 2006 a dozen of his "children" were senior supply executives at other companies:

Individual	UTC Business Unit	Post-UTC Position (2006)
Shelley Stewart	Hamilton Sundstrand	VP Operational Excellence and CPO, Tyco
Mike Rager	Hamilton Sundstrand	Director Enterprise Spend Mgmt., Diebolt
Jack Wagner	Carrier VP	VP Supply Chain, Gibraltar Steel
Ken Marcia	Corp. Supply Mgmt.	VP Supply Chain Mgmt., Dresser-Rand
Leo Diaz	Corp. Supply Mgmt.	Director Supply Chain Mgmt., Eaton Corp.
Ed Williams	Carrier	VP Supply Mgmt., Johns

		Manville
Tim Fiore	Corp. Supply Mgmt.	SVP Supply Mgmt., Celenase
Maurice Ghattas	Corp. Supply Mgmt.	VP Supply Mgmt., W. R. Grace
Rick Wize	Carrier	VP Sourcing & Supply Chain, Ingersall Rand
Steven Kim	Corp. Supply Mgmt.	Sr. Director, Paccar Corp.
Scott McKinnon	Pratt & Whitney	VP Indirect Spend, Ingersall Rand
Torsten Gessner	Otis	VP Operations, Thyssen Krupp

The talent flow is tough to control, so the best approach is to make it robust, so any losses become manageable. UTC did this. Brittan retired and twelve of his leaders left to head other organizations, yet UTC won *Purchasing* magazine's 2006 Medal of Professional Excellence!

Knowledge Flow: The Intersection of Information and People

The process to manage suppliers for value is fueled by data and information. They are the raw materials of sourcing strategy. However, no amount of data and information will equate to knowledge. Knowledge requires analysis and judgment that uses information to come to conclusions and drive actions. This blend of science (data and information) and art (human analysis and judgment) is also a flow. Everyone understands the information flow, but, once you understand that talent is a flow, the idea of a knowledge flow makes sense, too.

Unfortunately, early in the first decade of the twenty-first century, knowledge management was hijacked by the software industry in order to sell information collection, storage, and retrieval systems—most of which failed miserably because they underestimated the human aspect of knowledge flow. Unless people want to participate and see that sharing knowledge helps them, they are more likely to hoard than to share.

Suppliers are also entities constantly undergoing change—people, profitability/cost structure, business plans, etc. The biggest difference between supply side knowledge and talent flows is that knowledge is a two-sided flow. Huh? Two-sided in that internal knowledge must mingle with external knowledge in order for the flow to truly create value. Attempting to share knowledge between companies encounters another level of barriers to knowledge flow—intellectual property considerations coupled with distrust about who gets the benefit.

A classic example of knowledge flow is supplier development, where the buying company dispatches technical and operations experts to a supplier factory/office to implement improvement efforts by using methodologies like Lean, Six Sigma, and Total Quality. The buying firm has to decide that the potential benefits offset the fact that every other customer of that supplier, including the buyer's competitors, will also see some benefit. On the supplier side, the worries are about sharing intimate operational, economic, and technical information that it is far more comfortable to keep close to the vest. Will the buyer use that data to drive a tougher bargain? Will the supplier lose more than they gain?

Goodrich Engine Components (they make high-tech propulsion fuel nozzles for jets, not tires), has a major supplier value improvement program (SVIP) with eight strategic suppliers.[3] The idea is to transfer knowledge on Lean methods from Goodrich to the suppliers with the best potential to grow, both in terms of volume and technology. They train Lean practitioners and certified "change agents" at the suppliers and conduct value improvement workshops to deliver cost and quality improvements. These suppliers consistently deliver between 2 and 3 percent cost reductions without any profit margin reduction. However, the real knowledge flow goes more than two ways. Goodrich insists that the suppliers network best practices with each other— sometimes even between competitors—thus developing a more sustainable supply base overall. The next step is to move down into the suppliers' supply bases, training supplier Lean experts to work with their own suppliers.

Think of it as a flow of internal business and methodology knowledge combined with a flow of external business and methodology knowledge. Traditional management practices can erect barriers that reduce knowledge flow. Therefore, when the parties are able to address the barriers constructively, it presents an opportunity for competitive advantage.

Internally, knowledge needs to move across functions and business units relevant to both ongoing products and innovation—using internal teaming and collaboration methodologies. Externally, market, industry, supplier, and governmental knowledge also need to flow, using methodologies like Lean, Six Sigma, joint product development, and benchmarking. Given the added complexity of crossing company boundaries, intellectual property and relationship governance techniques are also important. Understanding where the knowledge resides and where knowledge gaps exist allows proactive efforts to channel the flow where it will do the most good.

The Electronic Flows: Money, Information, Connectivity/Analysis

Before discussing the last three "supply utility" flows, it's worth taking a moment to recognize that they all are intimately tied to electronics, computers, and data management, just like home heating (furnace fan), lights, telecom, and appliances (from refrigerators to computers) require electric power (lines or batteries). It is for this reason that the procurement-IT organizational interface and the ability of supply people (and companies) to use software applications effectively are pivotal to using these utility functions to manage the flows.

This ability is made up of a holistic range of capabilities in which the people (talent and knowledge) intersect with technology (software, hardware, mobile communication). The capability includes a range of tasks that must be done well—from transactional accuracy (data management, accounts payable—purchase-to-payment [P2P], logistical tracking, etc.) to complex strategic processes (decision support, intense collaboration beyond simple requirements planning, risk assessment, etc.). The array of electronic tasks shown in Figure 10.1 covers that full range. The point here is that even the most mundane parts of this pyramid must be done well (internally or via outsourcing) because each tier of capability builds on the one below it from data quality management to high-end joint supplier innovation.

The other aspect of the electronic capability pyramid shown in Figure 10.1 is that its elements need to parallel and support the firm's supply processes. Beware the temptation to buy software expecting that its process will provide you with your process. That takes a long time and, if the software is not user-friendly, will lead to a huge number of failed or underutilized supply applications. The long-term vision behind the entire pyramid is rarely visible to the everyday user. Often, that vision is simply not compelling when the day-to-day work is overwhelming. Grappling with a new technology application that does not flow along familiar work process paths leads to lengthy, expensive software implementations. Remember the ERP (Enterprise Resource Planning) implementations over the last fifteen years discussed in Chapter 9. Eventually the majority got done, but at great monetary and organizational cost, especially where the software did not parallel the basic corporate work flow. In some cases the failures resulted in major conflict between the customer and the software supplier, resulting in severed relationships and filed lawsuits.

Figure 10.1 Electronic Capabilities for Supply Value

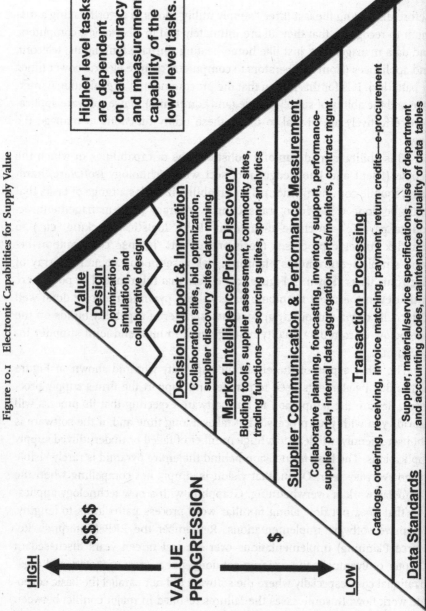

Higher level tasks are dependent on data accuracy and measurement capability of the lower level tasks.

Value Design
Optimization, simulation, and collaborative design

Decision Support & Innovation
Collaboration sites, bid optimization, supplier discovery sites, data mining

Market Intelligence/Price Discovery
Bidding tools, supplier assessment, commodity sites, trading functions—e-sourcing suites, spend analytics

Supplier Communication & Performance Measurement
Collaborative planning, forecasting, inventory support, performance-supplier portal, internal data aggregation, alerts/monitors, contract mgmt.

Transaction Processing
Catalogs, ordering, receiving, invoice matching, payment, return credits—e-procurement

Data Standards
Supplier, material/service specifications, use of department and accounting codes, maintenance of quality of data tables

VALUE PROGRESSION

HIGH

LOW

$$$$

$

—Practitioner's Take—

Witness the Waste Management/SAP lawsuit filed in March 2008.[4] When they sourced the ERP product in late 2005, Waste Management felt that the software was promised to be uniquely designed for the trash hauling industry supply chain and could be used "as is" without customization or enhancement. Hence, it would only take about eighteen months to install. Waste Management alleged that they were shown "fake software environments" as part of the sales pitch. (Early on in the software revolution at P&G, we were also fooled by a well-regarded supply chain software company's fancy—but fake—demonstrations. Lawsuits were talked about, but in the end we were able to find a "graceful exit" via a settlement; see Chapter 6 about exiting gracefully.) Granted, a lot of water has flowed under the software implementation bridge since the early supply chain applications came on the scene in the late 1990s, but these misalignments still happen a lot.

Waste Management and SAP had the benefit of years of ERP toil at other companies and, as any benchmarking of the industry would reinforce, ERP implementations are massive, complex, and intimately tied to the guts of daily work. Just getting to the finish line is a great accomplishment—and only the first step. Once it is in, then you need to use it. Once that is accomplished, it is often a great investment!! But that can be (and often is) years later. In this case, Waste Management sued for $100 million, alleging the project was completely wasted. As of this writing, the suit has just begun, so the final resolution is not clear.

What is the point of telling this story? While computer and software products are part of a firm's supply capability, they are also provided by suppliers. The previous chapters of this book apply to them as well as to other suppliers. Too often companies begin to think about software applications as part of themselves. In fact, they represent a sourcing and supplier management task that is vitally important to successful supply operation. Entire books have been written about the use of software to improve procurement and supply chain results (including *On Demand Supply Management*, which I coauthored with Doug Smock, former editor of *Purchasing* magazine, and Bob Rudzki, former CPO of Bayer Chemical and now president of Greybeard Advisors, LLC).

A detailed review of all these electronic tools is not within the scope of this book, but the key to remember is that they are provided by software companies and a joint sourcing/supplier management effort is required to manage that interface. Penetrating due diligence prior to the buy, ongoing project and cross-functional relationship management during the buy, rigorous qualification processes and ongoing management, including continuous improvement and more innovative step changes, all must be part of the IT tool deployment and usage process.

Money Flows: Keeping Score, Staying Solvent, and Delivering Efficient Value

The financial flows fuel the company. Typical supply side focus is on accounts payable because the linkage is directly with suppliers. However, upon further reflection, this flow really has several aspects beyond P2P. Tracking expenditures versus budgeted costs in the firm's profit forecast (an extension of cost savings measurement) and setting up supply chain financing to handle credit and cash needs back through the supply chain also fall here. The advent of global supply chains from low-cost countries makes this financing area ever more important.

P2P: The Basics

The order-to-payment system is a classic cross-functional flow.[5] P2P is also the transactional system that sends money out of the company in return for goods or services from suppliers. It crosses numerous organizational boundaries, both internal (using departments, procurement, receiving, accounts payable [AP], internal distribution, treasury, internal controls, and accounting), and external (supplier, bank, external delivery). As an area often offshored and outsourced, accounts payable and invoice processing areas can even represent another supplier—the outsourcing service provider.

Optimizing the P2P flow can be a lengthy process (years, not months or weeks) and requires ongoing training of the organization. The electronic system to streamline this flow requires five process elements:

1. User-friendly software interfaces.
2. Where catalogs or preferred suppliers are in place, solid sourcing behind the computer screen's interface with desktop requisitioners.

3. Embedded policy and procedures in the system to ensure accuracy and control of the spend (to avoid what is called maverick or renegade spending by users who go outside the preferred suppliers or approved limits for a buy).

4. Use of "supplier enablement" to make it work, where suppliers can electronically access the order and payment systems to help diagnose invoice payment problems and input their information into the system.

5. Tight software connections between the ERP system and other software for ordering/receiving and treasury connections with electronic payment systems.

Verifying that the firm only pays for what it actually gets requires weaving of information with cash flow. A growing number of companies seek to automate as much of this process as possible[6]—which requires that it become part of the money "utility flow." It is amazing where supplier invoices go after they arrive at a company. Aberdeen Group's "2006 Procure to Pay Study" found that 80 percent of invoices are still paper and so end up getting digitalized via scanning technology, but not before they find user desk drawers as paper invoice receptacles, often until well after they are due. That issue cascades into the financial and accounting reports, causing liability mismatches, month-end accounts payable accounting close inefficiencies, and unclear, sloppy procedures/policies that users don't know or understand. In most cases, this leads to late payments and lost discounts from suppliers, and sometimes, when suppliers reinvoice for the same shipment seeking missed payments, it leads to double payments and even fraud.

On the supplier end, lack of understanding on exactly what information must match the purchase order in order to get paid leads to invoice rejection at the customer's AP organization. Every customer has different rules and the supplier typically has its own standard invoicing process as well.

Automating the system seeks to solve all that and institutionalize the policies and procedures on both sides of the sale to make sure money flow matches the goods/services flow. Unfortunately, most companies struggle to make the basic system work and are forced to standardize payment terms with all suppliers (net sixty days, for example). The supplier builds that cash lag into its pricing and cash planning.

When competitive advantage is the objective, the ability to trade cash flow for cost of goods gains or vice versa, by tailoring supplier payment discount terms to both companies' financial goals, can enable either increased cash flow or lower cost. In one case, the supplier was cash rich and gave a major customer astonishing 180-day payment terms with no price change! In another, a German global auto subassembly company automated its system flexibly so they could pay each supplier based on uniquely negotiated cash/cost discount terms, modifiable as circumstances changed. That level of flexibility enables the money flow to be a source of competitive edge. It also feeds directly into the second money flow system—cost tracking for corporate financials and operational control relative to budgets.

Cost Tracking: Monitoring the Transactional Flow's Impact on the Business

In Chapters 6 and 9 we talked about metrics (savings/avoidance) and working with finance cross-functionally. While important, that is not what managing this part of the money flow is really about. Like the P2P system, truly managing the cost tracking system requires a tight connection between the company's budgets, profit forecasts, and the operation of the supply organization. Cost savings will not get to the bottom line or create funding for added value creating initiatives without this connection.

For direct spends (product components), the tie is easier to make (although not perfect) given the importance of cost of goods sold to financial statements and the fact that products require certain components that link amounts ordered to production and then to amounts in the sales forecast (for push systems) or customer orders (for pull systems). Sometimes these links take too long, but eventually someone notices the warehouse filling up. Indirect (overhead) is a far different proposition.

In order to create the discipline necessary to drive efficiency and effectiveness, tying the supply market for indirect goods and services directly to each overhead budget is critical. Unfortunately, most departments manage overheads as one general fund that must be met. Strong sourcing or supply management savings can easily be lost when reductions in one area are used to offset higher spending in another (e.g., a telecom price reduction is used up by either more telecom usage than budgeted, or the money gets spent on something else under the overall departmental budget umbrella). If the savings are spent on something that drives the business (perhaps an additional marketing event), value can be created. Too often, however, the mindset is to spend the budget so the same level is defensible next year.

The financial system, in collaboration with supply/procurement, needs to bring purchased goods and services budgetary savings into the profit forecast or to leadership attention to make a conscious decision on whether to spend it or save it to the bottom line. This must be done proactively, using supply market forecasts (and the inevitable adjustments to the forecast when unforeseen events occur) rather than only using purchase price variance (ppv), a historical result measure. The forecast is like driving by looking through the windshield, while ppv is more like driving while looking in the rearview mirror. Frequent cost forecast updates for all purchased items (at minimum monthly and certainly on an event basis when significant individual changes in market conditions occur) creates the kind of tight supply/finance interface that manages this part of the money flow.

—Practitioner's Take—

Part of this money flow is the budget of the supply organization itself. It is in supply's overhead budget where the talent, knowledge, and three electronic flows come together. Supply's budget process needs to be viewed as a combination of the cost to deliver competitive advantage through suppliers and, importantly, the investment to create competitive supply capability (human capital) for the future. This requires tough decisions about efficiency—such as adding people after the need is clear rather than in anticipation of new needs that may not occur or adding incremental headcount for projects that are not long-term needs, resulting in excess people when the project ends—and investing in sourcing/performance management software tools, travel (for face-to-face supplier meetings), training and skill development (external benchmarking, consultants, training classes, etc.), and market intelligence (knowledge) acquisition (e.g., market monitoring reports).

To cultivate supply-based advantage is like any other corporate priority—it must be resourced. Supply leadership needs to link its work to the business plan in order to justify resourcing the organization. Doing so with integrity and frugal spending (without being too cheap) represents the balance between planting for and harvesting high-yield supply value and eating your seed corn so you cannot plant value seeds in the future. If supply/procurement is seen by senior management as nothing more than a utility rather than a means to optimize and grow value, then the supply budget will be extremely tight—focused on efficiency rather than effectiveness and value creation.

Credit Flow: Financing the Supply Chain

The advent of global and low-cost country sourcing (long transit times with suppliers that are poor credit risks), plus the rise of demand pull working capital strategies like vendor managed inventory (VMI) and consignment/vendor owned inventory (VOI) seem simple on the surface. But in many long transcontinental supply lines that originate in low-wage, third-world countries, the ability to finance the flow of goods is beyond some suppliers. To gain the advantages of low-cost labor or use of supplier working capital, there has to be enough credit to cover the cash flow.[7]

As expensive physical letters of credit (often costing 2 percent of the inventory's value) have slowly fallen out of favor for less costly options, supply chain credit has emerged as the last part of the money flow. An Aberdeen study in early 2007 pointed out that the combination of software that automates the financing and payables process and third-party financial providers will, for a percentage of the savings or a flat fee, extend the buyer's payment terms by paying the supplier more quickly.[7] These third parties must have strong financials/credit ratings and deep supply chain service and software knowledge in order to extend this credit (banks with knowledge and insight into supply chains like Bank of America or J. P. Morgan Chase, and nonbanks like, Siemens, IBM, or UPS Capital). These players have visibility into the physical goods and cash financial flows. This allows them to extend credit and manage their credit risk along the supply chain.

These providers have a business model that gives the buying company extended payment terms, advances the supplier cash earlier and at an interest rate lower than many small third-world companies could get from a regular bank, thus carving out a rate tier between the buyer and seller's borrowing capability. The idea is to have the inventory owned by the people with the lowest cost of capital—typically a financial institution rather than a manufacturing company. Given all the regulations that govern this area, use of this "flow" must be a cross-functional effort, like most sophisticated financial approaches. Experts in procurement, logistics, accounting, auditing, and trade (import/export) all need to make sure the deals are structured correctly.

A division of Sun Microsystems uses this approach to enable several of its small Asian suppliers, who could not afford to wait for payment during the weeks of transit time between their plants and the Sun division's Puerto Rican delivery center. Essentially, Sun has put together several funding partners and a logistics company. Sun pays the funding partners when they would have paid the supplier. The funding partners then negotiate the payment terms with suppliers—either taking a percent or working out a time value of money that works for both parties. Sun has gained cash time flow value rather than having to pay suppliers to keep them afloat and experiences no parts shortages because supplier parts can be stored near the Puerto Rican plant rather than closer to Asia. Think of this as a less expensive option because it is less risky for the middlemen since they do not take responsibility for getting payment from the buyer. The global credit crunch in 2008 made this aspect of money flow even more important for those that need cash to fuel their supply chains.

Data Flows: The Raw Material of Sourcing and Supplier Management

Now we head into the more typical supply flows. Information based on market, supplier, and internal data is the raw material upon which supplier selection, contractual arrangements, and result measures are built. They extend across an enormous range of subjects—from market reports to supply chain movement (like RFID or bar code readers) to supplier portals, product catalogs, and buyer usage forecasts. The word "collaboration" has become an incredibly overused term. Early on in the e-commerce revolution, any sort of data transfer of forecasted needs, orders, acknowledgments, and shipping notices seemed to merit the descriptor "collaboration" and all the positives it implied. However, as e-commerce has become the norm, it is obvious that this level of collaboration is what has for years been called "just doing business," only electronically or Internet-enabled, not some special collaboration engine.

The back and forth movement of information from the market and particular companies allows analysis, operations, and communications. Inside the company, the ERP system holds much of that data and moves it around the organization—we've talked about the challenges that presents already. On the supply side (mirroring sales) these back and forth flows funnel through supplier and sales portals that allow suppliers (and customers) access behind your firewalls. All the collaboration information exchanges, noted above, move along this flow.

To manage this flow effectively takes two things:

1. Focus on data—its quality, its maintenance, and its ownership.
2. Use of technologies that become available and not being afraid to try some pilots. Laggards fall further behind because information flow innovation makes the new become old fast.

Think of data quality in terms of finding all the duplication, errors, and inconsistencies. The concept of "data cleansing" is critical to using this flow to manage the business. When e-procurement and e-sourcing hit big around 2000, the biggest barrier was the integrity of the data most companies had in their systems. The same supplier was found under several different names because computers see capital and small letters, spaces, full names versus abbreviations, and different subsidiaries as different companies. Similarly, different business units used different numbers as tags to describe the same purchased item or specification.

Once the inaccuracies and inconsistencies are cleaned up, the challenge becomes to keep them clean as the business creates ever more change; companies buy and sell products, plants, and businesses while outsourcing processes; suppliers change as fast or faster than the buying companies, and the need to look more than one tier deep in the supply chain becomes paramount for competitive superiority. Maintaining the cleanliness of the data is part of managing this flow.

Unlike a few years ago, software exists today that can dramatically improve the maintenance process as long as people have the foresight and discipline to use it. However, another aspect of this flow, data ownership, is commercial. Data is extremely valuable. Determining who owns it, who has access to it, and what they are allowed to do with it has become a critical aspect of managing the information flow.

As companies look to suppliers to provide more cost-effective information technology solutions—data center outsourcers, software providers using "on demand" software as their service models (much less expensive and less IT resource-intensive than a software license for mid-sized or relatively infrequent users of an application), telecom management including customer and supplier call centers, computer application help desks, etc.—getting clear on who owns what information (on both sides of the information management deal) and how each software deal's intellectual capital agreements intersect other software licenses becomes one of the most important aspects of any supplier negotiation in this space.

One major manufacturing company that outsourced its IT support to a third party suddenly woke up to find that the intellectual property agreements it had signed with the IT system provider (who also had a software business, as many do) conflicted with the intellectual property deals they had with several key software providers, including their ERP supplier. Inability to get all these players on the same page for a couple years led to some extremely difficult situations when upgrades and low-cost country data center shifts were to be made. The lesson: Map the full IT intellectual property "spider web" in parallel with the information flow to understand the intersection points. IP in this arena is multidimensional, not just a two-party agreement, because data and information are transparent when flowing across company boundaries. Knowing where it goes and who needs it is paramount to managing it.

As for trying out new technology, a simple example of a company that creatively took a risk on what is today a ho-hum technology is family-style Italian restaurant chain Buca di Beppo.[8] In 2000, the company had sixty-eight sites with about 5500 employees (today there are eighty-nine sites). Each location had about twelve regular phones and servers/hostesses handled calls for reservations at each location throughout the day. In 2000 VoIP (Voice-over Internet Protocol) was not all the rage and Buca was spending about $50 per line plus long-distance charges for dial-up access to database and e-mail systems in its Minnesota headquarters.

Buca moved early to VoIP and was saving between $300 and $400 per restaurant per month due to the change. For the small chain, it represented a $300K savings. However, the biggest difference was that VoIP allowed Buca to create a central reservation call center that, when compared to the individual restaurant phones, whose reliability depended on how busy the store was, delivered over 400 extra reservations per day ($1.5 million/year in additional revenue). Major companies like Dow Chemical and Merrill Lynch followed suit, moving to VoIP for huge savings as the technology transformed corporate telephone systems and is now penetrating the consumer market.

As is frequently the case, companies in tough businesses, with thin or no profit margins, often are willing to take the risk to try something new. Good ideas are not the sole property of strong companies but, when they are reapplied by the top players, help sustain an advantage, extending followers' catch-up time. Information management innovations like well-designed supplier portals (Hallmark has used its supplier portal to conduct global commerce for about ten years), smart phones for mobile work, and the use of "cloud computing" infrastructure options such as Amazon's S3 (Simple Storage Service) online storage business for small companies have enabled better connectivity and data flow—and changed the game, but only short term. Staying abreast of these technologies is easy to copy, giving advantage that is not really sustainable in the long run.

Finally, the concept of a supply dashboard, a way to see how all these flows come into and out of the business, is the final aspect of this information flow. The use of individualized portals tailored for the user—senior executives or particular spend category managers—is the capstone of the information flow because it allows visibility into the flows. This visibility allows control schemes and managerial interventions to take place because they are usable, not because they look good.

The Final Flow: Analysis/Interaction/Work Flow

It is this final flow that can make an enormous difference. Think of it as the application of software to the supply side of the business. Most companies were quick to invest in CRM (customer relationship management), Web marketing, and other customer-facing software products, in part because customers drive sales, and the logic of starting there is clear.

On the supply side, too many companies have a traditional view that internal efficiency is *the* driver—this "more with less" competitive pressure leads to the belief that the most important benefit of software is headcount reduction and internal efficiency. In 2004, *Managing Automation* magazine cited Forrester Research saying that 92 percent of the companies in its manufacturing survey were looking for incremental efficiency from supply chain software, not value adding potential from faster delivery to market or better customer service.[9] While efficiency is clearly part of the value equation for these kinds of software applications, never lose sight of the fact that, as the word "application" implies, applying these tools to supply's physical, financial, information, and knowledge flows is where the real payback lies.

There is an enormous range of supply side applications that focus on the three core processes in Chapters 5 through 7—sourcing strategy, supplier relationships, and supply chain; plus the three information-dependent flows mentioned above (knowledge, information, and money). Going forward, these tools (standard e-sourcing and supplier management suites) will become more and more important—and will continue to evolve—for two reasons. First, manipulating and using data is what makes supply market interventions work. As mentioned before, information is the raw material of supply activities and these applications are part of transforming that raw material into projects, strategies, and tactics that deliver business results that can be tracked. Second, future generations of the "talent flow" will arrive in corporations having already used these digital tools for years on their cell phones, computers, gaming consoles, and music players (one of Apple's iTunes store's largest products is podcasts, not music).

Today using the basics is still a contributor to competitive advantage from supply. But going forward, the basics will not be enough, as new, more sophisticated tools (many honed in the social networking of personal lives) and creative uses of "old" basic software tools will become the real difference between a "good" supply base and one that is "competitively advantaged."

Just as important is that tools are becoming more accessible to more companies. The shift to software as a service (SaaS) allows small- to medium-size companies to buy the level of service that they need/want (buy the drink) instead of the entire software license (buy the whole bar). This makes upgrades less costly and organizationally draining. In 2000 only big companies could use these tools. Today, entrepreneurs are far more savvy in reducing corporate infrastructure through the use of external as-needed capability (think about the "cloud computing" phenomenon that only a few major players [Google, IBM, Microsoft, Yahoo, and Amazon] sell, and think about open-source Linux software).

The Basics: Running the Supply Business

E-procurement tools continue to expand to cover the entire strategic sourcing platform from supplier data cleansing to spend analysis to spend management to supplier identification/assessment to the range of RFx's—request for information, proposals, and quotations—to reverse auctions, to contract management, to supplier performance management, to supply event alerts (that flag exceptions in what was expected), to supplier risk assessment, to payment settlement . . . the list of applications within any software "suite" is almost endless. The idea is that every step of the work process has its own tailored tool to help digitize the work and store the outcomes for future analysis. But as numerous studies confirm, very few companies use the full range of tools and, even when they cherry-pick two or three, they struggle to use them well. In 2007, I was talking with a well-known consulting firm that supports supply management implementations. A partner was presenting a webcast on the use of competitive bidding tools (RFx and reverse auctions), using a particular client as the example. Along the way it turned out that this example of excellent results was only a pilot, with just six electronic bidding events.

The firms that get the accolades often tout major gains for a particular tool after a successful implementation or even after just the first pilot before full rollout. Still, when fully implemented, results can be impressive. In 2007–08, when direct material costs skyrocketed, PPG Industries looked to indirect spend to offset some of the cost pressure.[10] They implemented the bedrock of "the basics," analysis of spending on the items that do not go into products. In 2003, PPG discovered that they had 307 suppliers of electrical supplies in North America alone for only $10 million of spend. Spend management software highlighted this and enabled a classic sourcing strategy of rationalizing the number of suppliers to apply volume leverage to negotiate lower cost and better terms with those that remained. Today PPG has six electrical supply providers and spends 15 percent less than five years ago.

Similarly, Chevron Corp. found that spreadsheet-based approaches to supplier negotiation were simply too complex, especially when considering that the spreadsheet attachments and in some cases, massive blueprints, were too big to move across regular e-mail.[11] They contracted with a procurement software provider to simplify the process and provide a workspace that would allow suppliers to make price changes as Chevron tweaked requirements and specifications. Chevron's IT cost to support supply management dropped by almost a third, partly due to software efficiency and partly due to use of SaaS as the means to deliver it, instead of internal server capacity.

Another software approach—an industrial e-Bay called MFG.com, a bidding site, deals with machine parts.[12] It is able to link access to computer-aided design (CAD) drawings with supplier selection. Major buyers—Apple, Ford, and Northrop Grumman—have all used it. For smaller companies like Bergmans Mechatronics, a control system development company that designs and manufactures custom equipment, MFG.com helps match the supplier responsiveness that major corporations demand—an element of competitive advantage. As an example, a customer needed a custom system with seventeen parts, comprising fifty-two pieces made of anodized aluminum and stainless steel, with tight technical tolerances, all in about a month.[13] John Bergman, the entrepreneurial owner, posted the drawings on the first of the month, MFG.com vetted the drawings and suppliers, the job was awarded on the fifth of the month to a company Bergman had never heard of (but that MFG.com had vetted), and delivery of machine parts with excellent quality occurred by the sixteenth, all for under $2000. Bergman says his requirements are typically for quality parts, competitive price, and speed. Interestingly, although he tries, he rarely uses the same supplier repeatedly because the combination of need for speed and available capacity are not there. Yet, the stable of machine shops that MFG.com has recruited (sellers pay to be on the site, buyers come for free) has resulted in repeated successful orders from a number of different suppliers.

Contrary to consultant/software provider sales pitches, big cost savings using these analytical tools does not always equate to ongoing market wins. In 2003, Motorola trumpeted its use of spend analysis software to consolidate thirty different supply chain databases into one and its procurement group's use of that information leverage to negotiate $2.5 billion savings from suppliers.[14] Three and half years later, that benefit was no longer a competitive edge as Motorola's market position was eroded by other competitors in a market where innovation re-creates the playing field.

Because supply software must parallel work processes deep in the bowels of the organization that connect with the supply side of the value chain—not the customer side that gets the most attention and is often less complex—it is not unheard of to have major failures that can badly penalize the business. Three of the most famous include Ford's use of Neverest purchasing software that was so hard to use that it had to be discontinued (cost of $400 million), Nike's 2001 rollout of i2 supply chain software that distorted customer orders (final cost of $100 million), and Hershey Chocolate's 1999 startup of an SAP supply chain product that caused them to miss the Halloween candy season (12 percent sales reduction during the biggest candy season).[15,16] It goes back to the importance of the talent and knowledge flows and the need to recognize that people, processes, and technology have to work together. For supply this is a complex intersection.

Beyond the Basics: Massaging the Data to Find More Value

The real edge comes from taking the basics and using their outcomes to dive even deeper into the data. We are talking about high-end analytics—combinatorial science—that can find subtle advantage hiding deep in the numbers. It makes use of deep collaboration in which customers virtually cooperate with suppliers on complex projects like product design (for product lifecycle management) and complex service-specific software systems (e.g., for temporary labor or telecom) that provide a comprehensive cross-functional work flow, accounting, and sourcing/procurement solution. It also involves total cost modeling—should cost and target cost analysis using sophisticated science-based software.

We are also talking about analysis of a range of supplier information that can help determine supplier risk levels via pattern recognition technology; supply chain visibility and tracking via radio frequency identification tags or satellites; and supply chain modeling, simulation, and optimization in which the various tiers of the chain are tested via computer simulation, using the output to redesign the end to end supply chain (e.g., Cisco systems engaged UPS to conduct such a model-driven redesign for its European distribution business). These tools go further than the basics.

Examples are frequently publicized in blogs, presentations, articles, books, and research studies but, as Sourcing Innovation blogger Michael La-moureaux (the Doctor) points out with some frustration, 75 percent of companies do not use advanced analytics on their supply side situation despite the complexity of multiple suppliers and multiple supply tiers that must routinely converge in order to meet fluctuating customer demand patterns.[17] His postings cite several resources and examples that document the advantages of these advanced tools—e.g., more than 10 percent incremental cost savings over regular bidding procedures when bid optimization is used. The Dairy Queen chain used technology to assess its distribution, transportation, and inventory management for a national rollout of new products. Result: $1.8 million or 29 percent cost reduction.

Add to that a growing development and use of new-generation electronic tools—project wikis to communicate across functions and companies, sophisticated web meeting technology to reduce travel and improve collaboration, corporate blogs, and social networks including network map creation to understand where experts reside and how knowledge flows through and across organizations. These adaptations of consumer network products represent a means to electronically interject a "people interface" into the electronic flows to better parallel traditional face-to-face business practices.

—Practitioner's Take—

More than any other flow; the software analysis area requires two important human processes to succeed—master planning and adoption support.[18] Master planning is the process that looks across all these analytical tools and decides how the corporation's business needs and strategy (not the supply function's) can best leverage the tools. This can often lead to a selection priority that is uniquely tailored to that firm's competitive approach. At P&G we chose PLM (product lifecycle management) efforts to support our innovation strategies and sourcing optimization ahead of spend analysis and e-procurement, which followed later. The paybacks were enormous. A generic answer to the question of what application should go first would, in my opinion, choose spend analysis, hands down. For many companies understanding what, how much, at what cost, from whom, for whom you buy is a clear imperative. Yet in my own company, despite that imperative, optimization of huge "obvious" spends and the competitive pressure to continually innovate to stay ahead of private label and branded consumer packaged goods competitors made for a more compelling business case.

Adoption is actually getting people to use the software. The adoption level is probably the real measure of success. So many times studies show that a minority of users actually apply the software to the problem. Costly software projects launch and get "semi-traction," petering out halfway through the implementation. The software investment might pay out, but the lost opportunities are what show up in the market. Even successful adoptions must continually reinforce adoption. In Chapter 6 we discussed Home Depot's supplier measurement system, but discussions with suppliers two years after the system was publicized continue to raise questions about data accuracy and user adoption. Adoption is an enormous task—beyond the scope of this book. However, recognize that it requires nine steps. Driving those steps is a hallmark of companies that use technology to help them create supply advantage.

1. Gain leadership support and alignment behind the software project.
2. Select user-friendly tools—the greatest functionality is worthless if no one uses the tool.
3. Spend time planning the training content and rollout of the plan.
4. Capture organizational emotion—find the pain and reduce it or find the joy and reinforce it. This requires understanding the working level experience with the tools and giving rewards that make successes visible.
5. Install a support structure for the change—expert troubleshooting, feedback mechanisms, etc.
6. Measure what matters—start with activities but then transition to results.
7. Leverage successes to convert doubters and manage the inevitable failures quickly to avoid losing those who were willing to risk trying the tool early.
8. Include the expansion challenges in the implementation plan. For example, going global means having the means to deliver training and knowledge globally.
9. Install sustaining support to provide ongoing training (given the dynamic nature of the talent flow); to track results; and, where slippage occurs, to take quick remedial action.

Good master planning and strong adoption support means the difference between IT tool success and failure.

The five supply flows discussed in this chapter are what make the supply base something that can be leveraged to improve a company's competitive position. We have consistently stressed that tailoring supplier efforts to the company's value proposition and "personality" is key to going beyond basic good work to gain advantage from suppliers. These streams, made up of a combination of people and information flows, in parallel with the work processes of the companies in the supply chain, should be thought of as the enablers of this supply-based advantage effort.

Notes

1. Thomas J. Oleson, "Supply Chain Competency Model: Sourcing Vertical," presentation by PNMR Company, Santa Fe, N.M., July 29, 2006.

2. David Hannon, "Professional Development: UTC supply management alumni branch out," *Purchasing*, September 7, 2006.

3. Robert A. Kemp, Susan K. Modeland, and Gerry l. VanDyke, "Strategies for Rewarding Your Best Suppliers in a Dynamic Supply Chain," presentation at Institute for Supply Management 93rd Annual International Supply Management Conference and Educational Exhibit, May 5, 2008, St. Louis, Mo.

4. Ann All, "Who's to Blame for Failed ERP Project that Prompted SAP Lawsuit?," The Visible Enterprise blog, *IT Business Edge*, April 1, 2008.

5. Douglas A. Smock, Robert A. Rudzki, and Stephen C. Rogers, *On Demand Supply Management: World Class Strategies, Practices and Technology* (Conyers, Ga.: J. Ross Publishing Inc., 2007), pp. 85–99.

6. "TOP 10 Reasons why you should automate AP," whitepaper by 170 Systems, 2007.

7. Karen M. Kroll, "Continuous Improvement—New Programs Help Manufacturers Free Up Cash Without Straining Suppliers," Industry Week.com, November 29 and December 13, 2005.

8. Dylan Tweney, "The Table Is Set for Web Telephony," *Business 2.0*, December 2001.

9. Jeff Moad, "The Rise of the Progressive Manufacturer," *Managing Automation*, June 2004.

10. Mylene Mangalindan, "As Times Get Tough, Firms Buy Online: 'Supply Management' Software Aims to Help Control Spending," *Wall Street Journal*, June 3, 2008.

11. Vauhini Vara, "Web-Based Software Services Take Hold," *Wall Street Journal*, May 15, 2007.

12. Erick Schonfeld and Chris Morrison, discussion of MFG.com in their column "The Next Disruptors," *Business 2.0*, September 2007.

13. "John Bergman's Secret Weapon," http://216.183.126.109/mfgq_live/marketing/Customer-Showcase-Program/CSP-case-studies/Bergman-Final.pdf.

14. Michael V. Copeland and Owen Thomas, "Hits and Misses: Never again to say 'We paid how much for that?'," *Business 2.0*, December 2003.

15. Alexei Oreskovic, "What's Next—When Bugs Attack," *Business 2.0*, September 2007.

16. Alexei Oreskovic, "Never Break the Chain—supply chain software—Industry Trend or Event?," *The Industry Standard*, July 2, 2001.

17. Michael Lamoureaux, "Optimization: Can You Afford NOT to Use It?," Sourcing Innovation blog, May 19, 2008.

18. Smock, Rudzki, and Rogers, pp. 205–228.

CHAPTER 11

Outsourcing

Using Suppliers to Maintain and Remodel Capability

> MAINTAIN: to keep in an appropriate condition, operation, or force.
>
> REMODEL: to reconstruct; make over.

If you deprive yourself of outsourcing and your competitors do not, you're putting yourself out of business.

—Lee Kuan Yew, first prime minister of Singapore

After moving into a house, the homeowner soon learns that ongoing mainte-nance, either to repair damage or refresh parts of the structure, makes living there more enjoyable and protects the owner's financial investment. As the family grows, there may even be remodeling projects—adding a patio or deck, redoing the kitchen or bathroom, adding a family recreation room or a garage for the car. The question becomes whether to do the work oneself or hire an expert to do it. If the owner has the skills, "do it yourself" is often cheaper and more satisfying. But when the project is beyond the owner's capability, hiring a builder or plumber is usually the better option.

Running a company is no different. In recent years, the concept of focus-ing on core competencies, while outsourcing routine tasks, has become quite common. The emergence of information technology, which enabled the out-sourcing of knowledge work, not just production, to lower cost and/or more focused firms has exploded on the scene—with political and economic conse-quences far beyond a single company. Still, competing in a world where com-petitors can add capability by outsourcing, or add cost competitiveness by offshoring, makes a firm's competitive position far more fluid. Once an in-dustry begins to outsource some of its work, its customers will buy what they perceive as best value. If best value is what companies using outsourcing offer, you can be sure that trend will continue.

Outsourcing, by itself, has been the subject of numerous books. The goal here is to incorporate the complexities of large service contracts into our sup-ply-based advantage discussion.

From a supply perspective, the outsourcing proposition means three things:

1. It creates new suppliers and new spends—sometimes by turning for-mer co-employees into supplier personnel, and other times by sim-ply adding a new service to the list of suppliers a company must manage.
2. It changes the control structure, which is different for internal func-tions than it is once a process is outsourced. This new supplier has multiple customers and different business goals and market rewards than when it was an internal function.
3. It presents the same choices to the supply function as it does to any other corporate function—should we outsource supply management or keep it in-house?

Early on, as the outsourcing wave began to surge, shifting work to an-other company was driven more by M&A (merger and acquisition) and corpo-rate finance aspects of the deal—selling corporate assets to get a better return on invested capital, shifting people to cut corporate cost, and anticipating scale advantages as the provider leveraged additional business to gain both people and asset productivity. Few companies really wanted a better work process—it was about shedding cost and assets. The finance organization drove the process and not enough thought was given to the fact that a new supplier had been created. Even though the new supplier was staffed by its customer's people, it did not take long for the two organizations to evolve into different cultures with different business strategies and goals. Today, the outsourcing industries have more established providers, and tighter credit limits the cash available for asset sales. Plus, companies are more cognizant of outsourcing's supplier management implications.

Many large outsourcing engagements (think remodeling, not fixing a leaky faucet) involve complex service arrangements where product delivery is much less tangible and more subjective than buying a "thing" where quality is physically measured. As a result, managing these relationships has become an enormous challenge. Outsourcing inserts another tier of suppliers on top of those that existed before the provider came on—the supply chain is one link longer, with the accompanying lack of transparency and visibility. Once thought of as an advantage—"We don't have to spend resources managing this anymore"—it's now considered a risk—"Is the outsourcer really managing the upstream supply base well?"

Outsourcing entails five major blocks of effort:

1. Decisions on what should be outsourced and development of work descriptions.
2. Supplier solicitation, selection, and contract negotiation—the deal making.
3. Measurement and governance of the relationship and its outcomes.
4. Ongoing upstream supply understanding and transparency.
5. Contingency planning.

Unlike simple purchases, for major outsourcing arrangements, the scope, length, complexity, and close user interpersonal interactions with the provider and its service requires more careful management. In this chapter, unlike the others, many of the examples are anonymous, in part because the operations are still underway and in part because they come from people who, while willing to tell the story, have asked that their companies not be identified.

Make Versus Buy: Politics Versus Judgment Versus Data in Decision Making

Professor Bob Monczka, the 2008 winner of the Institute for Supply Management's J. Shipman Gold Medal for lifetime achievement in supply management, says the highlight of his career is his leadership of the Global Supply Chain Benchmarking Initiative while at Michigan State University. The initiative, which included 150 companies, started in 1993 and continues today. In the late 1990s, one of those companies was Cummins Engine. They presented a decision matrix for outsourcing manufacturing operations, explained the approach, and how it helped them turn their business around. Then, as often happens on the conference circuit, once they made the rounds, new best practices on other subjects became the conference darlings. The widespread publicity about Cummins' approach faded away.

Importantly, their process changed Cummins' culture from one unwilling to outsource anything to one open-minded about the idea. Today, this decision matrix is still one of the best to force good thinking about outsourcing an operation—whether manufacturing or a business process.

In the 1990s, Cummins' situation was that it needed to upgrade its product line, but its financial circumstances precluded large capital investments and additional labor expenses for new plants. Its existing facilities were full and its manufacturing culture was strong and proud, believing that nobody could make their products with the necessary quality. Financial reality and strong manufacturing pride clashed when the only affordable option appeared to be moving some production outside to free up both physical and human capital for the new products.

Given these conditions, the heads of manufacturing and procurement joined forces to evaluate the outsourcing option. Manufacturing led the project. (Procurement insisted on this in the belief that the only way to get manufacturing as a group to buy into an outsourcing choice was to have the recommendation come from its leadership.) However, there was no formal make versus buy decision process, so the first step was to develop one.

They came up with a simple yet elegant model that captures the real issues of outsourcing—how good is the company at what it does and how competitively is it able to use that expertise. The axes were "Y"—strategic importance of the operation or business process in question—and "X"— Cummins' cost competitiveness relative to other providers of that operation. Using the model was much more challenging because it required significant analysis and fact finding to understand cost structures (internal and external) and real soul searching to determine whether a manufacturing operation met the "strategic importance test."

—Practitioner's Take—

With outsourcing in vogue more than ten years after Cummins' wrenching decisions, the idea that companies want to keep an operation seems almost quaint. The mindset today is almost the opposite of what existed when Cummins started their process. "If in doubt, outsource" has replaced "if in doubt, keep it." What has not changed is the need to carefully consider your goals for the outsourcing project (cost savings, access to technology or skill, focus on core/shed non-core, flexibility to adjust to demand volatility, or improved operations through supplier expertise), and then take the time to deeply assess the two sides of the Cummins' four-quadrant matrix (yes, another four-quadrant matrix).

Unfortunately, popular mindset and internal bias make in/out sourcing decisions quite political, regardless of which way a company is leaning. In my career, I've seen both sides: major resistance to outsourcing particular manufacturing processes as well as one business unit that decided it was right to outsource all production regardless of whether the in-house operations were more competitive than those outside. Luckily, after benchmarking with Cummins, we used their model (adjusted for our industry) to force better analysis prior to decision making.

Like most of the simple four-quadrant models, this one leads to four types of operations, thus, four decisions. Cummins had fabricated parts that fell in each of these quadrants:

1. *Strategic Processes That Are Done Well* (both operationally and at competitive/low cost). These are the basis of core competency and need to be kept and nurtured.

2. *Strategic Processes That Are Done Poorly.* This is the most critical quadrant—sort of the "hell on earth" area. These processes are imperative for competitive advantage, but the company is not good at performing them. Strategic options are all risky, given these operations' contribution to market victory. They include rebuilding the capability internally (usually a lengthy and costly process—the questions being can you afford it? do you have the time to do it? and, even with the time and money, do you have the skill to pull it off?) The second option is outsourcing, but very carefully. The outsourcing supplier needs to be excellent at the process and willing to help the buyer gain knowledge so they can better compete. This requires trust, but also puts the supplier in a power position, with significant leverage in the relationship. Not a place you necessarily want to be! Fixing this quadrant requires making the best of a very bad situation.

3. *Nonstrategic Processes Done Poorly.* These are outsourcing's "no brainers." Cost savings and better operation make the choice easy. These

processes sometimes allow the firm to sell some assets to the provider (harvesting), although this is far less lucrative than it was in outsourcing's heyday a few years ago. (A P&G process that fell in this quadrant was administration of the profit-sharing retirement program, which was outsourced to J. P. Morgan Chase. The result was better customer service for employees and retirees at lower cost than if done internally.)

4. *Nonstrategic Processes Done Extremely Well*. This, too, presents a bit of a dilemma—one that the consultants and academic outsourcing gurus dismiss as ridiculous. They say get rid of it. If operational performance is excellent but economic performance close to that available outside, maybe they are right, but it requires a governance system to ensure the operation's results do not erode as the provider changes things to integrate with its own work processes. However, if internal economics are better than that available outside, even for a nonstrategic operation, the question becomes, "Why pay more to do something nonstrategic?" The answer: Keep the nonstrategic operation until it requires significant investment to maintain or is bypassed by companies that see it as their core. Monitor market evolution, then reevaluate.

The question of how to decide when a process was strategic was the one Cummins spent the most time pondering. They settled on three very clear, simple, yet ultimately valid, criteria. If the process being evaluated strongly met any one of the following criteria, it was viewed as strategic.

➤ The process provides *customer-noticeable* differentiation. The key is that the customer has to see it; it can't just be an internal function of the corporation. Sometimes this customer visibility is indirect, such as when IT system maintenance makes the company use its information better, thus operating more effectively and efficiently—which is what the customer eventually sees. The indirect relevance would make this a less strategic process, but strategic nonetheless.

➤ The skills necessary to do the work are such that building them is difficult and replacing them very time consuming (think years, not weeks or months).

➤ The buyer has enough leverage in the relationship to avoid opportunistic supplier behavior. This requires an outsourcing market that is competitive and relationship exit barriers that are low enough to balance significant increases in the supplier's power position (due to its incumbency position on a process the buyer no longer has operational knowledge of). This was the most subjective criterion, since the buyer's power is highest during the evaluation and selection process, but after the deal, the potential exists to have that power shift to the supplier. If the supplier is opportunistic, this can result in price increases, performance erosion, or lack of ongoing innovation. Assessing this criterion requires looking into the future of the relationship, understanding the service market (other supply options), and considering potential exit strategies at the beginning, not during, the engagement.

For Cummins, the results helped lead a corporate turnaround—low-value processes were outsourced and the resulting internal resources were applied to new products that succeeded in the market. Still, the conclusion that a capability is strategic has to incorporate a great deal of judgment and is, in the end, a subjective call.

Sometimes a change in management or business reality can lead to a change in how strategic competencies are viewed. That can lead to enormous changes in outsourcing decisions. The outsourcing of J. P. Morgan Chase's (JPM) IT services in 2003 is one of the better known examples.[1,2] In 2002, JPM determined that their IT back office would require significant funds to upgrade and modernize. They saw IT as an important, but not core, competency and already had outsourced a portion of it. Rather than make that large investment, the bank undertook a major outsourcing project. Initially, they divided the requirement up into two technology service "blocks": (1) mainframe and midrange system management and (2) telecommunications and networking. There was also a third managerial area—distributed systems management.

The sourcing strategy was to award the deal to a series of providers. Halfway through the process, they stopped the RFP and decided to combine all three operations into a mega-quote, looking to award it to one provider. (This strategy was common at that time, as companies, often erroneously, believed that having one provider made deal governance easier than having more than one.)

This shift gave broad-range providers an advantage and IBM came out the winner, with a $5 billion, seven-year deal that moved 4000 JPM employees and their computer centers to the IT giant. Seems like a clear-cut outcome. However, a year later, Bank One CEO Jamie Dimon sold his bank to JPM and emerged as the driving force behind the new JPM. Dimon's view of

IT was totally different than that of the previous JPM leadership. He had just invested in Bank One's systems and firmly believed leveraging customer information (particularly on the consumer side of the bank) and supporting trading operations were to become a core competency for industry-leading banks—and that these areas would require excellent and efficient IT.

IBM was struggling to manage across a patchwork of systems from JPM's prior acquisitions. (Despite IBM's best efforts, JPM's overhead efficiency ratings were the lowest of the top ten global banks in 2004, largely due to legacy system inefficiencies that IBM had to network across.) Despite committing to a $3 billion cost takeout from the merger, Dimon chose to spend the cash to buy JPM out of the IBM deal (cancellation fee) and invested over half the $1.1 billion allocated for the bank's merger and acquisition's business expansion into in-house IT.

By 2006, JPM announced further in-house investment of over $1 billion to reduce its number of data centers around the world from ninety to thirty. The increased IT productivity allowed bankers to dramatically improve service and efficiency—instituting quicker, more rigorous loan approvals (remember, relative to many other banks, JPM has better handled the subprime loan fiasco), targeting new financial products at likely buyers more effectively, and building high-end trading analysis platforms capable of using sophisticated algorithmic models to speed up trading. The moral? One firm's nonstrategic support task can be another's strategic differentiator.

Provider Selection

The pre-Dimon JPM sourcing change, from multiple operations and providers to a single broad service arrangement, exemplifies weak sourcing strategy. In 2002, the company went to market without really understanding either its needs or the nature of the supply base it was approaching. (In fact, my view would have been to look at both options—bundled and unbundled—and then decide. Instead JPM more or less decided the kind of outcome it wanted and executed its strategy in a way that delivered that bias.) A key lesson I learned early on in my career is to never prejudge the market. You can't know exactly how it will turn out, so approach the supply base in a way that discovers how the options compare, not one that leads to a preconceived answer.

Selecting outsourcing providers requires some important preliminary steps:

> ➤ *Creating a statement of work that actually describes what needs to be done and, most important, does so in terms of outcomes rather than dictating*

the details of the process to get it done. The provider probably has its own work processes. If a customer insists on unique processes of its own, it forces its supplier to recreate the individuality and lack of scale that made the internal function uncompetitive or low performing in the first place.

▶ *Effectively vetting suppliers prior to entering into an agreement.* This includes visits, checking references, using industry-specific consultants in the outsourcing field, and holistic, cross-functional work execution criteria. Even when this is done, expect surprises. Do this early on because most complex outsourcing deals are very expensive for suppliers to bid on (bid compilation costs can easily be seven figures). Don't waste supplier time and money if they really are not an option.

▶ *Developing a sourcing strategy that provides a clear approach to the market and works out the decision-making process (including who calls the shots) before going to market, not during or after.* Make sure that any internal employees who will probably go with the operation are not in the decision-making loop (conflict of interest).

▶ *Weighing carefully the contract length that would be best.* For a while, long-term agreements (from seven to ten years) were preferred and, given the nuances of complex service delivery, short-term agreements (between one and two years) discouraged because it takes a while to get it right. Perhaps the middle ground (three to five years) makes most sense, but weigh the differences with respect to the intricacy of the work.

Too often, small details that are missed during the sourcing process become major issues later. The nature of these intimate work processes is such that the people who actually do the work often carry out the tasks differently than described in the work process diagrams used in supplier negotiations. An interesting example involves telecom management outsourcing.[3] Telecom includes a complex range of products (wireless, landline, local, long distance), equipment (office systems, mobile phones, smart phones, etc.), and phone "plans" (minutes, unlimited, domestic, roaming, etc.). Anyone who has seen a corporate phone bill that comes as a CD gets the picture. Cost control is difficult and value leakage insidious.

A major power and controls equipment company managed telecom internally. One full-time non-management staff person monitored company phone policy (type of phone, unauthorized use, discontinuation of phones of departed employees, etc.).

As part of his job he chose to include reviewing the phone bill line by line each month for a major office complex and sales organization (1500 users). After the decision was made to outsource policy administration, part of the SOW (statement of work) included his job. However, the ancillary bill checking was really not part of the policy work process—just an "extra" the employee performed on his own initiative. The company moved the activity, laid off the employee, and the rest, as they say, is history.

Six months later, telecom costs had increased $600,000 over budget, far outweighing the individual's $35,000 wage savings. The resulting crisis entailed several inexperienced people reviewing the phone bills—and finding clear reasons for only $250,000 of the overage. The rest included billing errors, inappropriate user plans, and the constant personnel turmoil of shifting job travel requirements that did not match operational budget expectations. Part of the problem is that most corporate users never even see their bill. A single individual making about $3000/month had been checking all this as a "favor" to his employer. The company was forced to add a second outsourcing deal. It hired a telecom software consultant to keep up with all the moving parts, using consultant/software products with telecom-specific sourcing, policy, and plan expertise plus invoice accuracy and reporting capabilities. It was an expensive (and embarrassing) lesson in accurate outsourcing specifications (which is why this story is anonymous).

Provider selection also requires that the process include some critical elements:

> ▶ *Let the supplier view the work in great detail during the due diligence period.* This helps ferret out when internal processes are a mess and will have to be modified, before the deal is done. Unlike short-term, one-off purchases, these service contracts last a long time. It's best to get the bad news out early rather than later. Seemingly counterintuitive in comparison to some simple commodity-like buys, this level of openness is critical when the work becomes part of the value delivery system (e.g., logistics planning, customer service call centers, sales promotion/advertising) or internal corporate management (accounting, order management, accounts payable, information technology). Problems here, such as an overloaded call center during a spike in customer complaints, have massive ramifications. It is best that the provider understand the work prior to the transition.

➤ *Negotiate a contract that can survive, not just one that squeezes short-term value out of the supplier.*[4] Extremely tight contracts that provide no leeway for changing business conditions are doomed to fail unless they are constantly sidestepped by the governance organizations. Then the conflicts between the written agreement and what actually happens open the door to significant performance and legal risk. Laying out "what if" scenarios on the front end to provide options is the best approach . . . with one watch-out. During the deal making, sometimes the parties cannot agree and so create "agreements to agree" on unforeseen conditions. The contract sounds collaborative and looks mutually crafted, but it fails to address what happens if the agreement to agree doesn't happen. Laying out the consequences of failure to agree on a situation avoids this false security and clarifies expectations enormously.

➤ *Transition control from the deal makers to the contract managers in a way that captures intent as well as outcome expectations.* A formal process with a launch event is far more likely to succeed than creation of a contract management group that is the only cadre that has read or understands the agreement. Even then, the reasons why something was agreed upon during the negotiation are often unclear unless the negotiating teams are forced to co-present to the main contract execution groups why certain things happened as they did.

In one case, an outsourcing provider's top management, in an effort to preempt its competition and avoid the often enormous cost of putting a comprehensive proposal together, proposed to waive the due diligence process. This was never explained to the working level leadership. The customer's working level employees assumed their negotiating team had pulled off an enormous coup by gaining guaranteed cost reductions without having to open the books. The supplier's people had the same misconception, and the resentment they felt when dealing with unexpected complications spilled over into the relationship. Two years later the deal makers returned and explained that "no due diligence" was part of the supplier's offer, not the buyer's demands. It was the first step in trying to improve what had become a very contentious association.

Because many outsourcing deals are longer term contracts, the ability to balance making the agreement a "living document" and fulfilling results commitments is extremely important. Wages, service volumes, and geographical business shifts will happen. There needs to be a means to deal with these changes over the life of the contract, without having to constantly renegotiate. One equipment supplier and its order management service provider spent 75 percent of their time renegotiating contract terms due to routine changes because the contract was too specific, with no mechanism to deal with volume or cost variability.

Too often, major outsourcing contracts, particularly for sizeable companies (mid-size and larger) end up being books with hundreds of pages and numerous subagreements (site-level agreements—SLAs—with specific measures). All this gets passed to the governance system. Make sure that the key performance indicators (KPIs) actually correlate with business results. One IT outsourcing deal started out with about fifty measures, but as time went on and business conditions changed (mergers, Sarbanes Oxley compliance requirements, and ongoing business changes) combined to add another fifty measures.

However, when KPI results were statistically correlated to desired quantitative business results, well over half the measures were simply not relevant. The two companies were spending enormous amounts of time and energy separately measuring the 100 KPIs, arguing about whose measurements were accurate, and poisoning their ability to move the business forward—all for metrics that really didn't matter to the customer's business results.

Governance: Where the Competitive Advantage Really Lies

All of which brings us to governance, which is where outsourcing either creates profit or cost. The Cutter Consortium's 2007 Sourcing Advisory Service Executive Report points out that poor contract terms are not the primary reason for outsourcing failures. Instead, poor business planning (37 percent of the time) and poor relationship dynamics between the firms (52 percent of the time) are the overwhelming reasons deals fail. While strategy and supplier selection are important, it is the governance approach that ultimately drives the relationship and how it works (or doesn't work).

A high percentage of major outsourcing agreements are viewed as failures by the clients that entered into them. A 2005 Diamond Management study of over 200 IT outsourcing suppliers and buyers, respectively, is representative. While three quarters of the companies expected to increase outsourcing, for the first time ever Diamond found that just under 10 percent were contemplating a reduction. With many well into longer term agreements, about half the buyers had terminated a major outsourcing agreement early—more than doubling previous years' rates.[5]

A conversation with the relationship owner at a client of a major employee services provider exemplified the typical "intense SLA measurement" view of governance, and why competitive advantage requires stepping beyond that limiting perspective. He complained, "I feel like a goalie. When you only play defense, you can't put any points on the scoreboard."

First let's define governance, especially for complex services like IT, employee relations, call centers, telecom, complex assembly/manufacturing, research, and so forth. As Paul Lynton, Director, Management of Change at Hewlett-Packard Services, sees it, governance is a work system for framing and managing the relationship—not just a measurement process.[6] The service provider (supplier) and its client (customer/buyer) use the governance system to mutually manage the relationship including expectations, contractual dependencies, and service delivery using a set of processes and practices that include relationship, contract, change, performance, and conflict management. This is where contract performance and long-term flexibility to deal with change must meet. Without performance and flexibility long-term competitive advantage will suffer, even if short-term advantage is gained.

An examination of major outsourcing deals brings a set of frustrations to the surface that is relatively universal. They are, in many respects, no different than those of internally performed processes that cross functional boundaries:

- ▶ Scope ambiguity (especially at the boundary of the process and when special cause situations arise)
- ▶ Different interpretations of what was agreed to (internally between functions and with the provider relative to the contract)
- ▶ Unanticipated costs
- ▶ Deterioration of service levels
- ▶ Difficulties keeping top staff and institutional knowledge about the particular firm in place

The contract, alone, is necessary but insufficient to manage these issues.

In large outsourcing agreements, the ability to manage results requires a blend of commercial (think procurement-like) and technical (think operations-like) people in the governance organization. A common fallacy is that the company that outsources a business process does not need to maintain knowledge about that part of the business. Such abdication results in "reality blindness" in the governance organization about how normal business change impacts the agreement. Maintaining a level of process understanding/knowledge is important to the governance task.

Governance best practices almost universally include a set of joint committees, each specifically designed to manage a different part of the relationship. When these deals involve "shared core processes," these joint governing committees are even more important. "Shared core" often falls in the "hell quadrant" of the Cummins' make versus buy model, where companies are forced or choose to outsource items or processes critical, but not central, to their ability to compete. Frequently, these are deeply embedded in the operation, impossible to extract, and move to the outsourcer in isolation. The goal is to select and manage relationships that allow rebuilding some internal knowledge over time, while maintaining a capable supply interface.

That means an outsourcing provider must co-locate, either physically or virtually, in order to make the intimate connections to the customer work. On the customer side, there can be no loss of control over the operation due to its mission-critical status. Typically the customer is unable to create a competitive advantage alone due to lack of skills or capital to invest at leading-edge levels. What emerges is a hierarchy to jointly lead the "service delivery entity," almost like a separate firm or a joint venture. As an example, a typical governance hierarchy would include:

1. *Executive Steering Committee.* Senior leaders that serve as the business alignment body for the joint effort. They provide joint direction and business oversight. (Think Board of Directors.)

2. *Relationship Management Committee.* Managing leadership that provides the direct management of the overall relationship and is cross functional. This includes operational, commercial/financial, technical, human resource management, and SLA metrics. (Think Management Committee in a business.)

3. *Service Delivery Committee.* The operational leaders of the various business processes that are included in the overall agreement. This includes ongoing management, change management, business planning, and SLA metrics for each of the processes to be jointly managed. (Think product division within a business unit.)

4. *Specific Process Teams.* Delivery of the ongoing work. (Think a production line team in a factory.)

These governance groups interact to drive the outsourced business and manage the culture of the joint relationship—providing infrastructural foundation. Shortchanging these efforts in order to cut headcount is a formula for value leakage, not value creation. The idea here is to approach the service outsourcing work as if it were a joint (buyer and supplier) cross-functional business unit selling its services to (internal) customers. Competitive advantage comes out of that mindset because it drives a set of relationship touch points to sustain communications and action as things change. These touch points include:

- ▶ Clear leadership connections and responsibilities, including principles for how to interact in the relationships and deployment processes to communicate with both companies' governance personnel.
- ▶ Regular meetings, with clear, joint agendas.
- ▶ Forums for process KPI (key process indicator) measurement, review, and joint reconciliation that avoid double-checking inefficiencies.
- ▶ Joint work forums along with space for independent work. There needs to be a balance between the dangers of working independently but efficiently and the risk of "too much togetherness" that wastes time.
- ▶ Problem-solving processes and forums. Remember that people both create and solve problems, so these forums need to focus on both solutions and problem anticipation/avoidance.
- ▶ Understandable conflict resolution processes. Too often, when conflict happens no one understands how it is supposed to be resolved. The process should be clear and relatively simple.
- ▶ Decision processes that lay out what, who, how much, and when decisions are made and whether specific decisions should be joint or independent.

All of this sounds quite collaborative but be clear, this is not a "group hug." As in a marriage or a sibling relationship, rivalry and disagreement are normal. The key becomes to try to make conflict constructive instead of destructive. That is where regular, meaningful touch points matter.

—Practitioner's Take—

In the years since leaving P&G, I have had some consulting engagements that involved troubleshooting large, long-term service outsourcing arrangements ranging from manufacturing to less visible processes like order management and IT. In addition, I managed P&G's manufacturing outsourcing in North America for five years and was involved in many service arrangements as a user. In these experiences a set of problems turned up repeatedly.

- *Language Differences.* Time after time, I observed simple terms carry widely different meanings in different companies. This can really get in the way. In one engagement, the parties reached an impasse when the client asked the provider for "transparency" into their business processes and supply arrangements, offering the same in return on their side. The supplier did not react well at all. Two days into a three-day "relationship improvement" work-shop—after much frustration on both sides that fed a misconception that the supplier wanted to hide bad news—the real issue came out and it was about semantics! It turned out that in the supplier's culture the word "transparency" meant "big brother" behavior and connoted distrust with intense scrutiny, looking over people's shoulders and second-guessing every action. In the client's culture it was a "norm" and high transparency was viewed as a positive. Until this "dictionary dispute" came to the surface and was resolved, the relationship battled instead of moving forward. (Amazingly, the simple decision to substitute the word "visibility," which had better "vibes" for the provider, created an atmosphere of cooperation instead of resistance. On such little things is leverage of supplier capabilities built!)

- *Internal Shielding.* Governance groups often view their role as the buffer and contract interpreter between each side's internal businesses. As a consultant, I repeatedly find the client governance group telling the supplier what is needed, while blocking any direct contact with the real internal customer—the business unit or function using the provider's service. In one case (call center), senior business management became more and more upset with "service outages," while the supplier was never told what was required—largely because the governance organization was not close enough to the changing competitive and business climate their internal customers were facing. Clearly, having a buffer is not always wrong and, in fact, is often right because unfettered contact can quickly cascade into anarchy with individual user groups requesting multiple, conflicting actions with no overall priority setting, cost estimating, or scope clarity. The problem was that the buffer masked the internal customer's dissatisfaction and its real needs. The answer in this case (and several others) was periodic, structured, controlled user/provider/joint governance committee meetings followed by clear prioritizing and decision-making processes to jointly determine actions coming out of the sessions across and between businesses on both sides.

- *Lack of Productive Client Presence at the Provider Operational Level.* In a call center the client had enormous supplier personnel turnover on its business. The reason? This particular client had a mindset that because they bought a service, the provider should provide it without any need for client involvement. This expectation caused the client to resist helping the provider be successful. Worse, the governance group was entirely made up of people who had done the work internally and had fought the outsourcing agreement and lost. They felt they did the work better (although much more expensively) and resisted any changes the outsourcer sought to incorporate from its standard processes. Result: A parallel process that the provider's employees hated and constant criticism with no praise from the client resulting in high turnover that hurt client customer service. (It turned out that the provider's best and happiest clients regularly met with the service module employees, in some cases even co-locating a two- or three-person cadre, to explain requirements and help solve ongoing issues directly. This client never bothered to ask what happy customers did differently than they did.)

- *The Contract Penalty Trap.* In an IT services agreement, the contract provided for penalties when service levels dropped below a certain minimum. However, when unexpected business crises caused surges in service usage well beyond those foreseen in the SLAs (e.g., a product recall spiked service centers' telecom requirements tenfold), there was no mechanism to reprioritize during the emergency. The provider, after shifting resources to meet the need, and getting financially penalized for dropping below several "routine" service levels as a result, changed its approach. First priority was meeting the letter of the contract, while second was addressing the client's real business need—the crisis, since those surges fell outside the penalty provisions. The client saw each crisis as a service failure (even though the contract said otherwise) while the provider saw no reason to take a revenue/profit hit to help the client solve a problem the provider did not cause. The client had forgotten that when it managed this process internally, it had informal communication links that suspended the routine to deal with the extreme. These informal communications traveled broadly and quickly so that routine service users recalibrated expectations almost automatically. Once outsourced, those links dried up and could not cross company boundaries, leading to penny-wise pound-foolish operating decisions. Once the real problem surfaced, SLA changes were needed to provide crisis management protocols.

- *Escalation Extremes.* Conflict is inevitable in processes where hundreds of interactions happen daily. Two conflict resolution extremes can emerge, each of which destroy long-term value creation. In one approach, everything gets elevated to the senior level for resolution, paralyzing the work until a "decision comes down" and creating the perception, which quickly becomes reality, that day-to-day interaction is poor. In the other, people advocate for their company instead of looking for solutions that can work or at least mitigate the problem. They resist escalation because it is interpreted as a failure by those above them. Neither extreme works. Paul Lynton at HP Services lays out a healthy escalation progression, saying 85 percent of the problems need to be resolved at the working level, another 10 percent at the service delivery level, 5 percent (major ones) at the Relationship Management Committee level, and fewer than 1 percent should reach the Executive Steering Committee level—only those that entail rethinking the nature of the joint business value proposition.

Many of these issues seem almost trivial in hindsight, but create major problems. Managing "invisible" business processes with lots of personal, subjective user/provider interaction can be harder than internally aligning across a company because two sets of business needs are involved. Assign top-quality people to these engagements. Periodically rotate them (Lynton recommends about 30 percent a year, after the first twelve to eighteen months, to avoid burnout) and publicize wins, not just problems.

Risks of Outsourcing

The next chapter will explore risk management more deeply, but within the outsourcing arena, there are some particular risks that must be anticipated and managed.

Upstream Supply Base Transparency

The first is balancing provider responsibility for managing the supply base that supports its work with the client's need to have situational transparency and direct contact with upstream supply tiers. This risk is easiest to visualize when considering manufacturing outsourcing—a physical process with inbound components, an assembly or product creation process, and customer order fulfillment.

Since buyers first outsourced manufacturing, the scope of the service has dramatically increased. What was once only nonunique, nonstrategic manufacturing outsourcing slowly evolved to include supply of components, sourcing those components, then product design, then product delivery directly to customers, including customer service—resulting in end-to-end outsourcing. It usually occurred over a period of years, as the enticement of cost savings from low-cost country suppliers incrementally encouraged scope creep.

The unexpected result can be a hollowing-out of upstream knowledge so that up-tier innovations start coming only through tier-one suppliers (the outsourcing contractor). If their contract manufacturers or supply chain management contractors filter the buyer's contact with sources of market differentiation, the buyer may lose the ability to see breakthrough innovations because the outsourcing provider does not see the customer's full business situation. This is even worse when providers are more interested in selling to the industry than tailoring for particular customers. Unchecked, this loss of contact leads to shifting upstream supply base leverage from the buyer to the service provider. For buyers that do not have the contacts to begin with, this is less of a problem. For those that have forged valuable connections into subcomponent supply tiers, this is a huge loss.

Part of relationship governance with a service provider needs to be the ability to have direct and joint contact with upstream suppliers and, if necessary, develop joint sourcing strategies with the outsourcing supplier. Scarce resources make it difficult to set up governance with the time, knowledge, and capability to look "through" the first-tier suppliers. Adding resources to understand where potential value or which finished product advantages lie in the upstream supply base is a hard sell to managers looking to maximize near-term profit. Yet those who have crafted a competitive advantage from the supply base allocate some resources to do just that—witness companies like HP, IBM, and Apple's product material, component, and software acquisition mastery that is part of their product design core competency. These companies do not relinquish total control to the tier-one contractors. Neither do the best footwear companies like Nike, Adidas, and New Balance.

The only way to manage this risk is a combination of contractual rights to upstream supplier communication and operating principles that make that direct communication okay for strategic components. Couple that with routine upstream market intelligence in search of potential differentiating technology. Sometimes the service provider can be of enormous help in this process, but other times they are looking to meet their business needs before their clients' needs. Maintaining supply contacts upstream of your core suppliers is vital to tailoring upstream developments into your business model. That means incorporating the expectation on both sides of the governance structure that periodic market benchmarking and upstream connections are normal parts of the business.

Scott Beth, a supply management executive with experience at Intuit, Agilent Technologies, and HP, lays out a good methodology to use with tier-one suppliers to determine ownership of routine upstream supply management interfaces. Each supply subprocess, from the search for innovation to quality control to logistics management, is identified. The question of who is best positioned, short and long term, to do this work needs to be asked of each subprocess, with a corresponding decision on which company—the outsourcer or the customer—should take the lead and which the support role. Work the supplier is best suited to do needs to be delegated, but even then, should have oversight from the customer—as the toy industry discovered when it delegated responsibility for raw material sourcing completely to its contractors and later found lead paint in its products. Upstream suppliers must know how this "direct" procurement or supply management responsibility has been apportioned so expectations for future involvement from the client are firmly in place. Finally, the choices that are made each year should be routinely reevaluated to fit ongoing business needs.

Creating a Competitor

The second unique risk is that of creating a potent competitor by outsourcing too much knowledge—essentially outsourcing your brains. The first time I really thought about this issue was at a purchasing conference in 2002 when the person next to me, from Black & Decker, commented that his group evaluated suppliers on several criteria, including competitive potential. I asked what that meant and he replied, "Some of these low-cost country suppliers could easily become our competitor in a few years. We have to assess that probability prior to doing any work with them."

A few years ago New Balance Athletic Shoe Company (NB) noticed that highly discounted shoes (some priced at $20) were showing up in stores across the world.[7] NB's long-time Taiwanese supplier's south China factory made NB sneakers, including low-tech styles for the local market. NB gave the supplier a license to produce NB shoes for the China market, and the Taiwanese owner began selling them locally. Eventually, NB concluded that these low-end products needed to be curtailed, as the company's marketing strategy shifted to focus on higher-tech models. Suddenly NB noticed that the supplier factory acquired materials for close to half a million pairs, including several colors and styles that NB never ordered. Low-price shoes started showing up in Japan and Western Europe, while U.S. retailers advised they were approached by middlemen with container-loads of similar shoes. Chinese courts found for the supplier due to the license agreement.

The dispute led the company to stop doing business with this long-term supplier and highlighted the cultural differences that make working globally difficult. More importantly, NB revamped its supply base, dramatically reducing the number of Chinese factories it used, monitoring them more closely, and shifting away from designs that were easy to knock off.

The same story has occurred in numerous industries. American vacuum manufacturer Royal (Dirt Devil brand) moved production offshore to TTI (Techtronic Industries) in an effort to save money. Within a few years, TTI bought Royal as it forward-integrated, looking for better margins than the competitive contract manufacturing business would bring. A couple of years later, the iconic Hoover name became part of the Hong Kong–based former contract manufacturer.

Palm received high accolades for its contract manufacturing approach to PDAs and smart phones. In 2001, the company was the darling of the high-tech world as it touted its "virtual manufacturing" approach of using contract manufacturers to make its products.[8] Then Senior VP of Global Operations, Angel Mendez, cautioned in 2003 that it kept an ironclad grip on the sourcing of critical commodities used in the assembly (microprocessors). Two years later, Mendez was using his contract manufacturing suppliers as ODMs (original design manufacturers) to do the mechanical and electrical design of the phone. He cited the "collaborative way design comes together" and reported cutting months off development times, lower defect rates, and higher margins.[9]

The supplier of choice for this work was Taiwanese ODM, High Tech Computer (HTC). HTC became the largest Windows-based smart phone manufacturer and began selling its own phones—including a line of four smart phones and five touch phones. Today it is the number three manufacturer, losing some volume as customers became competitors, but the choice to become a competitor has been made and the knowledge this supplier gained from its ODM position was clearly part of its long-term strategy.

General Motors' Chinese manufacturing partner, Shanghai Motors, made thousands of Buicks and Chevy's for the American company's Chinese business.[10] In 2006, it announced that it would begin producing its own four-door sedan under its name for sale in China, while at the same time announcing a long-term plan to export the product to the United States and Western Europe.

The examples go on. The point is that, as New Balance VP for international sales said about his company's experience, "Once you teach them how to make it, anyone could do it. It could happen to any of our suppliers anywhere in the world." Choosing extensive outsourcing and then expanding it into design and/or sales can create a potent competitor—the antithesis of competitive advantage.

Fraud: When Suppliers Steal Value Instead of Create It

Heavy use of contractors that work intimately with a company's organization have access to corporate data and, in some cases, source the firm's buys, requires vigilance. In any relationship, trust needs to be earned not just given. Procurement is no different. Sadly, the most extreme example of widespread supplier fraud is the experience of the U.S. military since 2002, with massive levels of "lost funds" in the Iraqi and Afghan wars and a large number of domestic no-bid contracts that have raised suspicions of illegal actions.[11] By mid-2008 there were ninety-five ongoing fraud investigations stemming from Middle Eastern and Afghan procurement practices, plus an additional 500 cases launched in the United States unrelated to war contracts. The allegations include double billing, illegal rebates, kickback payments, bribes, and conflicts of interest (awarding business to companies related to government employees without bidding processes).

Before simply damning the Pentagon's procurement operation, it is important to recognize that its search for value is much more complex than that of for-profit companies. Why? The value equation is different. In a war, running out is not an option. Furthermore, decision-making stakeholders are not just suppliers and buyers. They include elected officials whose value equation often includes domestic and district jobs; and appointed officials, for whom value is defending the powers that appointed them.

This means suppliers that lose business can (and frequently do) politically protest the award. Lobbyists also can exert significant pressure on the buy. The balance of ongoing spend (fighting a war) must be balanced with long-term, multibillion-dollar innovation projects, the outcomes of which will likely drive the ability to wage (and win) battles in the future. This leads to intense budget pressures in a system where elected officials (with attendant press coverage) must agree to budget appropriations in a politically charged atmosphere. These are no small tradeoffs! In comparison, the corporate search for competitive advantage is pretty straightforward.

Still, the level of fraud is outrageous and has grown dramatically since 2000. Again the question is, why? The answers are found in the quest for supply-based advantage. When unclear value definitions from conflicting stakeholders with very different goals are combined with skill shortages/outages and intense budget pressures, outsourcing agreements replace in-house staff to save money. That allows contractors to spend enormous amounts of money in an extremely ambiguous and fast-paced atmosphere—a recipe for supplier fraud.

In this case, the military spend more than doubled between 2002 and 2007, much of it overseas in very fluid situations. Yet, the military never authorized an increase in the number of people for contract governance and fraud investigation. With limited governance, weak information systems, and chaotic conditions, it is clear that good spend control is one of the first disciplines lost. Worse, the lack of strong skills and consistent sourcing and supplier management processes means that doing it right in the first place is more unlikely than the amount of money in question would warrant. The government is driven by rules, and, if you have gotten this far into this book, you have recognized that narrow rules don't work well in a dynamic commercial and operational environment.

Example: A Kuwaiti contractor responsible for feeding American military personnel in Iraq buys food from U.S. suppliers that are approved by the government. In military food contracts, the buyer typically procures the food from the approved sources at full cost and delivers it to the government— billing the government for the food plus delivery. The Kuwaiti firm negotiated early payment discounts of 6 percent and lenient payment terms of ninety days, and kept the discount for itself. (There was no specific rule against their doing this, but the normal discount the government had seen in the past was closer to 2 percent.) Government auditors concluded these were kickbacks, resulting in an investigation, which, at the time of this writing, has not been concluded. However, one result that did emerge was a change in military procurement rules to limit discounts to contractors for early payment to 2 percent.[12,13]

—Practitioner's Take—

Creative thinking and skill development in the private sector would lead to a different approach to the above problem. Rather than institute a rule limiting discounts, a more "value-creating" approach would be to allow whatever discount could be negotiated, share the savings in a manner that gives the supplier incentive to minimize the government's cost, and gain in the process. The fact that the military paid full (list) price regardless of the supplier's ability to get a discount was not strong procurement in the first place.

A second example is the ongoing sourcing of the Air Force aerial refueling tankers that began with the Darlene Druyan situation described in Chapter 4.[14] Seven years after the first RFQ was issued, no planes are on order. After numerous starts and stops, the Air Force awarded this politically sensitive contract to a joint Northrop–EADS (parent of European Airbus) supplier. Incredibly, despite the high visibility and likely scrutiny surrounding the award, Air Force procurement, after review by the General Accounting Office, violated its own evaluation criteria and even made mistakes in assessing one of the competitors' cost proposals. In other words, they botched the analysis (probably a complex one, but given the political stakes one would expect lots of careful checking). Again—poor supply management skills! Meanwhile, the Air Force still has no refuelers; it began another "accelerated" round of bidding in July, looking for a decision by December 2008, and then the Pentagon canceled the revised bidding yet again. As of this writing, they will likely start from scratch with decisions in 2009—eight years to run a bid!

Skill deficits, unclear or conflicting value definitions, and questionable practices often go hand in hand; when politics (governmental or internal corporate in the private sector) is added to the mix, the risks are even higher. The combination of weak supply capability and a lack of controls/contract governance capacity make a bad situation (dynamic wartime procurement) even worse. When these internal competencies are missing, fraud is a real potential. The military is heavily outsourced—so the potential for fraud is huge unless strong governance and contract management is in place.

Procurement Outsourcing:
Letting Somebody Else Do It

Like any other business process, supply management can be outsourced as well. In late 2007, Aberdeen Group published a report on procurement outsourcing, the title of which included the phrase "strategic imperative."[15] Outsourcing supply management can be done a number of ways, just like IT or HR—do the whole thing, do a particular process (e.g., spend analysis, sourcing, contract management, order placement, etc.), do a particular category of spend (e.g., indirect, as United Technologies did under Kent Brittan, discussed in Chapter 8), or do it incrementally with selected parts of categories and/or processes. The Aberdeen report said that while just over a quarter of companies outsource some procurement with another 15 percent expected to begin, of that 40 percent, about half chose the "selective incremental" approach and only 10 percent were willing to outsource the entire function.

A read of this book lays out why firms want to do this. Leveraging the supply base into a company strategy is no small task. While short-term savings due to provider supply scale and expertise tops the list of reasons to outsource procurement (56 percent cite it), the real reasons revolve around short-term savings goals, lack of expert resources, pressure to downsize headcount, reluctance to invest the time and effort to build capability, and need to improve particular processes—especially spend analysis on the strategic end and order placement on the transactional side.

MeadWestvaco (MWV), a major packaging company, concluded that it needed to dramatically improve its sourcing market intelligence.[16] The combination of a very lean organization, too much data for too few analysts, plus unforeseen commodity price spikes and supply chain disruptions caused organizational overload. The press of the business precluded gradual resource increases, so MWV chose to outsource supply market intelligence to an Indian firm, Beroe, in a way that integrated the supplier into its commodity strategy, sourcing support, and contract management processes.

The outcome worked well, driving better strategies that delivered supply availability in tight markets and better cost structures with minimal initial investment. The outsourcing supplier provided customized support to its client and became a joint member of MWV's sourcing teams. In the perspective of Tony Milikin, MWV Senior VP for supply, the reasons for the success were recognizing that the supply process is strategic and that its "shared core" aspects required an integrated approach rather than the traditional "delegate and let them do it" of many outsourcing deals.

The integration plan included ongoing market intelligence support (not short-term event-based sourcing), supplier incorporation into MWV's sourcing process as a participant (not just a data provider), and MWV involvement in the ongoing process. This was about the supplier tailoring its service delivery while utilizing backroom analysis resources for scale. Think of it as a computer system that has great user interface that makes people believe it was designed just for them, while sitting on a strong data infrastructure that is efficient and effective.

Net: Success in procurement outsourcing is about determining what you need and why, then investing in provider relationship management, ongoing client involvement, and governance—the cores of this chapter.

—Practitioner's Take—

Like the other tools available to manage the supply base, procurement outsourcing is a process tool to be used appropriately, not a silver bullet to fix everything or avoid the work. The bigger question is how it fits with the goal of competitive advantage. The trick is how customized the interface between provider and client is. Consistent with the tool perspective, like most CPOs in the Aberdeen study, my view is that incremental, carefully scoped and selected procurement areas (processes needing an injection of expertise or procurement of some nonstrategic spends) are the best use of the tool.

Competitive advantage is about differentiation and resistance to duplication by competitors. Straight procurement outsourcing to simply leverage scale for lower prices is unlikely to lead to sustained advantage. It might be okay for selected spends, but for important items, it won't deliver sustained advantage. Depending on the supply management ability of your competitors, such parity with large buyer leverage might be sustainable, but only if your industry has weak or limited supply resources. If another competitor chooses to invest in managing its supply base well and accomplishes that goal, procurement outsourcing could become a competitive rigidity that facilitates internal supply skill atrophy, leaving you unable to respond to the threat of a competitor's supply expertise, leading to disadvantage on a competency necessary to win (Cummins' hell quadrant).

The keys are, as MeadWestvaco described—prioritized targeting, governance, and ongoing relationship management of the provider. One of the revelations of researching this book was the creativity and agility of small entrepreneurial companies toward their suppliers, and their unwillingness to delegate the important supplier relationships and selection to others. Duplicating the value creation potential of that model means managing governance issues. Remember, each of the unique outsourcing risks mentioned above (lack of upstream visibility, creating a potent competitor, and fraud risk) includes procurement outsourcing where providers source large spends but the customer ultimately pays for it.

HP's Lynton puts it well.[17] Outsourcing is not about something as trite as "win-win." It is a far more complex ebb and flow of relationship advantage over time, during which each party will seek the upper hand. The real ability to win is about knowing when to share and never abdicating support for the work. Both parties need to own the process and its outcomes while respecting both parties' needs. Given the long term of many of these agreements, if one party consistently loses, it is time for both to get out of the deal. But winning may look a bit like a tug of war, which can work as long as each side has periods of enhanced results and remains committed to the relationship, and neither gets dragged into the mud puddle in the middle.

By the way, the Aberdeen report, "Procurement Outsourcing: A Strategic Imperative?" ends in a question mark, not a period.

Notes

1. Jeff Moad, "Consolidation Move Sealed $5B IBM Deal," *e-Week*, February 3, 2003.

2. Mara Der Hovanesian, "JPMorgan: The Bank of Technology," *Business Week*, June 19, 2006.

3. Douglas A. Smock, Robert A. Rudzki, and Stephen C. Rogers, *On Demand Supply Management: World Class Strategies, Practices and Technology* (Conyers, Ga.: J. Ross Publishing Inc., 2007), pp. 141–142.

4. Bill Deckelman, "Check Your FQ . . . Flexibility Quotient," *Outsourcing Journal*, October, 1997.

5. Tom Weakland, *2005 IT Outsourcing Study*, DiamondCluster International (now Diamond Management and Technology Consultants, Inc.), Spring 2005; study can be accessed at www.diamondconsultants.com/PublicSite/ideas/perspectives/downloads/Diamond2 005 OutsourcingStudy.pdf.

6. Interview with Paul Lynton, Director, Management of Change, Hewlett Packard Services, May 18, 2007.

7. Gabriel Kahn, "Factory Fight: A Sneaker Maker Says China Partner Became Its Rival," *Wall Street Journal,* December 19, 2002.

8. Jim Carbone, "Strategic Sourcing Is Palm's Pilot," *Purchasing,* April 17, 2003.

9. Pete Engardio and Bruce Einhorn, "Outsourcing Innovation," Business Week Special Report, *Business Week,* March 21, 2005.

10. Gordon Fairclough, "GM's Partner in China Plans Competing Car," *Wall Street Journal,* April 5, 2006.

11. Richard Lardner, Associated Press, "Military Struggles to Reduce Fraud," *Cincinnati Enquirer,* June 13, 2008.

12. Glenn R. Simpson, "Military Seeks Tighter Rules on Food Deals," *Wall Street Journal,* January 30, 2008.

13. Glenn R. Simpson, "As a Small Firm Takes a Top Role Supplying Troops, Questions Arise,"*Wall Street Journal,* December 8 and 9, 2007.

14. August Cole, "Surprise Ruling Gives Boeing New Shot at $40 Billion Job," *Wall Street Journal,* June 19, 2008.

15. William Browning III, "Procurement Outsourcing: A Strategic Imperative?" Boston: Aberdeen Group, November 2007.

16. Tony Milikin, Daniel McNally, and Vel Dhinagaravel, "Market Intelligence as a Critical Supply Management Tool," presentation at Institute for Supply Management 92nd Annual International Supply Management Conference, Las Vegas, Nev., May 6, 2007.

17. Paul Lynton, "MoC Relationship Transformation & Governance—Dealing with Result Accountability and Conflict Resolution," presentation at The Conference Board Supplier Relationship Management Conference, Atlanta, Ga., March 7, 2008.

CHAPTER 12

Risk Management in the Supply Base

Insuring Against Damage, Loss, and Liability

> INSURANCE: the act, system, or business of insuring property, life, one's person, etc., against loss or harm arising in specified contingencies, as fire, accident, death, disablement, or the like, in consideration of a payment proportionate to the risk involved.

There are risks and costs to a program of action. But they are far less than the long-range risks and costs of comfortable inaction.

—John F. Kennedy

Here and there throughout this book, we have talked about risks in various parts of the supply-based advantage proposition—supply chain disruptions, social responsibility outages, outsourcing loss of control, etc. Homeowners face the same situation. Insurance policies for fire, weather, natural disasters, vandalism, and accidents are the risk management mechanism of choice. But as Hurricane Katrina and natural disasters like the 2008 Sichuan earthquake made clear, risk management also needs to include foresight in building materials and codes, safe design layout, and occupant security. Most accidents occur in and around homes because people lower their guard in familiar surroundings. A company can't afford to make that mistake too often, especially if it is seeking supply-based advantage.

Supply chain risk has exploded on the scene with the advent of low-cost country labor sourcing, social responsibility issues, product safety recalls, and major corporate malfeasance investigations (resulting in the United States' Sarbanes Oxley [SOX] law and the European bribery investigations of Siemens and Alstom). What was, at one time, a second-rate task in supply organizations, centered mainly on supply assurance, has expanded to include everything from corporate reputation protection to price risk management (hedging) and extends far deeper into the supply network than just the tier-one suppliers that ship directly to the buying company.

Risks have become so wide-ranging and pervasive in a global supply network that many companies struggle to grapple with it. A March 2007 Aberdeen report labeled the best in class supply risk management companies as those with programs just three years old and concluded that 49 percent of companies have no formal supply risk plan in place.[1] Yet supply risks have been around forever—part of Ulysses S. Grant's military strategy for the American Civil war, about 140 years ago, was to shut down and destroy the South's supply lines—naval blockade of southern ports, Sherman's march to the sea destroying the South's crops, and capturing the Mississippi River to cut off Texas, a major food and leather supplier, from the rest of the south. Supply disruption as a military strategy worked. So, why is supply risk just now emerging? Perhaps because it is so easy to splinter into disconnected slivers managed independently.

Holistic Supply Risk Management Planning

Too often risk becomes an endless checklist of things to worry about that paralyzes those who ought to be managing it. Risks are rarely independent. Instead, they tend to slop into each other—a supplier financial risk quickly becomes a supply availability risk when that firm fails. A logistical risk quickly becomes a cost risk when fuel and shipping capacity limits cause major transportation price increases. A supply chain safety risk quickly expands to become financial liability, corporate reputation, supply availability, and regulatory intervention risks. A supplier commitment risk becomes a financial reporting outage risk, which evolves into a regulatory risk (witness SOX). Before somehow categorizing and describing supply risk into a set of workable tasks, start with a simple question: What does the firm want from risk management?

Step 1: Set Some Goals

If your objective is to avoid all supply risks, start over because you will fail. If the objective is to intelligently manage risk, including a decision about which risks matter most, then you are on the right track. Every company has its own appetite for business risk, of which supply risk is just one aspect. The decision, made in concert with senior management, needs to be how much risk do you want to take and what are you willing to spend to manage it? Old-fashioned cost/benefit analysis works well here.

Step 2: Assemble, Categorize, and Prioritize the Risks

Most supply risks are an outcome of tactical and strategic supply moves already made or contemplated. This is where long lists can become overwhelming. Categorization approaches to group and limit those lists include:

> *Nature of the Risk.* This category is typically broken into five large subcategories:
>
>   1. Legal (e.g., legal and ethical behavior, contracts, illegal pricing agreements, antitrust, intellectual property)
>   2. Financial (e.g., price volatility, supplier financial health, cost versus forecast, credit risk)
>   3. Operational (e.g., supply availability, supply interruptions, supplier quality, internal controls, project startups, fraud)
>   4. Regulatory (e.g., trade laws and tariffs, ingredient safety limits, financial reporting)
>   5. General business environment (economy, demand, etc.)

> *Internal Versus External.* Does the primary source of risk lie inside or outside the company? Kickback fraud, internal controls outages, and SOX compliance may lie largely inside, while commodity price volatility and supplier fraud are outside.

> *Proactive/Reactive Management.* Flowing out of Step 1's risk prioritization and the ability to foresee or control risks, this category looks at which risks can be managed largely up-front through efforts that

simply avoid the situation and that require a clear contingency and crisis management process that will only be executed in response to the risk occurring.

Step 3: Understand the Risks

Before risk can be managed it must be understood on two levels: as an individual risk and as a risk that interacts and integrates with other risks. For example, understanding the upstream supply chain delivery risk means having an appreciation for your suppliers' suppliers. That overlaps with regulatory, corporate reputation, safety, cost, and logistics risks. The devil is often in the details, so thoroughly understanding each major risk means penetrating it. If you have to start from scratch, the task can be overwhelming, so an important process intervention is to add risk assessment and management plans to your ongoing sourcing and supplier relationship efforts.

Step 4: Manage the Risks

Once understood, risks are better managed. Managing risk, generally, is a three-stage process, but in the supply arena, a fourth stage becomes the differentiator between competitive advantage and competitive parity.

1. *Risk Taking.* Understanding the risk and choosing to actually take it or not. Sometimes a path is too risky and needs to be avoided.

2. *Risk Mitigation.* Taking steps to lower the risk level before taking action. This involves contingency planning, installing redundancy (e.g., multiple suppliers or supplier locations), adjusting timelines, etc.

3. *Risk Management.* Monitoring and adjusting actions based on circumstances. It's important to implement mitigation plans, engage in problem solving, and, in extreme cases, stop to reevaluate.

4. *Risk Syndication/Collaboration.* Engaging suppliers to help manage the risks. Supply is inherently a two-sided coin, so enrolling the supplier in the risk mitigation/management stages can be quite powerful. The supplier's response, especially to highly strategic risks, can be enlightening. A strategic supplier who says, "You're on your own," may need to be reevaluated. Go through the same exercise internally with cross-functional peers as well.

Step 5: Integrated Reporting

Create a supply risk dashboard to monitor the health of the risk management system as well as adjust to major corporate or market environmental changes. Changing business circumstances can significantly change appetite for risk, leading to commensurate changes in the risk plan. Inherent in risk reporting is prompt, accurate communication when risks change or occur in the supply chain.

—Practitioner's Take—

While somewhat helpful in terms of creating an overview process, all of this remains heavy on theory and light on "how to's." Executives still get angry when business results are seriously impacted by a supplier mistake and rant about how supply managers could let this happen. Worse, during these situations, self-preservation makes it far easier to blame the supplier for problems than to shoulder the internal proportion of responsibility. Responsibility for most supply problems (not all) is a shared one, either through actions of commission (our contribution to mistakes) or omission (lack of planning or timely action—also often ours).

Supplier performance management, internal cross-functional collaboration, and strong communication channels, both internally and to suppliers, are the processes that support risk analysis and management. Once those have begun, the trick is to start by focusing on the basics: supplier quality, supplier delivery, overall cost competitiveness (total system, not just price), supplier responsiveness (time, ability to change), and supplier approach to legal and public relations issues.

Different companies determine different risk areas to address and then create their own approaches to do so. Prior to 2005, Dow Chemical's supply organization was predominantly focused on two things, savings delivery and efficiency improvement.[2] Then hurricanes Katrina and Rita hit their U.S. Gulf Coast plants hard and Dow became synonymous with "force majeure," as they failed to supply customers and repeatedly went on supply allocation. The organization's goals suddenly broadened to holistic strategic sourcing, of which supply risk management was a key component.

Dow used a combination of data and judgment to assess supply risks across four categories—supply market, suppliers, organization, and supply strategy, with a priority on mitigating the risk of supply disruptions. The result was the PRAM methodology (Procurement Risk Assessment & Mitigation). With 5000 materials coming into its plants, Dow first prioritized down to the most important 100, using likelihood of a disruption and Dow's profit/margin at risk in the event of a disruption to create a "heat map" for Dow products and business units. Size of the spend was not always predictive of "high heat." Some relatively small spends had disproportionate impact on financials.

Once the most important materials were found, the exercise became to evaluate each of the four risk types in terms of variables that could impact the risk. Example: Supply market risk might include number of qualified suppliers, location of the suppliers, whether the supplier had multiple plants, and whether other potential suppliers were available. Based on those evaluations, potential risk mitigation plans were developed (sometimes internally and sometimes with the suppliers) and costed out. Then the business and product management leadership were engaged to decide whether to "buy the risk insurance" by implementing the mitigation plan and thus absorbing its cost.

This kind of risk assessment and planning is no small task, requiring resources and a willingness to be thorough and engage the business.

Internal Risk Approaches: Controls, Contracts, and Intellectual Property

Supply risk does not always lie outside the company. The boundary-spanning nature of the supply chain makes internal risk management areas, when focused on interactions with suppliers, a key part of the control system. In fact, where established internal processes can pick up an external view, the efficiency of using existing infrastructure to support the supply side of the work is greatly increased.

Controls: Ensuring Supply Processes Work

The SOX legislation in the United States put a premium on internal controls, but long before that, competitively advantaged supply organizations recognized that staying on top of their internal processes was key to managing suppliers well. Internal controls procedures, intensified in recent years, simply allow that recognition to be clearly communicated and expected. The cost to implement these controls is generally inversely proportional to how far along companies already are in their process control procedures.

A comprehensive supply controls system needs to measure and enforce a set of ten key control areas:

1. Policies and principles toward the supply base are in place and in use. This includes ethical standards, broad training programs, legal guidelines, and conflict of interest reporting and investigation processes.

2. Adequate separation of duties is in place to ensure fraud will be prevented. The classic inbound supply duties—requisitioning, receiving, and invoice clearance—need to be done by different people to make perpetrating fraud more difficult (requires three people, typically in three different organizations). It also includes data management safeguards to separate supplier master data administration from any procurement activities. Extension of this concept into procurement outsourcing arrangements is also important—does the outsourcing supplier have good separation of duties?

3. Delegation of authority is in place to make sure that all commercial agreements are signed only by individuals with clearly delegated authority. This is a critical element because many times suppliers do not know who has legally delegated authority to buy, so they will accept orders from almost anyone at the buying company. Internal control is the only reasonable way to police the potential for unauthorized buying. Therefore spend analysis and electronic ordering systems need to be included in this control area.

4. Strategic sourcing processes that maximize company value need to be in place and utilized. This engages finance in the effort to use sourcing and supplier relationship management processes broadly to avoid poor placement of business. The processes extend from sourcing through to supplier performance measurement.

5. Information system data masters used to manage supplier purchases and performance need to be documented, managed, and up to date.

6. Purchasing commitments should conform to legal and corporate requirements and be communicated to users and suppliers in a timely manner.

7. The contract negotiation process should be monitored such that all contracts are signed (or terminated) effectively and decisions to work without a contract or buy while continuing to negotiate specific

terms and conditions are agreed to by the appropriate management level (per #3 above).

8. Invoice discrepancies are resolved in timely fashion and before payment (or, if after payment, with careful resolution follow-up).

9. Claims should be filed with suppliers and followed for settlement. The decision to cancel a claim must have proper authorization.

10. Information security protocols are in place, including computer security, intellectual property agreements, and business information safeguards.

For many supply practitioners, this is the somewhat boring underbelly of financial and operational supply base management. While it's not the energizing integration into the firm's business model and lacks the excitement of supply deal making, it does represent the bedrock discipline necessary to support those efforts. The importance of putting a system in place to train the supply organization and key cross-functional partners on each control area cannot be overemphasized. The effort needs to go beyond training by instituting a periodic self-auditing regimen, regular internal auditing controls, and the inclusion of supply and supplier management in the external auditor's annual reviews.

Contracts: A Commercial Framework

Contract management represents the connection between documentation of the commercial relationship's framework going forward and the means, through software applications, work processes, and authority delegation, to create a closed loop system between the deal's commercial conditions (price, transport, ownership transfer, volume, quality, payment terms, etc.) and the actual performance financials. For simple contracts this is quite workable. However, for complex agreements like the ones we discussed in Chapter 11, changing business conditions can greatly impact the relevance of some contract terms.

Developing a philosophy toward contracts and their connection to doing business is as important as the actual contract management process. Two overarching commercial approaches exist—the "sign my paper before you can do business with me" view and the "negotiate the details after finding how much value is possible" view. Companies often pick one or the other as their primary approach, falling back to the second when the situation requires it. Sounds like heresy!

For basic items and in situations where the buyer has the power, the former approach makes sense because it provides a stable set of supplier terms for the vast majority of purchases. However, when the buy is complicated or the markets put the supplier in the power seat, the likelihood of ending up there is minimal.

—Practitioner's Take—

During my career, I became a proponent of the second view—find the value and then work out the agreement. This often telescoped the negotiation process beyond when goods or services began to flow. The requirement of completed, signed contracts before doing any business can cause a lot of value to never make it to the table. But, moving forward with an unsigned, partially agreed-to contract is part of supply base risk management. For ongoing supply relationships, the business agenda keeps moving regardless of whether the contract is signed or not. Obvious exceptions are major outsourcing deals or massive supply arrangements that entail investments on both sides.

Having the completed agreement before anything ships is very clean, but competitive advantage lives in a gray world. Contract deadlines can create so much pressure to sign that it becomes a conduit to weak, poorly negotiated agreements that forfeit value, particularly when the supplier relationship has some adversarial elements or the attorneys and auditors on either side take "high ground" noncompromise positions that the commercial people are unable to overturn. Choosing the "find value, then a contract" approach means working through a risk mitigation plan:

- *Pick the commerce.* Taking the risk of working without a signed contract requires that the arrangement have two important elements: (1) a compelling business need for the buyer to move forward and (2) knowledge of, and history with, the supplier that gives context to the risk of opportunistic behavior or legal action.

  Don't do this when new suppliers, high-risk business plans, and known opportunistic vendors are involved! Then you need a documented framework that protects the buyer and clearly lays out all the standard contingencies. (The sales side is probably saying the same things concerning procurement organizations as I write this!)

- *Nail down the key provisions before anything starts. Always!* Understandings on cost, quality, delivery terms/process/responsibility, invoice payment terms, volume/capacity, and length/exit timing expectations must be in place and documented before any commerce begins. Interestingly, during the overwhelming majority of the time working without a contract, situations are driven by impasses on warranty, insurance, liability, regulatory, legal venue, and other important (but not commercial) clauses that deal with the many "what ifs" that surround the deal when things go wrong.

- *Continue to negotiate.* Really. Continue to talk and craft potential clauses for the provisions still in question. Don't just put the unfinished contract in a file and forget about it. This back-and-forth dialogue makes it clear, legally, that these terms are not agreed upon, just in case you end up in court or arbitration. They also present a chance to unearth mutual value—such as changes in insurance responsibility that can change the cost structure, or the ability to find middle ground on warranties. These negotiations are particularly important in litigious societies like the United States, but even where lawsuits are less likely or local country laws unenforceable, these negotiations bring clarity to the relationship's underlying expectations for commercial interaction. It incorporates contract clauses into relationship management.

- *Line up internal stakeholders.* Make sure the business leaders, lawyers, and auditors know what is going on—especially the business leaders. In the end, they must decide on risk taking. However, to do that they need to understand the tradeoffs a pressured contract signing would likely require versus delays in contract commencement versus working without a final signed agreement.

- *Don't forget about international culture.* Some places do not see the contract as the final deal. It's just "today's agreement," and is modifiable when circumstances change. Many Western companies learned this the hard way in emerging markets, after signing what they thought were ironclad contracts, only to discover that local legal and business contract norms were far more flexible. In this regard the "work without a signed contract" approach probably creates a more compatible mindset toward what could happen.

If your organization sees the goal of contract management as efficiency and legal "bulletproofing," then you are likely appalled by this line

> of reasoning. However, if the goal is a flexible, value-creating environment that can open additional doors, then contract management needs to become part of the commercial risk taking and risk mitigation process.

Intellectual Property: Intangible Value with Competitive Implications

The importance of intellectual property has become far greater today than ever before. As author Daniel Pink, in his best seller, *A Whole New Mind* (Riverhead Books, 2005), explains, winning products today incorporate both left- (logic and science) and right- (design, empathy) brain thinking, with the trend favoring the soft side. That broadens the range of intellectual property considerations dramatically to include traditional inventions, design patents, trade secrets on producing a product that incorporates an experience—you get the point. Add to that other proprietary information like customer preferences or new product business plans and the value of intellectual property grows. Intellectual property protection can look like a fortress wall that surrounds everything with any potential—that is what many intellectual property attorneys espouse. On the supply side, encouraging open innovation (described in Chapter 7), is the balancing factor.

Incorporating intellectual property considerations into the supply relationship has similar considerations to those just described in the Practitioner's Take above on unsigned contract negotiation. Laying out the principles first is what matters most. Unlike commercial agreements, however, intellectual property (IP) is about intangibles—ideas—and as such requires internal discipline. IP needs to be incorporated in any agreement (part of those ongoing negotiation clauses for most, but a prerequisite for commencement for those where innovation is the core of the contract's business focus). Internal processes need to exist that provide clear authority for these agreements (I strongly suggest that patent attorneys, not supply managers, review all intellectual property provisions) and an invention/idea registration protocol, protections where it is warranted, and most important, clear rights of use should all be firmly in place.

The purchase of software and complex outsourcing services are probably the most important areas to get clear on usage rights. The nature of those relationships can lead to the buyer not really knowing what technology or software the application/service they are using is based on. As software applications are strung together to create the IT infrastructure, it's imperative to understand this idea chain's flow through your platform and stay in control of how intellectual property can flow across your supply base. In one case, a company's IT service provider and its ERP software supplier had reached different and conflicting IP agreements with the client. When major business changes occurred—a big acquisition, a significant divestiture, and entry into new developing geographies with inconclusive intellectual property laws—chaos ensued. The client ended up in long sequential negotiations about license rights and data sharing with each supplier.

—Practitioner's Take—

Intellectual property can also be a potent competitive weapon that suppliers use in their industries to gain advantage relative to their competitors. IP becomes a problem, however, when the collateral damage from these patent wars endangers your business. In my own experience, we had a key class of ingredients that was supplied by two highly technical suppliers. These companies hated each other! Yet, as a major customer, we were able to have alliances with each—requiring the internal IP discipline mentioned above in spades, to ensure no cross-contamination of the two suppliers' ideas!

Things changed when both companies purchased the patent libraries of competitors exiting the business. Amid those patents were some that could call into question the other supplier's patents used in their exclusive materials. (The term "patent troll" has arisen in the electronics world to describe this practice.) Suits were filed by each supplier against the other. Our patent organization analyzed the situation and recognized that some of the litigated patents underpinned exclusive materials incorporated into our products. As a close customer of both firms, we were squarely in the middle, at risk of losing key performance attributes developed with each supplier.

Our technical/commercial/patent people kicked into high gear, seeking to negotiate with each supplier to no avail. We realized we needed to get all three parties together. Both suppliers initially refused to set foot in the same room. After weeks of delicate "shuttle diplomacy" they agreed to a small, narrowly focused meeting with lawyers present to avoid any illegalities.

Our point was that we did not presume to tell them not to sue each other. Rather, we explained that as their customer, we would be hurt if either or both won, and asked for them to come up with a means to keep us whole regardless of the legal outcome. They understood our situation and contingent licenses were worked out to allow our use of materials we had already been purchasing from each, even if the courts overturned any patents. Without the blend of strong relationships and astute intellectual property skills, this could have been more of a disaster for us, the customer, than for either supplier.

In 2004, the apparel industry faced a similar issue when longtime adversarial competitors, TAL Apparel Ltd. and Esquel Group, fought over the patents for no-pucker seams held together by high-tech, heat-sensitive adhesives. These seams are necessary for no-wrinkle garments because they stay smooth and flat in the washer and dryer.[3,4] TAL had the first patent, but Esquel, a big vertically integrated clothing maker (they grow their own cotton in China), came out with its own patented version in 2002.

Apparel buyers like Nordstrom and J.C. Penney, brands like Polo Ralph Lauren, Tommy Hilfiger, and Hugo Boss, and manufacturers like Japan's Diahoh all buy from these two suppliers—several from both. The suppliers' cross-suits raised the potential to leave the customers without enough supply if one succeeded in closing down the other's operation. The owners of the two firms, Harry Lee (TAL) and Y. L. Yang (Esquel), had an intense rivalry triggered by Yang having left TAL to start Esquel twenty-five years earlier. This time, no buyer-brokered deal emerged, but the apparel industry breathed a sigh of relief when, three years later, the courts declared TAL's patent unenforceable, leaving both suppliers' capacity in place.

Recognizing the importance of supplier intellectual property is only the first step in managing this risk area. Connecting the IP implications across multiple firms in a supply industry is the second.

External Risk: It's About Performance

The combination of lean production (inventory takeout), faster cycle times, and more spread out supply chains equates to greater risk. ChainLink Research, a supply chain research organization, made the point that each significant supply disruption carries an enormous negative impact (40 percent reduction in shareholder value).[5] The result is a growing brittleness in supply chains that leads to frequent small and occasional large outages. The Aberdeen Group's 2005 Supply Chain Risk Benchmark study cited 82 percent of supply chain executives experienced a supply disruption within the prior twenty-four months.[6] In my experience more than half the manufacturing plant shutdowns that occur are the result of supplier performance issues: delivery delays, capacity shortages, or quality problems. Supply risk involves more than figuring out where things are. It has to include what's going on with them. So, while emerging technologies like RFID (radio frequency identification) tags may matter, RFID and other tracking technologies are only one aspect of risk management.

The ability to manage these kinds of issues across a broad, multitiered supply base come down to the same old three factors: processes, relationships (people), and technology. Supplier performance risk arises from several sources:

- ► Supplier financial/credit viability
- ► Supplier geography (political and currency)
- ► Supplier operation outages (quality, plant breakdowns)
- ► Supply concentration (e.g., sole/single sourcing by choice)
- ► Supplier dependency (no backup options—sole/single *not* by choice)
- ► Supplier logistical delays/outages
- ► Supplier supply (upstream commodity shortages)
- ► Supply/supplier regulatory issues
- ► Supply chain labor disruptions
- ► Supply information errors

ChainLink's Bill McBeath conceptualizes the combination of processes, people, and technology better than most, combining the three in each of four categories:[7]

1. Management of the links via dual sourcing and flexible agreements (process), strategic relationships (people), and supplier performance reporting and event alerts (technology).

2. Proactive and predictive intelligence and management via risk analysis, including identification, assessment, prioritization, and planning (process and people) and monitoring systems with predictive analytics (technology)

3. Forecasting and design via volume forecast ranges (best and worst cases), scenario planning (people and process), and postponement

(process), product design for interchangeability (process), and supply chain modeling (technology).

4. Flexible supply via internal flexibility to incorporate multiple supplies and use of multiple underlying design platforms (process), multiple upstream sources with strong relationship linkage (people), and flexible operating option analysis such as optimization or simulation (technology).

Implementation of these approaches, however, is not a spare time exercise. In most companies, supplier information is scattered across functions, time zones, and business units. The same barriers we explored in Chapter 10, difficulties in moving information and knowledge across boundaries, plague this effort as well—and that is just on the internal side. Technology like supplier information management software (or supply intelligence software) has grown in response to the growing importance of this area. These applications overlay existing data/software across three areas—supply, sustainability (corporate responsibility), and risk—using portals, dashboards that allow both supplier involvement in maintaining the data, as well as proactive measurement by the buyers. The idea is to centralize all supplier data and provide user-friendly ways to analyze and review it.

Even more difficult is actually reaching into the supply base, where conflicting direction (be transparent and safe but be extremely low cost) sets up a reward system for suppliers to source their upstream requirements with a "squeeze" mentality in order to eke out a profit. Avoiding the risks of this dynamic requires the selection of suppliers that have the same principles and, as importantly, upstream monitoring interest and follow-up as you do. The complexity and breadth of these supply networks make 100 percent certainty virtually impossible. The task is to choose the supply base with risk management as a criterion, penetrate the high-probability, high-priority supply risks—both with suppliers and supply chains—and have a rapid-response plan for the outages that surprise you, because there will be some.

Suppliers get the blame, but they too face the same problem. Witness Mattel's 2007 lead paint toy recalls.[8,9,10] A combination of complex supply webs, intense cost pressure in a highly competitive market, and some unique aspects of Chinese business culture all combined to leave Mattel with a serious problem. Yet, the company's stock only fell about 4 percent after three recalls, as analysts noted that they had a relatively strong supply chain monitoring system and that the vast majority of the recalls were due to Mattel design problems (tiny magnets) rather than lead paint. The recalls cost Mattel

$30 million in addition to the stock price reduction—not small but not massive either.

Compare that to the supplier, Lee Der. Chinese authorities suspended the company's export license, leading to bankruptcy. Its 5000 employees lost their jobs. Its owner, a fifty-year-old entrepreneur named Zhang Shuhong, committed suicide in the company's warehouse within two weeks of the recall. In addition to business pressures, Zhang fell victim to a violation of the Chinese relationship code called *guanxi*, the single most important concept when doing business in China—your network of relationships.[11] It has concentric circles of influence—first family, then close friends, and only then, business partners.

Guanxi is built on four Confucian pillars—*ren,* a leader's obligation for his followers; *continuity,* the need to be in harmony with the past; *the market,* it's natural to bargain hard; and *obstacles* (China is a blend of cultures and working across them is itself an obstacle, and not just for Westerners). The paint factory that supplied the tainted pigment was owned by Zhang's best friend. Lee Der specified non-lead paint but put its trust in a high guanxi relationship with the owner's closest friend and awarded the business to a company that Mattel did not approve, without Mattel's knowledge. Zhang's loss of face was enormous—employees out of work, trust betrayed in a very competitive market with big cultural differences. He hung himself.

A second Mattel supplier, huge Early Light Industrial Co., also found some lead contamination. The company had subcontracted with another Chinese company, Hong Li Da, who contracted with yet another company for the paint supply. In this case, Early Light did not solely rely on traditional relationship management, but also incorporated the types of checks its long-term customer Mattel used—monitoring and testing. It found the problem and quickly reported it. It was an isolated instance that was traceable. The outcome, continued operation, no license suspension, and little, if any, loss of guanxi, was very different.

The point here is that a combination of traditional information tracking and analysis—monitoring and the use of technology—must be coupled with close, longstanding relationships. Circumstances change and with them relationships, whether due to changing business requirements or new leaders/ownership. Reliance on long-term corporate association, while a factor in operational risk management, is not enough. Two more examples make that clear.

At the Institute for Supply Management's 2008 global conference, Boeing gave an excellent presentation on its use of Lean in managing its suppliers.[12] During the Q&A afterward the inevitable question of how the supplier issues on the Dreamliner (Chapter 7) could have occurred given the rigor and philosophy (ask for help before you need it) of their program. The answer was thought provoking. The suppliers Boeing chose for the Dreamliner were ones with which they had long relationships, many of whom were taking on new tasks and technology. One of the common denominators across the suppliers in the most unexpected trouble was that they were the most proud of their capability and most confident of their ability to hit Boeing's performance targets. Overconfidence can create risk blindness at any tier of a supply network.

The second example is a much older story—the infamous Ford Explorer/Firestone radial tire scandal, which resulted in numerous consumer vehicle rollovers, injuries, and deaths even though the tire was specially designed for that SUV.[13] The Firestone/Ford relationship went back to the beginnings of the auto industry—Henry Ford and Harvey Firestone. But in the finger-pointing and intense public scrutiny this tire recall triggered, the gaps in the relationship and the lack of up-front, prompt risk mitigation processes led to disasters for both companies. In the end both announced they would no longer deal with the other, but they had ceased being close partners years before Japan's Bridgestone became the supplier instead of the original Firestone management.

At the height of the safety recall, several developments emerged that point to lack of rigor, probably due to complacency from the decades-long relationship, allowing small problems to grow into a monster. As Ford noticed a trend in its warranty data flagging a problem, its chief procurement officer, Carlos Mazzorin, contacted Bridgestone CEO, Yoichiro Kaizaki, urging the two companies to work together on the recall and for Bridgestone to search for the cause of the failures.

Instead, because alone among auto parts, tire warranties are owned by the supplier not the auto company, Bridgestone demanded that the lawyers negotiate a confidentiality agreement before releasing any product quality data, eating up valuable time. When Ford finally began analyzing their own data and the slowly released Bridgestone information, they found spec violations in an overseas market (a layer was left out of the tire by Bridgestone) and traced the source of the North American problem tires to a single U.S.-based Bridgestone plant (of three making the tires). Ford saw it as a tire problem.

Meanwhile, Bridgestone focused on the fact that Ford's tire inflation targets were significantly lower than Firestone's recommended levels as the cause, making the automaker and consumers that didn't check tire pressures the problems. Lower pressures improve traction and handling but cause more friction, the heat from which led to tire failures. (Interestingly, Goodyear, which also made Explorer radials with a spotless safety record, recommended the lower pressures.) The outcome was negative for both companies, but the lesson was that longstanding relationships are not always what they are perceived. Up-front risk management with rigorous agreed-upon standards and ongoing monitoring are also necessary.

While supply base risk is often equated to physical supply chains like toys and tires, the services chains are equally vulnerable to problems. In 2001, as the dot.com bust destroyed many Web-based companies, the U.S. Office of the Comptroller realized that banks had outsourced their IT functionality to contractor and software companies that were now at risk. As a result, the financial services industry started an IT working group (BITS—originally standing for Banking Industry Technology Secretariat) that developed a number of supplier management approaches and templates for services, particularly IT.

The BITS framework for managing technology risk in IT providers is one of the documents that emerged from this group.[14] It lays out a good thought process (although its language is quite legalistic and lengthy) by overtly incorporating a supplier's ability to maintain controls into the supplier evaluation and selection processes. The framework extends all the way to incorporating disaster recovery procedures, recommended governance, and risk testing.

Price Risk: Hedging

The advent of hedge funds as investment vehicles with high return potential, coupled with press reports of successful hedge strategies like those of Southwest Airlines (where hedge profit has, at times, offset a quarterly operational loss), has led to the belief that hedging is a cost savings strategy.

Nothing could be further from the truth, or more dangerous to the firm. Hedging is about risk management. Speculation is trading for profit. In neither case does the trader know the future. When commodity price volatility—crude oil, metals, agricultural products, natural gas, pulp/paper, and chemicals all spike, those who see hedging as a cost reduction approach are at great risk to lock in prices at the top of a bubble. While this provides price certainty it also can preserve a competitive disadvantage for as long as the hedge lasts. Before leaping into hedging at the direction of a beleaguered CEO looking to "stabilize the pain," recognize what hedging is:

> ➤ Supply hedging is a business strategy, not a supply strategy. The primary goal needs to be the reduction of earnings volatility stem-

ming from purchased commodity price volatility. The objective is to protect a business plan from potential cost surges, not save money.

▶ Hedging is about predictability of cost. It is meant to reduce uncertainty, not beat the market (although, in some circumstances it may extend favorable market conditions, as Southwest has done with its jet fuel hedges).

▶ Hedging requires cross-functional business involvement. Without it, expensive problems can emerge. For example, in 2000, Ford's finance, procurement, and product design organizations were not in good communication during a physical hedging program on palladium, which is used in catalytic converters.[15] In response to Russian producers' withholding supply, the purchasing guys started buying and storing metal (with senior management approval). Meanwhile, the finance guys did not know and thus did not help apply financial hedging tools (futures and options) to the problem, and the R&D guys began projects to drastically reduce the use of palladium without much communication with either purchasing or finance. Two years later, in a falling market, Ford took a $1 billion palladium inventory write-down. It had lots of inventory, significantly less usage, and a market price well below what they paid for the metal in storage.

▶ In a volatile commodity market, the decision *not* to hedge is as much speculation as the decision to hedge 100 percent. In both cases you are betting that you know what the price will be. The point is that not hedging puts you at the mercy of the market completely, while 100 percent hedging fixes a price when you really cannot predict what the market will do going forward.

▶ There are only five ways to manage price risk:

1. Be able to increase your price to recover supply price increases.
2. Stockpile physical inventory bought at a particular price.
3. Trade futures or options for the material on a commodity exchange.
4. Negotiate an "over-the-counter" hedging deal privately with a counterparty—similar in effect to using an exchange but less transparent and without the exchange's credit risk management.
5. Accept the price risk and don't hedge.

▶ Success needs to be measured in terms of risk reduction and business plan stability despite fluctuating physical prices. Therefore, success is, in part, determined by each firm's tolerance for supply price risk and the earnings fluctuations that risk creates.

► Understand what your competition is doing. If they are vertically integrated and you are not, their material volatility will be tied to their feedstock and production costs, while yours is essentially tied to the market price of what they make. For example, P&G for years bought the pulp used in its paper products, while competitors like Georgia Pacific and Kimberly Clark made theirs. In weak pulp markets, that gave P&G an advantage, while in strong markets the reverse was true. We learned to build those fundamentals into our business plans.

Like the other tools in this chapter, hedging starts with analysis, not action. The analysis has three views of commodity price volatility's business impact:

1. *Individual Commodity Risk Exposure.* This involves both directly purchased materials like fuel or power and indirectly procured ones like the plastic resin in a bottle, natural rubber in surgical gloves or industrial adhesives, the cotton in clothing, the ethylene monomer in polyethylene, or the grain needed to feed beef or chicken. The analysis entails looking at price data over several years and applies statistical tools to understand the mean, standard deviation and price distribution over time.

2. *Overall Business Risk Exposure.* This view looks across the business at all commodity impacted materials. In a large company, the various individual risks, when aggregated, can provide extremely valuable perspective. Some commodities are negatively correlated over time (much as stocks, bonds, and commodities are, and have different highs and lows that can partially offset each other, giving less earnings volatility in a diversified investment portfolio). Looking at the aggregated risks by commodity, business unit, geography, and product line is critical in prioritizing where risks have the greatest economic impact, how much risk is there, and which commodities are highest priority to manage. One chemical company concluded it had nine key commodities that were both "hedgeable" (instruments were available or could be developed) and strategically relevant. They were: aluminum and its derivatives, energy, precious metals in catalysts, petrochemical solvents, paper (packaging), olefin derivatives (plastics), corrugated linerboard, caustic soda, and transportation fuels.

Their hedging analysis helped them home in on four that mattered most for real protection.

3. *Market Analysis.* Using current fundamentals and historical trends to perform a market analysis offers a view that helps provide a perspective on the general direction of the market. It is important to stress-test this analysis, since unlike the historical price analysis above, it is a forecast, not a fact. Test what happens to the business if this forward look is very wrong—both on the high and low sides.

Once the overall exposure is determined, compare that with the risk tolerance of each business and the overall firm, to determine how much risk to take off the table. This is where individual exposure, aggregate exposure, and market view come together to set a business hedging strategy.

Hedging Price Risks Includes More Than Price

Financial hedging carries with it several complicating factors: accounting risk, index risk, and credit risk. Let's briefly address each one:

► *Accounting Risk.* The most bedeviling are the complex accounting standards that apply to hedges. Because they are derivatives, hedge instruments are subject to hedge accounting rules requiring close statistical correlation between the hedged commodity and the physical product actually bought. In the early days of its jet fuel program, Southwest did a great deal of work in this area, because when they began hedging, no hedge contracts for jet fuel, per se, were available. They had to work out the price correlations between heating oil and crude oil and their jet fuel to determine which mirrored their cost structure most closely. Some airlines hedge jet fuel directly using tailored over-the-counter hedges, while others use correlations with oil in the public exchange traded markets.

► *Index Risk.* In hedge contracts, the hedge price is compared to an index—in Chemicals, CMAI's index is often used; for crude oil, the commodity exchange closing price is often used. Depending on the wording of the contract, if the price falls below the hedge price, the hedging party has to pay its counterparty the difference between the two prices. Conversely, when the price goes up, the hedger "wins." If a market intelligence service's (e.g., CMAI) index is used, its accuracy is subject to error since the prices that go into it are self-reported by companies, averaged, and not posted publicly like commodity exchange quotes.

- *Credit Risk.* Since the parties must pay the difference between where the market closes (or index is reported) and the price specified in the hedge contract, having the money to pay is a big deal. When oil went far above anyone's estimates in spring 2008, companies that had hedged expecting $80 oil suddenly faced huge payments to make good on the financial hedges. This can happen to either a hedger or a speculator.

Always remember, every hedge must have two sides, so for every winner there is a loser. When the losers panic and the markets keep moving against them, companies can fail. In late 2004, China Aviation Oil (CAO), China's monopoly importer of jet fuel, set up a subsidiary in Singapore to trade jet fuel via oil futures.[16] The company hedged with a market view that oil would fall in price. When it didn't, rather than take the losses and reevaluate this view, the company negotiated to move back its positions in the continued expectation that prices would turn. The initial loss was just over $5 million, but as the market continued to move against CAO, in just over six months these speculative bets on 52 million barrels of oil exploded to 110 times the original loss. The company's Singapore entity went bankrupt, the Chinese government had to step in to stand behind and close out the hedges, and the CEO and several aides were suspended and put on trial for failure to disclose the losses to the Singapore exchange as they mounted.

—Practitioner's Take—

If all this sounds complex, it is! Derivatives are not something to entrust to inexperienced people or jump into because you are panicked over cost escalation. If you choose to use financial hedging, it is critical that best practices be followed, the most import of which are:

- Hedging should be integrated into the business strategy rather than functioning as a stand-alone supply economic strategy.
- Clear trading controls must be in place, listing specific individuals who are the *only* people who are authorized to trade derivatives, with clear limits (in terms of explicit commodity, volume, money, and length of hedge commitments) and there must be strict en-

forcement of those trading controls and policies, with routine re-porting of commitments daily. These markets can move swiftly, so turning your back on them is not smart.

- There should be joint physical and financial market connection—think linking physical procurement, physical volume estimates, financial instrument trading (hedging), and financial manage-ment (finance and accounting). This is a best practice that emerged after the Ford palladium debacle above—had they linked procurement, the financial organization, and R&D's usage reduc-tion efforts, their palladium hedge would have been both smaller and more effective.

- Traders need to be well-trained experts. The complexities of deriv-ative contracts are no place for amateurs. A couple years ago, the supply management blogosphere buzzed with comments about Sara Lee Corporation's addition of two experienced pork traders to help hedge commodity price inputs to their consumer product businesses.[17] The truth is that any food company that does not have pricing power with stores is, and has been, hedging for a while—the blogosphere just was not aware. The business implica-tions of a poor hedging strategy or bad execution of that strategy puts a premium on hiring or developing people that know what they are doing. The traders at Sara Lee were brought in by its new CEO from Pepsi, who was surprised to find they were not rou-tinely hedging their businesses that included meat- and grain-intensive products.

- Hedge instruments have a finite length. Eventually they end. When they do, there is no guarantee that you can renew them at a favorable price level. Business addiction to a "great" hedge is like drug addiction; you wish you had more, but if the market has truly shifted, you may not be able to find what you want—either price or quantity—in the new environment. This means the busi-ness unit needs to plan around both leveraging the current hedge and building a plan for when the hedge ends and the competitive price landscape shifts back to pre-hedge economics. Many compa-nies build a rolling hedge strategy that looks for predictability over time, rather than an opportunistic price target.

Hedging Strategy Elements

Development of a hedging strategy, the "sourcing strategy" (Chapter 5) for financial price hedging, is critical. It defines the business need and how price predictability plays into that need to support company strategy. Within that hedge strategy there are six levers that can be used—and they all will be shaped into a strategy that will drive specific use of each lever:

1. *Commodity.* What commodity should be hedged to reduce price risk the most?

2. *Business.* Which business should be protected first (what are the various vulnerabilities of different businesses or product lines)?

3. *Instruments.* Should you use exchange traded, "over-the-counter," or physical purchase commitments? Should you use futures, options and "plain vanilla" hedges (directly hedge the material involved), or "cross hedges" (hedge something to cover what you actually use like CAO did with oil and jet fuel).

4. *Volume.* How much of your volume should you hedge? Remember, the answer is either some type of rolling hedge that moves with the market over time or a portion of your volume between 100 percent and none at all, because each of those extremes is speculation, not hedging. You are betting the price you lock in will be competitive. If your hedge comes in under the market and you make money that is great, but if you are over, you just gave the competition a cost structure advantage. A position somewhere in between balances those competitive business risks.

5. *Price.* At what price level should you lock in (strike price)? This is where historical price statistical analysis, ability to pass increases to customers, and potential "bad outcome" scenario testing all matter.

6. *Length of Hedge (Tenor).* How far out do you want to go? Southwest Air's long hedges have kept them competitive and profitable for a while. But length also adds risk as Ford found out when its long position unraveled because its usage dropped, leaving way more material than planned in a down price market.

The combination and utilization of these levers is the heart of hedge strategy execution, once the business has determined what the hedging strategy actually is and how it relates to its business strategy. The advent of commodity-based investment funds have doubled and tripled the levels of hedge instruments used in these markets, causing both positives and negatives. On the positive side, there is a much wider range of commodities that can be hedged in 2008 than there were just five years ago. The negative is that speculators are a much bigger part of the market, making market fundamentals less predictive of where near- and mid-term prices will go.

This creates a user-based market view less tied to the fundamentals of physical supply and demand. In my career, I was a strong believer in fundamentals analysis (underlying supply and demand usage trends) as the dominant driver of hedge strategy. However, the second type of analysis, technical trading, uses statistical analysis to decide very short-term trends (often based on recent market activity, market momentum, and market emotion) and may become a bigger part of the strategy if these investment buyers stay a major force in the market.

Take the chocolate bar business. Cocoa (plus milk and sugar) is the commodity driver behind the cost of a chocolate bar.[18] In mid-2008, prices went up over 10 percent, driven in large part by a more than 50 percent cocoa price increase over early 2007 levels (from \$1700 a ton to \$2600). About 30 percent of a chocolate bar's cost lies in that cocoa, and candy makers have long hedged against cocoa price volatility (remember Mars in Chapter 2?). But a closer look at the dynamics of the market shows a growing investor influence:

▶ In 2005, chocolate producers held about 943 K tons of cocoa futures contracts on their hedging books, while speculators (hedge funds and other investors) held about 261 K tons, or 21 percent of the futures market.

▶ In 2008, the chocolate industry held 706 K tons, while the speculators held 655 K tons (48 percent of the market).

Some observations over the most recent three years: (a) despite a 25 percent fall in industry demand for hedge contracts to cover price uncertainty based on cocoa use, the overall financial market size is up about 10 percent; (b) speculators are half the market, up from a fifth; (c) futures prices are up 50 percent; and (d) when, almost inevitably, investor profit taking and the value of commodities in a diversified investment portfolio drops, these speculators will move out, reducing demand. The question is when and how to chart a market with steady fundamentals but high investor interest. That is the hedging environment that chocolate makers face when developing their hedging strategy.

—Practitioner's Take—

One last thought—there is a fundamental difference between physical contracts with suppliers and financial contracts with counterparties. In the physical product world, suppliers' business success is, in part at least, tied to your business success as their customer. If something in the agreements you have with physical suppliers puts you at a competitive disadvantage and your business slumps, so does theirs. That is why regular contracts are often renegotiated when the business situation changes. The risk is shared to some degree.

In a financial hedging contract, regardless of the commodity involved, you are not really buying and selling that physical good. Instead you are buying or selling the *price risk* around that good, which you will actually buy in the physical market. This is just a money transaction. Other than the potential for your bankruptcy (like CAO), the counterparty has no vested interest in whether your business slumps or not. They only want the money they are owed if the hedge goes against you. Renegotiating a hedge contract, other than in bankruptcy, simply does not happen.

On the other hand, physical suppliers can open contracts for renegotiation when their circumstances change. Force majeure declarations can change your physical availability and prices unilaterally in a physical contract. The financial hedge instrument counterparty does not have that option—the price stays firm.

Think about that when you make the choice between building inventory (with its cash and storage issues) and financial hedging (with its ruthlessly inescapable "don't care about your business" stipulation).

As we have seen, supply risk management is not simple. It requires tight business connection, careful analysis, thorough execution, and rapid response to the unexpected. Most of this chapter carries the perspective that the supply base is the source of the risk.

Another thought on the matter comes from the late management guru Peter Drucker, who, before his death in November 2005, related a conversation with a European client about the use of computers (reverse auctions) to buy things.[19] They were talking about how you go about choosing a supplier. The client said, "The last decision is, do I trust this person?" Drucker asked him why that was important, given the impact of the Internet on supplier selection and management. The client responded, "Because whenever you get in any kind of a crisis, you rely on your supplier to bail you out."

Drucker's observation was that there is a difference between a supplier that sees a quick buck and a supplier that sees a relationship. The computer does not provide that kind of judgment. Sometimes the supply base turns out to be a risk management technique, not the risk.

Notes

1. William Browning, III, Vance Checketts, and Andrew Bartolini, *Supply Risk Increasing While the Market Stands Still,* Aberdeen Group, March 2007.

2. Paulo Moretti, "Procurement Risk Assessment and Mitigation," presentation at The Conference Board Supplier Relationship Management Conference, Atlanta, Ga., March 6, 2008.

3. Rebecca Buckman, "This Patent War Really Involves Seamy Doings," *Wall Street Journal,* November 2, 2004.

4. PR release from K. L. Lee, Managing Director, Esquel Group, "U.S. Court Finds in Favor of Esquel in Court Case," Hong Kong, March 13, 2007.

5. Bill McBeath, "Resilient Supply Chains: The Next Frontier," *Parallex View Magazine,* April 2004, ChainLink Research.

6. Browning, Checketts, and Bartolini, Aberdeen Group, March 2007.

7. Bill McBeath, "Resilient Supply Chains: The Next Frontier," *Parallex View Magazine,* April 2004, ChainLink Research.

8. Jonathan Watts, "Chinese toy factory boss commits suicide over lead paint scandal," August 13, 2007; accessed at guardian.co.uk.

9. Nicholas Zamiska, "Toy Makers Face Dilemma Over Supplier," *Wall Street Journal,* August 17, 2007.

10. Nicholas Zamiska and Nicholas Casey, "Supplier of Toys to Mattel Is Investigated in China," *Wall Street Journal,* August 9, 2007.

11. Brian Robinson, "Creating Relationships That Last in China," presentation at The Conference Board Supplier Relationship Management Conference, Atlanta, Ga., March 7, 2008.

12. Rick Behrens, "Boeing Supplier Strategy and Lean," presentation at the Institute for Supply Management 93rd Annual International Supply Management Conference, St. Louis, Mo., May 6, 2008.

13. Robert L. Simpson, Norihiko Shirouzu, Timothy Aeppel, and Todd Zaun, "Tension Between Ford and Firestone Mounts Amid Recall Efforts," *Wall Street Journal,* August 28, 2000.

14. BITS Framework for Managing Technology Risk for IT Service Provider

Relationships, BITS Group, November 2003; www.bitsinfo.org/down-loads/Publications%20Page/bits2003framework.pdf.

15. Gregory L. White, "Precious Commodity: How Ford's Big Batch of Rare Metal Led to $1 Billion Write-Off," *Wall Street Journal*, February 6, 2002.

16. Matt Pottinger and Cris Prystay, "Rice to Riches: Behind a $550 Million Bad Bet: A Mystical Man with Ambition," *Wall Street Journal*, December 6, 2004.

17. Tim Minihan, "Do Recent Price Increases Portend the End of the World as We Know It?," August 1, 2006, and "And a Little Hedging on the Solution," Supply Excellence Blog, www.supplyexcellence.com, May 11, 2006.

18. Aaron O. Patrick, "Candy Companies Blame Higher Prices on Hedge Funds' Chocolate Cravings," *Wall Street Journal*, May 28, 2008.

19. Grant Delin, "The Guru's Guru," *Business 2.0*, October 2001.

CHAPTER 13

Building Supply
Base Advantage

A Long-Term Project

PROJECT: a large or major undertaking, especially one involving considerable money, personnel, and equipment.

Excellence in any department can be attained only by the labor of a lifetime;
it is not to be purchased at a lesser price.
—Samuel Johnson, eighteenth-century English poet, critic, and writer

We've designed the building—from the blueprints and structure to the internal layout and utilities positioning. We've thought about upkeep and insuring against property loss. But all this is still piecemeal—either separate areas of excellence not fully tied together, or just a conceptual plan. Like home building, eventually you need to have a house. The builder, using labor, materials, subcontractors, inspectors, and job site management skills, eventually produces the finished structure.

Anyone who goes through this process for a new house or major renovation will testify that it is complex, requiring the ability to manage flows of labor and materials. (The homeowner bemoans the fact that the building contractor never shows up on time, while the contractors respond that no job ever quite goes as planned, requiring field adjustments to make it work). But a really good house requires that the builder's mindset blends the work with high standards. Sounds sort of like managing a business' supply base, doesn't it? This chapter and the next seek to describe that mindset relative to integrating suppliers into a business plan and how it moves the organization up the curve over time.

The architect deals in "perfection" and concept. The builder deals with construction as hands-on work. That is why the details at the building project's end (punch lists) always seem to take forever and even then, some errors still get missed, latent defects emerge, or shifting ground creates foundation cracks that weren't there last week.

There is a difference between building a supply base for sustainable competitive advantage and launching a project that just improves supply management to make the firm's cost structure better. It is the difference between a home and a prefab trailer. For competitive advantage you need a building, and a good one at that. A lot of companies talk that game but are looking for something quick—we used to call it "instant pudding" at P&G—something fast with okay quality but not what a real chef would provide—the difference between pudding and crème brulée.

Companies, particularly top executives, are besieged with pitches to improve their supply organizations' results. CPOs looking to move to the next level are too. The instant pudding flavors of supply management are software (that will transform), consultants (who will transform), outsourcing suppliers (that will transform), recruiters (who will transform by changing all the people), and combinations thereof. All these options can be a transformation (think short-term makeover) and, importantly, a step along the journey to advantage building. But the real work is like building a house—funneling the right skills, resources, and effort against the right plan over a sustained period of time.

Supply Management Maturity

In the last couple years, a growing number of research houses and academics have created "supply maturity models." They are on to something, especially for those looking for sustainable advantage. Whether it is Hackett's four levels (reactive, planned, aligned, and strategic) based on how you respond to supply markets and business needs; IBM Services' five levels (static supply chain, functional excellence, horizontal integration, external collaboration, and "on demand" supply chain—where "on demand" is about the need for responsiveness, ability to change/tailor, focus, and resilience); or one that David Burt (retired professor of supply management at the University of San Diego) and Robert Lynch (see the Foreword and Chapter 6) came up with, which looks at supply's ability to deal with a rapidly changing external environment and deliver value over time—they all start at the lower left and move up and to the right with accelerating slope.

All are helpful frameworks, especially in terms of visualizing the length of the journey and the steepness of the path. (Figure 13.1 shows a representative sample put together after reading reports on a number of these models.) However, considered in the light of a construction project, the recognition becomes that each company will need to line up its approach to supply-based advantage to its position on the maturity curve. Someone at the bottom will not leap to the top overnight, while someone in the middle has the potential to move more rapidly because they have begun to connect the independent but interconnected dots.

Each stage means a different short-term target, all striving for the same long-range goal. At the risk of reopening the supply vocabulary debate we talked about so long ago in Chapter 2, I have used a set of terms to label each stage.

Purchasing. Mired in the past, an organization at this stage sees value as convenience, "good old boy" relationships, and price (not cost or the performance side of value). Firms with lots of maverick buying are, in part, here. The customer is internal and financial. The road ahead is long and will likely require some help (some of those "transformers" pitching improvement above), carefully selected for how much they will teach rather than just do. Beware consultant contracts solely tied to savings percentages instead of organizational development along with the savings.

Procurement. Corporations in this stage are also significantly focused on price, but beginning to understand the obvious parts of total cost and the value of fundamental quality/delivery. Relationships are about leveraging the size of the buy to lower cost and are somewhat adversarial and at arm's length as a result, but the external customer's demands are starting to penetrate the supply side. The journey is starting to evolve. Basic technology tools abound (e-RFx, electronic ordering, etc.) and consultants can be of real help. The most obvious strategic buys are where the learning and growth in perspective starts to grow.

Supply Chain Management. For firms at this stage, the dynamics of the business are clearer, causing a change in perspective. Value definition is

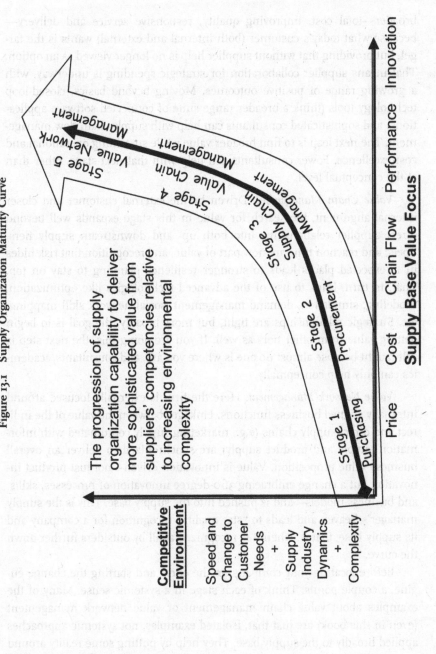

Figure 13.1   Supply Organization Maturity Curve

broader—total cost, improving quality, responsive service and delivery—because what today's customer (both internal and external) wants is the target, but providing that without supplier help is no longer viewed as an option. That means supplier collaboration for strategic spending is underway, with a growing range of positive outcomes. Moving beyond basics, closed-loop technology tools (think a broader range suite of connected software applications) and sophisticated consultants can help with supply chain flow management. The next leap is to find broader value while sustaining operational and cost excellence. Fewer consultants can help with that next stage, other than at the conceptual level.

Value Chain Management. Driven by the external customer and closer internal alignment, the search for value in this stage expands well beyond direct supplier relationships into both up- and downstream supply tiers. Speed and reaction time are now part of value, and recognition that risk hides in unexpected places leads to stronger resilience planning to stay on top. That, in turn, leads to use of the advanced technologies like optimization, modeling, simulation, demand management, social network skill mapping, etc. Strategic relationships are tight, but more broadly, the goal is to begin getting value from other tiers as well. If you are doing this, the next step is self-taught because almost no one is where you are, and consultants/academics can only help conceptually.

Value Network Management. Here the firm is externally focused around internally aligned business functions. Linkages between the value of the indirect and direct supply chains (e.g., marketing supply coordinated with information supply and product supply) are synchronized to deliver an overall business value proposition. Value is innovation driven—not just product innovation but a change embracing 360-degree innovation of processes, skills, and business models—and is pushed into the supply base. This is the supply manager's heaven and leads to "star quality" recognition for a company and its supply base, that is, when it is recognized at all by outsiders further down the curve.

Before locating your company on the curve and starting the change engine, a couple points: Think of each stage in a systemic sense. Many of the examples about value chain management or value network management (even in this book) are just that, isolated examples, not systemic approaches applied broadly to the supply base. They help by putting some reality around a concept, but that is not the same as repeatability across multiple areas. One of the elements of functional excellence in supply is the percentage of spend under professional (i.e, supply organization) management, called "spend under management." Even for something this basic, the best in class are below 100 percent—Aberdeen's 2007 CPO Agenda report pegged the best in class number at 61 percent. Systemic means nearly 100 percent, or at least *consciously deciding* when to *not* include a particular spend pool in the overall supply plan.

Then recognize that almost all companies are at maturity stages 2 and 3 ("procurement" and "supply chain"), not the 4 and 5 "value" stages. (Stage 1 is becoming the exception rather than the rule within most companies, but it is an exception that continues to occur.) Not many firms have seen stages 4 or 5, and if they have, the situational nature of what they observe makes simple reapplication tough. There is an element of appreciating beauty in the upper levels—you'll know it when you see it, yet there is also a science to it in terms of analysis, ability to sift the important few from the trivial many, and broad implementation capability across the firm. It also requires suppliers mature enough to see the point as well. That is part of why this is not often accomplished—supply has two sides and both sides have to "get it" and "keep it."

—Practitioner's Take—

A good friend, Leah Kalin, former supply director at Cardinal Health, points out that there is a supplier maturity curve as well, and if the buyer/seller maturity levels are out of sync, only the best buyers can bridge that gap. She thinks about supplier sophistication in grid form with the typical small to large size as one aspect, but a more interesting blend of type of company (sole proprietor, LLC, division of a publicly held company, etc.), business life cycle position (start up, wind down, for sale, etc.), business drivers (profit, revenue, cash flow, credit access, etc.) and business culture (entrepreneur, established corporate culture), financial ownership structure (venture capital or private equity) as the other side of the grid. Her point is that understanding these things is critical to finding effective middle ground for collaboration and evolution of the relationship. If the cultures are too alien for each other, expectations are probably unconsciously out of line, and will require overcommunication to compensate.

Finally, remember relativity—not Einstein's mass and energy equation, but rather that in your industry everything is relative. Too often these maturity charts are seen as a "top of the curve" success criterion. Not so. The requirements of an electronics company, with long networked supply chains and products subject to quick obsolesce, put it at a different place than an office stapler manufacturer. Both have challenges and innovation in their industries; and suppliers can provide them with competitive edge. Where that competitive edge lies along the maturity curve, however, can be very different. Winning is about what the customer wants, delivered better than the relevant competition—not some theoretical ideal.

Leaders Matter Most

To move from one maturity stage to another is not an inexorable upward march (no evolutionary mandate here) because, unless driven to change, capabilities will follow the path of least resistance—the status quo. For any capability that is important to the business, standing still means falling behind your peers. Therefore the leadership of the supply organization is the prime mover to make a step change in the systemic use of suppliers to gain competitive advantage. A single function (IT, manufacturing, whatever) can, if it believes in supplier importance, move its own supplier engagement performance, but that rarely delivers competitive advantage across the whole company.

With apologies to Jeffrey Krames (best-selling author of a book about retired GE leader Jack Welch's 4E leadership model), regardless of where on a maturity model you start, leadership combined with management make the difference. In a takeoff of Welch's four E's, it begins with *envision* (E#1), for you must create a visionary future state and a plan to go with it. You have to *energize* (E#2) both the organization and the company leaders around what can be and why it matters. Then you must *enable* (E#3), a critical step because without the resources—and that includes carving out expectations that time will be spent even when ongoing day-to-day brushfires beckon—the excitement generated by energizing will be lost or, worse, turn into cynical resistance to change. Then comes *execution* (E#4), which Welch said was the most important because that is what actually does something to get results. Finally, you must *evaluate* (E#5) the plan and its execution. Remember, these plans play out in competitive markets and can change in a heartbeat—a currency crash, a key supplier gets acquired, or a disruption changes the face of an industry. These E's are the five tasks a supply leader must carry out in order to build enduring excellence.

Without leadership, movement along the curve will not happen. This is not just about walking into the CEO's office and announcing that supply is a source of competitive advantage. That's a good way to get laughed off the floor. Occasionally, the CEO already understands and the project becomes a "pull" initiative. Be ready to move if that's the case, because the expectations are probably not realistic and have been set without your input by informal chats with other CEOs. (Consulting pitches to chief executive and financial officers often end up doing the same thing.) However, far more commonly, this is a "push" initiative, put together by supply leadership in a skeptical environment.

Maturity Curve Implications

Where a company sits on the maturity curve drives what the change looks like. There are two ways to think about supply performance: (1) best in class/leading edge and (2) competitive advantage.

They are not the same. Simplistically, think of the former as becoming "better" and the later as operating "differently."

For companies at the lower end of the maturity curve, improvement needs to look at the "best in class" idea. The trick is deciding what "best in class" looks like. The best in class loaf is being cut into ever thinner slices by research houses with best in class designations for every tool or subprocess in the supply management field—spend management, trade management, demand management, strategic sourcing, supplier performance management, and so on. The problem becomes integrating all that into something that is far-reaching enough to actually move the business, not just the supply function.

—Practitioner's Take—

A quick note: Trying to be best in class across a broad range of subprocesses all at the same time is a way to end up on the bleeding rather than leading edge. Best in class implies a level of risk taking to jump to the head of the class, which is on the edge of the unknown "next step."

One of my learnings from benchmarking a lot of companies over the years is that those making the most progress made the decision—often unconsciously—to be best in only a couple areas and "above average" on the rest, with almost nothing in the lower half as measured across the entire company (spend pools, business units, geographies). The real measure of value delivery thus becomes breadth of consistently strong capability rather than trying to be best in class in many narrow areas. Think of it as a straight B+ student with a couple A+'s versus one that has A's in a favorite class but low C's and D's in all the rest. I'll pick the consistent B+ player every time.

At the top end of the maturity curve, the game becomes competitive advantage, not an aggregation of "best in class" narrow supply silos. It's about how suppliers fit into the business model—and it's about operating differently so as to really leverage what suppliers can bring there, rather than using leverage as a hammer to beat value out of them. The tipping point along the curve is partway through stage 3—supply chain management. At its lower end, this stage addresses the fundamental flows that find and seek to improve the weak links in the chain that can cause a lot of narrow "near-best in class" performers to fail in the end. The upper end is beginning the transition from supply into value—waste elimination, customer service viewed as part of the product, bundled solutions, etc.

—Practitioner's Take—

In writing this book, one of the challenges was determining who the best in class companies were, and then getting meaningful insight into how they got there. Some of those who have the reputation don't talk much about it. Others get the press but upon deeper analysis, it turns out to be a pilot test that they "expect will expand well." Still others are great in their industry, but what they do doesn't translate well into other contexts.

Several consultants assess supply organizations for a living, with a comprehensive set of criteria including best practices and efficiency/effectiveness ratings. Two of the most well known are A. T. Kearney's AEP (Assessment of Excellence in Procurement survey of 400 companies) and Hackett Group's procurement performance benchmarks for effectiveness and efficiency. But these studies do not divulge company names. It became a dilemma to find enough different stories to cross-reference in order to look for real company road maps.

The one place that does provide some detail is the press, especially magazines. *Purchasing* magazine's Professional Medal of Excellence, which has an in-depth article about the winner each year, is the most accessible. Obviously, a problem is that not all the best supply management organizations nominate themselves for the award, but the winners at least provide some insight into successful journeys . . . and they ring true, correlating with my own observations and those of many CPOs I have met over the years.

This kind of analysis is especially valuable at the low end of the maturity curve, where building the skills and supply capability bring improvement. You can pick some lower hanging fruit. At the upper end, where competitive advantage lies, the task of more holistic integration with other successful business functions into an overall model expands the margin of victory. Some past medal winners are there and stay there while others stall or regress a bit, making these stories less predictive.

Example: In 2002 Lucent Technologies won the medal, using some extremely sophisticated approaches to outsourcing, business planning, supplier selection, supplier innovation access, and supplier segmentation and management. This supply excellence was not matched on the product side, where it was unable to distinguish itself versus competition, even with supplier help. Then, after it was acquired by Alcatel, the integration began dismantling the team that developed the supply practices that drove Lucent's excellence. Over lunch in Atlanta, just after deciding to leave the combined entity, Lucent's former VP of supplier management, Joe Carson, confided that one of the reasons for leaving was that in the new company, his position would be shared among six people.[1]

Lucent had learned that centralizing the management of suppliers across businesses was a key part of presenting a consistent face to the suppliers. As one of six doing the same thing, it would be like relearning a subject that you already passed in school. It was unlikely that the new owners would change many of their processes. Most of the rest of Lucent's award-winning team left as well and today the company is looking for another turnaround.

Road Maps from Some of the Best

A quick read of five recent winners of this award (2003–2007, inclusive) provides a fairly consistent list of accomplishments, each very tailored to the particular company's culture and situation.[2-6] Interestingly, with the exception of the 2004 winner, HP (the only two-time winner in the twenty-five-year history of the award), the other four all participate in the aviation industry as either a supplier or producer—Eaton Corp (2007), United Technologies (2006), Rockwell Collins (2005), and Cessna (2003). Their accomplishments are a list of the "usual suspects" cited for supply management excellence.

They include broad spend analysis, supplier rationalization, long-term supplier relationships, the extension of Lean, Six Sigma, and Total Quality concepts into the supply base as part of a supplier development program, extensive use of software, mostly at the "basic level" (discussed in Chapter 10; portals, e-sourcing, performance scorecarding) but some at the advanced level, cross-functional sourcing teams, cross-business volume leverage, intense supply chain improvement efforts (both operational and via connections to sales forecasting), and strong links between new product design and suppliers, often brokered by supply people dedicated to product development.

Okay, that all makes sense, and points out that the complexity of supply, due to the range of industries and market conditions it must deal with, requires the best to master a very wide range of tools and strategies to be that good. But deeper penetration reveals some clues (sometimes not directly articulated in each detailed description of accomplishments, but visible between the lines) about common elements of their road maps to get there. These provide the general path forward for those in the bottom half of the maturity curve and the underlying mindset to move up the top half.

Ten C's: Five to Build a Platform and Five to Leap Forward

The range of current states along the maturity curve is wide, so what works at one end will rarely help at the other. However, to manage the construction of supply-based competitive advantage there is a series of common conceptual mindsets that create a path forward, often in stepwise fashion from the bottom to the top. The use of consultants, software, and strong outsourcing partners are just an embodiment of these steps, not the steps themselves. Early on, we said small companies can extract competitive advantage because they are so connected to the business model and needs of their entrepreneurial leaders—in fact, the leaders often buy the important stuff themselves. The connection between suppliers and customers is wired in their brains. For bigger companies, that brain wiring is not there and has to evolve over time. Initially the evolution delivers stronger functional performance, but if the goal is sustainable competitive advantage, moving past the function into the business needs to be part of that advancement.

In this chapter we will only discuss the mindsets that lead to improvement in the lower half of the maturity curve, saving the upper half for Chapter 14.

Lower Maturity Curve C's: The First Five—Building Your Platform

The First C: Credibility. More important than anything else is for company leadership to believe that supply can deliver what they expect. At the low end of the maturity curve that is not a given. It requires a set of actions that both build a platform for the future while delivering the present.

- ► Acquire leadership talent and make it bond around a vision. Whether leadership talent came from inside (UTC, Eaton, and Rockwell Collins), outside (Cessna), or a blend (HP's Compac acquisition/merger), the first step was to find an overall leader and then add more horsepower across the supply leadership team to align and drive a mindset shift into the ranks of the organization.

- ► Talent management. The next talent need is at the working level. Leadership alone is not enough. The hands-on management of supplier relationships and sourcing initiatives require skills. Talent acquisition—recruiting from colleges, other companies, or other functions, plus creating a strong skill training system to create base-level skills in people already there—is necessary to build a credible group upon which to grow. Importing training masters or using internal leadership to train from within can both work at this level. Unfortunately, sometimes this C also requires cutting those that simply do not have the desire or ability to change their mindset.

- ► Establish a standard process (using leadership as a vetting mechanism) and drive it across and down the organization. The first one I would pick is sourcing strategy, since recognizing and selecting good suppliers is foundational. Use this effort to deliver against business cost reduction expectations.

- ► Focus on performance delivery via the basics of supply chain management—delivery, quality, and availability. This means setting standards with suppliers and following up when performance is not where you want it.

The point here is to build basic credibility by improving traditional measures. To do that takes talent and the will to develop it. From talent will come results.

The Second C: Communication. Examination of each Medal of Excellence winner's story reveals tireless communication with business unit management and senior company leadership. This one is critical. It is about identifying with the firm's values and strategies. The connection to the business units and their profit-generating business models begins to clarify the line of sight between what suppliers can provide and what the business needs. It also creates personal relationships with key business leadership teams that allow deep understanding of changing business conditions and how suppliers play in that value-creating equation. Functionally driven strategies can get results but without strong ties to business management, these strategies will not progress into supplier initiatives that can make a strategic difference.

The Third C: Cross-Functional Collaboration. Aside from getting a lower price or better efforts from a previously qualified supplier, procurement has little ability to influence results unaided by other functions. That's why Chapter 9 opened with the comment that internal collaboration might be the most important part of the book. Building bridges to other functions requires putting yourself in their shoes—what makes them look like winners and how can supply people and suppliers help do that. In return, these organizations will often pitch in to help supply reduce cost, especially when there is a profit crisis. Technical functions are the lifeblood of innovation.

The airline industry has faced higher than expected jet fuel prices for a long time—with forecasts seemingly always behind reality. Supply alone, under these circumstances, can do some smart things. When the fuel price issues began in 2004, for example, American Airlines' sourcing people used fuel price arbitrage (called "tankering") as a way to save money.[7] In the summer of '04 they figured out that the price of fuel in Dallas was $0.42/gallon less than in Los Angeles. They bought extra in Dallas, flew it to LA, and finished it off on the return flight—savings after taking into account the extra weight of the fuel was $400/round trip or $14K per day for that route alone. By the way, sophisticated computer modeling is part of this effort.

But more systemic approaches entail airline operations changes that require collaboration between procurement, airline engineering, airport ground operations, airport environmental control, and engine suppliers. As the price of oil continued to skyrocket, engine supplier Pratt and Whitney offered an engine washing technology.[8] It results in no environmental runoff after cleaning the toxic grime out of engines and works on its competitors' engines as well as its own. The fuel savings of a clean engine versus a filthy one is 1.2 percent and, given the law of big numbers, 1.2 percent of a billion-dollar quarterly fuel bill is also a big number—it makes sense. If procurement were to say "let's wash the engines" without the support of operations and environmental, it simply would not happen.

Still, for the airline industry, the advent of sustained expensive oil, which many believe is here to stay, will likely mean a business model change. The question will be how supply will play into the new business models that emerge (perhaps a return to an older model that saw it as a premium travel option rather than a medium- to long-distance competitor to the automobile).

The Fourth C: Change Management. All of which leads to the next C, change management. Given the dynamic nature of supply markets, the ability to embed an expectation for intelligent change into the organization is important to the mindset necessary for competitive advantage. Within any organization going through a change, there will be three types of people arrayed in something of a bell curve: those eager to embrace the shift, those who will fight it every step of the way, and the great middle—influenceable either way. One mistake often made is to focus on those who do not want to change (typically either due to lack of skills, resistance to acquiring new ones, or fear of anything different). There are many books covering change management, but there are a couple aspects unique to working with suppliers that can add to its complexity.

First, the change has to span two (or more) companies. Change can percolate from either side of the buyer/seller interface and can change more than just one company's approach to its supply partners. Change in business situation, if trapped in a rigid contractual interpretation, simply builds up pressure that will ultimately explode if not dealt with. (Witness the U.S. auto suppliers that have been forced into very different structures, ownership, and business strategies by the relentless pressure of its customer base.) Second, that relentless supply pressure forces major business strategy shifts. Sustained $100+ per barrel oil will bring that kind of change to most transportation industries and change some supply chain design parameters.

Earlier we talked about the iron ore industry and its relentless impact on steelmakers over a multiyear period. At the end of May 2008, the business impact of that pressure became startlingly clear when the largest steel company in the world, Arcelor/Mittal, took a radical step to gain some control over its iron supply through vertical integration.[9] The company launched a plan to rehabilitate an abandoned African ore mine in Liberia. This plan will require major infrastructure investment to build a highway from the mine, which was abandoned by a Liberian-Swedish-American company (Lamco) some twenty years ago. The investment will likely be $1.5 billion and is being made at the same time Arcelor/Mittal has a "from scratch" mine under way in Senegal (another country in West Africa)—price tag $2.2 billion. The iron ore industry is driving a "back to the past" steel supply base strategy that carries high risk and, perhaps, high reward. What had been a supply strategy based on ore relationships (and has turned adversarial) is shifting to one with a focus on major construction, heavy equipment, and local power station suppliers.

—Practitioner's Take—

As a former practitioner, I can't let the change management area pass without commenting on the biggest challenge to change management—when experts or high-ranking peers (and bosses) are simply not willing to change after agreeing to do so. The words and pictures do not match—the mouth says "yes" but the head is shaking a side-to-side "no." This is particularly difficult when a peer, over whom you have little or no control, chooses to voice assent and then tell his/her organization not to cooperate. There are three phases in solving this problem: finding it, trying to reason with it, and dealing with it. One model used in addressing it is the COD model—Cones of Darkness.

The imagery is to envision a bright light at the top of the organization, shining down on it. Where a peer leader is dragging his/her feet, the organization beneath will show up as a cone of darkness in which people never get the word, don't flow in the direction of sister organizations, or hunker down, hoping it will all go away. Each point of a cone represents a leader who is not supportive of the program. You have now completed phase one—you found it.

Once the recalcitrant leader is clear, you can: (a) discuss the situation and try to find out what is holding him/her back so it can be addressed; (b) use comparison results from other groups to publicly expose laggards broadly across the organization, hopefully raising questions of why; or (c) use leadership council meetings to exert peer pressure for change. This is phase two—reasoning with it.

The third phase is dealing with it. It involves escalating the issue and determining whether the management support that the first two C's—credibility and communication—are meant to deliver with senior management has resulted in real commitment to the business case. The outcome will either include "top-down reasoning" or disciplinary action. Sometimes this results in action—often a transfer of the dissenting leader. But just as often, nothing will happen. A sad reality is that such public actions are often ducked by senior management. When that happens, "dealing with it" consists of continuing to move forward where possible until the results discrepancies are great enough to raise questions again. Then the second and third phases will begin again.

Disappointed? So was I when I ran across this in my career, but it's a reality that must be faced. *If* the goal is change that will improve competitive position, and *if* the bulk of the leadership is making that move, eventually the resisters will be very visible and forced to either leave or act. But those are two very big ifs.

The Fifth C: Continuity/Constancy of Purpose. This C exists at both the lower (best in class aspirations) and upper (competitive advantage) ends of the maturity curve. In targeting best in class status it seems counterintuitive, almost a contradiction of the fourth C (change management). Yet, continuity is necessary because a supply-based strategy for advantage is a multiyear proposition. As with most long-term strategies, the general direction and ongoing foundational supply processes need to be maintained, while the firm moves along the maturity curve and deals with inevitable business climate changes (e.g., at the time of this writing they are high crude oil, mineral, and agricultural products—in the future they could even be the decline of those same prices).

With institutional memory at low ebb due to frequent personnel changes, the ability of a company to sustain its strategic vision when leaders and the "rank and file" frequently turn over is the challenge for long-range strategy execution. Intelligent change management, vivid descriptions of the plan, senior management expectations for that plan, and talent pipelining (see Chapter 8) are the means to sustain the momentum despite personnel turnover. Supplier relationships are also built off personal and company associations, so continuity requires injecting some redundancy and multilevel relationship connection into the seams between you and your strategic suppliers.

At the upper, competitive advantage portion of the curve, continuity extends beyond sustaining relationships and the long-term plan for the supply base. Continuity becomes constancy. It is about the external purpose to win with the customer, shift with the firm's strategies, and flex with external conditions. The idea is to build change and elasticity into the organization's mindset so that plans can shift with reality. Continuity connotes stability, while constancy means faithfulness to a higher vision; in this case, it means that suppliers are integral to business success and when managed well will make a competitive difference by augmenting the firm's own competencies in ways competitors will struggle to duplicate.

—Practitioner's Take—

Looking back over my own experiences, the first five C's must occur in a blended, sequential, and nonsequential fashion. The range of supply relationships across a typical corporation is such that different commodities and business applications drive situational "evolution by necessity." P&G was no different. For many years, direct materials were largely stages 2 and 3 on the maturity curve—with a few vital ones sneaking into stage 4, while some of the indirect spends stayed at stages 1 and 2, with a few sneaking into stage 4 as well.

To move forward required a strong focus on the "soft side" skills from Chapters 8 (Supply Organization) and 9 (Cross-Functional Alignment) plus the more human parts of Chapter 10 (Talent and Knowledge). The key became transitioning as much of the supply base management as possible along as many of the "lower end" maturity stages as possible. Be clear, we didn't have any neat visual model that told us which steps to take—it was more a logical expansion of our business needs that sparked a progression up the curve. Negotiation training shifted over several years from traditional approaches (win/lose positioning) to a spectrum from win/lose to win/win co-solution development.

The biggest shift started with a global sourcing initiative that made logical sense but struggled on the people side. Experienced American and European sourcing experts got into ego wars while the emerging regions (Asia and Latin America) were dismissed as inexperienced "children," even though they often understood their local suppliers' cultures better and were more willing to assimilate any expertise that worked from whoever offered it—qualities vital to continuous improvement.

We ended up placing senior leaders in close contact with the working levels to coordinate the global effort, an approach that was extremely uncomfortable for the line organization managers. The ability to grow internal trust and align on sourcing processes that were standard enough to drive continuity of approach were combined with enough diversity of process application to fit culturally across the world.

These steps quickly led to effective cross-functional involvement—for direct materials with groups from product development and manufacturing that qualified new suppliers, helped standardize specifications, and worked through the inevitable capacity planning/product delivery rough spots. The global scope helped trigger low-cost country sourcing projects like "Gold Mine," a China sourcing initiative that combined logistics and quality assurance with sourcing to tap into low-cost Chinese manufactured goods (chemicals and packages first, with equipment later on). The commitments made across the entire purchasing leadership team (and the fear of missing them), and the sweet recognition of successes, combined to overcome many of the major "people conflicts."

The ability to draw new entrants into our supply base and create material substitution strategies where they made sense was combined with the development of deeper relationships with some longstanding suppliers as well. All of this pushed us through the lower end of the maturity curve, but it was the people side that mattered most. As is often the case, the combination of people skill "art" and sourcing skill "science" is where the real win resides. Supply management methodology and information technology "science" was not enough until team building and internal collaboration "art" were added to the recipe to make the difference.

Nowhere do the mindset shifters of credibility, continuity, communication, cooperation, and change management come together more clearly than in the energy spend. Cemex, the Mexican cement supplier, has emerged as a global player in the construction industry.[10] However, in its home market, the firm relies on highly energy-intensive 2700-degree (Fahrenheit) kilns and over 40 percent of its operating costs are made up of the energy that feeds them. Cemex began dealing with this risk to their business years ago, when the cost of Mexico's fuel oil used to run these plants was deregulated and Mexico's power costs (60 percent higher than the United States) and currency devaluations made it uncompetitive with fuels its international competitors used. The answer became a substitute fuel called petroleum coke, a waste product from refineries that is relatively easy to ship and actually generates 20 percent more heat per ton than coal, but tends to clog kilns.

Cemex found a Spanish cement maker that had solved the engineering problems and installed the right processing equipment/techniques to use "pet coke" in its kilns. As part of its global expansion Cemex bought that company (and its expertise) and began sourcing the equipment to make it work around the world. At the same time, they opened a fuel sourcing office in Houston, Texas, to negotiate with oil companies to gain access to pet coke for their fifty plants worldwide through long-term commitments that would remove waste from the refineries and arrange its global shipment.

This became a competitive advantage that fueled Cemex's rise to the number three cement supplier globally. This "waste energy" strategy expanded to the purchase of other industries' high BTU production garbage—oily rags, cow-bone meal, old tires—to help fuel both kilns and power plants to support them. (In some cases Cemex is actually paid to take this fuel source and when they have excess pet coke supply and electricity from the power plants, they sell it at a profit on the open market.) The combination of engineering, sourcing, supply chain/logistics, and sales combine to give competitive edge by evolving beyond simple purchasing or procurement skills.

While each evolution will be corporately situational, there are some common lynchpins:

- Develop or import leadership for a visionary, yet staged, plan. Get the people piece right.
- Build business acumen—define value for the business, not the function.
- Create cross-functional involvement.
- Standardize key processes, starting with the basics.
- Build talent and skills and resource them when you have them. By resourcing we mean providing the organizational budget and training to embed supply improvement into the organization's mental model.
- Drive execution to get results.
- Move along the maturity stages following a path of "most value" and use those wins to breed others.
- Use continuity thinking to guard against "drift" and regression in mindset while avoiding rigidity on the particulars.

A single area of excellence that partially brings suppliers into the business model will drive results for a while, but often can't survive longer term. In Chapter 5, we described the sourcing strategy of retailer Steve and Barry's, which integrated its suppliers into its business model in terms of buying low-cost clothes that are not "fashion variable," thus allowing contracts that fill in supplier capacity during down seasons in return for good prices and payment terms.[11] Generally, that part of the business model worked well.

The other half of the business model, however, involved negotiating low rents and high renovation allowances from malls and hiring small suppliers to help refurbish the space and open the stores at costs below the allowances—and pocketing the difference. However, Steve and Barry's has not appeared to evolve up the best practice curve, credibility and communication were not followed by cooperation—and the competitive advantage blueprint began to top out because strong sourcing strategy was not followed by good supplier relationships. Failure to evolve began to undermine both credibility and communication.

The relationship aspects of off-season buying and long payment terms available from garment suppliers in less frequented geographies does not translate well in the use of small suppliers for carpentry and store shelving. Example: Eight-person Ottmans Services prepared stores before openings, but suddenly found that payment was never easy. They were asked to fill out different forms and talked to different people, but the check was always in the mail. The same was true for the University of Michigan student newspaper that sold the retailer lots of advertising while waiting over a year for some payments. Remember, a big part of Steve and Barry's product line is college logo wear—so they are messing with a valuable sales tool, the license from the University of Michigan to sell U of M clothes. Dangerous game—the escalator along the maturity curve is not a one-way ride, it goes both up and down.

This, coupled with a business model that essentially sold product at about a breakeven while generating profit from store expansion allowance savings, meant that without continuous expansion, the company could not stay profitable. Add to that alienation of the store renovation supply base, critical to profitability, and we find a bankruptcy filing in July 2008, purchase by a hedge fund affiliation between Bay Harbour Management and York Capital Management, and subsequent downsizing but not liquidation of the retailer.

Contrast that to the Cemex story, a basic material substitution sourcing strategy underwent a metamorphosis into a broader business strategy for a competitively advantaged business platform. That is how the best practice functional improvement level can suddenly transition into competitively advantaged "do it differently" supplier and commodity management. Suddenly you are there, sometimes understanding the route only in hindsight. Cemex made the leap (at least for now, since competitive advantage constantly changes), Steve and Barry's did not.

Notes

1. Interview with Joe Carson, former VP Supplier Management, Lucent Technologies, March 5, 2007, Atlanta, Ga.

2. Paul E. Teague, "Eaton Wins *Purchasing*'s Medal of Professional Excellence," purchasing.com, 9/13/2007; www.purchasing.com/article/CA6474828.html.

3. Susan Avery, "Supply Management Is Core of Success at UTC," purchasing.com, September 7, 2006; www.purchasing.com/article/CA6368274.html.

4. Susan Avery, "Lean But Not Mean, Rockwell Collins Excels," September 1, 2005; www.purchasing.com/article/CA6250270.html.

5. James Carbone, "Hewlett Packard Wins for the 2nd Time," purchasing.com, September 2, 2004.

6. Susan Avery, "Cessna Soars," purchasing.com, September 4, 2003; www.purchasing.com/article/CA451858.html.

7. Melanie Trottman, "Fill 'Er Up: Airlines Hop Around Cities for Cheaper Fuel," *Wall Street Journal*, November 12, 2004.

8. J. Lynn Lunsford, "Engine Washing Cuts Airline Fuel Costs," *Wall Street Journal*, June 11, 2008.

9. Natalie Obiko Pearson, "Arcelor, Liberia Share an Acid Test," *Wall Street Journal*, May 30, 2008.

10. John Lyons, "Power Play: Expensive Energy? Burn Other Stuff, One Firm Decides," *Wall Street Journal*, September 1, 2004.

11. Jeffrey McCracken and Peter Lattman, "Steve and Barry's Hits Trouble," *Wall Street Journal*, June 26, 2008.

CHAPTER 14

Situational Supply Base Flexibility

Achieving the Dream

DREAM: a vision sometimes voluntarily indulged in while awake, something of an unreal beauty, charm, or excellence.

Excellence is to do a common thing in an uncommon way.

—Booker T. Washington, educator

Every year in my hometown of Cincinnati, Ohio, over a dozen amazing houses, each outfitted by a major builder, are on display. People tour this special neighborhood—oohing and aahing over the rooms, decor, living space, and great home extras. It is called "Homearama" and draws thousands every year. People attend for entertainment to see dream houses they could never own, to look for ideas they can implement on a smaller scale, and in a very few cases, to actually buy one of those fully appointed homes for what is usually a large sum of money. Every year, there are some changes as the "fashion" of home design moves with time—kitchens, bathrooms, family entertainment centers, and garages all shift to both meet changing tastes and create new demand.

The upper half of the supply maturity curve we saw in the previous chapter is sort of like the houses in those Homearama exhibitions, each uniquely decorated, based on some standard floor plans, landscaped to provide "curb appeal" (looks good to a buyer driving by on the street), and designed to increase the business of the builders, decorators, furniture retailers, and land-scapers that put them together.

The supply analogy is about moving past lots of "best in class" focus areas into a more flexible, "shape-shifting" web that can adapt to change and move with the business needs for new products and business models. Once a company gets to this level, it begins to either distance itself from its compet-itors or find itself in a war with extremely elite companies. Competitors that stay up with such an industry leader have either adapted their supply base to also mesh with their companies or they possess another type of competitive advantage that boosts them over the rest of the market (e.g., patented technol-ogy or product design).

So, what does this "supply dream house" look like? As the word "dream" implies, it is often about mindset and, as the word "house" implies, that mindset creates tangibles that drive the business. That is where the second five C's come in:

Upper Maturity Curve C's: The Second Five— Leaping Forward

The Sixth C: Creativity. By creativity we mean going beyond internal original-ity. Think of this in the broader context of harnessing supplier innovation and linking it to internal ideas. At the more advanced levels, it also entails reaching through the members of the tier-one supply base to find and lever-age the innovation and creativity available in their supply bases.

The Seventh C: Co-Responsiveness. Again, think in broad strokes. In addi-tion to nurturing the relationships and skills necessary to jointly respond with a supplier when needed, this mindset also revolves around the foresight to have multiple suppliers, networks, and industry clusters of suppliers (like the car and apparel "cities" made up of co-located suppliers only) in more than one location. Without this broader level of responsiveness, the firm's supply base is unable to deal with major unexpected dislocations (natural disaster, currency distortion, wars).

The Eighth C: Customer Focus. This game is about customers. It gets back to the line of sight from suppliers to customers and users. "Customer" here means going beyond the internal customer's need, focusing instead on the firm's customers and how the various supply chains (and the supply bases contained in each) triangulate on the external customer in synchronized fashion.

The Ninth C: Concentric Connectivity. Visualize a set of concentric circles whose center is the firm, while each ring represents a tier of the supply/value chain, from tier-one direct suppliers to tier three or four further upstream. The ability to reach through tier one, either directly or through a supplier to influence upstream operations, is critical to the development of flexibility and innovation. The goal of concentric connectivity is to lead the supply network through influence and business opportunity to a value-enhancing position—a very difficult task indeed.

—Practitioner's Take—

Mining company Rio Tinto's aluminum business is often a "price taker," reacting to customer bidding events, rather than a "price setter" with market power to drive its desired price home.[1] This is quite different than its more dominating iron ore business (see Chapter 7) that dictated prices to its customers for several years. The construction of power stations on site at mines in emerging countries with poor infrastructure is the limiting factor for aluminum business expansion and increasing productivity in a tough cost environment.

Facing a three-supplier power station industry (one a regionally focused Japanese supplier, the second a Swiss/Swedish company dominant in emerging countries, and the third a French company focused more on replacement of existing stations), Rio Tinto launched an insightful sourcing strategy. The plan was to encourage the Japanese and French suppliers to expand their horizons into the third world in order to provide options instead of the dominant Swiss/Swedish player. When they were successful in soliciting a strong proposal with lower cost and better timing than the market leader from one of those firms, the next step was to find a way to dramatically improve productivity.

Rio Tinto catalyzed a meeting with the supplier's technical organization to discuss whether there was a way to change the traditional one aluminum production train per power station ratio. The supplier had no miracle fix, but turned to its supply base, calling them into the effort. As this expanded value chain grappled with the problem, innovation at the supplier's fuse supplier turned out to be the game changer. The develop-

ment of a higher capacity fuse allowed Rio Tinto to parallel-train two production facilities, almost doubling the productivity of the new operation
fueled by this purchased power station. The ability to connect with the
right companies in those concentric circles is the essence of this C and
brought with it a piece of the Creativity C as well.

The Tenth C: Common Sense. Over the last several years the concept of
"market bubbles" has come to the fore. Whether it was Internet technology,
the stock market (dot.com bust), or housing loans, when the bubble burst,
some companies burst with it. The nature of Tom Friedman's "flat world" is
that more new ideas and companies are showing up, sometimes creating a
wave of business expansion. Not all of them will make it. The same is true in
supply management. What seemed like a good idea one day can change overnight or with time. This C is about the mindset to run a "sanity check" before
locking in, and having a reasonable way to move if things change dramatically. This is a key mindset element, because the excitement of the collaboration can lead to "best case" thinking by both customer (the buyer) and
supplier (the seller)—but the world has few best cases.

In 2002 P&G was about to sign a huge outsourcing deal with EDS, when
the outsourcer announced an earnings miss after the NYSE closed. Its stock
price fell after hours and the asset transfer investment aspects of the deal
changed dramatically. P&G backed away and, in subsequent negotiations, so
did EDS. The game had changed in a night. (HP eventually got the deal and,
ironically [and "unrelatedly"], about six years later acquired EDS.)

Organizations that construct a sustained competitive advantage from
their supply base often find, in hindsight, that the "winning" advantages have
changed along the way. Rigid supply base strategies are often outflanked by
unexpected economic conditions or a savvy competitor's innovative new approach, much as the fixed concrete barriers of the French Maginot Line were
outflanked by German invasions through Belgium and the Netherlands and
the use of Luftwaffe aircraft.

The use of these second five C's is even less linear than the often overlap-
ping first five. The reason is that competitive advantage requires careful tend-
ing and periodic redesign. Maturity curve evolution for value chains and
networks is about multiple approaches, agility, and innovation. A eureka moment is seldom planned. Rather, it is the outcome of talent, resources, hard
work, ongoing analysis, and a flexible mindset.

Agility Personified

Li & Fung (L&F) is a century-old Chinese firm headquartered in Hong Kong. This $9 + billion trading company with over 10,000 employees, well known in the apparel and toy industries, exemplifies the value chain/value network management stages of the maturity model.[2] In 2006, Wal-Mart's first major attempt at more upscale fashion ended in failure, with excess inventories and missed sales estimates.[3] In 2008, as the retail giant regrouped, it contracted with L&F as a middleman to help manage its apparel supply chain. When a company viewed by many as the best supply chain operator in the world, and whose value proposition is based on everyday low prices, decides to outsource (and pay a fee for) part of its apparel supply chain management, it says something about the supplier that gets that business. In fact, several current Wal-Mart suppliers, finding its standards too hard to meet, had already sought out L&F's help on their own.

In Chapter 8's exhaustive discussion of skills, the final "systemesis" skill was described as supply network orchestration. In their book, *Competing in a Flat World*, Li and Fung's third-generation family leaders, brothers Victor (Group Chairman) and William (Group Managing Director) Fung, describe the company as a blend of traditional Chinese values (relationship-based cultural approach) and Western business management techniques (learned studying abroad).[4] Western approaches like compliance management, high-end computer technology, and strong accounting systems combine with entrepreneurial empowerment of people, long-term relationship building, and cultural diversity. They see Li & Fung as "network orchestrators," that assemble the capabilities of over 8000 primary suppliers in an "asset light" business model to move goods globally. L&F is not just a "Chinese" company; it has operations in forty countries and is constantly looking for new suppliers with lower cost structures, strong manufacturing capability, and innovative new products.

L&F's view of their network is that it must be flexible. That requires a blend of win-win supplier management philosophy with tough expectation setting and supplier selection criteria. The Fungs describe a value creation network that incorporates a global search for the right suppliers for each customer's product, on-site L&F presence at suppliers for both operational and social/environmental compliance control, and a shared benefit relationship approach, balancing empowerment of the entrepreneurial suppliers that make up most of the network with large enough business awards to provide L&F strong influence in the relationship.

Using what they call "the 30–70 Rule," the Fungs target having between

30 percent and 70 percent of a supplier's business in order to make them willing to listen; but not 100 percent so they are not solely reliant on L&F in the event that they are not the best fit for a customer's business. The combination of competitive cost, project timing, speed to market, adequate capacity, reliability, and operational capability must all match to make a supply network work. Getting all the members to match up time after time is nearly impossible in these high-speed markets.

The construction of parallel networks and multiple supplier matrices provides the agility and flexibility to react to change in the apparel, toy, and other retail markets. This global span is governed through a combination of human interactions (on-site representatives) and very strong (sometimes in-house designed) computer systems. During the SARS outbreak in 2003, many customers stopped traveling to China. L&F sent its own management teams to the customer and supplier home countries and used its IT capability (including video conferences and portable computer devices) to continue tight customer/supplier contact throughout.

The brothers also recommend a blend of big and small company culture—tying the scale of the back office (IT, accounting systems) to a small-firm-like customization of the front office (over 170 customer-specific divisions) with a compensation system that rewards company-wide results to avoid "Balkanizing" its operations. In the middle office lies the balance between the two (supplier compliance, shipping, and logistics, etc.—the functions where "customized scale" play out). To manage all this as an orchestra conductor means letting each "musician" play, but still directing them all toward the harmony and coordination of the musical score. To do that requires in-depth understanding of the suppliers, supply chains, and customers. It also requires what this chapter and its predecessor are focused upon—a mindset for reliable yet flexible operation using a network of suppliers that are shifted in and out of particular projects but sustained by the overall L&F project portfolio's breadth.

One example from the Fungs' book will illustrate how it all comes together.[5] Topper the Trick Terrier is a robot toy that can respond to commands in several languages for under $30. In 2003, a toy company came to L&F, who accepted their conceptual design in January and chose a south China supplier (Qualiman, where L&F's business is between 25 and 30 percent of the plant capacity). The first working model was available by March, the final model by April, when fabric sourcing, microchip development, and engineering development began—plastic parts from Malaysia and Taiwan, chips from Taiwan, stuffing from Korea, and the rest from China—and the first products shipped in July of that year. Not bad—in fact, pretty darn good!

Small Company Global Networks

For smaller companies dodging the scale of the big boys, this kind of agile flexibility is as much about survival as it is competitive advantage. Four Star Distribution is a small, focused skateboard footwear and apparel company.[6] It uses a blend of "on demand" computer software (see Chapter 10) to navigate the intricacies of global trade (tariffs, routing) and long-distance product design (specification setting) with on-the-ground human oversight and relationship building from offices in Hong Kong. If you have a skateboarding teenager, you may have heard of their brands—Quicksilver, Circa, DVS, and Vans—that are designed in the United States but managed as a supply base of low-cost suppliers in China and a software-enabled supply chain that includes electronic financing, which eliminates letters of credit (saving about half a percent of total cost—big in a narrow-margin industry). Sounds like a big company. Right? Well, Four Star is a seventy-five-person company with people on the ground in Asia and North America.

Obviously, not every business allows for the level of supplier interchangeability that toys or apparel might, and the world is not really flat, but has topography like governmental regulations, national biases, and logistical bottlenecks. Still, the concept of flexible rather than fixed supply networks is growing—the defense and pharmaceutical industries, despite heavy and fragmented regulation systems, are spreading out globally in the shift to low-cost countries for upstream components and raw materials in the former and clinical studies in the latter, respectively.

—Practitioner's Take—

The problem with maturity models is that they imply a skill and supplier relationship view that moves only in one direction—up the curve. But a modification to that approach would top the curve with a goal of "Situational Value Creation." Global competitive advantage is not just about creating a value network. Again and again, top supply organizations have shown the ability to be "situational" with their suppliers over time. Unlike many sales or marketing alliances and relationships, in supply you need to ride the relationship elevator both directions—up as well as down—because, as your needs from suppliers change, their importance to your business and your interest in their competencies and innovation can oscillate. The phrase I use to describe it is "exiting gracefully without really exiting." It is very hard to do. Once a supplier gets used to meetings with a customer's senior management, telling them that they are still valued, but not that valued, is tough to pull off without damaging the relationship (remember our discussion of the "graceful exit" in Chapter 6?).

Another reason for a situational approach is that well over 50 percent of a major company's spend falls with companies that are not strategic, so smart use of stages 2 through 5 capabilities is required and even stage 1 approaches can have their place. Supplier mindset is as important to the relationship as the buyer's. Using raw power in a loose market via a bidding process can be exactly the right approach in one situation, because your customers require you to be competitively sharp and the suppliers "expect" a hard bargain as long as it's a fair one. However, if the supplier is valued and their business situation is difficult, holding back may be right in another situation. Being too easy leads to disrespect, while being too hard leads to distrust—finding respect and trust in the middle is the supply manager's objective.

Over my career I cannot tell you how many times we had a close relationship and, based on the normal analytical techniques, were "sure" we were getting competitive price and service—only to discover when we bid the business that we were not as in touch with the market as we thought. Leaving too much money on the table due to "the strategic relationship" undermines competitive advantage. Net, we even got to the point where certain alliances were opened to market competition. One strategic "partner" was shown to be $15 million high (worldwide) at one point, which was simply not acceptable for our product cost structure. No amount of discussion got the necessary reductions until we bid the business and took some away. Yet, the alliance survived on new products, emerging with a clearer understanding of the competitive economics our customers and consumers required.

The trick in this is to have the supply maturity to be able to situationally toggle up and down the "maturity stage stairway" without cutting the ties that provide access to supplier competencies when you need them. Given the dynamic nature of markets, technologies, and cost structures you can easily need to reopen a relationship after pulling away previously. The ability to establish situational flexibility in a value network takes your capability to deliver a competitive advantage to a higher level than simply developing a "fixed" value network. Choosing the right value approach from along the maturity curve to redesign a particular supply/value chain without severing ties with suppliers that lose position is network orchestration at its best.

Another sign of maturity is the ability to conduct "network dissolution." This can mean severing relationships without severing the ability to have a relationship. That level of situational flexibility is a sign of a supply organization that is world class—tough but fair, using power but not to humiliate or annihilate, elevating and de-elevating importance and supplier skill access in time with market changes. That is what delivers competitive advantage—ultimately a level of relationship flexibility that suppliers respect and understand the reasoning behind.

Another Important Concept— "Customer of Choice"

The Corporate Executive Board (CEB) runs a series of functional excellence councils conducting research, benchmarking, and networking events for council members, who pay a five-figure fee to belong. In 2006, the CEB integrated its Sales Executive and Procurement Strategy Councils to publish some insightful research that was widely publicized.[7] Sales executives identified their most favored customers as "customers of choice." CEB defined it as "a company that consistently receives competitive preference for scarce resources across a critical mass of suppliers."

Procurement Strategy Council research showed that suppliers see only 14 percent of their customers as key accounts (making 86 percent just regular customers) and of that 14 percent, only 36 percent are customers of choice. The arithmetic says that just 5 percent of a company's customers are the strategically chosen and preferred elite. In the same research, sales executives consistently said less than a quarter of their customers worry about anything other than price and squeezing supplier margins. That eliminates a lot of customers from the "choice contest" because they are unwilling to pay the entrance fee—a willingness to work collaboratively to find value. Again, it gets back to balancing performance and cost.

The customer of choice concept is driven by three litmus tests:

1. *Consistency Test.* Your needs are consistently and reliably met and placed ahead of your competitors' when the supplier allocates resources.
2. *Scarcity Test.* The supplier will consistently give preference to your requirements even when their products and innovative ideas are in limited supply/high demand.

3. *Critical Mass Test.* This preferred position exists for your company beyond just the strategic level of the supplier segmentation matrix, to include the full range of suppliers.

That is a tough definition because most supply organizations aspire to this level of support from the strategic few, but, due to lack of resources, only expect solid performance from the rest. The sales executives were also clear that customers of choice get this preferred access to supplier capabilities more than 75 percent of the time. This preference includes supplier-provided productivity resources (think the reverse of supplier development—customer development where your supply group is the customer getting the development support).

—Practitioner's Take—

Of the three customer of choice tests, the one that is most difficult, but also the most telling, is, in my experience, the last one—creating these kinds of relationships with a critical mass of suppliers, not just the top few. Resources are limited and increasing your overhead to cover "just in case" relationship building is a business case that not many C-level executives will accept.

Three ways to extend relationship management deeper into the supply base are:

1. Outsource selectively to providers that are willing to provide transparency into their supply base for key customers (which means following the Executive Board's guidelines on how to become a customer of choice with those providers). Choosing a supplier like L&F, whose competency is network orchestration, helps put you closer to a broader range of upstream relationships typically worth every penny of what you would pay for that service.

2. Set the expectation that all levels in the supply organization establish contacts with higher level supplier management at the suppliers they work with (see Chapter 6), regardless of whether they are the important few. The experience of doing this will prepare less experienced supply managers for more important roles later on in their careers, plus provide intrinsic rewards at their current levels.

3. Regardless of where on the supplier segmentation priority list the commercial transaction falls, train into the organization to always ask the question, "Why do these guys want to do business with us?" The answer may surprise you. It is not always just volume or profit. Sometimes it is about your company's reputation and their ability to use it as a reference. Sometimes, for a small company, it is a low-risk/low-cost way to fund a possible growth opportunity. Sometimes it is access to your other suppliers and your customers. And sometimes it is as simple as a good personal relationship with a key leader at the other company.

A couple of examples illustrate this last point. One small auto parts distribution supplier holds an every-other-year supply chain conference that brings together five tiers in that chain. The company's sales are less than $100 million, but it still draws the big guys—Ford, GM, Nissan, Ashland Chemical, Schneider Logistics, etc. More impressive is that the funding for this event is from "supplier sponsors," which defray the cost of a multiday conference in return for the ability to describe their product lines for ten minutes during the conference (and it is timed). In talking with some of the sponsors, I learned that the host company's business, while of value to them, paled in comparison to the entrée into other industries as a potential customer base. They saw the event as a high ROI marketing investment and a way to support and supply value to a good customer.

In the software industry, companies willing to be the developmental customer or the "beta test" for emerging applications can provide an opportunity to purchase a product at a great discount, influence its final design, and use it before the market in general. Like anything else, however, it is a risk/reward tradeoff, so a couple of watch-outs on this approach are warranted. First, the product doesn't always work, so the investment of time and effort is wasted and the internal risk of "poisoning the well" for internal adoption of similar technology later increases. Second, sometimes a big software company talks the game, but nothing happens. Watching how the relationship develops and noticing when the words and the actions don't mesh should trigger a tough conversation to determine whether the application has enough potential to make the software company's top priority list, or it is just an experimental long shot.

So, how do you pass the three tests? Oil exploration, refining, and marketing company Hess Corporation discussed its approach, which is based on four pillars[8]:

1. Create an account team that manages the internal/external communication flows with the supplier in parallel with the supplier's sales account team.

2. Develop and use consistent global supply processes to avoid unpredictability and supplier confusion. Create processes that do not waste supplier resources.

3. Use Internet-based software to create more transparency and an easy collaboration forum.

4. Understand internal requirements and explain them clearly to suppliers. Use good forecasting models to communicate demand more effectively.

The Procurement Strategy Council's research recommends the following actions to gain customer of choice status[9]:

▶ Put some assets your supplier values into the game. Things like business predictability, loyalty in a crisis, supplier improvement resources, and frank, honest discussion about the business and its direction all count.

▶ Align your needs to theirs, or even let them help do that. The use of bidding optimization tools that let the suppliers create the bidding lots and supply options within a buyer's overall requirements is one way I observed P&G do this.

▶ Closely manage the relationships throughout the supply chain, maintaining contact with key supplier leadership.

A Last Caution: Avoid the Eleventh C

Unfortunately, for winners, press clippings are seductive. If you start to believe them, you are taking the first step toward mediocrity. The archenemies of sustained supply-based advantage are arrogance, rigidity, protectionism, and "not invented here" skepticism. Combined, they make up one last C, complacency.

The Eleventh C: Complacency! This brings more companies down than any other internal flaw, making them deaf and blind to warning signals. On the supply side, this is even more insidious, because unlike customers, whose votes count visibly on the revenue line, suppliers can be dismissed more easily. "They don't really understand our business." "They are just trying to sell us something! "We know better."

I once attended a three-day supply conference in Chicago with a peer, who voiced a real eagerness to attend and learn. Midway through the third presentation of the first day, he leaned over to say, "I know all this stuff. I am going to do some e-mails and see if I need to contact anyone back at the office." The rest of the day and into day two, his attendance was spotty and disinterested. Just before the last presentation of day two he announced he was going to try to catch a plane home to get back to the "firefighting tactical work" (my words, not, of course, his). The final presentation of that day blew my socks off, as a supply director from Medal of Excellence winner Lucent Technologies laid out an excellent methodology to combine supplier, market, competitive, and low-cost country intelligence into a supply base plan and supplier segmentation model.

After returning to Cincinnati, I looked up my unimpressed colleague and went over the presentation with him. He was impressed and sorry he missed it. Then I discussed some of the other presentations and what I had gotten out of them. He seemed surprised. "But you knew all that already." There is a difference between intellectually knowing something and actually knowing how to do it! In some of these presentations, the question and answer sessions that followed and the networking opportunities with the speakers gave great clues on actually making the "intellectually known" into "accomplished practice."

For companies at the bottom of the maturity curve, benchmarking is like opening a Christmas present—delightful surprises that can be used for great enjoyment. Further up the curve, the surprises are fewer (but there are typically a few nuggets), while the nuances of how to do things and what cultural context and intangible "tacit" knowledge is important for success become the more important insights—as are the contacts made that can provide valuable surprises later. The ah-ha becomes more about the how than the what.

The hallmarks of sustained supply-based competitive advantage are curiosity—what's new and how is that done?—and humility—focus on skill imperfections without ignoring the successes. These are complacency and arrogance fighters.

These two rather ordinary nouns—curiosity and humility—are the ultimate basis for adding the "sustained" to competitive advantage because they open the door for suppliers to bring what they are good at and find the reception warm. Yes, analysis, expectation setting, and discipline are all part of supplier management, but unless you avoid that eleventh C, competitive advantage will be a very brief moment rather than an ongoing position.

Every Christmas, the windows in high-end department stores are transformed for the holidays into something special. Most shoppers assume the stores do that work, but in Manhattan a small firm named Holiday Image "does" store windows at Macy's, Tiffany's, Cartier, The Gap, and Sephora (owned by LVMH—remember the champagne guys from Chapter 5?) at Christmas.[10]

Holiday Image's CEO, Mathew Schwam, says it well: "The way I see our business is not just as a Christmas decorating business. We are a global sourcing business." Holiday window sourcing begins fifteen months earlier when company executives travel overseas to research what's new in decorations. They tap into 500 factories in about two dozen countries, looking for the "fit" between a client's window and a range of decorations from simple trees to amazing LED light shows. Then each store's unique concept gets planned in the spring—nine months before "C-day"—and finalized by June.

When the hands-on work begins, Holiday Image triples its thirty-person staff, using contracted help—artists, actors, and freelance carpenters—to actually turn the concepts into reality. In 2007, Tiffany's transformation used thousands of frosted pine cones, red berries, feathers, garlands, and specially constructed substructures to avoid harming the store's stone exterior. Holiday Image stores each customer's decorations after the holidays in a heated/air conditioned warehouse, cataloged in detail by customer and subjected to routine maintenance (e.g., replacing burned-out lights and broken ornaments). The company sources an additional 15 to 20 percent extra decorations for each customer to make sure things don't look thin.

Customers keep coming back—and suppliers keep providing reliable and leading-edge decorating components. It's called competitive advantage and it comes from suppliers. This small company "gets it"—it's a global sourcing company not a decorating company and its place on the maturity curve is probably far above that of many bigger, better known outfits that are good at using procurement tools to leverage volume to get lower prices. Holiday Image understands how suppliers create value that customers appreciate over and above cost reduction.

That is what supply-based advantage is all about.

Notes

1. Discussion/interview with Greg Courts, Procurement Director, Rio Tinto Alcan, May 6, 2008, St. Louis, Mo.

2. "Supply 'China' Management: Superior SCM at Li & Fung Ltd.," China Apprentice Blog, http://screamingsushi.com/blog3/2007/06/30/supply-china-management; accessed on March 20, 2008.

3. Ann Zimmerman and Cheryl Lu-Lien Tan, "After misstep, Wal-Mart revisits fashion," *Wall Street Journal*, 4/28/2008; accessed at www.pantagraph.com/articles/2008/04/27/money/doc48121ce5941aa200254443.txt.

4. Victor K. Fung, William K. Fung, and Yoram (Jerry) Wind, *Competing in a Flat World: Building Enterprises for a Borderless World* (Upper Saddle River, N.J.: Wharton School Publishing, 2007).

5. *Ibid.*, pp. 131–133.

6. "Skateboarder Apparel, Footwear Firm Just Wants to Focus on Product Marketing," *Global Logistics and Supply Chain Magazine*, February 2008; www.supplychainbrain.com/content/nc/technology-solutions/saas-on-demand-systems/single-article-page/article/skateboarder-apparel-footwear-firm-just-wants-to-focus-on-product-marketing/].

7. Procurement Strategy Council, "Next Generation Cost Performance: Practices for Sustained Advantage," copyright 2006; www.spb.sa.gov.au/documents/Professional%20Development%20Seminar%201%20Summary %20(New%20Source).pdf.

8. Tim Minahan, "Are You a Customer of Choice?," Supply Excellence Blog, June 13, 2007 (summary of a presentation by Hess Corporation Supply Chain Specialist Carl Tatum at the Supply Management 2.0 Forum in Houston, Texas, June 4–8, 2007); www.supplyexcellence.com/blog/2007/06/13/are-you-a-customer-of-choice/.

9. Procurement Strategy Council, "The Customer of Choice Imperative: Securing a Disproportionate Share of Supplier Resources," www.psc.executiveboard.com/Public/FeaturedContent/CustomerofChoice.pdf.

10. Gwendolyn Bounds, "Decking the Halls (And Walls): How Small Firm Transforms Stores, Malls for Holidays," *Wall Street Journal*, December 4, 2007.

Afterword

You Can Get Competitive Advantage from Suppliers

Over the last two years, three retirees—one a former bakery owner, one a former small industrial equipment distributor, and the last, a farmer—had three stories that combined to help me think about suppliers and how they can impact a business, and through that, people's lives. All three stories are the kinds that get big play at a party or over a beer in a bar. I have no idea if they are true or not—I suspect that there is a lot of exaggeration (or at least selective memory) around a kernel of truth in each, but even if they are as fictional as Aesop's fables, the lessons embedded within them certainly ring true. So, let's get started . . .

The first conversation was at a retirement community party in Ft. Myers, Florida. The person I was talking to asked what the topic of the book I wanted to write was about. I told him—suppliers and how they help companies compete. He used to run a small bakery and hired suppliers that supported him. One day his oven stopped working due to an electrical problem. When he called the maintenance supplier he had used for years, he was told business was booming (a hurricane the prior year had created lots of repair and replacement demand) and the work would not be done for about a week. For a small business like a bakery, a week without an oven can equal bankruptcy. The loyal customer was not worth enough money to get any sort of preferred treatment—the relationship was about the supplier's profit, not a real relationship. The baker called another company and by mid-afternoon was up and running. The new supplier was a little more expensive, but really wanted

337

the business and continued to service his new customer. The baker's observation: Hire suppliers that care about you and your business, not the ones just looking for the cash. You won't know how reliable they are until the chips are down.

The second conversation was during a social event in Cincinnati. The retired equipment distributor related a two-sided story about what happens when people take something for granted. On the buy side, he had a relationship with a supplier who provided quick service and reliable supplies, but seemed to be a pretty routine vendor. The distributor was lured away by a lower price from another vendor. He never realized how much the original supplier's dependability contributed to his business until he was gone—and with him the business referrals that routinely attracted other customers for the distributor. On the sales side, this experience caused the distributor to evaluate his customers and find those that took him for granted and did not set high expectations. For that kind of customer, he found that he could routinely raise prices about 3 percent per year and never get caught because he was under the radar. The point, he explained, was if as a buyer you want competitive price and service you need to set and enforce that expectation with suppliers and, when you have a good supplier, really understand how much you are getting before walking away.

The last story is told by a crusty old farmer, who swears it is true. The farmer tells the story of a road contractor he knew. The contractor, after having a few beers, always bragged about the money he was making handling county road contracts. A friend in the county purchasing department made sure he got the contracts, which specified the use of a "six-bag mix," which has a higher ratio of cement to filler than some other mixes and is more appropriate for the freeze/thaw stress roads have to endure in the northern United States. When he put in the road, he shortchanged the mix one out of every six bags to shave costs and make more money. (This was a number of years ago, before more sophisticated core sampling would catch that kind of fraud.) Late one night the road contractor's pickup truck flipped over after hitting a patch of failed concrete. He died on his own stretch of road. The farmer's moral to the story was that a "shortcutter" got what he deserved. My own takeaway? Values count. Keep your standards high and find suppliers that have those same standards.

If you are still with me at this point, I can only hope it has been a good read. My goal was to describe supply-based competitive advantage in a way that includes a blueprint for what it takes. Then, to set the expectation that beyond a set of processes and skills, it also takes long-term commitment, not some kind of overnight alchemy. The goal was to bring the blueprint to life chapter by chapter and, more importantly, use examples to establish the right mindset to capture your imagination.

Making suppliers part of your business strategy, like all strategic choices, is about spending resources today in the expectation of a great economic return tomorrow. Sometimes tomorrow is near term and sometimes it is months or years in the future.

The choice to make suppliers a "strategic choice" requires you to:

➤ Resource the strategy with people and tools, both of which cost money.

➤ Get close to the business needs, not just supply's functional goals. Then make sure those needs are clear to suppliers. Meeting those needs creates a business case for supply as a corporate strategy.

➤ Build relationships both internally and externally. People still matter.

➤ Stay in touch with your own general management and be willing to tell it like it is, especially when markets are shifting.

➤ Expect hard work, both from your own organization to implement it and from suppliers to sustain it. Measure what matters to get the results from that work.

➤ Perhaps most important of all is to be able to apply *balance* to the supply base. Competition and collaboration; short and long term; risk and reward; extract and share value. Remember, balance creates flexibility and flexibility enables intelligent change.

One last story—one I can vouch for. At a recent P&G Alumni Network Cincinnati Chapter meeting, current CEO A. G. Lafley agreed to speak for a few minutes, sign his book about innovation (*Game Changer*, Crown Business, April 2008), and mingle with the alums, many of whom he knew personally. After his talk, which highlighted the challenges of rising costs and economically strained consumer budgets, he spent some time informally renewing relationships with former P&G people.

As we chatted for a few minutes the topic turned to writing books and he asked about the subject of mine. I explained that it was about how to tap into suppliers to help create competitive advantage. In that brief exchange, he reinforced that indeed, suppliers can be a source of competitive advantage when integrated into customer and consumer value. He went on to say that even in rising cost markets the ability to access supplier value, despite their price increases, remains a big part of the value supply organizations offer a firm.

Competitive advantage is fleeting—there is no guarantee that it will remain in place over time. Firms called out as exemplary models of supply-based advantage (including some of those in this book) can easily slide back into parity as business conditions change. Excellence breeds imitation and imitation reduces competitive differences. Companies will always copy those that stand out, so advantage must always keep changing, hence the idea of situational flexibility. This is especially true when massive forces come together to create a new competitive nexus. Past shifts like the Arab oil embargo, the emergence of China, India, and Brazil, the fall of the Soviet Union, and Russia's recent resurgence all have created those kinds of competitive nexuses.

Today we stand at the beginning of what could be another major business nexus shift. The forces of high-cost energy, global climate change (whether manmade or natural), food shortages/cost pressures, and the creation of global industry oligopolies in mining, steel, and chemicals (among others) are straining many business models and company strategies. Business paradigms will need to be revised to deal with the convergence of these forces. In 2008, for the first time I can remember, the Institute for Supply Management's annual conference had as many presentations about exiting strategic relationships as creating them. The nature of working with suppliers will continue to evolve and, in today's nexus, will probably take approaches from the past and present, and will no doubt fashion new ones in the future to propel that evolution. The supply strategies that have served companies well in the past will surely change as a new reality sorts itself out—and then, inevitably, changes yet again.

The key to dealing with an altered reality will be a combination of sustaining strengths and relationships that got you there while having the flexibility to change what will need to be changed. Mindset across the company and at the suppliers is everything when a new commercial reality emerges. Long global supply chains for physical goods will become more expensive due to the changes in transportation costs driven by energy prices. The residue of the last nexus change—electronic connections that allow knowledge work outsourcing and remote work from home—will continue to impact the future, especially in services supply chains. Fuel versus food tradeoffs will drive technology changes on one hand, yet make protectionism more attractive on the other, adding some mountains to the flat world.

In a world of oligopolies, the ability to establish new relationships and find extended value equations in old ones will become more important. There are some natural synergies—energy conservation and carbon emission reductions can go hand in hand, but other flexibilities such as substituting currently utilized plant-based fuels for petroleum-based materials may be largely played out, resulting in smaller arbitrage opportunities. Smaller arbitrage will drive exploration (and hopefully commercialization) of technology that unlocks a new plant-based source. Avoiding complacency and continuing to seek situational flexibility will remain vital.

Suppliers can and will play a major role at this nexus. The construction of supply-based advantage will still require the same structural elements that we discussed throughout this book:

- Blueprints—policies and principles toward suppliers/supply chains.
- Foundation—sourcing strategy.
- Walls—supplier relationship management.
- Rooms—supply organization design and skills.
- Doors and Windows—cross-functional integration and mindset.
- Utilities—the flows of talent, knowledge, information, money, and communication.
- Maintenance/Remodeling—make versus buy decisions and outsourcing governance.
- Insurance—supply risk management.

If anything in this book has inspired you, start building the house, because the timing may be exactly right to find supply-based advantage in an emerging new environment. Those who can harness, influence, and leverage their supply base's urgency to find new approaches and business models will unearth critical advantages. Those who can't may find their supply base adversely impacts their competitive position.

Good luck and I hope this book will help you along the way.

—Steve Rogers

Index

CPSIA information can be obtained
at www.ICGtesting.com
Printed in the USA
JSHW070802291222
35335JS00015B/109